Category: Planning

Objective	Sub-Objectives	Location: S~	
Choose an implementation strategy for Microsoft Exchange Server.	Server locations Address space	2.4 Exchange Se~~~~ ~~~~~~~~~~~~~~ Strategies, p. 56-59	Lab: p. ~~-~~ Appendix A, Sample Exam
Develop the configuration of an Exchange Server computer.		3.4 Creating and Configuring Exchange Server Recipients, p. 83-96	Lab: p. 105-113 Appendix A, Sample Exam
Identify strategies for migration from previous versions of Exchange Server to Exchange Server 5.5.		12.1 Migrating to Microsoft Exchange 5.5, p. 410-415	Lab: p. 438-442 Appendix A, Sample Exam
Develop a long-term coexistence strategy.	Protocols include: IMAP and LDAP	2.3 Exchange Server Infrastructure Design, p. 41-55 9.11 IMAP4, p. 334-336 9.10 LDAP, p. 331-333	Lab: p. 60-66 Appendix A, Sample Exam
Develop an infrastructure for Exchange Server.	Identify public folders, including server-side scripting. Identify private information store databases. Plan Internet connectivity and access.	2.3 Exchange Server Infrastructure Design, p. 41-55 10.1.3 The Private Information Store, p. 349-350 9.2 Planning Internet Access, p. 306-308	Lab: p. 60-66 Exercise: Developing an Infrastructure for an Exchange Server Messaging Environment, p. 64 Appendix A, Sample Exam
Choose installation and integration strategies for Exchange Server client applications.	Elements include: Network installation Client computer installation Scripted client application installation Forms interoperability Schedule+ interoperability Calendar interoperability	6.2 Understanding Exchange Server Clients, p. 196-198 6.5.2 Creating a Customized Setup Script with the Network Installation Wizard, p. 215-216 6.3 Client Interoperability, p. 198-201 6.4 Installing and Configuring Outlook, p. 202-212	Lab: p. 222-228 Appendix A, Sample Exam Exercise: Setting Up an Outlook Automatic Upgrade, p. 227
Develop long-term administration strategies.	Plan: A backup strategy A disaster recovery strategy Information store maintenance Remote administration Information retrieval strategies	4.1 Developing a Backup Strategy for Exchange Server, p. 116-121 4.4 Developing a Disaster Recovery, p. 124-125 4.5 Planning Information Store Maintenance, p. 125-132	Lab: p. 142-147 Appendix A, Sample Exam
Develop security strategies.		Day 11, p. 370-407	Lab: p. 397-406 Appendix A, Sample Exam Exercises: Turning on Object Permissions, p. 403 Adding a New Exchange Administrator to an Exchange Site, p. 403-404 Changing LDAP Security, p. 404-405
Develop server-side scripting strategies.		4.8 Understanding the Exchange Scripting Agent, p. 141	Lab: p. 142-147 Appendix A, Sample Exam

Category: Installation and Configuration

Objective	Sub-Objectives	Location: Section	Hands-on Material
Install an Exchange Server computer.		3.1 Installing Microsoft Exchange Server, p. 70-77	Lab: p. 105-113 Appendix A, Sample Exam

continues on page 2

Category: Troubleshooting

Objective	Sub-Objectives	Location: Section	Hands-on Material
Diagnose and resolve upgrade problems.		14.1 Upgrades to Hardware and Software, p. 490-493	Lab: p. 514-520 Appendix A, Sample Exam
Diagnose and resolve server installation problems.		14.2 Troubleshooting Installation Problems, p. 493-495	Lab: p. 514-520 Appendix A, Sample Exam
Diagnose and resolve migration problems.		13.11 Mail Migration Issues, p. 478-479	Lab: p. 480-486 Appendix A, Sample Exam
Diagnose and resolve connectivity problems.	Elements include: Foreign connectivity; Site-to-site connectivity; Internet connectivity; Connectivity within a site	13.5.1 Troubleshooting Foreign Mail Connectors, p. 455-456 13.7 Site-to-Site Connectivity, p. 456-464 13.6 Internet Connectivity, p. 464-469 13.8 Directory Service Connectivity, p.469-473	Lab: p. 480-486 Appendix A, Sample Exam
Diagnose and resolve problems with client application connectivity.		13.9 Client Connectivity, p. 473-476	Lab: p. 480-486 Appendix A, Sample Exam
Diagnose and resolve information store problems.		14.3 Troubleshooting Directory and Information Store Problems, p. 496-505	Lab: p. 514-520 Appendix A, Sample Exam
Diagnose and resolve server directory problems.		14.3 Troubleshooting Directory and Information Store Problems, p. 496-505	Lab: p. 514-520 Appendix A, Sample Exam Exercise: Troubleshooting Directory Store Problems, p. 518
Diagnose and resolve server resource problems.		14.5 Server Resource Issues: Diagnostics and Recovery, p. 507-513	Lab: p. 514-520 Appendix A, Sample Exam
Diagnose and resolve message delivery problems.		13.8 Directory Service Connectivity, p. 469-473 13.8.1 Message Transfer Agent, p. 471-473	Lab: p. 480-486 Appendix A, Sample Exam
Diagnose and resolve backup problems and restore problems.		14.4 Diagnosing Backup and Recovery Problems, p. 505-507	Lab: p. 514-520 Appendix A, Sample Exam
Diagnose organization security problems.		11.8.5 Troubleshooting Advanced Security, p. 395-396	Lab: p. 397-406 Appendix A, Sample Exam

Category: Configuring and Managing Resource Access

Objective	Sub-Objectives	Location: Section	Hands-on Material
Manage site security.		10.5 Overall Site Security and Management, p. 363	Lab: p. 364-369 Appendix A, Sample Exam
Manage users.		6.1 Understanding MAPI Compliance, Windows Messaging, and Profiles, p. 194-196 10.1 The Information Store, p. 346-356	Lab: p. 364-369 Appendix A, Sample Exam Exercise: Using Directory Import to Create Mailboxes, p. 367
Manage distribution lists.		10.3 Distribution Lists, p. 359-361	Lab: p. 364-369 Appendix A, Sample Exam
Manage the directory.		10.2 The Microsoft Exchange Server Directory, p. 356-359	Lab: p. 364-369 Appendix A, Sample Exam
Manage public information store databases.	Elements include: Server locations; Rehoming of public folders	8.1 Overview of Public Folders, p. 274-283 10.1.2 The Public Folder Container, p. 346-349	Lab: p. 297-301 Appendix A, Sample Exam
Manage private information store databases.		10.1.3 The Private Information Store, p. 349-350	Lab: p. 364-369 Appendix A, Sample Exam Exercise: Managing the Private Information Store, p. 367
Back up and restore the Exchange Server organization.		4.1 Developing a Backup Strategy for Exchange Server, p.116-121 4.2 Restoring an Exchange Database Offline Backup, p. 122 4.3 Restoring an Exchange Server Online Backup, p. 123 4.4 Developing a Disaster Recovery Strategy, p. 124-125	Lab: p. 142-147 Appendix A, Sample Exam Exercise: Performing a Full Server Recovery, p. 147
Manage connectivity.		10.4 Managing Connectivity, p. 361-362	Lab: p. 364-369 Appendix A, Sample Exam

Category: Monitoring and Optimization

Objective	Sub-Objectives	Location: Section	Hands-on Material
Configure a link monitor and a server monitor.		5.1 Microsoft Exchange Server Tools, p. 152-170 5.1.1 Server Monitor, p. 152-160 5.1.2 Link Monitor, p. 160-164	Lab: p. 182-190 Appendix A, Sample Exam
Optimize Exchange Server.	Tasks include: Hardware optimization; Operating system optimization	5.1.4 Performance Optimizer, p. 168-170 5.2.6 Performance Monitor, 174-180	Lab: p. 265-270 Appendix A, Sample Exam Exercise: Running the Performance Optimizer, p. 187
Optimize foreign connections and site-to-site connections.		7.3 Optimizing Connections, p. 261-264	Lab: p. 182-190 Appendix A, Sample Exam
Monitor and optimize the messaging environment.		5.1.3 Message Tracker, p. 164-168	Lab: p. 182-190 Appendix A, Sample Exam Exercise: Turning on Message Tracking, p. 187
Monitor server performance by using SNMP and MADMAN MIB.		5.3 Configuring Exchange Server to Monitor Server Performance Using SNMP and the MADMAN MIB, p. 180-181	Lab: p. 182-190 Appendix A, Sample Exam Exercise: Using the Performance Monitor, p. 187

Category: Installation and Configuration   continued

Objective	Sub-Objectives	Location: Section	Hands-on Material
Configure Exchange Server for message recipients	Configure: mailboxes; custom recipients; public folders; distribution lists; site addressing; container-level search controls; Address Book views	3.4.1 Creating and Configuring Mailboxes, p. 83-87 3.4.4 Creating and Configuring Public Folders, p. 91-96 3.4.3 Creating and Configuring Distribution Lists, p. 88-91 3.7 Understanding Address Book Views, p. 102-104	Lab: p. 105-113 Appendix A, Sample Exam Exercise: Creating a Mailbox Template, p. 109
Configure connectivity to a mail system other than Exchange Server.	Connector types include: X.400 Connector; Microsoft Exchange Connector for Lotus cc:Mail; Microsoft Mail Connector	7.2 Connecting Exchange Server to Other Mail Systems, p. 247-261	Lab: p. 265-270 Appendix A, Sample Exam Exercises: Using the Site Addressing Properties to Modify SMTP Addresses, p. 268; Setting Up and Configuring the Dynamic RAS Connector, p. 269
Configure synchronization of directory information between Exchange Server and other mail systems.	Types of directory synchronization include: Manual Automatic	8.2.4 Synchronizing Directories with Other Email Systems, p. 287-291	Lab: p. 297-301 Appendix A, Sample Exam
Configure directory replication.		8.2 Configuring Directory Replication, p. 283-291	Lab: p. 297-301 Appendix A, Sample Exam Exercise: Configuring Directory Replication, p. 300
Import directory, message and scheduling data from existing mail systems.		12.2 Migration Planning and Strategies for Foreign Mail Systems, p. 415-417	Lab: p. 438-442 Appendix A, Sample Exam
Install and configure Exchange Server client computers.		Day 6, p. 192-228	Lab: p. 222-228 Appendix A, Sample Exam
Configure address lists and accounts by using the Administrator program.		3.3 Using Exchange Administrator, p. 79-83	Lab: p. 105-113 Appendix A, Sample Exam
Configure the message transfer agent within a site.		8.3.1 Configuring the MTA Within a Single Site, p. 292-293	Lab: p. 297-301 Appendix A, Sample Exam
Configure the message transfer agent among sites.		8.3.2 Configuring the MTA Between Multiple Sites, p. 293-295	Lab: p. 297-301 Appendix A, Sample Exam
Configure Internet protocols and services.	Protocols and services include: POP3 and IMAP4; Active Server and HTTP; NNTP; LDAP	9.4 Internet Messaging Protocols, p. 315 9.3 How to Implement the Internet Mail Service p. 308-315	Lab: p. 337-343 Appendix A, Sample Exam Exercise: Viewing Internet Protocol Settings, p. 341-342
Configure message tracking.		8.4 Tracking Messages, p. 295-296	Lab: p. 297-301 Appendix A, Sample Exam Exercise: Tracking a Message, p. 300
Configure server locations.		3.6 Configuring Organizations, Sites, and Servers, p. 98-102	Lab: p. 105-113 Appendix A, Sample Exam
Configure security.		11.5 How to Use Exchange's Built-in Security Features, p. 376-383 Configuring Site Security, p. 393	Lab: p. 397-406 Appendix A, Sample Exam

continues on page 3

Keith A. Powell

Chris Miller

William N. Matsoukas

Brad M. McGehee

Stephen L. Wiles

Syed Hussain

Sams'
Teach
Yourself
MCSE
Exchange
Server 5.5
IN 14 DAYS

SAMS
PUBLISHING

Copyright© 1998 by Sams Publishing

International Standard Book Number: 0-672-31276-X

Library of Congress Catalog Card Number: 98-84471

01 00 99 98   4 3 2 1

Interpretation of the printing code: The rightmost double-digit number is the year of the book's printing; the rightmost single-digit number, the number of the book's printing. For example, a printing code of 98-1 shows that the first printing of the book occurred in 1998.

Printed in the United States of America

Trademarks

Executive Editor
John Kane

Acquisitions Editor
Danielle Bird

Development Editor
John Sleeva

Technical Editor
Jay Adamson

Managing Editor
Sarah Kearns

Project Editor
Tom Dinse

Copy Editor
Alice Martina Smith

Indexer
Chris Barrick

Cover Designer
Tim Amrhein

Book Designer
Gary Adair

Production
Betsy Deeter
Lisa England
Nicole Ritch
Lisa Stumpf

Overview

Contents

About the Authors

Keith A. Powell

Keith has over nine years of experience in the industry and is presently employed as a Senior Consultant for KPMG Consulting in Chicago as part of the Electronic Commerce practice. As a Microsoft Certified Product Specialist, he devotes much of his time in the Microsoft Windows and BackOffice arena, focusing on LAN/WAN assessments and architectures. He has worked with clients in designing and implementing the Microsoft Exchange Server messaging environment, as well as aiding others in the documentation of Exchange Server implementations. Keith can be reached via the Internet at kpowell@kpmg.com.

Brad M. McGehee

Brad is a full-time computer trainer, specializing in Microsoft Windows NT Server and Microsoft BackOffice products. He is a Microsoft Certified Trainer (MCT), a Microsoft Certified Systems Engineer (MCSE), Microsoft Certified Professional + Internet (MCP+I), and a Certified NetWare Engineer (CNE). He has passed over 20 Microsoft Certification tests and is working to attain his Microsoft Certified Systems Developer (MCSD) certification, among several other industry certifications. After receiving a bachelor's degree in Business and Economics in 1981, his first job was to teach introductory computer and BASIC programming at a community college. He is the author of four books on computers, contributing author of seven additional books on computers, and over 100 magazine articles. He has also worked for several computer integrators over the years, first becoming involved in networking and relational database management in the mid-1980's. He received his masters degree in business in 1992. Throughout his career, Brad has been a computer consultant, developer, writer, and trainer, switching roles in order not to get too bored with any one task. Currently, Brad lives in Overland Park, KS, with his wife Veronica, who is a network engineer and C++ programmer. He can be reached at mcgehee@msn.com.

Chris Miller

Chris is an MCSE who has consulted and trained on Exchange Server since its release. Currently, he is a System Engineer for a nationwide wireless telecommunications company, providing support for a variety of Microsoft BackOffice products.

William N. Matsoukas

Bill is a Principal Consultant with an international firm where he specializes in network implementation and migration. He is an MCSE and a CNE as well as a perpetual student at Regis University in Denver. He lives in Westminster, Colorado with his wife, Teri, and his three children, Dee Dee, Kim, and Bryan, where they all take advantage of Colorado life by fishing, hiking, and camping.

Stephen L. Wiles

Steve is a Technical Trainer, currently with Empower Trainers & Consultants. His foci include MS Exchange, TCP/IP, and the core O/S courseware in Windows NT and Windows 95. His IS background includes PBX and call processing, DEC VAX/VMS systems, maintaining multiple messaging systems from both client and server ends, and tier I and II technical support for MS Office and BackOffice products. He received his BS in Microbiology from UT Arlington, and worked as a certified Medical Microbiology Lab Technologist for several years before moving into the equally exciting, but substantially less lethal environment of Information Technology. Steve also spent twelve years in the Texas Army National Guard both as an Armor Officer and as a Chemical Officer. Currently, he lives in Shawnee, Kansas with his fiancee, Corrie, and two dogs.

Syed Hussain

Syed is a consultant working for Whittman-Hart in Indianapolis. He is an MCSE with extensive experience in planning and implementing large Microsoft Exchange Server environments. His last project involved integrating Microsoft Exchange Server with MS Mail for a large Fortune 500 company. Syed is currently working on a project involving an upgrade from Microsoft Exchange Server 4.0 to Exchange Server 5.5 in a mid-size chemical company.

We'd Like to Hear from You!

As part of our continuing effort to produce books of the highest possible quality, MCP would like to hear your comments. To stay competitive, we really want you, as a computer book reader and user, to let us know what you like or dislike most about this book or other Macmillan products.

You can mail comments, ideas, or suggestions for improving future editions to the address below, or email us at **networking.mcp.com**. The address of our Internet site is **http://www.mcp.com** (World Wide Web).

Thanks in advance—your comments help us to continue publishing the best books available on computer topics in today's market.

> Although we cannot provide general technical support, we're happy to help you resolve problems you encounter related to our books, disks, or other products. If you need such assistance, please contact our Tech Support department at 800-545-5914 ext. 3833.

Introduction

Whether you're new to Exchange Server or an old pro at it, taking the Microsoft certification exam may be a stressful event. Passing depends not only on what you know, but also how well you are able to take tests. In this book, you will find everything you need to pass the Implementing and Supporting Microsoft Exchange Server 5.5 exam (70-081). Not only does this book cover how Exchange Server works, it also offers tips on taking the exam.

Of the many electives potential MCSEs can take, one of the more popular series is *Implementing and Supporting Microsoft Exchange Server 5.5*. Microsoft provides two different versions of the course, one for Exchange Server 5.0 and one updated for Exchange Server version 5.5. This book is designed specifically to give you all the information you need to pass the Exchange Server 5.5 version of this course. In addition, the study of this book combined with real-world experience using the product itself should equip you to confidently implement network solutions using the Microsoft Exchange Server messaging system. Also, this test counts as one of six exams toward MCSE certification.

This introduction looks at the MCSE certification process and examines where this course fits in. We will examine how this book is designed to help you pass the course, give you some suggestions on using this book to prepare for the exam, and discuss some tips and strategies when it comes time to take the test itself.

Why Take Microsoft Certification Tests?

If you have looked in the help-wanted ads lately, you probably have seen ads searching for Microsoft Certified Professionals (MCPs) and especially Microsoft Certified Systems Engineers (MCSEs). No matter where you go, MCPs and MCSEs are in demand. Getting your Microsoft certification is a powerful way of demonstrating your mastery of Microsoft products, and this is exactly the kind of expertise the job market is seeking.

Even if you are not looking for a new job, Microsoft certification can help you by giving your current company a reason to increase your pay. After your company discovers you are more valuable, it will probably be more motivated to keep you happy.

Why Is the Exchange Server Exam an Important Part of the MCSE Tests?

Whether your reason for taking the MCSE tests is for personal enrichment, desire for promotion, or just more money, it is important to realize where the Exchange Server exam fits into the picture. Exchange Server is one of the specialty electives available as part of the Windows NT 4.0 MCSE certification track. Other certification options include SQL Server, Internet Information Server, TCP/IP, SNA Server, and Site Server.

Although the Exchange Server exam is just one of the various MCSE electives, the authors of this book feel that the Exchange Server exam is a more useful part of the MCSE certification. By taking your Exchange Server exam, you are not only exposed to the testing format, but after passing it, you will become certified in one of the fastest growing messaging systems on the planet.

How the Exam Works

Microsoft has developed each of the MCP/MCSE exams with the help of instructors, network administrators, and respected members of the networking community. Each test question represents a mastery level of the operating system; questions are not designed to be tricky. This does not mean, however, that the test questions are easy. In fact, the test questions generally require a lot of thought. Often, you are asked to evaluate which of the listed criteria are important, and which solutions will work.

To some test takers, the questions that ask for the "best" answer are tricky. For these questions, Microsoft wants only what it considers to be the "best" solution to a problem. Look for these questions in this book and make sure that you read *all* the answers. Microsoft has made a point of providing possible, but not optimum, solutions to these questions, so it is vital to evaluate each answer to see how it weighs against the other answers. Also, Microsoft will sometimes toss extra information into an exam question that is frivolous. Do not worry that some of the information given in a question may not pertain to the answer in any way; it is probable that you have chosen the correct answer already.

The other curve most people find is that every exam is unique. Just because your friend does not get any questions on troubleshooting or connectivity does not mean that you do not have to study these topics. It could be that most of your questions come from the troubleshooting or connectivity objectives.

Speaking with other people who have passed the exam is an important part of preparing for the test, but do not focus on only those topics with which others had trouble. Study every topic area in as much detail as possible. A single area of weakness can bring down your score enough to cause you to fail the exam. Another important thing to remember is that the test covers the base product; it does not cover service packs or any other add-ins.

About Exam 70-081

The Exchange Server exam, as it is referred to, is officially known as *Implementing and Supporting Microsoft Exchange Server 5.5*. It is computer administered and is intended to measure your ability to implement and administer the product in an enterprise environment. It builds on basic knowledge and assumes that the test candidate possesses a good deal of experience with the product.

There are two types of multiple-choice questions on the exam: single answer (always readily identified by a radio button) and multiple answer (with the correct number of answers given). There are a limited number of "click-on" questions (where you are given a property sheet and told to click the item you would choose to meet the specifications given). The questions, overall, are verbose, include a large number of exhibits, and provide choices from A to D.

The exam is divided into five objective categories:

- Planning
- Installation and Configuration
- Configuring and Managing Resource Access
- Monitoring and Optimization
- Troubleshooting

Note Although the exam is multiple choice, and you need only click radio buttons and boxes to answer questions, the act of taking the exam is called "writing."

Organization of This Book

As you may have guessed by its title, this book was designed from the ground up specifically to help you pass the *Implementing and Supporting Microsoft Exchange Server 5.5* exam. We have combined our experience both with the test itself and with competing preparation materials available on the market to design the best possible tool for giving you the skills and confidence necessary to pass the exam with flying colors.

The book is divided into three core parts:

- **Introductory materials.** This part of the book includes this Introduction, which is designed to help you prepare for studying and taking the exam, along with the standard publishing and legal mumbo-jumbo you find at the beginning of any book.
- **The 14 Days.** This is the heart of the book. We have divided the material needed to pass the exam into digestible chunks; each is designed to be learned in one day. Like a good classroom course, each day provides a mix of descriptive text, concept demonstrations, and review. Each day also includes a number of questions designed to help reinforce and solidify your knowledge and to help you get used to the question format used on the test.
- **Appendix.** The appendix contains a sample exam.

To help make your study time more productive and to allow you to review after taking assessment tests, this book is divided into 14 chapters—one for each day. Each chapter will probably take a couple hours to complete, not including the software installation time (it is further assumed that the Windows NT Server operating system software on which Exchange Server is installed, has already been successfully implemented). If you study just a few hours each day for two weeks, you should be ready to take your Microsoft Exchange Server certification exam.

How to Use This Book

Passing the exam requires broad understanding of Exchange Server. The exam will not ask specific questions about quirks of Microsoft Exchange Server or the workarounds that might be necessary in certain environments. To get this broad understanding of Exchange Server, you should read and re-read each section until you completely understand all the major topics. Each topic covered in this book may or may not be included on your exam. As mentioned previously, each test taker gets a unique exam. Wherever possible, you will find examples of how Exchange Server works.

There are two ways you should approach this book. The first is to read it linearly, chapter by chapter. This will give you an understanding of all the topics on the exam and will give you a firm foundation for taking an evaluation exam. The second way is to use this book as a reference for issues that occur after you have passed the exam. In several places, we have included information that may not be necessary for the exam, but that is nonetheless useful for the real world.

It is recommended that you take the Microsoft self-assessment test before taking the exam at a Sylvan Prometric testing center. The assessment test approximates the exam and will familiarize you with the testing engine. The testing engine used for the sample tests is the same as the one used at the testing center. In addition, the test will report your correct and incorrect answers in each objective. If you look at the results of the self-assessment test, you will know which parts of this book you need to review before taking the exam. Thus, this book can be used as a resource to improve your understanding of specific topics.

Taking the Exam

After long, arduous hours of study and practice, you feel ready to accept the challenge of the *Implementing and Supporting Microsoft Exchange Server 5.5* exam. There are a few things you should know when you schedule your exam and on the day of the exam that can make your process much smoother.

Scheduling the Exam

The certification exams are administered entirely by Sylvan Prometric. Call 1-800-755-EXAM to schedule your exams. You need the following information the first time you schedule a exam:

- Your full name
- Your social security number
- Your address
- Your telephone number
- An appropriate method of payment (Sylvan accepts credit cards or checks)

If you call again to schedule future exams, you will be asked for your social security number and your payment information. The operator will help you pick the Sylvan testing center most convenient to you and help you schedule an exam during a free time slot at that location.

Each exam costs $100.00. You can schedule exams whenever there are slots available at your chosen testing center (although you must give at least one business day's notice to register). You can also call back and change a planned testing date as late as one day in advance. You may also find it convenient to pay for all your exams ahead of time and then schedule the specific exams later when you have a better idea of when you will be available to take them.

Preparing for Exam Day

We hope that when the time for your exam comes around, you will be prepared to pass the exam. The day before your exam, do a final review of the course material; glance over everything but focus primarily on any areas on which you feel a little shaky. Make sure that you eat a healthy meal and get a good night's rest before your exam.

The morning of the exam, eat healthy meals and relax; your preparations should leave you with a feeling of optimism and confidence for the exam. It's not a bad idea to go over last-minute review items again before your exam, but don't panic and race through everything, or try to cram new material.

If there are any specifics about which you are not 100 percent confident, it is easy to think, "I do not need to go over that. I'm sure I will remember it or they won't cover it much in the test." This attitude is most often found in relation to specific configuration options or syntax issues that are easy to look up in a real-world situation—so you tend to believe that you will not be heavily questioned on those topics. We have all found ourselves in this position before, and each time we do, we receive a nasty surprise when we sit down to take the exam. If you feel this way, take a few minutes to glance over the specifics again. The few minutes you take can add some needed points to your score and prevent your confidence from being shaken when you sit down to take the exam.

The Exam Specifics

The exam consists of a number of different question types:

- Multiple choice, with one correct answer
- Multiple choice, with more than one correct answer
- Scenarios, in which you evaluate a given solution
- Scenarios, in which you provide the most appropriate solution
- Fill-in-the-blank questions
- Simulation questions, in which you select the correct option from a simulated dialog box

Some questions are ambiguous, and you are expected to pick the best possible answer. Some questions are actually poorly written and very difficult to answer.

Each question has a Mark option that allows you to mark the question for later review. Each question can also be left incomplete.

Once you have run through each of the questions (generally 54 questions for the *Exchange Server* exam), you are given a chance to review your answers. The testing engine highlights any questions you marked for review as well as the ones you did not complete (although you can review and change any answer).

Once you are confident you have done the best you can, you submit your questions, and your answers are recorded. Then you are given the opportunity to comment on individual questions. When your comments are submitted, your test is graded, and you are told whether you passed or failed; you are also given your percentage score for each section of the exam. You cannot review and find out which questions you missed.

After reviewing your score, you are given the opportunity to comment on the test itself, and you're asked to fill out a survey about yourself and your test preparation process.

Test Strategies

The strategies for taking the MCSE exam are very similar to those for taking any standardized test. Perhaps the most important is attitude. Coming into the exam confident in your knowledge and excited about getting your certification is critical to passing the test. You can gain this confidence and excitement by taking care of yourself and by allowing yourself plenty of time before exam day to study, review, and prepare.

Once the exam begins, make certain that you read each question carefully and thoroughly before selecting an answer. If you are not sure about a question, make your best guess and mark the question for later review (sometimes, other questions give you the knowledge to help you make a more informed decision). If you have no idea about a question, leave it incomplete.

If you run into a question about which you have no clue, do not let it blow your concentration. Just mark it and move on; you will probably be able to make an intelligent guess later based on information from other questions.

Frequently Asked Questions

Q. If I have already taken an exam for a previous version of Exchange Server, how much studying do I have to do for this exam?

A. A great deal of information is carried forward from the previous versions' exams because Exchange Server 5.5 is based on version 4.0 and 5.0 of the product. You will want to study the differences between Version 5.5 and the previous versions because these will probably appear in some form on the test.

Q. If I fail the exam, what is my next course of action?

A. The results of the exam are divided into the five major objective categories. Look at your weakest areas and better your skills in those. The tear-out card in this book will show you where coverage for each of those objectives is found. Study that material until you know it thoroughly, and then retake the exam. Microsoft imposes no limitation on the number of times you can take an exam.

Q. Is there a way to prepare for the style of questions that are asked?

A. A number of electronic test engines emulate the Microsoft exam. A quick glance at the back pages of any higher-end computing magazine shows half a dozen companies marketing such products. Some of these products are exceptional, and some are very poor. The differences in quality relate to how well the engines test your knowledge and emulate questions on the actual exam.

In addition, the questions at the end of each chapter of this book mirror exam questions. These questions will help you test your knowledge, even though they appear in a medium not found in the exam (that is, they appear in written, not electronic, form).

Q. Is the Exchange Server exam a good one to choose if you have never taken a certification exam before?

A. The ExchangeServer exam is probably not suited as a first exam. The topics you are tested on are generally not confined to one product (unlike say, the Microsoft Windows NT Workstation 4.0 test), and may lead to some confusion.

Q. If I have questions about the exam that are not addressed in this book, where should I turn?

A. We have made every attempt to cover all exam-relevant material in this book. Nevertheless, you may have questions that are not addressed in a way that rings true to you. If that is the case, feel free to contact the authors by email; we will make every attempt to respond to you in a timely fashion.

Good luck with the exam!

Day 1

Microsoft Exchange Server 5.5 Concepts and Guidelines

by Keith Powell

The purpose of this first chapter is to properly acquaint a new administrator with the Microsoft Exchange Server messaging environment. It has long been a good idea that when you are learning a new subject, such as how to ride a bike or how to drive your first car, you start with the basics and work upward. When it comes to gathering new wisdom regarding a Microsoft BackOffice product, I like to start with baby steps. Consider this chapter, Day 1, as those first baby steps.

Before we can be expected to install the software, configure it properly, add hundreds or even thousands of new users—let alone convert an existing email system over to Exchange Server—it is surely a great idea to gain a better understanding of it all. Yes, I thought you would agree. We will start with the basic terms and components of Exchange Server. Next, we will move into an in-depth discussion of the more important components, such as the purpose of the Exchange organization, its sites, and its servers.

Having all that behind us, we'll then discuss the differences between Exchange Version 5.5 and the previous versions. Although this discussion will be of more significance to experienced Exchange system administrators, new administrators will enjoy it just the same (especially because the MCSE exam may pop a few questions concerning some of these items).

Following the discussion of the newest features and updates, we will move into a detailed (but still relatively high-level) discussion of the Message Transfer Agent (MTA). The MTA is one of the core components of Exchange Server. Without it, nothing works. It probably does not get more key than that. *Hint:* Pay close attention to the MTA; you'll probably see it again on a certain exam! So, let's get started!

Objectives

The objectives for this chapter are as follows:

- To provide readers with an understanding of the terminology used throughout the Microsoft Exchange messaging environment, including that of organization, sites, and servers

- To inform readers of the many new features available in version 5.5 of Microsoft Exchange Server

- To assist readers in understanding the Exchange environment's Message Transfer Agent (MTA)

1.1. Introduction to Microsoft Exchange Server

Microsoft Corporation has a vision for an electronic messaging system that can work effectively across the corporate enterprise. That vision is the messaging system software known as Microsoft Exchange, which is presently in its third public release (Version 5.5).

Microsoft Exchange Server has been in the marketplace for nearly two years, ever since its public debut, at Version 4.0, in April 1996. Although to some people it may appear to be a newly worded upgrade to the older Microsoft Mail electronic mail software, Exchange Server is actually much more than just another email system. The Exchange Server messaging environment, when viewed as an integrated messaging and collaboration platform, provides organizations with numerous capabilities, including these:

- Electronic mail and forms, including a relatively uncomplicated migration path from many other email packages
- Task management
- Document routing
- Groupware capabilities such as scheduling, online discussions, and real-time conferencing
- Internet messaging connectivity

The email features of Exchange are consistent with those of the many other electronic messaging packages on the market today, such as Lotus cc:Mail and Novell GroupWise. However, Microsoft Exchange adds many additional bells and whistles that separate it from these other packages. Exchange includes a Forms Designer function that permits the modification of the GUI presentation of Exchange to those who use it. Additionally, the electronic forms allow additional intelligence to be coded into them for groupware and document management purposes.

The task management capabilities found within the Microsoft Outlook client software for Exchange Server include the capability for the end-user to manage ongoing tasks and projects efficiently and easily. All of this can be done without the trouble of purchasing and learning how to use a full-blown project management software package such as Microsoft Project.

The document routing feature provides for the intelligent routing of messages across the messaging infrastructure. If one site is down, another can automatically move the message along to its destination. Likewise, Exchange supports simple document routing, which permits companies to set up special routing paths for specific purposes. For example, in a purchasing department, the product planner can issue a requisition that is then automatically routed to the buyer. From there, the requisition may have to go to one of several finance department persons for purchasing authorization (for example, if it exceeds any one of a number of predesignated buying levels). Following the approval of the purchase, the message that began as a requisition request, that now has a purchase order attached to it, and that has been approved, can now automatically be routed to the vendor. To support such routing of a message within a standard email system is not possible without special software coding.

The groupware capabilities of Microsoft Exchange—such as online discussions, real-time conferencing, and scheduling—also differentiate it from the standard email systems on the market today. These include the capabilities for company personnel to post messages on an internal bulletin board and to access HR-specific information from a shared human resource folder. These capabilities also include the scheduling of personal time, department-wide meetings, and the conducting of messaging conference calls both within the company as well as across the Internet, if need be.

A topic of interest that has been growing rapidly over the past few years is that of connectivity to the phenomenon known as the Internet. For most companies, the Internet is an opportunity to send and receive electronic messages and documents without having to first build their own private internetworks. Although many view the Internet as a way to cut communications costs, many others view it as an "unsafe" manner in which to send or receive messages from others (be they internal employees or corporate customers). Microsoft Exchange goes a long way to quell these concerns.

The Internet presents a number of unique opportunities, as well as challenges, for firms seeking to use it as a part of their normal business day. Although the Internet can be used to limit telecommunications costs (because it does not require expensive leased lines across great distances), the security challenges for protecting data remain numerous. Additionally, although standards for data exchange exist, these standards and technologies change so rapidly that it is difficult, at best, to maintain a sane pace. It is in these areas that the Exchange electronic messaging environment excels.

Microsoft Exchange Server was designed from the ground up with the Internet in mind. It includes support for many Internet protocols such as SMTP/POP3, HTTP,

NNTP, LDAPv3, IMAP4; it also supports numerous Internet connectivity security standards such as SSL, E/SMTP, S/MIME, and RSA digital key encryption.

•To learn more about Internet protocols, see Day 9, "Internet Connectivity Strategies."

The Internet uses the Transmission Control Protocol/Internet Protocol (TCP/IP). Although a good many corporate LAN and WAN infrastructures have been built around TCP/IP, most host systems revolve around IBM's SNA protocol. Microsoft Exchange Server can connect right in to access BackOffice technologies and information, especially for those companies that have existing email systems built on these legacy platforms.

The Exchange product consists of a client/server messaging architecture that differs from standard email-only type systems. Microsoft Exchange is designed for the distributed environment, as opposed to the centralized processing environment found in a mainframe or LAN-based environment. Although Exchange Server can thrive in a centralized processing structure, it is better suited to a distributed messaging environment, such as the one the Internet makes available.

Exchange's integration into the Microsoft Windows NT network operating system infrastructure is complete. Exchange's distributed messaging capabilities can take full advantage of the Microsoft Windows NT security features, such as single network logons and user administration. When a user is added to a Windows NT domain, part of that administration process includes a series of screens for adding that same user to the existing Microsoft Exchange Server environment.

Other areas in which Exchange can take advantage of Windows NT include Exchange's support for remote users, system reliability and monitoring, connectivity to disparate network operating systems, and backup and retrieval of information. Optimization of the remote connection is possible when users are supported remotely with the Windows NT RAS and dial-up networking, coupled with the Exchange clients' use of remote procedure calls (RPC).

Another advantage of Microsoft Exchange is that it revolves around its integrated design with the Windows NT operating environment. This integration permits easy scalability—because it is compatible with Microsoft Cluster Server (MSCS). Scalability of a messaging environment is usually associated with the thought that a product suitable for "mom and pop" businesses will never be useful in the corporate world.

Exchange changes this perception dramatically. Exchange Server works well on a small Windows NT Server (for a small company with just a dozen or so users) running with just one Intel CPU, 32MB of DRAM, and a single EIDE hard drive. In a

1

large, multinational business, such as Microsoft Corporation, there are a few hundred Exchange Servers supporting over 100 physical locations. These servers are powerhouse Windows NT Servers with multiple CPUs, quite a bit more memory, and multiple SCSI hard drives with RAID support. The user community is a bit larger as well, supporting tens of thousands of users across multiple national boundaries and continents.

Microsoft Cluster Server permits the use of clustering to provide fault tolerance for each pair of servers, allowing for high availability operation. MSCS within an Exchange Server environment is presently limited to two Windows NT Servers. It is important to note that MSCS requires the use of Windows NT Enterprise Servers, which offer a different level of robustness for the Windows NT operating system. Users on the failed server do not see a change in their email service. They can continue to send and receive mail and browse public folders as usual.

1.2. What's New in Microsoft Exchange Server Version 5.5

Microsoft Exchange Server Version 5.5 is an update to Version 5.0; Version 5.5 was released by Microsoft Corporation in early 1997. Version 5.5 sports a number of notable improvements over its previous release:

- An unlimited message store size in the Enterprise version
- Several new message connectivity choices:
    - Exchange Connector for Lotus Notes
    - Exchange Connector for IBM OfficeVision/VM
    - Exchange Connector for SNADS
- An improved backup application program interface (API) that increases the speed of Exchange system backups to up to 25 gigabytes of data per hour
- Support for Secure/Multipurpose Internet Mail Extensions (S/MIME)
- Support for X.509 v3 certificate-based authentication
- Support for the Microsoft Cluster Server (MSCS) capability
- Support for MHTML, which encapsulates HTML content in MIME
- The capability to download only the deltas of an offline Address Book, as opposed to performing a complete download each time
- Support for ETRN

ETRN is a new Internet Request-for-Comment (RFC 1985)—an SMTP Service Extension for Remote Message Queue Starting. ETRN will assist a remote SMTP server in starting the processing of its outbound message queue. ETRN will become especially important in Exchange dial-up environments where full time connectivity is not the norm.

1.2.1. Exchange Server Message Store Sizing

The unlimited message store size, available only in the Enterprise version of Exchange Server, is a most welcome addition. Many Information Services departments within the corporate community were using this liability as the primary reason that they were not moving toward a Microsoft Exchange messaging solution. The previous limit for an Information Store was 16 gigabytes of data. The new information store size boundary is limited only by the hardware for any installation of the Exchange Server enterprise software.

1.2.2. Exchange Server Connectors

The three new connectors added to Exchange Version 5.5 include support for connecting an Exchange Server environment to Lotus Notes, to IBM's OfficeVision/VM product, and to a new Exchange Connector for SNADS. The first two connectors (Lotus Notes and OfficeVision/VM) came as part of an acquisition Microsoft announced in June 1997. Microsoft purchased a company previously known as LinkAge Software, Inc., a Canadian-based vendor of messaging connectivity software. Both the Exchange Connector for Lotus Notes and the Exchange Connector for IBM OfficeVision/VM were part of the LinkAge product line and have been enhanced for inclusion into the Microsoft Exchange Server Version 5.5. Microsoft Corporation developed the third new connector for Exchange Server 5.5, an Exchange Connector for SNADS.

1.2.3. Exchange Connector for Lotus Notes

The Exchange Connector for Lotus Notes supports a messaging connection—with support for directory synchronization—between an Exchange Server and Lotus Notes (Version 3 or 4), as well as Lotus Domino (Version 4.x). Other features include the capability to preserve colors, fonts, and formats of documents when they are transported between Microsoft Exchange and Lotus Notes; a Notes email address generator; complete support for message status, including confirmation of read receipts, delivery, and nondelivery reports; and the capability for Notes document links to be sent to Exchange users as rich text format (RTF) or object linking and embedding (OLE) attachments, as well as in the form of web hyperlinks (for Domino users only, of course). It should be noted, however, that the Exchange Connector for Lotus Notes cannot provide a connection between an Exchange Public Folder and a Notes database.

Exchange Connector for IBM OfficeVision/VM

The Exchange Connector for IBM OfficeVision/VM also originates out of a LinkAge product (LinkAge Version 3.2 OfficeVision/VM). Although Microsoft includes it with the Exchange Server 5.5 Enterprise Edition, it is initially offered only in English and only for use with the Intel platform. Microsoft plans to release future localized versions, as well as one for the Alpha platform. This connector's primary features include the following:

- The capability to transport messages between an Exchange Server and an IBM OfficeVision/VM (a.k.a. PROFS) messaging system
- An option to suppress attachments sent from an Exchange user up to the host OfficeVision/VM system
- Support for both CMS and PROFS messages and documents
- Support for host OfficeVision/VM users to send messages to the Internet using Microsoft Exchange's Internet Mail Services system component
- Current support for a PROFS email address generator for Exchange on the Intel platform; support for the Alpha platform will be provided as soon as the connector is available for it

No coding is required on the host system to make this connection possible. However, it should be noted that there is a requirement for Microsoft SNA Server to be used to make this connection to the host possible.

Exchange Connector for SNADS

As is the connector for OfficeVision/VM, the Exchange Connector for SNADS will initially be available only in English and only for use with the Intel platform. Microsoft plans to release future localized versions, as well as one for the Alpha platform. The Exchange Connector for SNADS allows users to send messages between a Microsoft Exchange Server and a SNADS-compliant message system such as the following:

- IBM OfficeVision/VM
- IBM OfficeVision/400

- NBS TOSS
- Fischer TAO
- Software AG Connect
- Verimation Memo
- SoftSwitch Central and LMS

Other features of the Exchange Connector for SNADS include the capability to connect Exchange Server to an IBM host system using the Application Program-to-Program Communications (APPC) protocol, an option to suppress attachments from Exchange users when sent to a SNADS-compliant host, and the capability to avoid the writing of any host-side code (except for the SNADS-compliant transport mechanism). It should be noted, however, that there is a requirement for a Microsoft SNA Server implementation to make a connection to the host environment possible.

1.2.4. Exchange Server Backup Capabilities

The next new feature of Exchange Server Version 5.5 is its capability to perform hot backups of the Exchange messaging environment more quickly. The improved backup API permits an Exchange system backup rate to be increased to a top-end limit of 25 gigabytes of data per hour. Unlike many other messaging systems, a system administrator does not have to down the Exchange Server to back it up, which means that Exchange users can have access to their messaging system 24x7 (24 hours per day, 7 days per week).

1.2.5. Exchange Server MSCS Support

As mentioned earlier in this chapter, Exchange Server 5.5 supports the new Microsoft Cluster Server (MSCS) capability. This enhancement to Exchange means that two Windows NT Server computers can be clustered together for improved reliability of an Exchange messaging environment. MSCS allows for single-node fail-over support in the event of a downed server, whether that failure is caused by a hardware or software catastrophe. However, it should be noted that the Enterprise Edition of Microsoft Windows NT Server 4.0 is required for this feature.

1.2.6. Exchange Server Internet Security Support

Exchange Server 5.5 offers many Internet/intranet enhancements, which revolve around Exchange Server's security and connectivity capabilities. Exchange supports the S/MIME protocol, which permits an S/MIME-aware client software package (such as Microsoft Outlook Express or Netscape Communicator) to exchange encrypted or digitally signed electronic mail with Exchange Server.

Another aspect of Internet support offered by Exchange Server 5.5 is X.509 v3 certificate-based authentication. This feature permits the Exchange Server to authenticate the validity of a message based on the message's security certificate. The certificate required is generated by a third party—such as the Certificate Server that comes with Windows NT's Internet Information Server (IIS) Version 4.0—or is created by an Internet certificate company such as VeriSign. In any event, the X.509 v3 certificates allow for the use of security certificates with the creation, sending, and receipt of Microsoft Exchange Server email messages.

Microsoft Exchange Server provides for the SSL encryption of SMTP connections between hosts and SASL for authenticating SMTP logins. Additional security features permit an Exchange administrator to reject or accept inbound SMTP connections, depending on the type of security those connections use. In addition, Exchange prevents spoofing by using an authenticated login.

1.2.7. Exchange Server Internet Connectivity Support

Other Internet connectivity support by Exchange involves its support for MHTML, which encapsulates HTML content in MIME. This feature permits an Exchange Server to store HTML messages.

Microsoft Exchange Server's support for ETRN (when Exchange must act as both an SMTP client and server simultaneously) allows an Exchange Server to solicit messages for a particular Internet domain that have already been queued on another SMTP server. ETRN simplifies dial-up connections for servers and clients that rely on this type of connection for receiving queued mail after establishing the connection with their Exchange Server.

The topic of collaboration isbecoming a larger issue all the time. Microsoft Exchange Server provides for additional Internet support in the form of the Microsoft Exchange Chat Service. This service permits real-time collaboration, because it permits any client browser using standard Internet Relay Chat (IRC) software to connect with other IRC users using an Exchange Server. Additionally, the Microsoft product NetMeeting has been integrated into the Outlook client, thereby permitting Outlook users to initiate meetings directly from Outlook. Through the use of Collaboration Data Objects (CDO), formerly known as Active Messaging, Exchange developers can create Exchange Active Server Pages (ASP) applications that make it much easier for users to access Exchange Server information from a web browser interface.

1.2.8. Exchange Server Synchronization Updates

The last notable improvements of Exchange Server Version 5.5 over its previous releases revolve around the client side of Exchange. Exchange 5.5 provides the new capability for end users to download just the changes (or *deltas*) of an offline Address Book, as opposed to having to download the complete Address Book each time. For remote users, this feature alone can save hours of connect time over the course of a year. For WAN-based users, this enhancement may amount to only a few minutes of additional productivity each time a download is performed.

1.2.9. New Exchange Clients

Next come the two new versions of the Microsoft Outlook client: one for Windows 3.x and the other for the Apple Macintosh operating system environment. These versions both include the Outlook user interface and provide interoperability with the 32-bit Outlook scheduling environment. The drawback to the Macintosh version, however, is that it cannot use Exchange forms created with the Exchange Forms Designer. This limitation exists because Exchange forms are based on the Visual Basic (VB) development environment, and VB executables are not available for the Macintosh platform.

1.3. The Base Microsoft Exchange Messaging System

To start a proper review of the Exchange messaging system environment, you have to be able to visualize the many different components an Exchange Server implementation can contain. You also have to be able to understand how each of those components are used. Additionally, you should possess a basic awareness of the functionality for each of those components. This book discusses each of the following components in detail; the following chapters give proper instruction in the installation and configuration of each piece, where appropriate.

- Administrator program
- Address Book
- Custom recipients
- Directory

- Distribution lists
- Enterprise
- Exchange Server connectors, including:
    - Site Connector
    - Internet Mail Services
    - X.400 Connector
    - Microsoft Mail Connector
    - Dynamic RAS Connector
    - Schedule+ Free/Busy Connector
    - Exchange Connector for Lotus Notes
    - Exchange Connector for IBM OfficeVision/VM
    - Exchange Connector for SNADS
    - cc:Mail Connector
- Information store
- Internet messaging protocols, including:
    - Network News Transport Protocol (NNTP)
    - Simple Message Transport Protocol (SMTP)
    - Post Office Protocol 3 (POP3)
    - Internet Message Access Protocol 4 (IMAP4)
    - Lightweight Directory Access Protocol v3 (LDAPv3)
    - Hypertext Transfer Protocol (HTTP)
    - Multipurpose Internet Mail Extensions (MIME)
    - Secure Multipurpose Internet Mail Extensions (S/MIME)
- Private folders
- Public folders
- Mailbox
- Message Transfer Agent (MTA)
- Organization
- Site addressing
- Sites

- Security components, including:
    - Key Management Server (KMS)
    - S/MIME
    - Secure Sockets Layer (SSL)
    - X.509 v3 certificates ·
- Servers

This list of topics isintended to demonstrate the complexity of the Microsoft Exchange Server's components, as well as to get you thinking about the most important pieces of your Exchange messaging environment. When an organization wants to scale its Exchange Server deployment across its enterprise information systems at a future date, it first must have a solid architecture on which to build. In the Exchange messaging world, failure to plan properly up-front may very well result in a costly "do over" down the road.

1.4. Microsoft Exchange Server Structure

The structure of an Exchange Server implementation consists of a single organization, with one or more sites below it, followed by one or more servers below each site (see Figure 1.1).

Figure 1.1.

Associations between Exchange Server organization, sites, and servers.

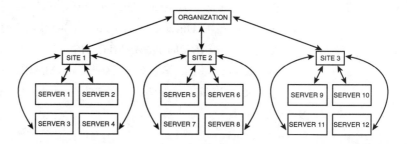

Typically, there will exist a single organization within any deployment of Microsoft Exchange Server. The organization name cannot be changed without reinstalling Exchange Server. Therefore, it is very important when planning an Exchange implementation that you choose a unique organization name that can be used in perpetuity for the company or group at which Exchange Server is implemented.

Once an organization name has been chosen, it cannot be changed without reinstalling Exchange. The Exchange Organization name is used to generate the users' email addresses.

1

Exchange Server uses the organization's name to generate email addresses. Additionally, note that although the organization name can consist of a total of 64 characters, it makes life a bit easier for the user community if the organization name is much shorter than the maximum allowed.

Within an organization, there may be one or more sites. The Exchange term *site* can be thought of as a collection of one or more Exchange Server computers that share the same directory information. Typically, these computers are physically located within a close geographical proximity, but this is not a requirement.

For administrative purposes, it may make more sense to choose unique site names based on the physical location or business function of a site's Exchange user community instead of using randomly generated site names. For example, the organization name can be the name of a company (for example, Microsoft), and the unique site names might be Chicago and Milwaukee or Purchasing and Accounting. Just as with organization names, a site name can contain up to 64 characters.

Within a site, there may be one or more servers. The Exchange term *server* is an aggregation of users. An Exchange server name is, by default, the same as the Microsoft Windows NT Server's computer name. Although you can change the server name to any unique name, for simplicity's sake (and to help maintain the sanity of the system administrators) it is not recommended that the server name differ from the Windows NT computer name. Unlike the organization and site names, a server name cannot exceed 15 characters in length.

At the bottom of the Microsoft Exchange heap are the users. An Exchange Server *user* is the human being who sits down and writes, sends, or receives the electronic mail messages transmitted around by the Microsoft Exchange messaging system(s).

•Information about the limitations of user capabilities per server, suggested naming conventions for user mailboxes, and the like can be found in Day 2, "Planning and Designing an Exchange Messaging Environment."

Table 1.1 describes additional important components for the Exchange Server messaging architecture, including some of the more typically used, but discretionary, components of Exchange Server.

Table 1.1. Primary Exchange Server components.

Component Name	Description
Administrator program	The system administration software, which has a GUI interface that allows for easy systems administration of a Microsoft Exchange Server computer. The primary features of the Administrator program include, but are not limited to, Server, Connector, Folders, and Mailbox Maintenance.
Address Book	This piece of the Exchange Server displays recipient names within the directory including mailboxes, public folders, custom recipients, and a user-defined number of address lists.
Connector	Connectors are used for the routing of messages between Exchange Server sites, as well as between Exchange Server sites and non-Exchange messaging systems.
	For example, the IBM OfficeVision/VM Connector permits Exchange Server users to transmit messages between an Exchange Server site and a legacy system's messaging system.
Custom recipients	A non-Exchange messaging system recipient whose email address is in the Address Book.
Directory	This component contains a list of all the Exchange organization's resources and users, similar to how an index of a road atlas provides city and street location information to a lost driver. Used by other Exchange system elements, the primary purpose of the Directory is for addressing and routing messages to the appropriate destination(s).
Directory replication	The Exchange process required for maintaining directory data for all servers within a single site, as well as between all sites.
Directory synchronization	Required only if a non-Microsoft Exchange messaging system is operating alongside the Exchange Server messaging system. That is, if there are at least two different messaging systems in the mix, at least two distinct directory structures must be maintained. Exchange Server automatically maintains the addressing information between Exchange and the

1

Component Name	Description
	non-Exchange system, provided that the other system conforms to the Microsoft Mail directory synchronization protocol standard.
Distribution lists	A list of users' mailboxes contained as an individual recipient. This list can then be referenced by a user to send a single email message to one or more users without having to manually specify every single user required.
Forms Designer	The purpose of this Exchange component, which actually resides on the client side, is to permit end-users to create special forms or applications. The Forms Designer permits customization of the Exchange messaging environment in any way that makes sense for a company that implements Microsoft Exchange Server.
Information store	The Exchange storage component that contains the mailboxes, replicates the public folders, and acts as the "policeman" for Exchange (it is the system's security enforcer). This component consists of two separate databases: the Public Information Store and the Private Information Store. In the Standard Edition of Microsoft Exchange Server, there is a 16-gigabyte Information Store storage limit; the Enterprise Edition has no upper storage limit.
Internet Mail Services (IMS)	The primary function of the Internet Mail Services is to enable Exchange Servers to connect to the Internet. The IMS Connector can be configured to link an Exchange Server with another site that supports the SMTP, MIME, RFC-822 plain text, or MS Mail Server-compliant messaging types.
Key Management Server (KMS)	The centralized point of security within an Exchange organization. KMS controls the encryption keys necessary to unlock secured messages. It is important to have only one KMS within an organization; multiple occurrences of the Key Management Server may cause authentication or encryption errors.
Mailbox	The Private Information Store in which all Exchange users' messages are located.

continues

Table 1.1. continued

Component Name	Description
Personal folders	A folder that enables an Exchange user to store messaging data on his or her own hard drive, as opposed to having to keep information on an Exchange Server. Personal folders permit the offline reading or creation of messages without having to maintain a connection to an Exchange Server.
Public folders	A collection of messaging data stored in the Public Information Store. Public folders can contain a variety of information including email messages, binary files, graphics, voice-mail messages, workflow documents, and so on.
System Attendant	A maintenance service that must be operational for Exchange services to function properly. The System Attendant can generate message tracking logs and automate proxy address generation. There are no major changes in the System Attendant from Exchange Version 5.

1.5. Introduction to the Message Transfer Agent

The Message Transfer Agent (MTA) is the nucleus of the Microsoft Exchange messaging architecture: It is one of the core components of Exchange Server. The MTA is the function that submits, routes, and delivers messages across the Exchange architecture to other Exchange Server MTAs, to gateways for non-Exchange messaging systems, and the Exchange Information Stores. Additionally, MTA can be used for the same functionality to any of the ten Microsoft Exchange connectors.

For example, in the case of the Microsoft Mail Connector MTA, the MTA performs the task of moving the required messages from the Exchange Server's Information Store to one or more Microsoft Mail post offices. In this way, the Exchange messaging system permits its users to send mail to Microsoft Mail post office users on the same LAN without first having to convert the messages into the MS Mail format.

1.6. Exchange Server Connectors

Microsoft Exchange Server provides a series of connectivity options that make it possible to connect Exchange sites with each other as well as with numerous other non-Exchange Server messaging systems. These connectors include the following:

- **cc:Mail Connector:** Used to provide connectivity and directory replication between an Exchange site and the Lotus cc:Mail electronic mail system.

- **Directory Replication Connector:** The principal mechanism used to configure directory replication between Exchange sites.

- **Dynamic RAS Connector:** Used to connect two or more Exchange Server sites across a dial-up remote access services (RAS) link, without having to first convert messages into a different format.

- **Exchange Connector for IBM OfficeVision/VM:** Used to create the connection between an OfficeVision/VM (PROFS) email environment and an Exchange Server.

- **Exchange Connector for Lotus Notes:** Used to create the connection between Lotus Notes and an Exchange Server.

- **Exchange Connector for SNADS:** Used to create the connection between a SNADS-compliant messaging environment and an Exchange Server.

- **Internet Mail Services:** Used to connect an Exchange Server with the Internet for the transmission of SMTP-compliant messages. These services can also be used to provide connectivity and directory replication between an Exchange site and an SMTP-compliant messaging system.

- **Microsoft Mail Connector:** Used to create the connection between an older Microsoft Mail post office and an Exchange Server. This connector can also be used to establish a connection between Exchange and a Microsoft Mail-compliant messaging system such as the Microsoft Mail for AppleTalk network email system.

- **Schedule+ Free/Busy Connector:** Used to manage free/busy scheduling information from Schedule+ for Microsoft Mail connections.

- **Site Connector:** Used to connect two or more Exchange Server sites across a LAN or WAN link, without having to first convert messages into a different format.

- **X.400 Connector:** Used to provide connectivity and directory replication between an Exchange site and an X.400 messaging system.

It is important to note that although each connector serves a distinct purpose, the Microsoft Mail Connector can be used for linking Exchange with non-Microsoft electronic messaging systems, provided that those systems are Microsoft Mail-compliant. Furthermore, the Internet Mail Services connector can be configured to perform similar tasks for SMTP, MIME, RFC-822 plain text, and other MS Mail server-compliant messaging types.

1.7. Summary

This chapter provided you with a basic understanding of Microsoft Exchange Server and introduced some of the more complicated items of an Exchange implementation. As you move into the next 13 days, you will fully comprehend the details of the concepts presented in this chapter. If you take this knowledge one step further, you can discover the various intricacies of Exchange Server and how to use those details to install, configure, and maintain an Exchange Server messaging environment.

These details form the basis of the understanding required to successfully pass the Microsoft Certified Systems Engineer examination. Although this exam can be viewed as the culmination of the learning process, it should not be seen as the end-all of Microsoft Exchange Server 5.5 knowledge. Regardless of your goals, this book starts your acquisition of Exchange Server 5.5 knowledge.

Lab

This lab consists of review questions pertaining to this chapter and provides an opportunity to apply the knowledge you've gained in this chapter.

Questions

1. The hierarchical order of an Exchange messaging environment is
   _____.

   A. Sites, servers, and organizations

   B. Organization, sites, and servers

   C. Organizations, servers, and sites

   D. None of the above

2. An Exchange Server Enterprise Edition information store may not exceed
   _____.

   A. 16 megabytes

   B. 16 gigabytes

   C. 16 terabytes

   D. Information stores are unlimited in size

3. The new Exchange Connector for IBM OfficeVision/VM and for SNADS are both available through _____.

   A. The Standard Edition of Microsoft Exchange Server

   B. The Global Edition of Microsoft Exchange Server

   C. The Enterprise Edition of Microsoft Exchange Server

   D. None of the above

4. The _____ is the component responsible for submitting, routing, and delivering messages across an Exchange messaging environment.

   A. Directory Connector

   B. Routing Connector

   C. Message Transfer Agent

   D. MS Mail Connector

5. Information stores contain _____.

    A. Public folders, private folders

    B. Public folders, private folders, messaging folders

    C. Public folders

    D. Private folders

6. The _____ is used for connecting two or more Exchange Server sites across a LAN or WAN link, without having to first convert messages into a different format.

    A. Dynamic RAS Connector

    B. Site Connector

    C. X.400 Connector

    D. All of the above

7. The centralized point of security within an Exchange environment is the _____.

    A. Certificate Server

    B. Key Management Server

    C. Security Server

    D. None of the above

8. The improved Exchange backup API allows for a top-end backup limit of _____ of data per hour.

    A. 5 gigabytes

    B. 10 gigabytes

    C. 25 gigabytes

    D. 50 gigabytes

9. A well-designed Exchange messaging system contains _____ Key Management Servers for security purposes.

    A. 0

    B. 1

    C. 3

    D. 5

10. Which of the following Internet protocols does Exchange Server support?

   A. SMTP, HTTP

   B. LDAP

   C. NNTP

   D. Both **A** and **B**

   E. All of the above

Answers to Questions

1. **B** The top level of the Exchange hierarchy is an organization, so A and C cannot be the correct answer. Because B is the correct choice, D is obviously not right.

2. **D** Answer A is way too small for almost any Exchange implementation. For the Exchange Server Standard Edition, B is the correct answer, but we are seeking the answer for the Enterprise Edition. Under any Exchange implementation, answer C is an extremely large information store. The correct answer is D, because Exchange Server information stores are now limited only by the amount of free hard drive space available to the Exchange messaging system.

3. **C** Answer A is incorrect because the Standard Edition contains nearly all the Exchange connectors except for these two. Answer B is incorrect because there is no such thing as a Global Edition of Microsoft Exchange Server.

4. **C** Answer A is incorrect because there is no such thing as a Directory Connector for Microsoft Exchange Server. Answer B is incorrect because there is no such thing as a Routing Connector for Microsoft Exchange Server. Answer D is incorrect because the MS Mail Connector is used to permit a non-Exchange system (such as Microsoft Mail for either the PC or Macintosh, or Novell GroupWise) to communicate easily with an Exchange messaging system.

5. **A** Answer B is incorrect because there is no such thing as a messaging folders component for the Exchange Server system. Answer C is incorrect because the public folder is just one piece of the information store—another is necessary. Answer D is incorrect because the private folder is just one piece of the information store—another is necessary.

6. **B** Answer A is incorrect because the Dynamic RAS Connector is used to connect two Exchange Server Sites with a Windows NT RAS dial-up connectivity method. RAS would not be used by two Exchange Servers on the same

LAN. Answer C is incorrect because the X.400 Connector is used to connect an Exchange Server environment with a non-Exchange messaging system that supports the CCITT's X.400 email format.

7. **B**   Although a certificate server is recommended, technically answer A is not correct because it is the Key Management Server component that generates certificates for an Exchange messaging system environment. Answer C is incorrect because the term "Security Server" is a make-believe component (that is, it does not really exist and therefore cannot be the correct answer).

8. **C**   Answer A is incorrect because just 5 gigabytes per hour is quite slow for most enterprise messaging systems. Answer B is incorrect because although 10 gigabytes per hour is better, it is not quite what is possible for Microsoft Exchange Server. Answer D is incorrect because although we would love to see this speed available in a future version of Microsoft Exchange Server, this may just be wishful thinking.

9. **B**   Answer A is incorrect because not having a Key Management Server is not a recommended choice. Answers C and D, having more than a single Key Management Server, is not a wise idea in the current release of Exchange Server because it may cause valid certificates to be read as invalid by a different Key Management Server (for example, a server that did not create it) and so is not the correct choice. It is rumored, however, that the first Service Pack release for Exchange Server 5.5 will finally support multiple Key Management Servers, an important feature for those enterprise-size Exchange implementations with numerous sites.

10. **D**   In answer A, SMTP and HTTP are both valid Internet protocols available to an Exchange Server administrator. However, there are more protocols, so this is not the right choice. LDAP is a valid Internet protocol available to an Exchange Server administrator. There are more protocols, however, so this is not the right choice. The NNTP protocol is a valid Internet protocol available to an Exchange Server administrator. There are more protocols, however, so C is not the right choice.

TEST DAY
FAST FACTS

Here are a few fast facts about this chapter that you may want to know ahead of time. These facts provide great last-minute study material.

- The Exchange Server naming conventions comprise an extremely important piece of the Exchange Server infrastructure design and should not be taken lightly.

- The organization name must be unique and cannot be changed after it has been selected.

- Exchange site names must be unique and cannot be changed after they have been chosen.

- Exchange Server names must be unique; although they can be changed at any time in the future, doing so is a very difficult and tedious process, fraught with multiple points of failure.

- An Exchange directory name is generally created from the alias name and cannot be modified after it has been generated.

- More is better when it comes to hardware requirements for an Exchange Server messaging system environment, especially in terms of multiple hard drives and controllers, as well as additional system memory.

- The three factors for a successful Exchange Server implementation are design, design, and design.

Day 2

Planning and Designing an Exchange Messaging Environment

by Keith Powell

Microsoft Exchange Server is more than just another electronic mail system. It is a full-blown, enterprise-level messaging system designed by Microsoft to handle every type of business from a mom-and-pop retail outlet to one of the largest corporations on the planet. In addition, because Exchange Server can scale from the very small to the very large, it is imperative that you plan your Exchange Server messaging environment very carefully. This chapter delves into the planning and design steps you should take before actually implementing Exchange in a production environment.

Objectives

This chapter addresses the following Microsoft exam objectives:

- Choose an implementation strategy for Microsoft Exchange Server
- Develop a long-term coexistence strategy
- Develop an infrastructure for Exchange Server

2.1. Exchange Server Installation Requirements

Microsoft Exchange Server Version 5.5 changes the licensing possibilities from earlier versions of the product. With Exchange Server 5.5, the "per server" licensing mode is the only one available. Along those same lines, when you install an Exchange Server, it is important to enter the proper Product ID Code (PID) for each server being installed instead of just typing all 1s or using the same PID for every server installation. One of the reasons for doing so is that it makes support calls and software licensing updates easier if the PID number exists on each Exchange Server within your company's messaging environment.

The installation requirements for a Microsoft Exchange Server implementation vary by type of installation (Standard or Enterprise Edition) as well as by processor type (Intel or Alpha RISC). Microsoft publishes a minimum set of system requirements in its Microsoft TechNet product (available from Microsoft directly; call 1-425-635-7035 for additional information). Through experience, you will realize that although the Microsoft-suggested standards usually work for the initial installation of Exchange, more is usually better. Table 2.1 lists the base installation requirements for Microsoft Exchange Server.

Table 2.1. Exchange Server installation requirements.

Exchange Server Type	CPU Type	Operating System
Standard Edition	Intel or compatible system	Windows NT Server 4.0, with Service Pack 3 or later

- 60 MHz Intel Pentium or faster (133 MHz recommended)
- 24M memory (32M recommended)
- 250M available hard disk space (500M recommended)
- CD-ROM drive

Exchange Server Type	CPU Type	Operating System
Standard Edition	RISC-based systems with an Alpha processor	Windows NT Server 4.0, with Service Pack 3 or later
■ 32M memory (48M recommended)		
■ 300M available hard disk space (500M recommended)		
■ CD-ROM drive		
Enterprise Edition	Intel or compatible system	Windows NT Server 4.0, with Service Pack 3 or later
■ 60 MHz Intel Pentium or faster (133 MHz recommended)		
■ 64M memory		
■ 250M available hard disk space (500M recommended)		
■ CD-ROM drive		
Enterprise Edition	RISC-based systems with an Alpha processor	Windows NT Server 4.0, with Service Pack 3 or later
■ 64M memory		
■ 300M available hard disk space (500M recommended)		
■ CD-ROM drive		

Deciding on the "correct" hardware requirements for an Exchange Server implementation is a difficult task. Although the concept of "more is better" holds true for nearly any computer systems implementation, this is not a completely solid piece of advice. Nobody should just throw money at a problem until it becomes a solution; instead, you will probably have a "trial and error" approach to find the most acceptable environment for your organization.

As with any software application, there is a method to the madness of determining the proper hardware requirements to support a deployment of Microsoft Exchange Server. One of the better approaches for Exchange is to review hard disk requirements and optimization first, then consider memory requirements, and then look at system processor needs.

Let's discuss the hard disk requirements first. Exchange Server operates on a single hard drive, of any of the following types: IDE, EIDE, EISA, and SCSI. Additionally, Exchange requires a minimum of 250M of disk space on an Intel-based system; it requires 300M of disk space on an Alpha-based system.

The differences between the Standard and Enterprise Editions of Exchange Server 5.5 are slight. The Standard Edition consists of the following components:

- Exchange Server Version 5.5 software
- Microsoft Outlook 97 client software
- Microsoft Exchange Connector
- Internet Mail Services Connector
- cc:Mail Connector
- Lotus NotesConnector
- MS Mail Connector
- Internet News Service
- Collaboration Data Objects
- Microsoft Visual InterDev
- Microsoft Exchange Chat Service

The Enterprise Edition contains all the components of the Standard Edition plus the following elements:

- Unlimited Storage
- X.400 Connector
- Exchange Connector IBM OfficeVision/VM
- Exchange Connector for SNADS

2.1.1. Exchange Server Address Space

An Exchange Server *address space* is a routing entry that identifies a certain type of message to a specific Exchange Server Connector. Exchange uses each address space entry as a filter to determine how a message should be moved through the Exchange messaging architecture (for example, to determine whether the message is passed through a gateway or a connector). For example, the Internet Mail Service (IMS) Connector permits the addition of a series of Internet domain names, X.400 names, and other Exchange Server IMS names in the address space properties. This allows for the routing of messages through the newly installed IMS Connector of the Exchange Server.

2.1.2. Exchange Server Hardware Suggestions

Your Exchange Server messaging infrastructure design team should focus specifically on the Exchange servers that will be hosting the public folders for the organization. The sizing of the hardware for the public folders depends on the users' usage patterns, so you should conduct a careful analysis of the Exchange Server pilot implementation. If this implementation is to be for a large corporation, it is wise to consider using a pool of Exchange public folder servers. Remember that the Public Information Store is really a separate database, so there are two areas on which you, as the Exchange system administrator, can focus your attention:

- If there appears to be a lot of Read activity (as is usually the case for Internet newsgroups public folders), turn your focus toward the disk drives that contain the Information Store's Public database.

- If there appears to be a lot of Write activity (such as the storing of network newsfeeds on the public folders), turn your attention to the disk drives that contain the IS Public logs.

Again, the focus for creating additional Exchange Servers across your business's messaging infrastructure depends mostly on usage patterns. User activity in an Exchange implementation will drive the loads of both the Exchange Server and the network. Here are some of the usage patterns to analyze:

- The number of messages sent and received daily
- Use of distribution lists
- The percentage of messages that stay on the server from which they were sent; also the reverse (the percentage of messages that go to recipients on other Exchange Servers)
- Use of public folders; on the average, how much information (in megabytes) is copied to and from the public folders on any one Exchange Server in a given day? week? month?
- The mean, median, and mode sizes of standard messages as well as messages that have file attachments
- The number of users just browsing, moving, or rereading messages on a given day, in a week, and each month

- Where is the work done for the typical user? Does it occur on the same Exchange Server on which that user's mailbox is assigned, or is it on another Exchange Server, or even another Exchange site?

Continually updating these answers enables an Exchange administrator to properly administer the Exchange Server messaging environment. Other considerations when sizing the hardware configurations of the Exchange Servers include the following:

- What else is running at the Exchange Server's site?
- What else is running on that particular Exchange Server?
- Will the Exchange Servers to be deployed run other loads, such as other Microsoft BackOffice applications, file or print services, domain controllers, and so on?
- How will the CPU utilization of each Exchange Server be controlled? This issue becomes especially important if LDAP searches, server-side scripts, and ActiveX object applications activated from Active Server Pages (ASP) are permitted on any of the Exchange Servers within your messaging environment.

For Exchange Server computers that directly support users, there are several tips and tricks for making an Exchange deployment a bit smoother:

- Use a separate, fast disk drive and controller for the Information Store log and the IS database. Doing this can easily result in a 25-to-30-percent increase in hard drive system performance.
- Use dedicated hard disk drives for both the IS logs and the database. Information Store logs grow linearly because each transaction writes to the disk in order. If the logs use separate hard drives, the log can always quickly resume exactly where it left off, thereby improving system performance.
- Strongly consider using the RAID 5 level of fault tolerance. Not only can this improve the Exchange Server's performance, it is also a safety precaution for your organization's messaging information. Because both the IS logs and database are on the same hard drive, if that drive fails, the only recovery option is from tape backup (a possibly slow, time-intensive, expensive recovery process).
- Use the fastest CPUs your group can afford.
- Use multiprocessor-ready machines, especially those with large L2 caches.
- Ensure that there is adequate memory in the Windows NT Server computer on which Exchange is installed (check memory use with a series of Windows NT Performance Monitors over a period of time).

- Ensure that there is adequate network bandwidth for the Windows NT Server computer on which Exchange is installed (check bandwidth use with either a series of Windows NT Performance Monitors or a network sniffer/management device).

- Use the FAT file allocation system instead of NTFS for all Information Store logs, where possible. There is much less system overhead associated with FAT than there is with NTFS; security should not be a concern if the only items on that hard disk drive are the Microsoft Exchange Server's IS log files. Like a lot of other things, this tip also has a "gotcha": If the hard drive partition is greater than 512M, NTFS will be more efficient than FAT. Therefore, it is a good idea to select the file system based on the actual size of the drive partition on which the log files will be stored.

Perhaps the ideal Microsoft Exchange Server public folders hardware configuration is as follows:

- A single fast-wide SCSI-3 hard disk drive (mirrored) for the Exchange Server Information Stores transaction logs.

- A single fast-wide SCSI-3 hard disk drive (mirrored) for the Windows NT Server operating system, including the swap file.

- Multiple striped-with-parity, fast-wide SCSI-3 hard disk drives for the Information Stores database.

- More than one Intel 300 MHz Pentium II CPU or a 500 MHz DEC Alpha CPU for system processing power.

- Lots and lots of memory for the server, starting at 256M of EDO or better DRAM. When it comes to Microsoft Exchange Server implementations, the more memory the merrier.

2.2. Exchange Server Naming Conventions

Naming the various components of an Exchange Server implementation may seem trivial, but, in fact, it is a very important piece of an Exchange Server infrastructure design. Most first-time administrators and users of Microsoft Exchange fail to fully grasp all the implications of creating a precise naming convention for their organization, a fact that usually comes back to haunt them somewhere down the road.

One of the first steps in creating a naming convention for an Exchange Server design is figuring out exactly what needs naming. Several pieces of Exchange require specific names:

- Organization name
- Site name(s)
- Server name(s)
- Mailbox names
- Custom recipient name(s)
- Connector name(s)
- Monitor name(s)
- Container name(s)
- Public folder name(s)
- SMTP address format
- MS mail address format
- X.400 address format

A few ground rules first: With Windows NT Server Version 5.0 (and Active Directory) right around the corner, so to speak, it is wise to follow a simple guideline that will make the transition to Windows NT 5.0 that much easier in the future. This guideline is for any Exchange Server component name (as well as for the Windows NT domain and server names), do not use any of the reserved DNS and NetBIOS characters. If you are not sure what these characters are, refer to Table 2.2.

Table 2.2. DNS and NetBIOS reserved characters.

Character Symbol	English Name
+	Plus
~	Tilde
\	Backslash
	Space
]	Right Bracket
[	Left Bracket
<	Less Than
>	Greater Than

Character Symbol	English Name
,	Comma
$	Dollar Sign
^	Carat or Accent Circumflex
}	Right Curly Brace
{	Left Curly Brace
*	Asterisk
¦	Broken Vertical Bar
•	Bullet
§	Section Sign
=	Equal Sign
/	Solidus
¶	Paragraph Mark
:	Colon
$	Currency Sign
;	Semicolon
?	Question Mark
#	Number Sign

Microsoft has also stipulated a few other characters you cannot use when assigning Windows NT Server names. Table 2.3 lists the other invalid characters for server names.

Table 2.3. Invalid characters for a Microsoft Windows NT Server name.

Character Symbol	English Name
•	Bullet
$	Currency Sign
"	Curly Quotation Mark
^	Carat or Accent Circumflex
}	Right Curly Brace
{	Left Curly Brace
§	Section Sign
¶	Paragraph Mark
,	Comma

continues

Table 2.3. continued

Character Symbol	English Name
$	Dollar Sign
¦	Broken Vertical Bar
~	Tilde
;	Semicolon
#	Number Sign

As you can see, most of the characters you cannot use for Windows NT Server names are also DNS or NetBIOS reserved characters. Avoiding any combination of the characters listed in Tables 2.2 and 2.3 is a good practice.

2.2.1. Organization Name

Let's start at the top with what is usually the easiest naming convention to select: the organization name. This is an essential name for Exchange Server deployment and is typically the name of your group or business. Because this is the name used to create email addresses, it should probably be kept as short as possible while still reflecting the proper name of the business or group.

For example, a company such as KVP Consulting may use the organization name KVP, which enables the creation of email addresses such as jdoe@kvp.com (for John Doe, a user at the company known as KVP Consulting). The only Exchange Server restriction is that the organization name cannot exceed 64 characters; however, if connectivity to legacy systems is either wanted or just plain unavoidable, you are wise to limit the organization's name to less than 9 characters. No matter what name is selected, the Exchange Server infrastructure design team must be sure of that name. After the organization name has been specified in Exchange, you cannot alter it without completely reinstalling the entire Exchange messaging system (not a good or cheap task).

2.2.2. Site Names

Moving down the list, site names are next to be specified. Once again, the Exchange Server restrictions are that site names cannot exceed 64 characters and that all site names must be unique. For the sake of simplicity, name sites according to their geographic or physical location or by their functionality within the company. For example, an Exchange designer may pick Midwest as the site name for the Exchange Server locations in Chicago, Cisne, Owatonna, and Nashville (see Figure 2.1).

Figure 2.1.

Selecting an Exchange Server site name.

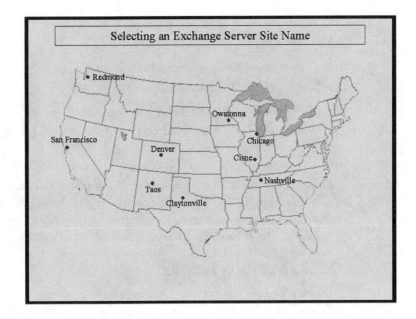

Selecting an Exchange Server Site Name

Redmond
Owatonna
San Francisco
Chicago
Denver
Cisne
Nashville
Taos
Claytonville

2

Other site names that make sense may revolve around business functions. For example, within a single physical location, you may have an Electronic Commerce department, a Sales department, and an MIS department. Because these user groups tend to work together but do not co-mingle, creating a site for each separate function might be a good idea. Following that same logic, it would make sense to name the sites `EC`, `Sales`, and `MIS`. It is important to remember that the Exchange Server site name is used to generate directory names and foreign email addresses, so be careful when selecting each unique name. Also, as is true for the organization name, once you select a site name, you cannot change it without reinstalling that Exchange Server. Make it right the first time!

2.2.3. Server Names

Next on the list of things to name are the Exchange Server names. Microsoft Exchange uses the Windows NT Server computer name as its default Exchange Server name. Although you can change this name, it is wiser to select the server name at the Windows NT Server level rather than at the Exchange Server level. The Exchange Server name must be unique, so to, the organization and site names. However, unlike those names, the Exchange Server name can be changed if necessary.

To change the server name, the Exchange Server/Windows NT administrator must follow these steps:

1. Remove the Exchange Server from the site.
2. Rename the Windows NT Server.
3. Reinstall Microsoft Exchange Server.
4. Reconfigure the Microsoft Exchange Server as it was before you took this severe course of action.

Keep in mind that it is very time-consuming, complex, and expensive (in terms of time) to rename an Exchange Server computer; plan the names carefully. Exchange Server names can contain up to 15 characters but should not contain any of the DNS or NetBIOS reserved characters listed earlier in Table 2.2.

2.2.4. Mailbox Names

The next Exchange Server item requiring a naming convention is that of the Exchange users' mailboxes. There are five parts to a mailbox name:

- First name
- Last name
- Alias name
- Display name
- Directory name

A user's first name and last name each cannot exceed 64 characters (for a total of 128 characters) and can be changed without much difficulty. The purpose of these two mailbox fields should be obvious to even the casual user of Exchange.

The alias name can be considered a nickname for the user and should be much shorter than the 64 characters permitted. Note that the default manner in which directory names are created is based on mailbox alias names, so it is important to be careful when creating the alias naming standard. For example, the Exchange user Genevieve Snow may have an Exchange mailbox alias of genevieves. Mailboxes can have more than one alias name, and alias names can be changed on the fly. However, it is *very* important to remember that if your Exchange implementation uses the mailbox alias to create the directory names, the directory names cannot be changed once they have been established. So once again, be careful when creating this naming convention.

Because the display name for an Exchange mailbox should be consistent across the Exchange messaging enterprise, it is important to choose a standardized naming convention for your group's Exchange Server display names. Display names can consist of up to 256 characters and can be changed at will. The display name is the name shown in the windowof the Administrator program and in the Exchange Address Book; the display name should accurately reflect the Exchange user's true identity. For example, the display name can be formatted in any of the following ways:

- First Name, Last Name (Frank Snow)
- Last Name, First Name (Snow, Frank)
- Last Name, First Name, Middle Initial (Snow, Frank J.)
- First Initial, Last Name (FSnow)
- First Initial, Middle Initial, Last Name (FJSnow)

The final piece of the mailbox name is the Exchange directory name. By default, the directory name is created from the Exchange alias name, but this is not required. An Exchange system administrator can alter the method in which directory names are created by using the Tools Option menu. Whatever method is used, it is essential to note that once a directory name has been selected for a particular user, that name can never be changed because Exchange Server uses the directory name as a permanent way to identify that user's object in the directory structure. The directory name can consist of up to 64 characters, but is unalterable once it has been selected for any Exchange user.

2.2.5. Custom Recipient Names

Next up is the Exchange naming convention for custom recipient names. Simply put, a *custom recipient* is an Exchange user whose email address is actually located on a foreign (that is, a non-Microsoft Exchange) messaging system but who exists in the Microsoft Exchange Server directory. Persons who access the Exchange Server use their custom recipient name with an address in a format that the other email system can readily understand. The custom recipient name is limited by the foreign email system, not by Microsoft Exchange Server. Therefore, it is important for an Exchange system administrator to properly configure the custom recipient name following the standards of the foreign email system.

2.2.6. Miscellaneous Exchange Names

The Exchange Server naming conventions for Exchange system connectors, monitors, containers, and public folders should be consistent across the Exchange messaging infrastructure. These names should also make sense for each individual item. For example, the Dynamic RAS Connector between the Owatonna and Redmond locations might be named Owatonna RAS on the Redmond Exchange Server and Redmond RAS on the Owatonna Exchange Server. Likewise, it makes more sense to name public folders according to their use instead of giving them generic names such as PublicFolder1, PublicFolder2, PublicFolder3, and so on. For example, the three public folders attached to the Exchange Servers in the Chicago office might be named EC Clients, Internet Newsgroups, and CVM Sales Prospects.

So that the users of an Exchange Server messaging deployment can communicate with other electronic mail systems, email-naming standards are necessary (Exchange users must have addresses that other systems can understand). For MS Mail (PC, not Macintosh), X.400, and Internet (SMTP) addresses, Microsoft Exchange Server automatically generates an email address for each of its users (see Table 2.4). These addresses are based on the user Genevieve Snow (alias GenevieveS), whose Exchange mailbox is located in the Midwest site, in the KVP organization.

Table 2.4. Email addresses automatically generated by Exchange Server.

Exchange Address Type	Email Address Generated
Microsoft Mail (PC)	KVP/MIDWEST/GENEVIEVES
Internet (SMTP)	Genevieves@midwest.kvp.com
X.400 address	g=Genevieve; s=Snow; o=Midwest; p=KVP; a=mci; c=us

Other Exchange Server names that may require standards are those for any third-party gateways, which may exist for establishing connectivity to other systems. The Microsoft Exchange Server default is for the gateway to use the Exchange alias name in the creation of these foreign addresses.

To sum up, there are several concerns when you are establishing a solid Microsoft Exchange Server naming convention:

- The naming convention should make it easy to identify sites, servers, and connectors—especially if the names are to make it easy to use and administer the Exchange Server messaging system

- Each site must use the same organization name
- All the site names must be unique
- All the server names must be unique
- The display names for a user's mailbox should be consistent throughout the entire organization
- There should be unique top-level public folder names
- There will exist unique Message Class IDs for the Organization Forms Library
- No DNS or NetBIOS reserved characters can be used for any organization, site, Exchange Server, or Windows NT Server names anywhere in the entire Exchange messaging enterprise
- Alias names must be unique so that the unique directory names created automatically will make sense to any Exchange Server system administrator

Now that you understand the importance of creating an Exchange naming convention, it is time to begin designing the remainder of the Exchange Server architecture.

2.3. Exchange Server Infrastructure Design

Planning a Microsoft Exchange Server implementation takes time—lots of it. Numerous tasks are necessary, including time spent thinking about those tasks, and then intensely debating them with others on the project team. The time to change your mind is during these planning stages and not following a rollout.

The primary reason for planning any project, such as an Exchange Server messaging system, is to minimize the risk of something going wrong. It is usually the intention of everyone involved in any project to do it right the first time, so that they don't have to go back and perform the same task twice. Designing a Microsoft Exchange Server infrastructure is no different. The designing or planning phase is all about risk aversion. As with most other systems projects, there are three levels of risk aversion to an Exchange Server deployment:

- Do not do any planning now and just deal with the consequences as situations arise in the future.
- Use the design stage to try to reduce the likelihood of anything going astray; but if anything happens, have a planned response to such issues. For example,

design a backup and recovery system into your Exchange environment and test itthoroughly to make sure that it works. Then, if you ever experience a disaster, the planned response is to use the backup tapes as necessary.

■ Create such a thorough and complete Exchange System design that there can be no problems. This option is also known as the full risk-aversion methodology. It is also by far the most expensive to implement (some would argue that it is impossible to implement).

Another piece of the design phase that helps ensure that the Exchange Server messaging implementation will go smoothly is the notion of a true "pilot" project. A *pilot installation* is a minimal install of Exchange Server along with a few of the client types that will be present in the full rollout of your organization. The pilot part of the design phase is where questions regarding a particular design segment can be tested and proven.

For a pilot implementation to be truly successful, it should be seen as a "throw-away" installation. That is, when the pilot time frame is complete (usually a 4-to-6-week period), the software configurations are deleted from both the client and the server computers. Using an existing pilot installation of Microsoft Exchange Server as a starting point for the full implementation is downright foolish. Many companies do this only to find out later down the road that it was an avoidable and costly mistake.

2.3.1. Planning for Exchange with a Windows NT Server Design

The first piece of a complete Exchange Server messaging environment is actually its non-Exchange Server component: the Windows NT Server operating system (OS). Windows NT Server is Microsoft's premier 32-bit network operating system, a multithreaded, multitasking OS that provides a very scalable and robust platform for an Exchange Server messaging environment.

Microsoft Exchange Server 5.5 requires Microsoft Windows NT Server Version 4.0 with Service Pack 3 (or later) loaded. The hardware requirements for an Exchange Server can get very detailed and messy, so that discussion comes later in this chapter. Configuring the Windows NT base of an Exchange Server implementation can be difficult and confusing for the first-time user, so these subjects are covered first.

Planning the Windows NT Domain Architecture

At the heart of any Exchange Server implementation is its Windows NT operating system domain architecture. Windows NT is responsible for managing the users and user groups, as well as the file security and access authentication for the network. Microsoft Exchange Server is tightly integrated into the Windows NT security model, so the configuration of the Windows NT domain becomes as vital to Exchange as it is to Windows NT itself.

What is a Windows NT domain? A Windows NT *domain* can be thought of as a logical group of Windows NT servers and workstations, with all the authentication functions being handled by the domain controllers. The Windows domain architecture structure can range from the very simple to the extremely complex. However, every domain created possesses a Primary Domain Controller (PDC) and probably at least one Backup Domain Controller (BDC)—although a Windows NT domain does not require a BDC. The PDC is the primary server whose function is to control the Windows NT network operating system environment. The purpose of a BDC is twofold: To act as a backup to the PDC should it ever fail, and to help with the authentication of users as necessary.

There are multiple types of Windows NT domains:

- Single domain model
- Master domain model
- Multiple Master domain model
- Complete Trust domain model

To understand these various Windows NT domain models, it is important to first grasp the concept of trust relationships among Windows NT domains.

Understanding Windows NT Trusts

The *trust relationship* between a Windows NT domain and one or more other Windows NT domains is the basis for this discussion. Microsoft created two types of trust relationships—one way and two way—for the purpose of permitting users from one domain to use resources from another domain without the cumbersome administrative issues of creating user IDs and passwords for the same user across multiple servers in different domains. Compared to other available network operating systems, this feature alone is reason enough to use Windows NT over any other network operating system on the market today.

A Windows NT administrator can establish a one-way trust between two domains; the first domain is the *trusting domain*, and the second domain is the *trusted domain*. The trusted domain is the domain that contains the users and user groups who will be able to use the resources contained within the trusting domain. This arrangement permits the second, or trusted, domain to continue to manage its users and resources while remaining completely autonomous of the first, or trusting, domain. Figure 2.2 shows an example of a trusting and trusted domain structure.

An easy way to remember the difference between "trusting" and "trusted" domains is by taking the word *trusted* and breaking it into two words: *Trust Ed. Ed* is the name of a user, so the trusted domain must be the one that contains the user accounts and global groups. Therefore, the trusting domain must be the one that contains the resources.

Figure 2.2.

Basic Windows NT Server trusts.

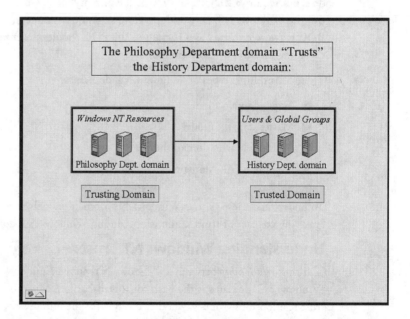

The other type of trust is a two-way trust between domains. (Actually, there is no such thing as a two-way trust; the arrangement is two one-way trusts between the same two domain controllers.) Taking what we have learned about the one-way trust, a two-way trust is simply an extension of that: both domains involved now share resources fully between them. A Windows NT administrator can create two-way trusts between any number of domains in order to grant the access rights necessary for each of those domains. A two-way trust between all domains is not a common Windows NT architecture, but it does exist and can work well.

2.3.2. Windows NT Domain Models

As stated earlier in this chapter, there are four Windows NT domain architecture types: the Single domain model, the Master domain model, the Multiple Master domain model, and the Complete Trust domain model. To keep these models straight in your mind, think of the four in relation to the size of the Exchange Server messaging system that you are implementing. Of course, a larger organization may already have an existing Windows NT domain architecture in place. This can make your job as the Microsoft Exchange Server messaging system designer a bit easier because you will be "fitting" Exchange to the existing Windows NT domain structures already in place.

If no Windows NT domain structure is present, you have to choose one. If this is going to be a relatively small implementation (for example, a single department or a small proprietorship business), a single domain model is probably the right one to choose. If it is for a larger organization that prefers a centralized point of administration, the Master domain model is probably the correct one to select.

Consider using the Multiple Master domain model when there are many core points of contact, such as can be found in a university environment. For example, the university's organizational structure may have many colleges that each want better control of their users, global groups, and domain resources. The College of Arts and Sciences may have tens of thousands of users and resources, and the College of Business may have only a few thousand users and resources to manage.

The Complete Trust domain model is similar to the Master domain model except that its administration points are distributed across the organization. The Complete Trust model permits multiple distributed administration points of contact (unlike the Master model's single point of administration). It is important to note, however, that the Complete Trust domain model brings with it a whole series of security issues that may not be appropriate for larger organizations.

To help you gain a better understanding of these domain models, the following sections graphically restate these domain modeling definitions. Starting with the Single domain model and moving to the Complete Trust domain model, study these pictures closely so that you can choose the correct model for your Exchange Server messaging environment. Again, it is very important to note that once you select a domain model and install the Microsoft Exchange Server, it is very difficult and complex to change your mind about the domain architecture. Take the time up front to select the Windows NT structure that best fits your organization to avoid costly and time-consuming changes somewhere down the road.

The Single Domain Model

As stated previously, the Single domain model (see Figure 2.3) is best suited for smaller organizations, especially because it uses only a single PDC and no trust relationships. Additional Backup Domain Controllers (BDCs) can be added to the infrastructure as required for processing additional users to the Windows NT domain architecture.

Figure 2.3.

Windows NT Server trusts: Single domain model.

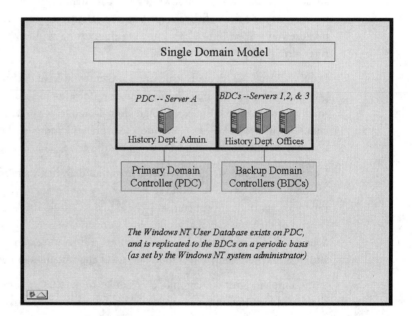

The Master Domain Model

The Master domain model (see Figure 2.4) is a good fit for a small-to-medium-sized user community, especially if centralized system administration is a requirement. If an organization grows too large, an authentication bottleneck may occur with the Master domain model because all users have to authenticate to only the master domain. The master domain contains the PDC with all the user accounts but permits the existence of resource domains for its users to access. One-way trusts are established between the resource domains and the master domain, with the resource domains acting as the trusting domain and the master domain acting as the trusted domain.

Figure 2.4.
Windows NT Server trusts: Master domain model.

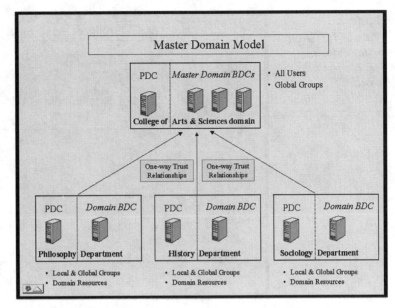

The Multiple Master Domain Model

The Multiple Master domain model (see Figure 2.5) is quite complex, considering all the trust relationships that must be maintained. Obviously, the more master and resource domains you add to the design, the harder it is to administer the Multiple Master domain model. This is also the first domain model that uses two-way trusts. The Multiple Master domain model is a solid infrastructure design that can handle tens of thousands of users, provided that the hardware exists to support the software architecture.

The Complete Trust Domain Model

The Complete Trust domain model (see Figure 2.6) is aimed at those organizations in which each domain fully trusts all the others. Because of security concerns, the Complete Trust domain model is not really appropriate for medium-to-large-sized firms. In the university example, an administrator in each college would have full control over the users and resources in each of the other colleges. This is probably not an appropriate level of administration for non-Housing Office administrators.

Figure 2.5.

Windows NT Server trusts: Multiple Master domain model.

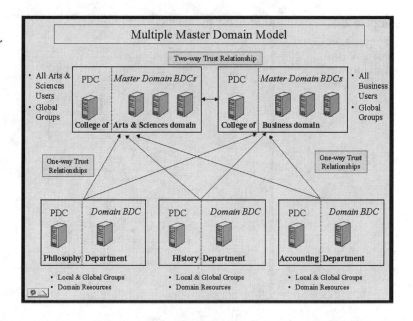

Figure 2.6.

Windows NT Server trusts: Complete Trust domain model.

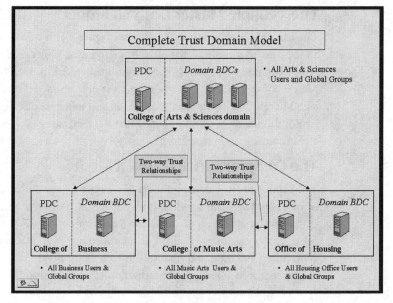

2.3.3. Exchange Server Infrastructure Design

Now that we have settled the Windows NT architecture issues, it is time to get back to the heart of the matter: the Microsoft Exchange Server messaging infrastructure design. It is time to make another choice—this time, the Exchange Server model that will best fit into your organization. Exchange is more straightforward than is Windows NT; it offers just two choices:

- Symmetric functionality
- Partitioned functionality

Symmetric Functionality

Symmetric functionality is the default for an Exchange Server implementation. *Symmetric functionality* is simply a design structure in which the Exchange Servers within the organization all fulfill the same purpose. That is, each server contains the exact same features and connectors and performs the same functionality as all the other Exchange Servers. This structure of an Exchange messaging environment is ideal for small businesses, groups, and organizations because it is easy to design and deploy. However, if the Exchange Server messaging infrastructure design is for a large organization with multiple locations—especially one with international sites—the Symmetric design is not the one to pick. These much larger implementations of Exchange require the Partitioned functionality of Exchange Server.

Partitioned Functionality

Partitioned functionality is simple in concept, yet very complex in planning, design, and deployment stages. It is this choice on which most of the remainder of this chapter focuses. In a Partitioned functionality structure, the Exchange Server's parts and pieces are essentially divided among multiple computers and locations to best optimize the Microsoft Exchange messaging infrastructure across all levels and locations of the organization.

To begin the design process for the Partitioned functionality Exchange infrastructure, the Exchange designers must first decide on a few basic issues:

- What are the physical locations for each of the Exchange Servers?
- What are the backup and restore requirements, including frequency, public folders versus private folders (or both), and the reasoning for restoring any aspect of the Exchange system?
- Which services will run on each Exchange server?

- What are the incident escalation policies and procedures? That is, when something goes wrong, at what level is it considered severe enough to warrant a response, and exactly what is that response, and who is responsible for conducting the response?
- Who are the allowed system administrators? Will there be more than one location performing the administration of users, services, and the like?
- What are the hardware requirements for each server?
- How many servers are required for the organization, and what are their purposes?

These issues are not listed in any particular order; they are here merely to begin to show you the complexity you face when attempting to deploy a Partitioned functionality Exchange infrastructure. To make this process a bit easier, we'll start with the easier issues and work toward and through the more complex topics. Having said all that, let's start with the server types.

You can have many server types within an Exchange Server messaging environment: mail servers, public folders servers, distribution lists expansion servers, site directory bridgehead servers, site connector bridgehead servers, a Key Management Server (KMS), an event scripting server, and Microsoft Outlook Web Access servers that run the Internet Information Server (IIS) feature of Windows NT Server. Just because we have listed eight different types of servers does not mean that each Partitioned functionality deployment of Exchange Server requires eight file servers in addition to the primary Exchange Server computer.

At this point, a small, experimental pilot implementation of Exchange Server may be useful. Much of the design process can be by trial and error, so it is important not to become too wrapped up in placing the blame when mistakes are made. Just figure out what can be learned from an error and move on. Do not worry about major issues when you are working with an Exchange pilot because it is to be completely discarded after the testing is completed anyway. Therefore, view the pilot strictly as an educational tool.

The first piece of the design is to determine the size of the complete Exchange Server infrastructure. How many total users will be expected to use Exchange once it is fully operational? Perhaps it is easier to see this from a range of users:

- Small deployment: Less than 500 users
- Medium deployment: More than 500 users but less than 25,000 users
- Large deployment: More than 25,000 users

Just knowing the precise number of users is not an end in itself because there are so many variables that play into the Exchange design based on the various types of users. The sheer size of the user community has a definite impact on the design of the Exchange Server messaging infrastructure, as does the types of users. It is important to either survey the potential user community and its leadership to determine whether the users are simply looking for electronic mail capabilities or more of the groupware information sharing features proffered by Exchange. Straight email lends itself to numerous and large distribution lists, larger mail server requirements, and heavy use of site connectors—especially if Internet email connectivity is of high importance.

Users who want to use the new Exchange deployment for its groupware and information sharing capabilities will add server requirements of their own. Heavy use of the public folders is the first bottleneck Exchange Server will hit with this user community. Site directory replication bridgehead servers and site connector bridgehead servers also tend to slow down from these types of users.

A standard way to view the eight possible servers is from a bottleneck perspective. From a bottleneck perspective, the following lists the server types in the order in which they will probably occur:

- Mail servers
- Public folders servers
- Distribution list expansion servers
- Bridgehead servers: site directory and site connector bridgehead servers
- Key Management Server
- Event scripting server
- Microsoft Outlook Web Access servers

Mail Servers

A *mail server* is the Exchange Server that supports user or recipient mailboxes. The configuration of this server depends on the methods of access established for the Exchange user community. For example, will the users be permitted to access the Exchange Server through the MAPI protocol, through IMAP, POP3, or even HTTP? These access types are generally decided by default (when the Exchange infrastructure designers select the Exchange client software types that can be used within their messaging environment). These access types are discussed later in this book.

The mail server is mail servers;hardware requirementsa time-critical server that has very high (read *expensive*) hardware requirements. Basic Exchange hardware requirements were covered earlier in this chapter; specific suggestions for all these additional Partitioned functionality servers will be discussed later in this chapter.

Public Folder Servers

The public folder server is the Exchange Server that hosts the public folder replicas across an Exchange Server deployment. Public folders, as you should remember, are centralized locations from which information is shared across the organization. It is important to spend the time necessary to size the public folders servers as accurately as possible. Because no two companies (and probably no two departments or divisions) are alike, it is vital that these servers be designed as accurately as possible. Once again, a pilot implementation of Exchange Server can aid in the determination of the public folders server configurations; without testing, the server sizes you come up with would be vague guesstimates.

The key points to remember about public folders servers are that they are very harddisk and I/O intensive and, although they are similar to mail servers, a public folders server can cause a bottleneck faster because of its higher level of disk I/O processing.

Distribution List Expansion Servers

In Exchange Server design, a distribution list expansion server is nice to have. Distribution lists propagate themselves throughout an Exchange organization; the distribution list expansion servers are usually found in a hub-and-spoke type of environment. If the network bandwidth is flaky, for performance reasons it is a good idea to place a distribution list expansion server in each of the spokes (see Figure 2.7).

As you can see from the figure, a hub-and-spoke network can get quite large and complex. However, this is probably the most common form of local-area network for today's businesses. The single computer in the middle of each circle represents the Windows NT Server that controls each LAN. The largest circle is the "hub" (where the Exchange Server typically appears). However, if the network connections between each circle do not provide adequate bandwidth for the Exchange distribution list expansion environment, it may be prudent to add an additional server to each "spoke" LAN. An obvious downside to doing this is the cost. Implementing a distribution list expansion server in each of the spokes can be quite expensive, especially for a large corporate network.

Figure 2.7.

An example of a hub-and-spoke network.

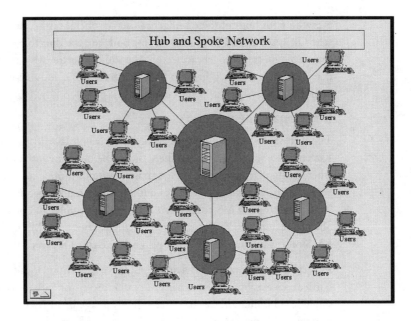

2

Distribution list expansion servers can create bottlenecks in an Exchange environment quickly, so it is useful to add additional Exchange Servers to your infrastructure design to cover these areas. It is important to note, however, that the Microsoft Exchange Server Optimization program does not cover this topic at all, leaving it up to the Exchange design team to optimize this server. Another concern is that, although these servers can be changed on the fly, doing so increases confusion for the user community. That is, once users become accustomed to finding information in one area of the Exchange messaging environment, moving the data source to another area leads to increased technical support calls and additional training for end users. Therefore, it is best to plan, plan, and plan some more up front to avoid changes down the road.

Bridgehead Servers: Site Directory and Site Connector

The next two Exchange add-on servers are the site directory replication bridgehead server and the site connector bridgehead server. The function of the *site directory replication server* is to connect two Exchange Server sites for the purpose of replicating directory information back and forth periodically. The function of the *site connector bridgehead server* is to swap information, such as email messages, between two Exchange sites. Typically, a single Exchange server is configured to handle both of these bridgehead server functions (supposing that there is sufficient hardware processing power and bandwidth available to handle the tasks at hand). Timing is everything for both of these bridgehead server operations. A standard replication schedule is set at four-hour intervals for both the site directory replication server and the site connector bridgehead server. The site connector, which is discussed in greater detail later in this book, handles SMTP, X.400, X.25, and dial-up (RAS) types of connections.

Key Management Servers

The next server type is the Key Management Server (KMS). In the current release of Exchange Server (Version 5.5), there should be only one instance of the KMS anywhere in the Exchange messaging infrastructure. If more than one Key Management Server exists, a message may fail to authenticate properly because it was unable to "find" the proper KMS computer that created its public and private keys. The most obvious reason for using a separate Exchange Server for KMS duties is to get the KMS processing overhead off the primary Exchange Servers.

In very large organizations, having a single KMS computer leads to administrative bottlenecks because everyone has to use that server for authentication purposes. The single KMS limitation can be quite a disadvantage in an Exchange messaging environment with dozens or perhaps hundreds of Exchange Servers (especially for environments with international locations). Microsoft may, in a not-too-distant future release of Exchange Server (or one of its Service Pack releases), provide the capability to have multiple Key Management Servers within the same Exchange messaging environment.

Event Scripting Servers

The next Exchange Server add-on server to consider is an event scripting server. In a e messaging environment, the system administrators will probably not write any event-driven scripts to process user information. However, in larger organizations, event-driven scripts are almost a necessity to process information on a timely basis, as well as to limit necessary administrative overhead. These event services can include folder-based events (including Add, Move, and Delete timers). To put it more succinctly, an event service permits the addition of business logic to Exchange folders by using various built-in components and third-party applications.

You can execute various types of scripts on an Exchange Server, including the Visual Basic 5.0 Scripting Edition, Java, C++, Visual InterDev (included with Exchange Server 5.5 Enterprise Edition), Outlook scripts, and the Microsoft Exchange Scripting Agent. The Microsoft Exchange Scripting Agent is a new feature of Exchange Server Version 5.5 that improves the collaboration capabilities of the earlier versions of Exchange Server. The new Collaboration Data Objects (CDO), formerly known as Active Messaging, make it possible to create even more versatile Exchange Active Server Pages (ASP) applications. Most of these types of applications and activities would probably be run from an Exchange event scripting server to alleviate the processing load on the primary Exchange Server.

Microsoft Outlook Web Access Servers

The eighth and final add-on server you may find necessary in an organization's Exchange Server infrastructure design is the Outlook Web Access/IIS server. This server permits users to access their Exchange Server email boxes using an Internet web browser such as Microsoft Internet Explorer or Netscape Navigator. Through the use of the CDO library's calendar objects, it is now possible for Exchange users to gain admission and make changes to personal and group schedules.

Adding to the user size concerns of an Exchange design is the issue of how the connectivity is to be accomplished. That is, the Exchange infrastructure design team must determine all the methods by which an Exchange user can connect to the messaging environment. Will the users be using plain Microsoft Exchange Server 5.5 clients, or will they be using Microsoft Outlook as the client software? Moreover, if they are using Outlook, which versions are going to be permitted? Many versions of Outlook are available, from the ones found in Microsoft Office 95 and 97, to the Outlook Web Access (OWA) client software, to the Windows Messaging/Exchange clients built into Windows NT Workstation 4.0, 5.0, and Windows 95/98. The permissible client software becomes more of an end-user support issue, with the possible exception of the Outlook Web Access client.

OWA clients are extremely hard on network bandwidth requirements, especially when it comes to wide-area network (WAN) links. It is suggested that Exchange infrastructure designers take care when designing an Exchange Server implementation in an organization that has branch offices located across WAN links—even if a Web IIS server is located in the branch locations—because of the sheer number of RPCs generated back to the Exchange Server for each connected user. For example, if 200 OWA clients are sending and receiving mail an average of 12 times per day, these 200 users can very easily overwhelm a 56K WAN link. So although it may be easier to administer OWA clients than it is to administer users with the full Exchange client software, there is a price to be paid in the form of heavy WAN/LAN traffic.

2.4. Exchange Server Implementation Strategies

Once you have decided on the additional servers and client software types, the Exchange messaging infrastructure team must determine where all these servers are to go. Most companies probably have at least a vague idea of how to answer this question, based on the spread of the user community. The physical locations of the servers plays an essential role in determining the various Exchange Server sites that have to be created. For example, it may make sense within your group to name sites based on the physical locations of the firm's offices, as shown in Figure 2.8.

Figure 2.8.

Designing Exchange Server site boundaries.

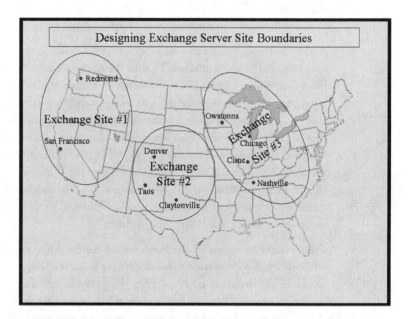

For an initial Exchange messaging system design, it is better to make sites too large rather than too small for two reasons: First, it is much easier to administer a limited number of larger sites then it is to administer a large number of smaller Exchange Server sites. Second, it is quite a bit easier to split large Exchange sites than it is to merge two or more smaller ones. Typically, someone who is designing an Exchange Server infrastructure takes a map of the company's physical locations and writes down the number of users in each location. It is then a matter of drawing separation lines between the locations to create the site boundaries, as shown in Figure 2.8. Of course, you also have to take into consideration the WAN links between each of the locations whendetermining whether or not enough bandwidth exists to support an Exchange Server site.

Figuring out whether there are enough users at a branch office to warrant a physical Exchange Server and determining whether the bandwidth exists to support those remote sites is not an exact science. The basis for determining the answers to these questions is found in Table 2.5.

Table 2.5. Typical Exchange Server bandwidth requirements versus users supported.

WAN Link Available	Number of Average Exchange Users	Server Required?	Acceptable Bandwidth?
Slower than 64K	Less than 10	No	Yes
Slower than 64K	10 to 30	No	No
Slower than 64K	More than 30	Yes	N/A
128K or faster	Less than 10	No	Yes
128K or faster	10 to 50	No	Yes
128K or faster	More than 50	Yes	N/A

Note

Additional details on determining Exchange Server user requirements, especially how they relate to server performance, can be unearthed in Microsoft's "Microsoft Exchange Server Capacity Planning and Performance" whitepaper, available in the January 1998 issue of *Microsoft TechNet*.

Another rule of thumb for determining WAN bandwidth links is that approximately 1.5K of bandwidth is required for each connected Microsoft Outlook user for an Exchange implementation. These "general" users are light users of the public folders and other collaboration activities.

To maintain the budget when it comes to costing an Exchange Server infrastructure deployment, this aspect of the design phase is most crucial. It is important to keep in mind that Exchange Server sites require permanent network connections that support synchronous RPCs, which sometimes means expensive connections between sites. This also goes back to the Windows NT domain trusts scenarios in that all the servers in a site must be able to authenticate Exchange Server users and service accounts. Moreover, the only way a user can be authenticated is by being in the same domain as the servers or through trusted domains.

There are a few more considerations to pore over when creating the company's Exchange Server sites. These fall into the categories of Exchange Server performance, directory replication, and organization topics.

2.4.1. Exchange Server Performance

Performance is always an important issue when deploying messaging systems. End users are usually not very receptive to long response times, undelivered mail or slow mail delivery, and sluggish collaboration efforts. The simple fact is that people seem to lose their sense of humor when a problem has a direct impact on their work.

One easy way to maximize site performance is to create sites in which all the network or WAN links are of the same or similar sizes. For example, consider Figure 2.8. If there are T-1 links between Chicago, Owatonna, and Cisne, but only a 56K link between those locations and Nashville, you should not include the Nashville location in site #3.

Other factors that affect Exchange Server performance include the number of servers per site (try not to exceed 50), the location of the Information Stores (for desktop users, make their default store a personal folders file—a PST file—thereby alleviating much of the work the server must otherwise perform), and the hardware purchased to run the Exchange Server (the focus should be on CPU power, memory, and multiple SCSI hard drives).

2.4.2. Exchange Server Directory Replication

Directory replication should occur more frequently within an Exchange site than between Exchange sites. If the site locations have been determined properly, this will be the case. If the site locations have not been properly determined, your business will incur greater operational costs caused by increased replication across WAN links and will also see decreased performance for the Exchange user community.

2.4.3. Exchange Server Organizational Issues

The organizational topics to be covered during the Exchange Server infrastructure design phase include grouping onto servers the users who interact with each other most frequently. Although this can have the greatest impact on Exchange system performance, it is the most difficult to achieve from just pure planning. The Exchange Server messaging pilot implementation can go a long way in determining user patterns, but only on a very limited scale. Unfortunately, organizing users onto servers is virtually impossible to do correctly if this is a brand-new messaging rollout. However, if this new deployment of the Exchange Server infrastructure is replacing an existing email system, perhaps the usage logs and network monitoring tools of the old messaging system can help you determine usage patterns.

Another organizational issue is that the grouping of other Windows NT Server services and applications on the same physical computers as the Exchange Server services and applications. Although Windows NT services such as DNS, DHCP, and WINS do not require much overhead and can probably exist on the same box as Exchange, other Windows NT Server applications such as Microsoft SQL Server, Microsoft Site Server, and XcelleNet RemoteWare should not be located on the same computer as Microsoft Exchange Server. These types of applications demand heavy overhead in terms of disk space, memory requirements, and CPU processing.

2

Lab

This section consists of review questions that pertain to this chapter and provides an opportunity to apply the knowledge you acquired in the course of this chapter.

Questions

1. A(n) ___ is a routing entry that identifies a certain type of message to a specific Exchange Server connector.

   A. ETRN Router

   B. Exchange Server address space

   C. X.400 entry

   D. All of the above

2. In Microsoft Exchange terminology, *KMS* means what?

   A. Keep Messages Short

   B. Key Management Systems

   C. Key Management Server

   D. None of the above

3. The Exchange Server site connector handles which type(s) of connections?

   A. SMTP, dial-up (RAS)

   B. X.25

   C. X.400

   D. All of the above

4. The function of the ___ server is to connect two Exchange Server sites for the purpose of replicating directory information back and forth on a periodic basis.

   A. Site Directory Replication

   B. Site Connector Bridgehead Server

   C. Both **A** and **B**

   D. None of the above

5. What is the purpose of the OWA/IIS server within an Exchange Server infra-structure design?

    A. It is never necessary, under any circumstances

    B. This server permits users to access their Exchange Server email boxes using an Internet web browser

    C. This server permits users to access their Exchange Server email boxes using an Outlook client instead of the standard Exchange client software

    D. It permits use of the CDO library's calendar objects

6. Collaboration Data Objects (CDO) were formerly known as ___ in an Exchange Server implementation.

    A. Common Business Objects

    B. Exchange Data Objects

    C. Active Server Pages

    D. Active Messaging

7. An Exchange Server implementation can be installed on which type(s) of Windows NT servers?

    A. Primary Domain Controller

    B. Backup Domain Controller

    C. Server

    D. All of the above

8. What will probably occur if a separate hard disk drive and controller are used for the Information Store log and the IS database?

    A. Nothing

    B. The Exchange Server administrator will probably realize a 25-percent increase in hard drive system performance

    C. The Exchange Server administrator will probably realize a 25-percent decrease in lost email messages

    D. Both **B** and **C**

2

9. Information Store logs grow ___.

    A. Linearly

    B. Horizontally

    C. Randomly

    D. None of the above

10. Which file allocation system should be used on drive partitions that are less than 512M in size for all Information Store logs?

    A. NTFS

    B. HPFS

    C. FAT

    D. FAT32

11. An Exchangeimplementation can have multiple ___.

    A. Organizations and sites

    B. Organizations and servers

    C. Sites and servers

    D. Servers

12. The minimum size CPU on which Exchange Server will operate is either an Intel ___ or a(ny) RISC-based ___.

    A. 80386, RS/6000

    B. 80486, RS/6000

    C. Pentium II, CPU

    D. Pentium, Alpha

13. Public folders should have ___ names.

    A. Unique

    B. Consecutive

    C. All alpha (nonnumeric)

    D. All of the above

14. The ___ name is used in the creation of email addresses in an Exchange Server messaging system.

    A. Site

    B. Organization

    C. Server

    D. Alias

15. Exchange Server names can have up to ___ characters but should avoid using any of the DNS and/or NetBIOS reserved characters.

    A. 64

    B. 15

    C. 32

    D. 8

2

Exercises

Developing an Infrastructure for an Exchange Server Messaging Environment

 Note   This exercise addresses the following Microsoft exam objective:

■ Develop an infrastructure for Exchange Server

The goal of this exercise is to ensure that you can properly design an infrastructure for your Exchange Server messaging environment. There are a few steps to perform when you develop an Exchange Server messaging infrastructure. These tasks take the knowledge you accumulated when learning how to choose an implementation strategy and develop a long-term coexistence strategy and builds on these topics so that you can effectively format an Exchange Server infrastructure.

1. Perform a Microsoft Exchange Server deployment risk assessment (which level is most appropriate for your environment).

2. Design the Windows NT Server domain architecture by deciding which domain structure is best for your company (Single domain, Master domain, Multiple Master domain, or Complete Trust domain).

3. Determine whether the Symmetric or Partitioned functionality is the correct architecture for your Exchange Server environment.

4. Determine the proper hardware configuration necessary to maximize Exchange Server performance but still balance any budgetary concerns (you probably do not have a million dollars to spend on server hardware, so balance loads wisely).

Answers to Questions

1. **B**   Answer C is correct because it identifies a certain type of message to a specific type of Exchange connector. Answer A is incorrect because there is no Exchange component known as an ETRN router. Answer B is incorrect because X.400 is an email addressing format, not a routing environment. Because Answer C is correct, obviously D cannot be correct.

2. **C**   KMS stands for Key Management Server.

3. **D**   SMTP is used for Internet mail. Dial-up connections permit two sites to connect, even though they do not have a permanent WAN connection. X.25 and X.400 are valid Exchange messaging transport types.

4. **A**   Answer A is correct because the site directory replication server connects two sites for the purpose of replicating directory information. Answer B is incorrect because the site connector bridgehead server is used to connect two Exchange Server sites for messaging connectivity. Because Answer A is correct, Answers C and D cannot be correct.

5. **B**   OWA is used for Web access of an Exchange Server. Answer A is incorrect because the Outlook Web Access/Internet Information Server definitely has a place within an Exchange Server design. Answer C is incorrect because the OWA provides web access through an Outlook client. Answer D is pretty much a nonsensical answer.

6. **D**   Active Messaging was the old term. Answers A and B are invented terms. Answer C is incorrect because Active Server Pages are still usable within an IIS server's Web site.

7. **D**   Answer D is correct because Exchange can be installed on all types of Windows NT servers.

8. **B**   Answer B is correct because log growth can occur simultaneously with server use. Answer A is not true because there should be some sort of performance increase. Answer C is incorrect because adding hardware does not reduce lost messages (that is a configuration issue).

9. **A**   Answer B is a nonsensical answer. Answer C is incorrect because Information Store logs definitely grow in a structured order. Because the correct answer is A, Answer D cannot hold true.

10. **C**   Answer A is incorrect because NTFS adds too much overhead without benefiting anyone. Answer B is incorrect because HPFS is used on OS/2 systems. Answer D is incorrect because FAT32 is becoming more popular on OEM versions of Windows 95, as well as becoming a standard for Windows 98 implementations on large hard drives.

11. **C**   Answers A and B are incorrect because there can be only a single organization. Answer D is incorrect because there can be multiple sites as well.

12. **D**   Answers A and B are incorrect because the starting point for Intel systems is a Pentium. Answer C is incorrect because the starting point for Intel systems is a Pentium and only the Alpha RISC-based CPU is supported.

13. **A**   Answer B is a nonsensical answer. Answer C is incorrect because numbers can be included in public folder names. Because Answers B and C are not true, answer D cannot be correct.

14. **B**   Answer A is incorrect because a site is the second level in the top-down hierarchy of an Exchange Server messaging architecture. Answer C is incorrect because a server is the third level in the top-down hierarchy of an Exchange Server messaging architecture. Answer D is incorrect because an alias is used to generate the directory name for a recipient, among other things.

15. **B**   Answer A is the right number for organization and site names. Answers C and D are pretend numbers.

TEST DAY FAST FACTS

Here are a few fast facts about this chapter you may want to know ahead of time. These facts provide great last-minute study material.

- To install Exchange Server, the computer must be a member of a domain, and the primary domain controller must be available.

- A special domain user account, called the *Site Services Account*, is used by Exchange Server to run services.

- As part of the Exchange Server installation process, you should enhance Exchange Server's performance by using Performance Optimizer.

- Exchange data is kept in two stores: the Directory Store (DS) and the Information Store (IS).

- Exchange's Information Store consists of a Public Information Store and a Private Information Store.

- The primary tool used to configure and manage Exchange Server is the Exchange Server Administrator program, which is shipped with Exchange Server.

- Exchange Server has four primary recipient types: mailboxes, custom recipients, distribution lists, and public folders.

Day 3

Exchange Server Installation and Configuration

by William Matsoukas

This chapter covers the fundamentals of Exchange Server installation and configuration. The exercises in this chapter build a complete, single-server Exchange mail system that uses the default configurations. After finishing this chapter, you should understand the Exchange Server installation process as well as the basic Exchange Server configuration.

Objectives

After reading this chapter, performing the exercises, and answering the lab questions, you will be able to meet the following Exchange Server exam objectives:

- Develop the configuration of an Exchange Server computer
- Install an Exchange Server computer
- Configure Exchange Server for message recipients
- Configure server locations

3.1. Installing Microsoft Exchange Server

Once all the hardware, software, and licensing requirements described in Day 2, "Planning and Designing an Exchange Messaging Environment," have been met, you are ready to install Exchange Server.

The exercises in this chapter assume the following:

- You are working with a Windows NT network that has a domain name of Ionia.
- The Windows NT network has at least the user accounts listed in Table 3.1 and the groups described in Table 3.2. To successfully follow along with the exercises in this chapter, you must create these global users and groups.
- The Windows NT network is connected to the Internet and has the IP domain name Ionia. The IP domain name for the Exchange Server is Western.

Table 3.1. To complete the exercises in this chapter, create the users in this table on the Windows NT domain.

User Name	Full Name
lguzor	Lauren Guzor
vnessa	Vicki Nessa
tfoolery	Tom Foolery
arubino	Annette Rubino
mfarrell	Margaret Farrell
tdavis	Taylor Davis
imullen	Ian Mullen
hgallagher	Hanna Gallagher
tday	Tricia Day

Table 3.2. The groups in this table are used in the exercises in this chapter.

Group Name	Members
Editors	tfoolery
	arubino
	imullen

Group Name	Members
Accountants	lguzor
	mfarrell
	tdavis
Artists	hgallagher
Writers	vnessa
	tday

3.1.1. Installation Preparation

To install Exchange Server, you must have administrative rights to the target Windows NT Server. That is, you must be a member of the local group Administrators for the target server, either directly as a user member or as a member of a global group that belongs to the local group Administrators.

The target computer for the Exchange Server installation must be a member of the target domain and connected to the network. If you plan to use web client access, it is recommended that you configure the Exchange Server as a backup domain controller. This approach simplifies user authentication for web clients. The primary domain controller must be connected to the network and running.

 Note When Exchange Server is installed, the current user account is granted Administrator rights for the Exchange Server computer. This user account in turn has permission to assign other user accounts permission to administer Exchange Server.

If this is the first Exchange Server installation for a site, a service account must be created. A *user* account that is permitted to log on as a service under Windows NT is referred to as a *service account*. The service account created for Exchange Server is called the Exchange Server *Site Services Account*. To create an Exchange Server Site Services Account, run User Manager for Domains and create a user with the following attributes:

- User cannot change password
- Password never expires

> **Note** The Site Services Account is used by all Exchange Servers installed in a site. There is no real reason to change the password for the Site Services Account, however. But because it is a domain user, the password can be changed. It is critical, however, that the password never expire. This service account is used to start critical Exchange Server services. If the password expires, the services cannot be run.

When Exchange Server Setup runs, the Exchange Server Site Services Account is granted the following additional permissions:

- Log on as a service
- Act as part of the operating system
- Restore Exchange files and directories

> **Note** A single Exchange Server Site Services Account should be used for all Exchange Servers within a site.

3.1.2. Installing Exchange Server

There are two ways to access the Exchange Server Setup program. The Exchange Server CD-ROM includes an AutoPlay wizard that offers the menu options shown in Table 3.3.

Table 3.3. The Exchange Server CD-ROM uses an AutoPlay, HTML-based wizard to facilitate access to Exchange Server Setup options.

Menu Item	Functions
Setup Server and Components	Installation for the following components: Exchange Server Chat Services Applications & Authoring Tools Internet Location Services Resource Kit Connector for Lotus Notes Connector for IBM OfficeVision/VM Connector for SNADS
Release Notes	Exchange Server and Outlook release notes in HTML format

Menu Item	Functions
Documentation	Exchange Server
	Chat Service
	Connectivity
	Quick Setup
	Clustering with Exchange Server
Online Resources	Web links to the following:
	More Information on Exchange Server
	Online Community
	Interactive Newsgroups
	Service Packs & Hot Fixes
	Application Farm
	Exchange ISV Database
Exit	Quit Exchange Server Setup

The other way to access Exchange Server Setup is to run SETUP.EXE for the appropriate processor. This is the method used in the following exercise. This exercise steps you through the installation of Exchange Server. The exercise assumes that you are logged on to the target server with administrative rights.

> **Note** This exercise describes an installation using a CD-ROM drive physically attached to the target server.

1. Insert the Microsoft Exchange Server CD-ROM.

2. Locate the SETUP.EXE file for your server's processor type. SETUP.EXE is located in the directory `<drive>`:\SERVER\SETUP\`<processor>` where `<drive>` is the drive letter designation for the target server's CD-ROM drive and `<processor>` is the directory name that represents your server's processor type. If your server is an Intel platform computer, then the correct SETUP.EXE is found in the directory named I386.

3. Execute SETUP.EXE. The Setup Welcome message box appears. Click Accept to continue.

4. The Microsoft Exchange Server Setup dialog box appears. You are prompted to select both the target installation directory for Microsoft Exchange Server and the installation type. Table 3.4 describes the standard installation options

available. For this exercise, accept the default installation directory and the Custom/Complete installation option by clicking the Complete/Custom button.

Table 3.4. Microsoft Exchange Server offers three installation options.

Installation Option	Features Installed
Typical	Microsoft Exchange Server Exchange Administrator
Complete/Custom	Microsoft Exchange Server Exchange Administrator Connectors: Microsoft Mail, cc:Mail, X.400 Books Online (online documentation), and Active Server components
Minimum	Microsoft Exchange Server

5. The Microsoft Exchange Server-Complete/Custom dialog box appears. The Options pane displays the installation options described in Table 3.5.

Table 3.5. Microsoft Exchange Server installation options are listed as logical groups of features.

Option	Description
Microsoft Exchange Server	The core Microsoft Exchange Server components required for installation.
Microsoft Exchange Administrator	Programs used to administer Microsoft Exchange Server.
Books Online	Online help for Microsoft Exchange Server.
Outlook Web Access	Facilitates access to Exchange using the Internet Information Server.

6. For this exercise, click Continue to accept all options.

 Note

If the target Windows NT Server has Internet Information Server installed, Outlook Web Access is already installed. In this case, Exchange Server Setup issues an error message, clears the Outlook Web Access option, and continues.

7. The Licensing Mode dialog box appears. You should have already determined the licensing mode for your site as described in Day 2. For this exercise, select the Per Seat option. Click Continue.

8. The next dialog box prompts for the CD-ROM key. Enter the key and click OK to continue.

9. A message box displays Exchange Server's product ID number. Click OK to continue.

10. Because per-seat licensing was used for this Exchange Server installation, an Exchange Server Licensing dialog box appears. Note the terms of a per-seat license, select the I Agree checkbox, and click OK.

11. The Organization and Site dialog box appears. You should have determined before beginning the installation whether you are creating a new site or joining an existing site. For this exercise, create a new site. Click the Create New Site option.

12. In the same dialog box, you are prompted to enter an organization name and a site name. Type **Ionia** for the organization name and **Western** for the site name. Click OK to continue.

13. You are prompted to confirm the creation of a new site. Click Yes.

14. The Site Services Account dialog box appears. Click the Browse button and then select the account you created as the Exchange Site Service Account. Click OK.

15. Setup informs you that the Site Services Account has been granted the following rights:

    ■ Log on as a service

    ■ Restore files and directories

    ■ Act as part of the operating system

16. Click OK. Setup copies the required files from the CD-ROM and then starts Exchange Server services.

17. From the next dialog box, you can either exit Setup or run the Performance Optimizer. For this exercise, click Run Optimizer.

18. Setup closes, and the Microsoft Exchange Server Performance Optimizer wizard welcome screen appears. Click Next to continue.

19. Performance Optimizer stops all Exchange Server services and then displays a configuration dialog box (see Figure 3.1). The available configuration parameters are listed in Table 3.6.

3

Figure 3.1.

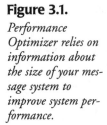

Performance Optimizer relies on information about the size of your message system to improve system performance.

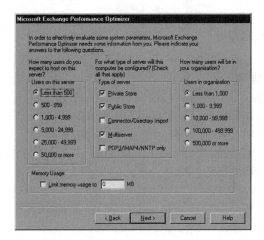

Table 3.6. Performance Optimizer configures Exchange Server based on information about the size and type of server being installed.

Parameter	Settings
Users on This Server	Estimated number of users on this server. Performance Optimizer configures resource allocations based on this value.
Type of Server	Types of messaging services provided by the Exchange Server: **Private Store.** Server contains a private store for recipient data. **Public Store.** Server contains a public store for public folders. **Connector/Directory Import.** Server is configured for foreign directory replication or site and foreign mail connectors. **Multiserver.** Server belongs to a site that contains more than one server. **POP3/IMAP4/NNTP only.** This Exchange Server is used only for Internet mail and newsgroup recipients.
Users in Organization	The range of user counts.
Memory Usage	Configurable to memory usage limit.

20. Set the Performance Optimizer options as follows:

   ■ **Users on This Server:** Less than 500

   ■ **Type of Server:** Private Store, Public Store, Multiserver

   ■ **Users in Organization:** Less than 1,000

   ■ **Memory Usage:** (no restrictions)

21. Click Next to begin optimizing Exchange Server.

> **Note**
>
> If Exchange Server is installed on a computer with only one hard drive available, Performance Optimizer issues a warning message. This message appears because Performance Optimizer prefers to distribute data files across two or more disk drives to improve disk I/O. Acknowledge the warning by clicking OK and continue the optimization.

22. Performance Optimizer configures Exchange Server as necessary, saves the configuration, and restarts Exchange Server services. Click Finish to end Performance Optimizer.

23. Confirm that Exchange Server is successfully installed and running by verifying that the following core Exchange services are running:

   ■ Microsoft Exchange Directory

   ■ Microsoft Exchange Event Service

   ■ Microsoft Exchange Information Store

   ■ Microsoft Exchange Message Transfer Agent

   ■ Microsoft Exchange System Attendant

As you have seen, there is nothing particularly difficult about installing Exchange Server. The real work is done up front when you plan the Exchange environment. By the time you are ready to install Exchange Server, you should already know the answers to Setup's prompts and questions, especially when configuring for performance optimization.

3.2. Default Exchange Server Directories and Files

This section describes the directory structure, directory shares, and file locations for a default Exchange Server installation. This information is often useful for capacity planning or troubleshooting. If you encounter a corrupted file, Exchange Server does not usually reference the file location. Knowing file locations can also be helpful for checking executable and library versions, modification dates, and file sizes.

3

3.2.1. Default Exchange Server Directory Structure

Table 3.7 describes the Exchange Server directory structure and shares for a default installation. The default main directory for Exchange Server is \EXCHSRVR. The directories in Table 3.7 are subdirectories of \EXCHSRVR.

Table 3.7. The default directory structure for an Exchange Server installation.

Directory	Contents
ADD-INS	Exchange Server application extensions
ADDRESS	Program files used to generate foreign addresses
BIN	Binary components of Exchange Server and Exchange Administrator
CCMCDATA	Support files for the cc:Mail connector
CONNECT	Connector files
DOCS	Supplemental Exchange Server documentation
DSADATA	Directory data files
DXADATA	Microsoft Mail directory synchronization
IMCDATA	Internet Mail Service (IMS) working files
INSDATA	Internet News Service data files
KMSDATA	Key Management Server application and data files
MDBDATA	Private Information Store, Public Information Store
MTADATA	Message Transfer Agent and related files
RES	Message string files used to write log messages
SAMPAPPS	Sample applications and forms
TRACKING.LOG	Message tracking files generated by Exchange Administrator's message tracking
WEBTEMP	Web Connector files

3.2.2. Exchange Server Files of Note

As with the directory structure and share points described in the preceding section, it may be useful to know the purpose and location of the more important Exchange Server files. Table 3.8 describes some important Exchange Server files in terms of purpose and location in a default Exchange Server configuration. With just a little experience troubleshooting Exchange Server or any other complex system, you soon learn where the "trouble spots" for that system are located. You can often identify the source or a symptom of a problem by looking at the size, time stamp, or content of one of the system's key files. You can use this table as a first step in tracking down those files.

Table 3.8. Knowing the location of some important Exchange Server files can prove useful for troubleshooting.

Filename	Description
\EXCHSRVR\DSADATA\DIR.EDB	Directory Service database file
\EXCHSRVR\DSADATA*.LOG	Directory Service database log files
\EXCHSRVR\DXADATA\XDIR.EDB	Directory synchronization database
\EXCHSRVR\MDBDATA\PRIV.EDB	Private Information Store database
\EXCHSRVR\MDBDATA\PUB.EDB	Public Information Store database
\EXHCSRVR\MDBDATA*.LOG	Transaction log files for the Public Information Store and the Private Information Store
\EXCHSRVR\TRACKING.LOG*.LOG	Message tracking logs created by the Microsoft Exchange Server Administrator message tracking option

3.3. Using Exchange Administrator

Exchange Administrator is the graphical tool used to manage your Exchange organization. Exchange Administrator can be installed on the Windows NT Server as part of the Exchange Server installation, or it can be installed on any Windows NT computer at any time using Exchange Server Setup. Exchange Administrator is installed on the target server in Exercise 2 at the end of this chapter.

3.3.1. Starting Exchange Administrator

The purpose of the following exercise is to get you started using the primary Exchange Server administrative tool, Exchange Administrator. Subsequent exercises in this chapter that use Exchange Administrator (most of the exercises do) simply instruct you to start Exchange Administrator.

1. Log on to the Exchange Server using an account that is an Exchange administrator.

Note If you completed the first exercise in this chapter, "Installing Exchange Server," the user account that was used to install Exchange Server has Administrator rights for the site to which the Exchange Server belongs.

2. Select Programs|Microsoft Exchange from the Start menu.

3. Choose Microsoft Exchange Administrator. If this is the first time that Exchange Administrator has run, a Connect to Server dialog box appears.

4. Enter the name of the Exchange Server; optionally, check the Set as Default checkbox. Click OK.

Note You can connect to any Exchange Server on your network (assuming that you have the appropriate rights) by choosing Connect to Server from Exchange Server's File menu. Each time you connect to another server, you are offered the option to set that server as the default server. When Exchange Server Administrator is started, it automatically connects to the default server.

Figure 3.2 shows the Administrator window. The left pane of the Administrator window shows the hierarchical structure of the organization's objects; the right pane shows any children of the selected object.

Figure 3.2.

Exchange Administrator is used to configure and manage all components of Exchange Server.

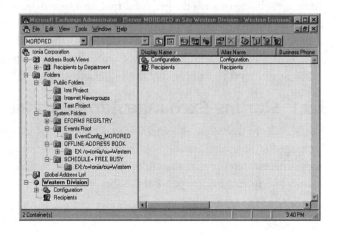

Table 3.9 defines the objects that may be displayed in the left pane of the Administrator window.

Table 3.9. Exchange Server object types are represented by unique icons in the Administrator window.

Object Type	Description
Organization	The primary container for the entire Exchange organization
Address Book Views	Contains Address Book views
Folders	Contains the public folder structure
Public Folder	Shared information folder within the public folder structure
Global Address List	Database of all recipients in the organization
Site	Site container
Site Configuration Container	Contains configuration objects
Add-Ins	Contains third-party add-in products
Addressing	Contains site addressing information
Details Templates	Contains templates that define how object details are displayed in the Address Book
E-mail Address Generators	Contains tools that generate email addresses for installed connectors and gateways
Custom Recipient	Recipient that uses a foreign email system
Distribution List	List of recipients that can be addressed as a group
Mailbox	Private container for email and other messages
Mailbox Agent	Application written to facilitate messaging-enabled applications
One-off Address Templates	Contains Exchange Server-specific templates that can be used to define the information that must be specified when a user creates a new email address
Connections Container	Contains connectors for the server
Site Connector	Connects two Exchange sites within an organization
X.400 Connector	Connects an Exchange Server to an X.400 backbone or another site using Transport5 Class 4 (TP4), TCP/IP, or X.25 transports
Other Connectors	Provides connectivity to messaging systems other than X.400 and Exchange sites
Directory Synchronization	Directory synchronization tool used between Exchange and Microsoft Mail (PC)

continues

Table 3.9. continued

Object Type	Description
Remote Dirsync Requestor	Emulates a Microsoft Mail (PC) Dirsync Requestor for Directory Synchronization object; Microsoft Mail post offices send directory updates to other Microsoft Mail post offices when they receive a request; the Remote Dirsync Requestor sends this request
Protocols Container	Contains Internet protocol information
Certification Authority (CA)	Exchange Server Key Manager service
Directory Site (DS) Configuration	Properties for site's directory
Encryption	Advanced security configuration for the site
Information Store Site Configuration	Properties for site's information store (IS)
Message Transfer Agent (MTA)	Message routing tool that moves messages between servers
MTA Site Configuration	Properties for site's MTA configuration
Link Monitor	Status monitor tool for Exchange Server connections to other messaging systems
Server Container	Contains site's Exchange Servers
Server	Exchange Server
Server Monitor	Status monitor tool for Exchange Server as well as for other services running on one or more Windows NT Servers
Private Information Store	Contains all mailboxes that use the current server as their home server
System Attendant	Exchange Server system maintenance services
Public Information Store	Contains all public folders
Recipients	Contains mailboxes, custom recipients, distribution lists, and public folders (all recipient types)

3.4. Creating and Configuring Exchange Server Recipients

An Exchange Server *recipient* is an object that can receive messages. Exchange Server has several recipient objects:

- Mailboxes
- Custom recipients
- Distribution lists
- Public folders

As with other objects in the Windows NT world, Exchange Server recipient objects have attributes, or properties. The following sections describe the preceding recipient objects in terms of creation and configuration.

3.4.1. Creating and Configuring Mailboxes

A *mailbox*, the most commonly used Exchange Server recipient object, is the delivery target for messages addressed to the mailbox owner. Messages contained in a mailbox can include information such as email, spreadsheets, and documents. The Inbox is the client-side representation of an Exchange mailbox.

After completing the following sections, you will be able to do the following:

- Identify mailbox properties
- Create a new mailbox using Exchange Administrator
- Configure a mailbox using Exchange Administrator

Understanding the Mailbox Properties Pages

When you use Exchange Administrator to configure an Exchange mailbox, you will find all the mailbox settings contained in a Properties dialog box that consists of several pages (see Figure 3.3).

Table 3.10 lists mailbox properties, grouped by Properties page, with brief definitions.

Figure 3.3.

The Exchange mailbox recipient offers a rich set of configuration options.

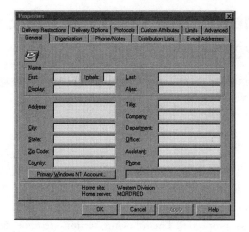

Table 3.10. Exchange Server's mailbox Properties dialog box has 13 pages.

Properties Page	Properties Stored
General	Basic properties pertaining to mailbox identification and ownership such as display name, company name, company address, and primary Windows NT user account.
Organization	Mailbox owner's manager and direct reports.
Phone/Notes	Pertinent phone numbers and notes for the mailbox owner.
Distribution Lists	List of distribution lists to which the mailbox belongs.
E-mail Addresses	Alternate email addresses for the mailbox.
Delivery Restrictions	List of addresses from which the mailbox will or will not accept messages.
Delivery Options	List of recipients that may send on behalf of this mailbox and name of alternate recipient to receive mail sent to this mailbox.
Protocols	List of protocols that can be used by a client to connect to the mailbox.
Custom Attributes	Ten definable properties for the mailbox. These properties can be used, for example, to add detail to the recipient information for use with Address Book views or for scripting.
Limits	Mailbox message limits such as maximum incoming message size.
Advanced	Miscellaneous properties such as home server name, directory synchronization trust level, and administrative notes.

Creating and Configuring a New Mailbox

For a Windows NT user account to receive messages, a mailbox must be created and associated with that user account. Exercise 1 at the end of this chapter steps through the creation and configuration of an Exchange mailbox using Exchange Administrator.

There are three methods for creating a new mailbox:

- Use the Exchange Server Administrator to create a mailbox for an existing Windows NT user account.
- Use User Manager for Domains to create a mailbox for a new Windows NT user account.
- Use Exchange Server extraction and import tools to create mailboxes for existing NetWare, LAN Manager, and Windows NT user accounts.

The following exercise explains how to create a new mailbox for an existing Windows NT user account using Exchange Administrator.

1. Run Exchange Server Administrator.
2. From the Administrator window, select the Recipients object for the site Western.
3. Choose New Mailbox from the Exchange Server Administrator File menu. The mailbox Properties dialog box appears.
4. Assign a primary user to the mailbox. Click the Primary Windows NT Account button. A dialog box offers the option to create a new Windows NT user account or to use an existing Windows NT user account.
5. Click Select an Existing Windows NT Account. The Add User or Group dialog box appears (see Figure 3.4).
6. Select a current user account. Click Add, then click OK.
7. Complete the Properties dialog box with the information shown in Table 3.11.

Figure 3.4.

Windows NT users are associated with Exchange mailbox objects.

Table 3.11. These Properties page values are commonly used properties.

Properties Page	Property	Value
General	Display	Taylor Davis
	First (name)	Taylor
	Last (name)	Davis
	Company	Speed Productions
	Department	Accounting
	Alias	tdavis
Phone/Notes	Business	(311)887-7878
	Fax	(311)887-7801
Limits	Incoming Message Size	4096(KB)

Note that the Display name field and the Alias name field are filled in automatically when the First and Last fields are entered. Save the new mailbox configuration by clicking OK.

> You can configure Exchange Administrator to create both the alias name and display name in any format. Choose Options from the Exchange Administrator Tools menu. Choose the Autonaming Properties page and select a format for the alias name and display name.

8. Create a mailbox for all the users listed in Table 3.1, earlier in this chapter. Be sure to enter the correct department for each of these users, based on their respective groups as defined in Table 3.2. These mailboxes are used in subsequent exercises in this chapter.

The purpose of this exercise was to demonstrate the basics of creating a new mailbox. Adding new mailboxes is a simple process if you are working with a limited number of users. However, if you are installing Exchange Server at a large corporation, consider creating mailboxes *en masse* using Exchange Server's import processes. Also, remember that mailboxes can be created automatically when adding new users to your network with User Manager for Domains.

3.4.2. Creating and Configuring Custom Recipients

A *custom recipient* is a foreign recipient. A custom recipient is not within the Exchange local post office, site, or organization. When a custom recipient is created, it appears in the address book and can receive messages sent by Exchange clients. Custom recipients are useful for providing Address Book entries for persons outside the company. Custom recipients are most often used to connect Exchange users with foreign post offices within a company.

There are two ways to create a custom recipient:

- Using the Exchange Server Administrator
- Using Exchange Server's directory import feature

The following exercise shows you how to create a custom recipient using the Exchange Server Administrator. In this example, the custom recipient is an Internet recipient that uses an SMTP address.

1. Run Exchange Server Administrator.

2. Select New Custom Recipient from the Exchange Server Administrator's File menu.

3. Select Internet Address from the Choose E-mail Address Type dialog box. Click OK.

4. The Internet Address Properties dialog box appears. Type `wpowell@msn.com` as the email address for the custom recipient.

5. Click OK. The Properties dialog box appears (see Figure 3.5).

6. Enter the following property values on the General Properties page for the newly created custom recipient:

    First (name):   `Will`

    Last (name):   `Powell`

    Alias: `wpowell`

    Title: `Consultant`

    Company: `CAP Gemini`

3

Figure 3.5.

The customer recipient object facilitates foreign addresses in the Address Book.

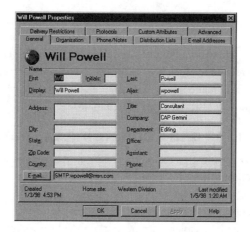

7. Click OK. The custom recipient is displayed as Will Powell in the Address Book(s). Any mail sent to Will Powell is sent to the Internet address wpowell@msn.com.

Custom recipients are often used as a stop-gap trafficking point when migrating from another mail system to Exchange Server. You can also use custom recipients for temporary users (consultants working at your site, for example) who maintain a primary mailbox at another location. In any case, the custom recipient is a useful way to provide connectivity to other mail systems.

3.4.3. Creating and Configuring Distribution Lists

Distribution lists are simply electronic mailing lists to which other Exchange recipients (including other distribution lists) belong. When a message is sent to a distribution list, all members of that list receive a copy of the message.

After completing the following sections, you will be able to do the following:

- Identify and define distribution list properties
- Create and configure a distribution list

Understanding Distribution List Properties Pages

The Distribution List Properties dialog box is used to configure the selected distribution list. The dialog box contains the Properties pages described in Table 3.12.

Table 3.12. The Properties pages for distribution lists.

Properties Page	Description
General	Contains basic configuration information such as display name, alias, list members, and notes
Organization	Optional information about your organization: manager for the custom recipient owner and persons that report to the custom recipient owner
Phone/Notes	Phone number information for the custom recipient and related notes
Permissions	Permissions granted to the custom recipient are specified on this page
Distribution Lists	List of distribution lists to which the custom recipient belongs
E-mail Addresses	List of foreign email addresses by which the custom recipient is known to gateways and connectors
Delivery Restrictions	List of recipients from which messages will be accepted, and a list of recipients from which messages will be rejected
Protocols	List of protocols that may be used by a client to connect to the mailbox
Custom Attributes	Ten administrator-definable properties to store additional information about distribution lists
Advanced	Miscellaneous configuration options such as maximum message size, directory synchronization trust level, and simple display name

Creating and Configuring a Distribution List

The following exercise demonstrates how to create a distribution list for the Accounting department at the Western site:

1. Run Exchange Server Administrator.

2. Select a recipient container.

3. Choose New Distribution List from the Exchange Server Administrator's File menu. The Distribution List Properties dialog box appears (see Figure 3.6).

4. Select the General page from the distribution list Properties dialog box.

5. Set the Display name property to Accounting Department.

6. Set the Alias name to acctdept.

7. Add members to the distribution list. Click the Modify button. The Distribution List dialog box appears (see Figure 3.7).

Figure 3.6.

The distribution list Properties dialog box.

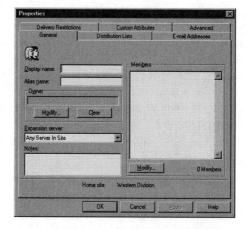

Figure 3.7.

Exchange recipients are added to a distribution list.

8. Double-click these user names to move them to the Add list: Lauren Guzor, Margaret Farrell, and Taylor Davis.

9. Click OK to return to the distribution list Properties dialog box.

10. Configure the distribution list so that SMTP clients can send messages to the accounting department. Select the E-mail Addresses Properties page.

11. Add the email address acctdept@western.ionia.com to the email addresses list.

12. Limit the size of messages that can be sent to this distribution list to 4 megabytes. Select the Advanced Properties page, then click the Max(K) radio button. Enter **4096** in the Max(K) property field.

13. Click OK. The creation of the Accounting Department distribution list is complete

Creating distribution lists is as simple as adding users to a Windows NT group. Remember that the distribution lists you create on Exchange Server are added to the Exchange Directory and are normally available to all users. Users can also create personal distribution lists in their personal Address Books.

3.4.4. Creating and Configuring Public Folders

A *public folder* is a container object that holds information shared among all users and groups. Public folders can be configured to facilitate different applications including discussion forums, cooperative scheduling, collaborative development, and bulletin boards.

After completing the following sections, you will be able to do the following:

- Identify and define the contents of public folder Properties pages
- Create a public folder using Microsoft Outlook
- Configure a public folder using Exchange Administrator

Understanding Public Folder Properties Pages

The public folder Properties dialog box is used to configure the selected public folder. It consists of the pages described in Table 3.13.

Table 3.13. Some of the properties for public folders listed here are configurable from an Exchange client.

Properties Page	Description
General	Basic configuration items such as folder name, address book display name, and client permissions. All these attributes (except the folder name) can be configured from the Exchange Server client or Outlook.
Replicas	Used to manage replication of the folder to other Exchange Servers, configurable only from Exchange Administrator.
Folder Replication Status	Per-server information about the replication updates such as last received time and transmission time. This Properties page is informational only.
Replication Schedule	Used to configure the frequency of replication. Use Exchange Administrator to set the replication schedule.

continues

Table 3.13. continued

Properties Page	Description
Distribution Lists	Shows any distribution lists to which the folder belongs. Also used to add the folder to distribution lists.
E-mail Addresses	Used to display and configure foreign email addresses.
Custom Attributes	Contains up to 10 administrator-defined fields. Custom attributes can be configured only using Exchange Administrator.
Limits	Settingsfor deleted items retention, storage size limits, and age limits for messages in the folder. Use Exchange Administrator to set these properties.
Advanced	Miscellaneous settings including home server, directory synchronization trust level, and simple display name. These properties can be configured only from Exchange Administrator.

Creating a Public Folder Using Microsoft Outlook

Public folders are created by Exchange clients. The following exercise demonstrates how to create a public folder using Microsoft Outlook.

When a client creates a public folder, the logged-on user is assigned ownership of the folder. Folder owners have complete administrative control of the folder. Configuration of the folders is limited by the options offered by the Exchange client. Microsoft Outlook has a subset of the configuration options that can be performed using Exchange Administrator.

The following exercise walks you through the creation of a public folder using Microsoft Outlook. You will also set some configuration settings. It is assumed that Microsoft Outlook is configured to connect to the Exchange Server you installed at the beginning of this chapter.

1. Start Outlook.

2. If it is not the default view for your configuration of Outlook, set the view to Folder List. From the View Menu, choose Folder List.

3. Double-click the Public Folders folder in the folder pane.

4. Right-click the All Public Folders option and choose Create Subfolder. The Create New Folder dialog box appears (see Figure 3.8).

Figure 3.8.

Public folders provide group access to messages and other information.

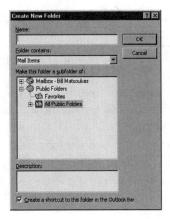

5. Type **Test Project** in the Name field.

6. Click OK. The new public folder is created.

7. As the owner, you can now configure the Test Project folder. Right-click the Test Project folder and choose Properties from the pop-up menu. The Properties dialog box appears (see Figure 3.9).

Figure 3.9.

Many public folder configuration options can be accomplished using Microsoft Outlook.

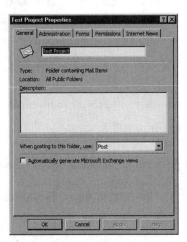

8. Review the user-configurable Properties pages described in Table 3.14.

3

Table 3.14. Public folder properties available in Microsoft Outlook.

Properties Page	Description
General	Basic settings such as folder description, forms selection, and view configuration.
Administration	Used to configure initial view, availability to users, and drag-and-drop actions. Also contains the Folder Assistant, used to define rules for messages sent to the folder.
Forms	Forms management: used to associate forms with the folder.
Permissions	Used to set access permissions for users. This is the same as the Client Permissions option offered on the General Properties page in Exchange Administrator.

Exchange Server and Outlook provide limited administrative access to public folders. This approach allows the Exchange Administrator to delegate public folder management to users. Many administrators create a public folder for each department at the company and assign a user from each department as the owner of that department's folder.

Configuring a Public Folder Using Exchange Administrator

Although Exchange Administrator cannot be used to create a public folder, it can access and configure a number of public folder properties. The following exercise demonstrates how to configure a public folder using Exchange Administrator.

1. Start Exchange Administrator.

2. From the Administrator window, select the public folder Test Project.

3. Choose Properties from the File menu. The Test Project Properties dialog box appears (see Figure 3.10).

4. Choose the General Properties page and then click Client Permissions. The Client Permissions dialog box appears (see Figure 3.11). Note that user Default has Author permissions. This means that any user can add, edit, and delete his or her own items in this folder. The information in this folder is to be contributed to by the accounting department, but is available for review by all users.

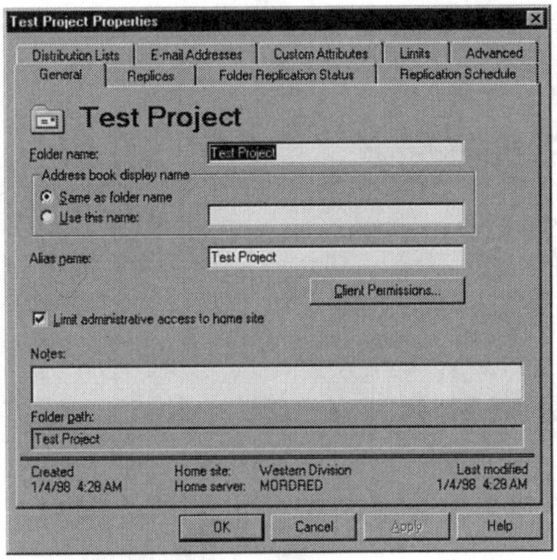

Figure 3.10.

Client permissions are configured from the public folder Properties dialog box.

Figure 3.11.

Exchange recipients can be granted access to public folders.

5. Select the user Default from the user list, and then change the role from Author to Reviewer by selecting Reviewer from the Roles drop-down menu.

6. Enable the Accounting department to add, edit, and delete any item in the folder. Click Add; the Add Users dialog box appears (see Figure 3.12).

7. Double-click the distribution list Accounting Department and then click OK. You are returned to the Client Permissions dialog box.

8. Select Accounting Department from the user list, then set the permissions to Editor by selecting Editor from the Role drop-down menu.

9. Click OK. You are returned to the Properties dialog box.

Figure 3.12.

The Add Users dialog box.

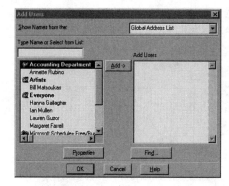

10. Set the messages posted to expire in 30 days. Choose the Limits Properties page.

11. Check the Age Limit for Replicas checkbox and enter **30** in the associated field.

12. Click OK.

3.5. Understanding Exchange Permissions and Roles

If you have been exploring Exchange Administrator, you may have discovered an option that displays a Permissions property page in all object Properties dialog boxes. The subject of permissions was omitted in the earlier discussion of recipient objects to simplify the recipient configuration.

The following sections describe the permission scheme used by Exchange. After completing these sections, you will be able to do the following:

■ Identify Exchange object permissions

■ Identify permission roles

3.5.1. Understanding Exchange Permissions

Microsoft Exchange permissions, referred to as *directory permissions*, have three important attributes:

■ Directory permissions are assigned to Windows NT user accounts or groups. They should not be confused with Windows NT permissions: Exchange directory permissions apply only to access to objects within Exchange. This means that an ordinary user can be assigned permission to administer a group of Exchange recipients.

■ Directory permissions, like file permissions, facilitate varying levels of access to Exchange objects. The different permissions discussed in this section are combined to create permission *roles*. Roles are discussed in the next section.

■ Directory permissions can be inherited by subordinate (or child) objects. Whether permissions are inherited depends on the target object.

Table 3.15 describes the Exchange directory permissions. Note that all directory permissions do not apply to all Exchange object types.

Table 3.15. Directory permissions facilitate access to Exchange objects.

Permission	Description
Add Child	Allows the user to create objects within the container.
Delete	Provides user with permission to delete the object. If the object is a container, the user can delete objects within that container.
Logon Rights	Facilitates access to the directory. This permission is required to use Exchange Administrator.
Mailbox Owner	Allows user to read and delete messages in the mailbox object.
Modify Admin Attributes	Allows user to change administrative-level properties such as display names.
Modify Permissions	Allows user to change permissions for the object.
Modify User Attributes	Allows user to change user-level attributes such as phone numbers associated with a mailbox.
Replication	Allows user to replicate directory information with other servers.
Search	Allows user to view contents of the container object.
Send As	Permits user to send messages with the sending object's return address.

3.5.2. Understanding Permission Roles

Exchange directory permissions are combined to create a set of default Exchange *roles*. Roles are used to simplify assignment of permissions to Exchange objects in much the same way that Windows NT user groups simplify assignment of file permissions to users.

Table 3.16 shows these roles and their associated permissions.

Table 3.16. Exchange directory permissions are organized into roles.

Role	Permissions Assigned
Admin	Add Child Modify User Attributes Modify Admin Attributes Delete Logon
Permissions Admin	Add Child Modify User Attributes Modify Admin Attributes Delete Logon Modify Permission
Search	Modify User Attributes Search
Send As	Send As
Service Account Admin	Add Child Modify User Attributes Modify Admin Attributes Delete Logon Modify Permission Replication Mailbox Owner Send As
User	Modify User Attributes Mailbox Owner Send As
View Only Admin	Logon

3.6. Configuring Organizations, Sites, and Servers

Organization, site, and server objects are not very complex objects. Their primary purpose is to serve as containers for other objects and to provide a point of permission assignment for administrative purposes. After completing the following sections, you should be able to do the following:

■ Assign display names and permissions to organization, site, and server objects
■ Understand the details of the server object properties

3.6.1. Configuring the Organization Object

The *organization object* is the root of the Exchange hierarchy. Its primary purpose is to hold all the other objects that make up Exchange Server. As such, there is little to configure. After completing the following exercise, you will understand how to change the organization object display name and assign permissions to the organization object.

> **Note** The display name assigned to the organization object and site objects appears in the Exchange client Address Book. It is a good idea to assign a recognizable name to these objects.

1. Start Exchange Administrator.
2. Select the organization object from the Administrator window.
3. Choose Properties from the File menu. The Properties dialog box for the organization object appears.
4. Change the name displayed for the Exchange Administrator and Exchange Client. Choose the General Properties page and enter a new name in the Display Name field.
5. Assign user `Ian Mullen` permission to change the organization object display name. Choose the Permissions Properties page.

> **Note** Permissions assigned to the organization object *are not inherited* by any child objects.

6. Click Add. The Add User or Group dialog box appears.
7. Double-click user `Ian Mullen` in the Names list and then click OK to return to the organization object Properties dialog box.

8. Select Ian Mullen from the user list and choose Admin from the Roles drop-down menu.

9. Click OK.

The folder name assigned to an Exchange object is used internally by Exchange Server. The display name is used to convey the meaning or purpose of the object to the human viewer. For objects that are viewed by users, the display name should be descriptive and concise. Display names for objects seen only by administrators should follow some order or standard to help maintain logical structure for your Exchange environment.

3.6.2. Configuring Site Objects

Site containers are child objects of the organization container object. As is the case with the organization object, the site object serves exclusively as a container. The site container holds two very important objects: the configuration and the recipients objects.

The exercise that follows steps through changing the site container name from Western to a more eloquent name: Western Division. This exercise also demonstrates assigning permissions to the site object.

> Unlike the organization object, there are ramifications to assigning permissions to a site object. Site object permissions *are inherited* by any child recipient container objects and by the Address Book Views container object. This means that any user assigned permission to a site object has the same permissions to any recipient container object and recipient object within that site.

1. Start Exchange Administrator.

2. Select the Western site object and choose Properties from the File menu. The site Properties dialog box appears.

3. Change the display name for the site object to **Western Division**. Choose the General Properties page and enter **Western Division** in the Display Name field.

4. To grant Hanna Gallagher permission to administer all recipient objects within the Western Division site, grant her Admin permission to the Western Division site object. Choose the Permissions property page and then click Add.

5. The Add User or Group dialog box appears. Double-click Hanna Gallagher in the user list and click OK to return to the site object Properties dialog box.

6. Select Hanna Gallagher from the account list and then select Admin from the Roles drop-down menu.

7. Click OK.

Like the organization object, the site object is a "pure container" object. Its purpose is to hold other objects. Both the organization object and the site object have very few properties.

3.6.3. Configuring Server Objects

Each server object represents a single installation of Exchange Server. *Server objects* are child objects of the site/configuration/servers object.

Server object configuration is centered around operational parameters such as services, logging, and database configuration. Table 3.17 lists the Properties pages and descriptions for the server object.

Table 3.17. Exchange Server object Properties pages.

Properties Page	Description
General	Contains general configuration information and properties such as software version, directory name, server location, and administrative notes.
Permissions	Contains security configuration for the server object.
Services	Contains tools to configure services monitoring.
Locales	Date, time, and currency display is configured on this page.
Database Paths	Paths to log files and database files can be configured on this page.
IS Maintenance	Contains a tool to schedule maintenance hours for Exchange Server.
Advanced	Circular logging, directory, and Information Stores synchronization is configured here.
Diagnostics Logging	Logging levels for various components of Exchange Server are configured on this page.

3

3.7. Understanding Address Book Views

Address Book views are a kind of filter through which Exchange clients can view recipients in the Address Book. Address Book views allow the Exchange administrator to group recipients in an organization by recipient properties such as Company, Department, or one of the Custom Attributes.

The following exercise explains how to create an Address Book view based on Department (meaning that a client can look up a user based on his or her department within the organization).

It is important not only to understand how to create and configure an Address Book view, but also to see the end result of the effort. In the first part of this exercise, you install and configure an Address Book view; in the second part of the exercise, you view the end result of the Address Book view using an Exchange client.

1. Start Exchange Administrator.

2. Choose New Other/Address Book View from the File menu. An address view Properties dialog box appears.

3. Choose the General Properties page and then set both the Display Name property and the Directory Name property to Department.

4. Choose the Group By Properties page. Note that you can group recipients up to four levels deep (see Figure 3.13).

Figure 3.13.

Address Book views allow you to group recipients by various properties.

5. Choose Department from the topmost Group Items By drop-down menu.

6. Choose the Advanced Properties page. Confirm that the Confirm Entries to Parent Containers checkbox is selected. This property allows recipients to be listed in more than one Address Book view.

7. Confirm that the Department Address Book view will be available to Exchange clients. Make sure that the Show This View in the Client Address Book checkbox is selected.

> Address Book views are useful tools for administering recipients. Recipients that appear under the Address Book Views container object are the same recipient objects stored in the Site/Recipient container objects and are assigned the same permissions. A large recipient population can be segregated by up to four recipient fields. Administrative Address Book views can be hidden from Exchange clients.

8. Click OK to save the Department Address Book view.

9. Check the Department Address Book view in Exchange Administrator. Open the Address Book View/Department object in the Administrator window. Four departments should appear as child objects under the Department container object (see Figure 3.14).

Figure 3.14.

Exchange automatically creates Address Book views for group criteria.

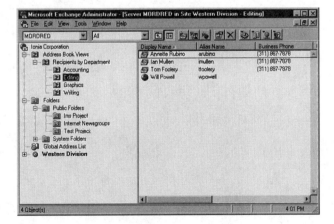

10. Close Exchange Administrator.

11. Confirm that the Department Address Book view is accessible to Exchange clients. At a client workstation, start Microsoft Outlook (or a mail client configured for Exchange Server).

12. Choose Address Book from the Tools menu. The Address Book window appears.

13. Open the Show Names drop-down menu. Note the addition of the Department Address Book view (see Figure 3.15).

Figure 3.15.

Address Book views can be added to the client Address Book.

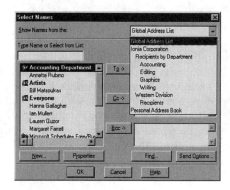

14. Close Exchange Administrator.

Address Book views are a powerful tool for providing easy access to recipients and as an administrative tool. This exercise stepped through a very simple configuration of an Address Book view. The power of this tool underlines the importance of carefully planning recipient configuration for your Exchange organization.

Lab

This lab consists of review questions pertaining to this chapter and provides an opportunity to apply the knowledge you've gained in this chapter.

Questions

1. You are installing a second Microsoft Exchange Server for your site. This server is administered remotely and is used strictly to distribute the mail processing load for the site. There are no foreign mail connectors required for this server. What standard installation option best meets the requirement for this server?

    A. Minimum

    B. Complete/Custom

    C. Connectors-Only

    D. Remote

2. What tool can be used to create a new mailbox on an Exchange Server?

    A. Exchange Server Administrator

    B. User Manager for Domains

    C. Exchange Extract and Import Tools

    D. All of the above

3. You are installing the first Exchange Server at a site that consists of two domains: DomainA and DomainB. There are approximately 120 users in each domain. You are installing the server as a member of DomainA. For a single Exchange Server to service all the users at this site, which of the following statements must be true?

    A. DomainA must trust DomainB.

    B. DomainB must trust DomainA.

    C. DomainA and DomainB must trust each other.

    D. Exchange Servers cannot cross domain boundaries. You must install an Exchange Server in each domain and configure a connector between them.

4. You are installing Exchange Server at a location that is already using Lotus cc:Mail. Management has indicated that they want you to migrate the 500 cc:Mail users to Exchange over a period of time, moving the users one

department at a time. To facilitate a smooth transition, you have decided to set up the Exchange Server, connect the cc:Mail server, and then begin to migrate users. Other than Exchange Server, what additional software must you install to create a connection between the cc:Mail server and the Exchange Server?

    A. You must install the cc:Mail client service on the Exchange Server.

    B. You must install the System Attendant to manage foreign email.

    C. No additional software is required. The cc:Mail connector is part of Exchange Server's Custom/Complete installation.

    D. A connection cannot be made between Exchange Server and cc:Mail. The cc:Mail users must be migrated using Exchange Administrator's import feature.

5. Your company wants to implement web access to your Exchange Server's email system. Other than Exchange Server, what additional software must be installed on any Exchange Server used to service web clients?

    A. You must install Web Access Components using Exchange Server's Custom/Complete installation option.

    B. You must install Internet Information Server.

    C. You must install both the Web Access Components and Internet Information Server.

    D. No additional software is required for the Exchange Servers; however, a web server must be connected to the network.

6. You have discovered that using Address Book views is a useful way to group mailboxes in your Exchange organization. However, the ways in which you are grouping mailboxes is not useful to anyone but you. Is there a practical way to set up administrative Address Book views?

    A. No, because the Address Book views are visible to all clients within the organization, and they will clutter up the Address Book.

    B. No, because even though you can group mailboxes in Address Book views, the mailboxes are only configurable from the site container.

    C. Yes, because Address Book views can be hidden from client Address Books, and the mailboxes in the Address Book Views container are completely configurable.

    D. Yes, because Address Book views can be limited by site, and the mailboxes in the Address Book Views container are completely configurable.

7. What tool is used to configure Exchange Server container objects?

    A. System Attendant

    B. Exchange Administrator

    C. Object Manager

    D. None of the above

8. You have been asked to create a distribution list that includes local Exchange users as well as several users with Internet email addresses. How will you create the distribution list?

    A. Create the distribution list, add the local Exchange users, then manually add the addresses for the foreign users.

    B. Import the foreign user addresses using the Internet Connector, create the distribution list, add the local Exchange users to the list, then add the imported Internet addresses to the list.

    C. Create the distribution list, create a custom recipient for each of the foreign users, then add both the custom recipients and the local Exchange users to the distribution list.

    D. Create a foreign distribution list, add the Internet addresses to the foreign distribution list, create an Exchange distribution list and add the local Exchange users to the Exchange distribution list, then tell the users that they must send email to both lists.

9. You must create a public folder that can be viewed by everyone at your site, but only persons in the Accounting department can contribute to or modify contents of the folder. What is the best way to group users to grant the appropriate permissions?

    A. Create a distribution list for the Accounting department and use the Default user for all others at your site.

    B. Create a Windows NT global group for the Accounting department and use the special group Everyone for all others at your site.

    C. Create a Windows NT local group on the server on which the public folder is homed and use the special group Everyone for all others at your site.

    D. None of the above. Groups and distribution lists cannot be assigned permissions to a public folder.

3

10. For security purposes, how often should the Exchange Server Service Account password be changed?

    A. At least every 30 days.

    B. Al least every 90 days.

    C. Never. Exchange Server automatically changes the password periodically.

    D. None of the above. The password can be changed, but it is not required.

Exercises

Exercise 1: Creating a Mailbox Template

This exercise addresses the following Microsoft exam objectives:
- Configure Exchange Server message recipients
- Configure address lists and accounts by using Exchange Administrator

Mailboxes created for a given site usually have a significant number of properties in common. A mailbox *template* can be used as a properties framework for new mailboxes. Mailbox templates are an ordinary mailbox that is used to copy common information such as company name and security information to a new mailbox.

This exercise demonstrates the creation of a mailbox template using Exchange Server Administrator. After completing this exercise, you should be able to do the following:

- Create a mailbox template
- Create a new mailbox using a mailbox template to set site-specific defaults for the new mailbox

1. Run Exchange Server Administrator.
2. From the Administrator window, select the recipient object where you want to create the mailbox template.
3. Choose New Mailbox from the Exchange Server Administrator File menu. The Properties dialog box for the new mailbox appears.
4. Select the General page in the mailbox Properties dialog box.
5. Enter the name for the mailbox template in the Display field.
6. Enter the default, or common, properties to be used for all mailboxes (see Table 3.18) using this template.

3

Table 3.18. Site-specific defaults set in a mailbox template are copied to new mailboxes created using that template.

Tab	Field	Value
General	Company	Speed Productions
	Phone	(311)887-7878
Limits	Outgoing Message Size	Max(K) 4096

7. It is a good idea to hide mailbox templates so that they are not viewed in the Address Book and users cannot send mail to the template. Choose the Advanced Properties page and then select the Hide from Address Book checkbox.

8. Click OK.

To use the template, select the mailbox template from the Administrator window and then choose Duplicate from the File menu. A new mailbox dialog box appears with all the information you added to the template.

Exercise 2: Installing Exchange Administrator on a Windows NT Workstation Client

Note | This exercise addresses the following Microsoft exam objective:
■ Install an Exchange Server computer

It is more than likely that users assigned to administer Exchange for an organization will log directly onto an Exchange Server to perform their jobs. They run Exchange Administrator from a connected workstation. This exercise steps through the installation of Exchange Administrator on a Windows NT Workstation. After completing this exercise, you should be able to do the following:

■ Perform an over-the-network installation of Exchange Administrator

■ Configure Exchange Administrator with a default server

■ Use Exchange Administrator to connect to any Exchange Server within the organization.

> **Note** This exercise assumes that you are using a Windows NT Workstation that belongs to the same domain as the Exchange Server(s) or a trusted domain.

1. Log on to a Windows NT Workstation with a user account that has administrative rights on the workstation as well as appropriate rights to the Exchange Server.

2. Connect the workstation to the share point where the Exchange Server CD-ROM or install directory is located.

3. Run SETUP.EXE. The Exchange license agreement screen appears. Click Accept.

4. The first setup dialog box that appears prompts for both the install directory and the installation type. Set the install directory to C:\Program Files\Exchsrvr and choose the Complete/Custom installation option.

5. If the target directory, C:\Program Files\Exchsrvr, does not exist, you are prompted to create the directory. Click OK.

6. The Complete/Custom configuration dialog box appears. Clear all option checkboxes except for the Exchange Server Administrator option and click Continue.

7. You are prompted for your CD-ROM key. Enter the key number and click OK. The Product ID message box appears.

8. Click OK. After Exchange Administrator is installed and configured, Setup informs you that the installation has been completed successfully.

9. Click OK. Exchange Administrator has been installed and added to the Start menu.

10. Run Exchange Administrator by choosing Programs|Microsoft Exchange|Microsoft Exchange Administrator from the Start menu. Because this is the first time that Exchange Administrator has run on this computer, you are prompted for the name of target Exchange Server (see Figure 3.16).

Figure 3.16.

The Connect to server dialog box.

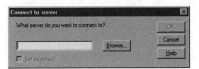

11. Enter the name of the Exchange Server.

12. Set the target Exchange Server as the default server for this copy of Exchange Administrator by selecting the Set as Default option.

13. Click OK. Exchange Administrator connects to the target server, and the Administrator window appears.

14. Connect Exchange Administrator to a different server. Choose Connect to Server from the File menu. You are prompted for the name of the target Exchange Server.

15. Enter the name of the Exchange Server, confirm that the Set as Default option is cleared, and click OK. A second Administrator window appears (see Figure 3.17).

Figure 3.17.

Exchange Administrator can be used to view more than one Exchange server simultaneously.

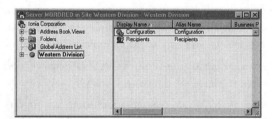

16. Quit Exchange Administrator by choosing Exit from the File menu.

The next time you start Exchange Administrator, it will connect to the server you assigned as the default server the first time you started Exchange Administrator. You are offered the option of changing the default server each time you connect Exchange Administrator to a different server.

Answers to Questions

1. **A**   The minimum installation installs the Microsoft Exchange Server software only. Because this site is administered remotely, there is no need for the Exchange Server Administrator software. Connector-Only and Remote are not Microsoft Exchange Server installation options.

   Note that the same results can be achieved by setting the appropriate options using the Custom/Complete installation option. The question is which option best meets the requirements, not which option merely meets the requirements.

2. **A**   Although Exchange Server Administrator, User Manager for Domains, and Exchange Extract and Import Tools can all be used to create a new mailbox, the important thing is understanding which tool is *best* used for a given scenario. Exchange Server Administrator is useful for creating a small number of

mailboxes for a few existing users; User Manager for Domains is best used for creating a new mailbox while creating a new user; Exchange Extract and Import Tools is best applied to creating new mailboxes *en masse*.

3. **A**   The Exchange Server in DomainA is a resource that must be available to users in DomainB for the users in DomainB to use the Exchange Server services.

4. **C**   The cc:Mail connector is part of Exchange Server's Complete/Custom installation. The cc:Mail connector is a gateway that permits Exchange Server to process cc:Mail messages.

5. **A**   This question is a bit tricky: When you install Internet Information Server, the Web Access Components are installed.

6. **C**   Using hidden Address Book views is a good way to administer a large number of mailboxes.

7. **B**   Exchange Administrator is used to configure all components of Exchange Server.

8. **C**   Custom recipients are recipients with foreign addresses such as Internet and cc:Mail addresses. Because custom recipients are recipient objects, they can be added to a distribution list.

9 **A**   The permissions used for access to a public folder are Exchange client access permissions, not Windows NT groups. Distribution lists can be assigned access permissions to public folders, as can the global Default recipient.

10. **D**   The Exchange Server Service Account password should never expire and should not be changed.

TEST DAY FAST FACTS

Here are a few fast facts about this chapter that you may want to know ahead of time. These facts provide great last-minute study material.

- Exchange Server backup processes are handled differently than ordinary file-level backups.

- Exchange Server databases are updated using transaction log files.

- Circular logging configuration is important to the Exchange backup scheme.

- Exchange data can be backed up in either online or offline mode.

- The two primary categories of Exchange data are the Directory Store (DS) and the Information Store (IS).

- Replication is used to keep Exchange directories and public folders up to date throughout an organization.

- Exchange Administrator provides a rich set of statistics about Exchange Server's performance and capacities.

- Public folders can be configured to be user-manageable.

- Efficient public Information Store replication can be configured using public folder affinity, replication scheduling, and server groups.

- Directory replication is automatic among servers within an Exchange site, but must be configured between sites.

Day 4

Long-Term Exchange System Administration

by William Matsoukas

The default installation of Exchange Server as described in Day 3 provides a foundation configuration that can meet the needs of a small network. As a network and its associated messaging system grows, the management of Exchange becomes more critical in terms of performance, growth management, and system security.

This chapter describes the primary configuration strategies that can be employed to provide ongoing performance and reliability as the network and the messaging system grows.

Objectives

This chapter addresses the following Microsoft exam objectives:

- Develop long-term administration strategies
- Develop server-side scripting strategies

- Bridgehead servers act as communication centers for replication between sites.

- All associated replicas are peers. There is no master replica.

- Public folder structure is always replicated between servers within an Exchange site; public folder content replication must be configured.

- Directory updates between servers within an Exchange site work differently than Directory updates between sites.

- Inbound sites are Exchange sites from which the local site directly or indirectly receives Directory updates.

- Outbound sites are Exchange sites to which the local site provides Directory updates.

- A new feature included with Exchange Server 5.5 is Server Scripting Language, which facilitates application development for Exchange Server using VBScript, JScript, and other supported scripting languages.

4.1. Developing a Backup Strategy for Exchange Server

Exchange-related data requires special backup and restore procedure considerations. Because of the way in which Exchange Server processes and stores data, ordinary file-level backups are not adequate for ensuring data recoverability. To develop good backup and restore procedures, you need an understanding of Exchange data and processes, including the following:

- The location and types of Exchange data
- How Exchange processes data
- Backup types
- How Windows NT Backup handles Exchange data
- How Exchange data is restored

4.1.1. Understanding Exchange Server Data

To develop a functional backup process, you must know the nature and location of the Exchange-related data. This section describes the purpose and location of Exchange data.

Exchange data can be categorized according to its location on the network. Exchange data stored on user workstations, referred to as *local data*, is usually one of the following four data types:

- Personal message stores
- Offline message stores
- Personal Address Book(s)
- Microsoft Schedule+ files

> **Note** It is normally the user's responsibility to back up local data. User data can also be stored on a file server so that it is backed up during the course of regular server backups.

Most Exchange data is stored on the Exchange Server and is referred to as—believe it or not—*server-based data.* Server-based Exchange data is stored in the following databases:

- The Directory Store (DS)
- The Information Store (IS)
- The Key Management Server (if installed)
- The Windows NT Registry

Exchange Server stores a significant amount of information in the Windows NT Registry, such as service and connector configuration information. The Registry is crucial to an efficient and reliable disaster recovery.

In addition to configuration information stored in the Windows NT Registry, Exchange Server data is stored in three databases as shown in Table 4.1. These files store Directory (Directory Store) and message (Information Store) data. These database files also have a transaction log file associated with them. Log files are discussed later in this chapter in "Understanding Exchange Server's Transaction Log Processing."

4

Table 4.1. Three database files (and the associated transaction file —not shown here) comprise the most critical Exchange data.

Filename	Default Folder	Data Type
DIR.EDB	\exchsrvr\DSADATA	Directory store
PRIV.EDB	\exchsrvr\MDBDATA	Private store
PUB.EDB	\exchsrvr\MDBDATA	Public store

If the Key Management Server is installed on the Exchange Server, its data is stored in folder \exchsrvr\KMSDATA. Exchange Server 4.0 and 5.0 require that the Key Management Server be installed *after* Exchange Server is installed. The Key Management Server is an integrated option on Exchange Server 5.5.

In addition to the data described in Table 4.1, other information stored in the exchsrvr folder that should be included in a backup plan are MTA transient message data and message-tracking log files. All data stored in the exchsrvr folder should be included in a file-level backup plan.

4.1.2. Understanding Exchange Server's Transaction Log Processing

To provide recoverability and improved performance, Exchange Server uses transaction log processing to maintain both the Directory Store and Information Store databases. This section describes transaction log processing and its relationship to backup and recovery of the Exchange databases.

When Exchange Server processes a transaction such as deleting a message or creating a new recipient, the transaction is not written directly to one of Exchange's random-access database files. Instead, the transaction is first written to a sequential transaction log file and then to the appropriate database file. This update scheme yields two performance advantages over directly writing to a database:

- The initial transaction write to the sequential log file is faster than a write to a random access database file.
- Exchange Server can write the transaction to the database file(s) when CPU time is freed from higher priority tasks, and the order in which the transactions are written to the database file can be (and is) optimized.

To further improve performance, transaction log files are fixed-length files. This means that the entire file space is allocated when the file is first created. This eliminates the need for the operating system to continually allocate disk space as the transaction log file grows.

> Exchange Server transaction log files are always 5,242,880 bytes. If a transaction log file is any other size, it is probably corrupted.

Transaction log files contain a signature record that matches its associated database file. The current transaction log file, EDB.LOG, is located by default in the folder with its associated database file (refer to Table 4.1). If an Exchange Server service attempts to update a database file with a transaction log file when the signatures do not match, the service fails, and an error event is written to Exchange Server's system event log.

Log files can be viewed as scripts that are played back against a database file. This is useful when today's database is corrupted: You can restore yesterday's database file and then "play" today's transaction log against the database file, recovering the database and updating it to the last transaction that was committed before the database file became corrupted.

 When an Exchange Server is stopped abnormally, the Information Stores are recovered automatically when the server is restarted. The Exchange Server database services determine which transactions in the log file were not completed. The Information Store is then rolled back to the point at which all transactions were completed.

In addition, each transaction log file has a *checkpoint file* associated with it. The checkpoint file functions as a pointer for a transaction log file. It contains information about what records in the transaction log file have and have not been committed to the database file. The checkpoint file is located, by default, in the folder with its associated transaction log file. Checkpoint files are an optimization feature and are not required to perform a restore using transaction log files.

Exchange Server has a circular logging option (which is turned on by default). With circular logging enabled, when the transaction log file is full, Exchange Server begins writing transactions at the beginning of the file, overwriting the oldest transaction. With circular logging disabled, when a transaction log file fills up, it is renamed and a new transaction log file is created.

4.1.3. Understanding Backup Types

Exchange Server can be backed up in two modes:

- **Online.** Online backups are performed while Exchange Server services are running and the databases are open. Backing up Exchange Server online requires special backup software such as Windows NT Backup, which ships with Exchange Server.
- **Offline.** Offline backup is an ordinary file-level backup performed while Exchange database services are not running.

The four traditional file-level backups (full, full copy, incremental, and differential) are described in Table 4.2. These backup processes translate differently when you are backing up Exchange Server data online, as described in the following section.

Table 4.2. The traditional backup processes described in terms of a file-level backup.

Backup Process	Description
Full	All files on the target are backed up, and the archive flag is cleared for all files.
Full Copy	All files on the target are backed up, but the archive bit is not changed for any files.
Incremental	All files on the target with the archive flag set are backed up, and the archive flag is cleared.
Differential	All files on the target with the archive flag set are backed up, but the archive bit is not changed for any files.

4.1.4. Understanding Exchange Server Online Backups

In the preceding discussion of file-level backup types, changes in files were described in terms of the *archive flag*. Exchange Server online backups are described in terms of *log files* (see Table 4.3).

Table 4.3. Exchange Server online backups defined in terms of log files rather than archive flags.

Backup Process	Description
Full	Database files and transaction log files are backed up, and transaction log files are purged. Circular logging must be disabled.
Full Copy	Database files and transaction log files are backed up, but transaction log files are not purged. Not normally used in a backup scheme, but to take a snapshot of the database.
Incremental	Transaction log files are backed up and then purged. Circular logging must be disabled.
Differential	Transaction log files are backed up, but the transaction log files are not purged. Circular logging must be disabled.

The four backup processes described in Table 4.3 can be used in various combinations to create backup schemes. As with most things in life, there are performance and ease-of-recovery tradeoffs when designing backup schemes. Full and Full Copy backups take the biggest performance bite (or is it byte?) out of your Exchange Server because they back up the database files as well as the log files. Incremental and Differential backups save only the log files and are therefore the fastest and least resource-intensive backup process.

4.1.5. Designing a Backup Scheme

This section looks at some commonly used backup schemes. Backup schemes are typically based on a seven-day cycle. A *cycle* is a period of time in the backup scheme marked by a full backup. Table 4.4 charts three of the most commonly used backup cycles.

Table 4.4. Backup cycles usually reflect the business week and include at least one full backup.

	Sun	Mon	Tue	Wed	Thu	Fri	Sat
Scenario A	Full	Full	Full	Full	Full	Full	Full
Scenario B	Full	Inc	Inc	Inc	Inc	Inc	Inc
Scenario C	Full	Diff	Diff	Diff	Diff	Diff	Diff

Backup Scenario A is a one-day cycle; that is, a full backup is performed every day. This backup scheme offers good data security because you need only restore data from a single full backup and possibly the most recent transaction log file in the event of a database failure. Scenario A is also very inefficient because of the amount of data that must be written to backup media every day.

Backup Scenario B is a seven-day backup cycle that uses incremental backups between full backups. This is a very efficient backup scheme. All database files are backed up once a week. Incremental backups purge backed-up log files, minimizing the number of log files to be backed up each day. The downside to this backup scheme is that you may have to restore data from up to seven backups in the event of a database failure.

Backup Scenario C is a seven-day backup cycle that uses differential backups between full backups. Recall that differential backups do not delete the transaction log files. This means that as differential backups progress through the cycle, the amount of data backed up increases. The advantage to this backup scheme is that you never restore data from more than two backups in the event of a database failure.

It is recommended that regular file-level full backups be performed on Exchange Servers in addition to Exchange online backups. It is imperative that they be performed for disaster recovery purposes.

4.2. Restoring an Exchange Database Offline Backup

Performing a complete Exchange Server restore from an offline backup is a two-step process: First you restore the Directory Store, and then you restore the Information Store. These two steps are different procedures. The Information Store and the Directory Store can be restored independently.

To restore the Directory Store, follow these steps:

1. Restore all files located in the DSADATA directories.

2. Start the Exchange services.

> If Exchange Server Optimizer was run on the target machine, the DSADATA and MDBDATA directories may be located on a different disk volume than the default location or the same volume with Exchange program files. You can use the Windows NT Registry to locate the directories.

To restore the Information Store, follow these steps:

1. Restore all files to the MDBDATA directories.

2. Run an Exchange Server utility program named ISINTEG.EXE (Information Store INTEGrity) with the -patch command-line option. ISINTEG.EXE starts the Exchange Server services.

3. Stop the Exchange Server services. They should start again automatically.

4. Confirm that the correct data was successfully restored.

If you are performing file-level backups, restoring the Exchange database is probably the most common restore procedure that is required. In terms of the Microsoft exam, you will likely not be quizzed on the exact procedure for restoring Exchange data from file-level backups. You may be tested, however, for your understanding of the location of critical files, the ISINTEG tool, and the general restore procedure (that is, that the Directory Store and Information Store are restored differently).

4.3. Restoring an Exchange Server Online Backup

Restoring an Exchange database using an online backup is much simpler than restoring an Exchange database using an offline backup. Because the backup software supports Exchange Server online backups, the restore process is simply to restore data from the last full backup, and then bring the databases up to date with the subsequent incremental or differential backup data.

4.3.1. Restoring a Single Item

In addition to full database recovery, Exchange Server 5.5 provides for single-item recovery. A single item can be any Information Store item, such as public folders or messages. The single-item recovery does not recover mailboxes. When Exchange Server is configured to hold deleted items, the items are not deleted from the Exchange Information Store; instead, they are simply hidden until the specified hold time has transpired, at which time the objects are truly deleted.

Follow these steps to restore a single item:

1. Start Exchange Administrator.
2. Select the Public Information Store object.
3. Click the Properties button on the Administrators toolbar. The Public Information Store Properties dialog box appears.
4. Choose the General properties page.
5. Configure the public information store so that deleted items are kept for 10 days before they are purged: Set the Deleted Item Retention Time [Days] field to 10.
6. Configure the Public Information Store so that deleted items are purged only after they have been backed up, regardless of the time limit: Check the Don't Permanently Delete Item Until the Store Has Been Backed Up checkbox.
7. Click OK to close the dialog box.

Single-item restore is performed using a new client extension. It may or may not be a feature of the Exchange client you are using. If the single-item restore feature is not available to you, you must restore a single item by restoring the entire backup Information Store to a spare Exchange Server and then copying the appropriate files to the production Exchange Server.

4.4. Developing a Disaster Recovery Strategy

The preceding sections were devoted to Exchange data backup and recovery. The next few sections cover disaster recovery. Disaster recovery encompasses all Exchange Server failures other than database failures. This usually means hardware failure, system environmental failure, or acts of God. The following sections cover reducing the risk of a disaster and recovering from a disaster.

4.4.1. Minimizing Your Disaster Risk

Risk minimization means simply that: eliminate as many risk factors for your computing environment as available resources allow. This includes hardware selection, server environment, and security.

Matching computing hardware to a task is the best way to reduce risk of failure and to enhance recoverability. Table 4.5 lists the recommended hardware configuration for Exchange Server. Keep in mind that Exchange Server is very disk I/O-intensive, so the better the hard drive configuration in terms of data integrity, the less the risk for your organization. Notice that the transaction log files are stored on a different physical drive than the database files. This is done for two reasons: First, this configuration optimizes performance. Second, using separate drives for the transaction log files and the database files reduces the likelihood that you lose both sets of files simultaneously.

Table 4.5. The minimum hardware requirements for Exchange Server after Windows NT 4.0, Service Pack 3, is installed.

Item	Minimum Required	Recommended Minimum
Processor	Intel P90, Alpha 4/275	Intel P166, Alpha 5/500
Disk Space	250M: 50M + installed RAM for page file	
	Depends on number of mailboxes, messages, and public folders	100M + installed RAM for page file
RAM	24M platforms, 48M for RISC platforms	32M for Intel

Any mission-critical computing equipment should be in an environment conducive to long and reliable service. This means placing such equipment in a temperature-controlled environment and providing that equipment with clean power backed up by batteries.

Exchange Server (and any other mail server) should be physically and logically secure. Physical access to the computer should be closely controlled. Access to the Exchange Server program and its utilities should be closely controlled and monitored.

• For more information on Exchange Server security, see Day 11 "Security."

4.4.2. Recovering Exchange Server from a Disaster

Disaster recovery requires a complete Exchange Server recovery. In addition to disaster recovery, a complete Exchange Server restore is used to upgrade server hardware.

In a nutshell, the new Exchange Server must be installed on the network with the same name as the old server, and then the Directory Store and the Information Store are restored to the new server. The specific steps for this process vary from network to network; Exercise 1 at the end of this chapter steps through a full server build.

4.5. Planning Information Store Maintenance

Exchange Server data consists of the Private Information Store, the Public Information Store, and the Directory. To ensure efficient and reliable operation of Exchange Server, it is important that this Exchange data is managed and maintained.

The Private Information Store stored in `PRIV.EDB` keeps all data for users configured as recipients on the Exchange Server. The Public Information Store kept in `PUB.EDB` is all public folder information. Public Information Store data can be replicated to other servers; Private Information Store data is kept only on each user's home Exchange Server.

4.5.1. Planning Information Store Status Displays

Exchange Server provides several status information objects for both the Public and Private Information Stores. These configurable objects are an important part of Exchange Server administration. The status for Information Stores can be viewed using Exchange Administrator.

Planning Private Information Store Status Displays

Table 4.6 defines the default status items available for the Private Information Store. This next exercise demonstrates how to access status information for the Private Information Store for an Exchange Server.

1. Start Exchange Administrator.

2. From the Administrator window, select the Logons item from the Private Information Store container for a server as shown in Figure 4.1.

Figure 4.1.

Selecting the Logons item displays all accounts currently logged on to the Private Information Store.

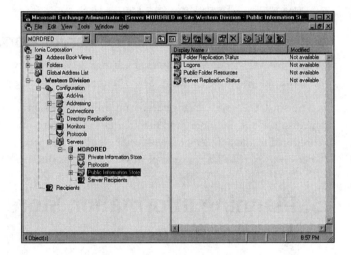

3. Review the status information available for the Logons item: From the Administrator window, select the Columns option from the View menu to display the Columns dialog box (see Figure 4.2).

Figure 4.2.

The Columns dialog box displays status information that may be added or removed from the Administrator window.

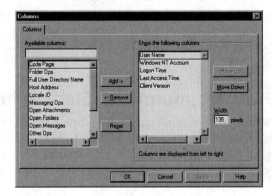

4. Click Cancel to close the Columns dialog box.

5. Select the Mailbox Resources status item from the Private Information Store. Mailbox status details are displayed as shown in Figure 4.3.

Figure 4.3.

The Mailbox Resources status item is accessed from Exchange Administrator and provides information about resource usage for mailboxes.

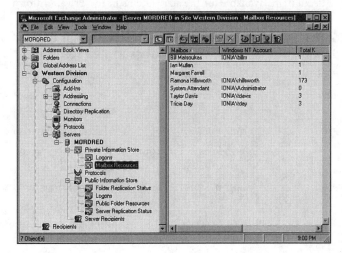

6. From the Administrator window, select the Columns option from the View menu to display the Columns dialog box for Mailbox Resources (see Figure 4.4). Just as is true for the Columns dialog boxes associated with other status objects, the Mailbox Resources Columns dialog box lists all status information fields that can be displayed when the Mailbox Resources object is selected. The fields currently configured to be displayed are shown in the list box on the right; fields that are available but not selected for display are shown in the list box on the left.

Figure 4.4.

The Columns dialog box shows available display information for the selected status object, in this case Mailbox Resources.

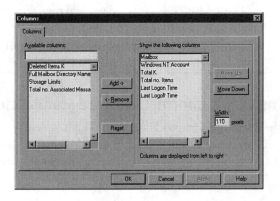

7. Click Cancel to close the Columns dialog box.

As you probably discerned from this exercise, a substantial amount of status information is available for Information Store items. Table 4.6 lists the default status detail items available for the status items in the Private Information Store container.

Table 4.6. The default Private Information Store status detail items are displayed in the Administrator window when the associated status item is selected.

Status Item	Status Detail	Description
Logons	User Name	Network name associated with the recipient object
	Mailbox	Mailbox display name
	Windows NT Account	Windows NT account that last logged on to the mailbox
	Logon Time	Date and time that user last logged on to the mailbox
	Last Access Time	Date and time that user last accessed (read from or wrote to) the mailbox
	Client Version	Version of the Exchange client that last logged on to this mailbox
Mailbox Resources	Mailbox	Mailbox display name
	Windows NT Account	Windows NT account that last logged on to the mailbox
	Total K	Disk space used by the mailbox in the information store
	Total no. Items	Number of messages in the mailbox, exclusive of associated messages
	Last Logon Time	Date and time that the user last logged on to the mailbox
	Last Logoff Time	Date and time that the user last logged off the mailbox

Planning Public Information Store Status Displays

As does the Private Information Store, the Public Information Store contains a great deal of status detail information. This exercise demonstrates how to customize the status display for the Public Folder Resources status item.

1. Start Exchange Administrator

2. Select the Public Folder Resources status item in the Public Information Store. When selected, the Public Folder Resources detail items are displayed in the right pane (see Figure 4.5).

Figure 4.5.

The default configuration of the Public Folder Resources status object provides an "at a glance" display of the most important status details for public folders.

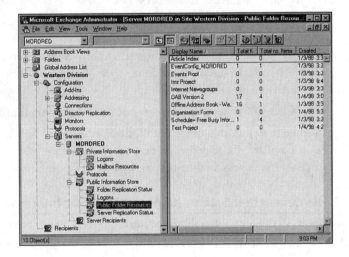

3. Choose Columns from the View menu. The Columns dialog box appears (see Figure 4.6).

Figure 4.6.

The Columns dialog box is used to configure status object displays.

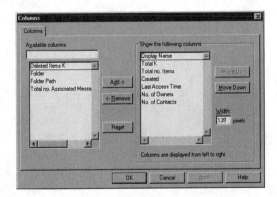

4. You are interested in tracking the amount of disk space used by deleted messages and the number of associated messages stored in the various public folders. Select Deleted Items K from the Available columns list and then click Add.

5. Select Total no. Associated Messages from the Available columns list and then click Add.

6. You are not interested in knowing the last time a public folder was accessed, nor do you care when the public folder was created. Press and hold the Control key, select Created and Last Access Time from the Show the Following Columns list, and then click Remove.

7. You want the total number of items in each folder displayed immediately after the public folder display name. Select Total no. Items from the Show the Following Columns list, and then click Move Up until the selected item is the second item on the list.

8. Click OK to apply the changes and close the Columns dialog box.

In addition to public folder resources, status information for the Public Information Store is available for folder replication, server replication, and logons. Table 4.7 describes the default detail status items for the Public Information Store.

Table 4.7. The default detail status items for the Public Information Store.

Status Item	Detail Status Item	Description
Folder Replication Status	Display name	Display name for the folder
	Last Received Time	Date and time the folder received an update
	Number of Replicas	Number of replicas for this folder within the site, including the local folder
	Replication Status	Set to either In Sync or Local Modified: In Sync means that data in the folder is up to date; Local Modified means that the data has changed on the current server and has not yet been replicated to its replication partners
Logons	User Name	Network name associated with the recipient object
	Mailbox	Mailbox display name
	Windows NT Account	Windows NT account that last logged on to the mailbox

Status Item	Detail Status Item	Description
	Logon Time	Date and time that user last logged on to the mailbox
	Last Access Time	Date and time that user last accessed (read from or wrote to) the mailbox
	Client Version	Version of the Exchange client that last logged on to this mailbox
Public Folder Resources	Display Name	Public folder display name
	Total K	Disk space in kilobytes used by the folder in the Public Information Store
	Total no. Items	Number of items in the public folder, exclusive of associated messages
	Created	Date and time the folder was created
	Last Access Time	Date the folder was last read from or written to
	No. of Owners	Number of users with Owners permission to the folder
	No. of Contacts	Number of users defined as folder contacts
Server Replication Status	Server Name	Name of the Exchange Server
	Replication Status	Set to either In Sync or Local Modified: In Sync means that data in the Public Information Store is up to date; Local Modified means that the data in one or more public folders has changed on the current server and has not yet been replicated to its replication partners
	Last Received Time	Date and time replication updates were received by the local server

4

continues

Table 4.7. continued

Status Item	Detail Status Item	Description
	Average Transmission Time	The average time required to update the selected server from the local server
	Last Transmission Time (sec)	Time in seconds required to update the selected server by the local server

Using the status information for Public Information Stores is important to long-term maintenance of the data. You should review all the status information available and configure the status information items to display the information most relevant to your Exchange installation.

4.6. Planning Public Folder Configuration

In addition to configuring status information displays, several other considerations affect public folder maintenance. These design decisions include the following:

- Designing public folder access using replication, public folder affinity, and server groups
- Configuring replication
- Organizing the public folder
- Planning public folder permissions

4.6.1. Planning Public Folder Access

The whole purpose of public folders is to provide shared access to Exchange messages for groups of users. There are two ways a site can be configured to access remote folders: by replicating folders between sites (in which case the remote public folder becomes a local public folder) or by setting public folder affinity.

By default, users are connected to the public folders located within their site. Usually, public folders that are often accessed by a substantial number of users in an organization are replicated to all sites. In many cases, there are public folders that are accessed primarily within a site and only occasionally by users located in a foreign site. In such cases, public folders can be configured to facilitate access by users located in another site. This is referred to as *public folder affinity*.

This exercise steps through configuring public folder affinity:

1. Start Exchange Administrator.
2. Select the Configuration object in the site container.
3. Double-click Information Store Site Configuration. The Information Store Site Configuration Properties dialog box appears.
4. Select the Public Folder Affinity tab.
5. From the Sites list, select the site for which you want to set affinity and click Add.

When the public folder affinity is set, users belonging to the local site can access public folders on the remote site. Additionally, if public folder affinity is set for more than one remote site, a cost value of 1 to 100 can be set for each site so that remote sites will be accessed in least-cost order when a local user attempts to access a remote public folder.

Setting site costs for public folder affinity allows you to optimize intrasite performance. Intersite public folder access can also be optimized using server location grouping. Each server in a site can be assigned a location value. When a user attempts to access a public folder replication, servers within the group are searched first.

To assign a server to a group, perform the following steps:

1. Start Exchange Administrator.
2. Select a server object in the site container and click the Properties button on the Exchange Administrator's toolbar. The server Properties dialog box appears.
3. On the General page, select the desired group from the Server Location drop-down menu. Alternatively, create a new location by entering a unique location name in the Server Location drop-down menu field.
4. Click OK.

4.6.2. Planning Public Folder Permissions

Exchange users can be assigned permissions to public folders at any level, in much the same way that Windows NT users can be assigned Directory permissions on an NTFS volume. Additionally, the public folder permissions are inherited in the same fashion as NTFS directories. The design decision for public folder permissions should be a determination of how much public folder management is to be done by

Exchange administrators versus the amount of public folder management to be left to the Exchange user community.

Directory permissions and roles are defined in Day 3,"Exchange Server Installation and Configuration." Public folders also have permissions and a set of roles. Table 4.8 defines public folder permission roles. Combinations of permissions other than the built-in roles can also be used.

Table 4.8. Public folder permissions roles are used to control access to public folders.

Role	Create Items	Read Items	Create Sub-folders	Edit Own Any Items	Edit Any Item	Folder Owner	Folder Contact	Folder	Delete Visible Items	Delete Own Item
Owner	Yes	Yes	Yes	Yes	Yes	Yes	Yes	Yes	Yes	Yes
Publishing Editor	Yes	Yes	Yes	Yes	Yes	No	No	Yes	Yes	Yes
Editor	Yes	Yes	No	Yes	Yes	No	No	Yes	Yes	Yes
Publishing Author	Yes	Yes	Yes	Yes	No	No	No	Yes	Yes	No
Author	Yes	Yes	No	Yes	No	No	No	Yes	Yes	No
Nonediting Author	Yes	Yes	No	No	No	No	No	Yes	Yes	No
Reviewer	No	Yes	No	No	No	No	No	Yes	No	No
Contributor	Yes	No	No	No	No	No	No	Yes	No	No
None	No	No	No	No	No	No	No	No	No	No

Because permissions can be assigned at any level in the public folder container, any number of users can be assigned the equivalent of administrative permissions for any combination of public folders. Some Exchange administrators take advantage of this fact and "farm out" public folder administration to one or more users. Other Exchange administrators prefer to manage the entirety of the public folders.

How public folders are organized depends a great deal on how your company organizes data, how the public folders will be administered, and how public folders will be replicated. In most cases, public folders are organized by organizational workgroups such as project teams or departments.

4.6.3. Planning Public Folder Replication

Public folders can be configured to reside on multiple Exchange Servers as replicas. *Replicas* are peer copies of one or more public folders. When the contents of one instance of a replica are changed, the changes are sent to all other replicas. The structure, or hierarchy, of public folders is replicated to all public folder servers in an organization. The data contained in public folders is only replicated to public folder servers where replicas have been configured.

When planning public folder replication, you must determine which public folders to replicate across sites, when to schedule replication, and which public folders should be assigned affinity. These three configuration options should be used to balance the load between Exchange Servers, to minimize network traffic, and to provide the user with good performance.

Public folder replicas can be created by configuring either the Public Information Store object or any public folder object. This exercise describes how to add a public folder replica to the local Exchange Server.

1. Start Exchange Administrator.
2. Open the server object for the server to which you want to add a replica.
3. Select the Public Information Store for that site.
4. From the Exchange Administrator File menu, choose the Properties item. The Public Information Store Properties dialog box appears.
5. Choose the Instances Property page.
6. From the Site drop-down menu, select the site that contains the public folder you want to replicate.
7. From the Public folders list, select the public folder you want to replicate.
8. Click Add to add the public folder to the local server's Folder on the Information Store list.
9. Click OK.

In addition to configuring public folder replication in terms of connections, you should also configure replication scheduling. Replication scheduling can be configured on a per-server basis by using the Public Information Store object properties or by configuring the individual public folder objects.

Scheduling replication using the Public Information Store object effectively sets the default schedule for the local server. By default, the Public Information Store object is set to update associated replicas using the Always option; public folder objects are configured to use the Public Information Store replication schedule. This means that all changes to information in all replicated public folders are replicated every 15 minutes.

4

The default replication schedule is probably adequate for very small organizations with limited amounts of replicated public information. It is a better idea to configure public folders on an individual basis depending on the volume and timeliness of the data being replicated. For example, order information shared with the sales department should probably be replicated more often than changes to the employee handbook shared with all company employees.

The volume of replication data sent between servers is controlled by the Replication Message Size Limit setting on the Advanced properties page for the Public Information Store object. This setting restricts the amount of replication data that can be sent between two Public Information Stores, but does not restrict a single public folder item that exceeds the size limit. This size limit should be set larger than most replicated public folder items in the Public Information Store.

The other replication setting on the Advanced properties page for the Public Information Store object is Replicate Always Interval (Minutes). This setting specifies the amount of time in minutes between replications that is used when a replication schedule is set to Always. This setting can be used to fine-tune the replication schedule if you use Always for any public folder or folders.

4.7. Planning for Directory Replication

The Exchange Server Directory contains information about an organization's structure, resources, and recipients. To achieve a current and manageable Exchange environment, the Directory must be replicated among all servers within an organization in a timely fashion. After completing the following sections, you should be able to do the following:

- Describe the Directory replication update process within sites and across site boundaries
- Understand configuration differences between LAN site replication and WAN site replication
- Configure bridgehead servers and define their role in site replication
- Configure site replication scheduling
- Define inbound and outbound sites and their role in Directory replication

Directory replication planning is an important factor in long-term administration strategies. The Directory should be configured to provide your entire organization with timely information, minimize the load on the enterprise network, and allow for enterprise growth. After completing the following sections, you should have a clear understanding of Directory replication for most enterprise network circumstances so that you can develop strategies that take advantage of Directory services replication options.

4.7.1. Understanding the Directory Update Process

The Directory update process begins within five minutes of a change to the Directory on any server within a site. When Directory information is changed on a server, the server notifies all other Exchange Servers in the site using a Remote Procedure Call (RPC). All servers that received the update notification reply to the calling server with an update request. Update information is sent to all servers that responded to the original RPC notification.

Directory updates between sites works a little differently. Scheduled update requests are sent from one site to another. The called site responds with update information. Note that the timeliness of the update schedule impacts the accuracy of the organization's Directory at any given time.

Directory replication among servers within a site is done automatically. Directory replication between sites within an organization must be configured. Directory replication between sites comes in two flavors: replication between sites connected to the same LAN, and replication between sites connected over a WAN link.

4.7.2. Configuring Directory Replication Between Sites on the Same Network

Setting up replication between sites connected to the same LAN requires that you have administrative permissions for the sites to be connected and that you have a message connection between sites. The message connection is usually a site connector. Once a messaging connection has been established between the sites, you must configure a replication connector for each site.

The following exercise demonstrates creating and configuring a replication connector.

1. Start Exchange Administrator.
2. Select Directory Replication for one of the replicating sites.
3. Select the Directory Replication Connector item from the File | New Other menu. The New Directory Replication Connector dialog box appears.

4. Enter the name of the server at the remote site and then click the Yes, The Remote Site Is Available on This Network button.

5. Because the target replication server is on the same network, you can configure both servers simultaneously. Click Configure Both Sites.

6. Click OK. The Directory Replication Connector Properties dialog box appears.

7. Select a bridgehead server for each site. The bridgehead server is used to process updates between sites. There is a one-to-one relationship between bridgehead servers. One and only one Exchange Server can connect to one and only one Exchange Server at another site to process updates. You can, however, have more than one bridgehead server within a site if each is connected to a different site. Because the replication is between two sites on the same network, the bridgehead servers are automatically configured. To change the bridgehead servers, you can enter the server names in the Local Bridgehead Server and the Remote Bridgehead Server fields.

When establishing a connection between two bridgehead servers, be sure that their clocks are synchronized to ensure that scheduled updates execute in a timely manner.

8. Configure the Directory replication schedule. Select the Schedule properties page from the Directory Replication Connector Properties dialog box and then set the replication times.

It is important to match replication schedules with the volatility of the Directory and the efficiency of the physical connection between the bridgehead servers. When connecting sites over a WAN connection, this becomes very important in terms of network traffic.

9. Review the sites associated with this replication connector. Select the Sites properties page (see Figure 4.7).

Figure 4.7.

The Sites property page for a replication connector displays a list of connected sites.

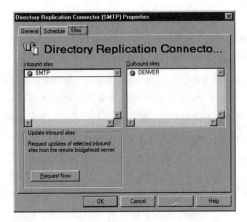

10. The sites listed as inbound sites for this Directory replication connector are sites that directly or indirectly provide Directory information to the local site. The sites listed as outbound sites are sites to which the local bridgehead server sends updates.

> The Sites properties page for Directory replication connectors can be used to force updates from a remote site to the local bridgehead server. Simply select the remote site from which you want update information and then click Request Now.

11. Click OK to save the configuration.

Configuring Directory replication between sites on the same network is the simplest replication process to configure—primarily because you can configure both bridgehead servers from a single Exchange Administrator session. The important points in this replication are that the two bridgehead servers are configured simultaneously, bridgehead servers have a one-to-one relationship, and there are several scheduling options.

4.7.3. Configuring Directory Replication Connectors Between Sites on Different Networks

Creating and configuring a Directory replication connector for sites that are not on the same network requires that you have a message connection between the two sites and that you have administrative rights to the remote site. The message connection between two sites is a connector used for remote sites, usually an X.400 or Internet Mail connector. Because the sites are not connected to the same LAN, the Directory replication connectors cannot be configured simultaneously.

The next exercise steps through creating and configuring a Directory replication connector for two remotely connected sites. It is assumed that the connector that facilitates messaging between the sites is in place and working correctly.

1. Start Exchange Administrator.

2. Select the Directory Replication object and then choose Directory Replication Connector from the File|New Other menu. The New Directory Replication Connector dialog box appears.

3. Enter the name of the target remote server in the Server in Remote Site field, Click the No, The Remote Site Is Not Available on This Network button, and then click OK. The Directory Replication Connector Properties dialog box appears (see Figure 4.8).

Figure 4.8.

A Directory replication connector must be configured on both the source and the target Exchange Servers.

4. Select a bridgehead server for each site. Enter the server names in the Local Bridgehead Server and the Remote Bridgehead Server fields.

5. Review and optionally modify access to this connector by selecting the Permissions properties page.

6. Configure the Directory replication schedule. Select the Schedule properties page from the Directory Replication Connector Properties dialog box and set the replication times.

It is important to match replication schedules with the volatility of the Directory and the efficiency of the physical connection between the bridgehead servers. When connecting sites over a WAN connection, this becomes very important in terms of network traffic.

7. Click OK to save the configuration.

The configuration procedure described in this exercise must be repeated on the remote site before the replication configuration is complete and the sites can exchange Directory updates.

4.8. Understanding the Exchange Scripting Agent

One of the most useful administrative tools added to Exchange Server 5.5 is the Exchange Scripting Agent. Simply put, the Exchange Scripting Agent allows script-based applications such as VBScript, JScript, and other supported scripting languages to be associated with public and private folders. These scripts are triggered by events such as sending, creating, or deleting a message.

Exchange Server scripting can be used to create complete applications (called *Collaborative Data Objects*, or CDOs) that can automatically process messages. For example, a mailbox can have a CDO associated with it that is triggered when a message is received. The CDO script can examine the message and process the information stored in the message based on its content. The message can be associated with a form that is sent to the target mailbox in a predetermined format.

It is important to understand that Exchange Server can be used to build full-scale collaborative applications using the Exchange Script engine and that Exchange scripting can be used to perform small administrative jobs.

4

Lab

This section consists of review questions that pertain to this chapter and provides an opportunity to apply the knowledge you acquired in the course of this chapter.

Questions

1. One of the Exchange Servers at your site fails because of a corrupted Information Store database file. Which two of the following files is probably corrupted?

   A. PUBLIC.EDB

   B. PRIV.MDB

   C. PUB.EDB

   D. PRIV.EDB

2. Why does Exchange Server use transaction log files to facilitate updates to its databases?

   A. Transaction log processing is faster than directly writing to a database because writes to a transaction log file are faster.

   B. Transaction log processing offers a high degree of data recoverability.

   C. Transaction log processing is the accepted standard for updating flat database files.

   D. Exchange Server does not use transaction log processing.

3. You are performing a cursory scan of the database directories on one of three Exchange Servers at your site. You notice that the transaction log file in the Private Information Store folder is larger than the file in the Directory database folder. Is this a problem?

   A. No, transaction log files often vary in size, depending on the size of the database with which they are associated.

   B. Yes, the transaction log file associated with the Directory database is always larger than the information store transaction log files. The Directory database log file is probably corrupted.

C. Yes, valid transaction log files on Exchange Server are always exactly the same size. One or more of the log files is corrupt.

D. Yes, one transaction log file is used for all Exchange Server database files; there should be only one transaction log file in the information store folder.

4. You are configuring your Exchange Server for a seven-day online backup cycle using a full backup on Sunday night and incremental backups for the rest of the week. How would you configure Exchange Server's circular logging feature?

A. Incremental backups require that circular logging be enabled so that old log files are saved to tape.

B. Incremental and full backups require that circular logging be disabled to facilitate recovery using backed-up transaction log files.

C. The backups described here will work regardless of the circular logging configuration.

D. Circular logging should be scheduled as enabled for the Sunday night full backup and disabled for the incremental backups performed for the remainder of the week.

5. You have configured Windows Backup to perform a full file-level backup of your Exchange Server every night. This backup procedure includes shutting down Exchange Server's services so that all database files are closed before the backup begins. How does this backup scheme affect your transaction log files if circular logging is disabled?

A. The full file-level backup will save only the transaction log files and then delete them.

B. All files on the server including transaction log files are backed up and the archive flag for all files is set.

C. A full file-level backup cannot be performed if circular logging has been disabled.

D. All files on the server including transaction log files are backed up and the archive flag for all files is cleared.

6. How might you check disk space used by public folders for a given server?

   A. Look at the Public Folder Resources status for the Public Information Store associated with the server.

   B. Use Windows Explorer to look at the General properties page for the folder \exchsrvr\pub on the server.

   C. Use the Windows NT Disk Administrator to view file allocation for the file PUB.EDB.

   D. Check the Server Replication Status object.

7. Your network consists of two physical sites connected by a WAN connection. You have three Exchange Servers at each physical site. Your Exchange organization is configured as a single site. All public folders are configured to replicate to two Exchange Servers at each physical site. What configuration option should you use to ensure that users accessing public folders not replicated on their home server are accessing public folders across the WAN link only as a last resort?

   A. Set the public folder affinity for all Exchange Servers that hold replica public folders.

   B. Disable the public folder affinity for all Exchange Servers that hold replica public folders.

   C. Assign servers at each site to a server group.

   D. Remove all servers at each site from server groups.

8. The network you administer is three LANs: LAN1, LAN2, and LAN3 (see Figure 4.9). Each LAN site is also an Exchange site. LAN1 is connected to LAN2 with a full T1 (1.44M). LAN1 is connected to LAN3 by a 256K data line. You are configuring public folder affinity for folders that reside on both LAN2 and LAN3. If the same public folder exists in LAN2 and LAN3, how would you configure public folder affinity to use the faster WAN link when a user in LAN1 attempts to open the folder?

Figure 4.9.

LAN2 and LAN3 are indirectly connected, but have a common public folder that can be accessed by users on LAN1.

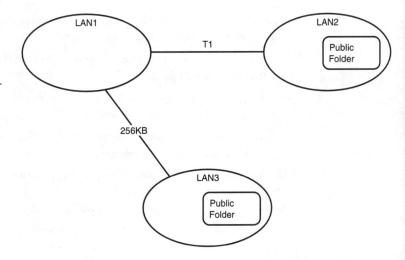

A. Set the public folder affinity cost for LAN2 higher than the cost for LAN3.

B. Set the public folder affinity cost for LAN1 higher than the cost for both LAN2 and LAN3.

C. Set the public folder affinity cost for LAN2 lower that the cost for LAN3.

D. None of the above: Public folder affinity is used between servers within a single Exchange site.

9. You have a single-site Exchange organization that has three Exchange Servers. The physical network is a single LAN. Assuming that recipients are evenly distributed among the three servers, how should you configure Directory replication?

A. You should configure replication to all servers within the site.

B. There is no replication configuration for the Directory within a site.

C. You should not configure any replication because all servers are on the same LAN and there is no access or performance problem.

D. You should leave the Directory on one server and set affinity for the other servers.

4

10. Why is a site connector required before Directory replication can be set up between two sites within an organization?

   A. Because Exchange requires a messaging connection between the two sites to transmit updates.

   B. A site connector is not required. The site replication connector provides the communication channel between the two sites.

   C. Because the site replication connector will replicate to all servers at the remote site without the messaging connection, causing traffic problems.

   D. A site connector is needed to assign a bridgehead server.

11. In terms of configuration, what is the difference between a replication connector between sites connected by a WAN link and sites that reside on the same network?

   A. There is no difference.

   B. The replication connector between two different networks requires bridgehead servers.

   C. Sites on a single network require only one replication connector; sites connected by a WAN link require a replication connector at each site.

   D. When configuring the replication connectors for two sites on the same network, they can be configured simultaneously.

Exercise: Performing a Full Server Recovery

This exercise addresses the following Microsoft exam objective:

■ Develop long-term administration strategies

A full server recovery is performed when you replace an Exchange Server. Typically, this is either an upgrade or a disaster recovery task. This exercise steps you through a full server recovery.

A lot of work is involved in this seemingly short exercise. That is because the exercise steps must be generalized. This exercise focuses on bringing up Exchange Server, but keep in mind that most Windows NT Servers are used for other work in addition to messaging services.

After completing this exercise, you should be able to do the following:

■ Have a clear understanding of the full server restore process.

■ Identify the minimum configuration requirements for a full server restore.

4

Understanding and, more importantly, planning for a full server recovery is an important part of a long-term administration strategy for Exchange. The Microsoft exam will likely query you about some part of this process, probably as a situational question. It is important to understand the full server restore process and when it is used.

1. To replace an existing Exchange Server with a full server recovery, the new server must have the same name as the old Exchange Server and must be added to the same Windows NT domain. Therefore, you must remove the old server from the network before restoring to the new one.

2. Use Server Manager to delete the old Exchange Server's account from the domain, and then add the account for the new Exchange Server. You must use the same server name for the new server.

3. Install Windows NT Server on the target computer, along with any service packs that were part of the old server's configuration. This new server must have the same name as the old server and must belong to the same domain.

4. Install Exchange Server and any service packs that were installed on the old server. Use the same installation options as the old server but *do not* join the existing site: create a new site instead (the new site name is unimportant).

5. If the old server has a Microsoft Mail Connector configured, install and configure one on the new server.

6. Restore the Directory and the Information Store, confirm the integrity of the Information Store using ISINTEG.EXE, and then restart the Exchange Server.

Answers to Questions

1. **C, D**   PUB.EDB and PRIV.EDB are the database files that comprise Exchange Server's Information Store.

2. **A, B**   Transaction log processing affords better performance than writing directly to a database file for a number of reasons including the fact that writes to a sequential transaction file are faster than writes to a random access database; transaction log files can be run against a database to bring the database up to date ("up to date" being any single transaction point in the log file); Exchange Server does not use flat database files; Exchange Server does use transaction log processing.

3. **C**   Transaction log files are always exactly 5 megabytes (5,242,880 bytes) in size. If two Exchange Server transaction log files are different sizes, at least one of the files is corrupt.

4. **B**   By definition, both full and incremental backups back up and then delete old log files during an online backup, so circular logging must be disabled at all times.

5. **D**   A file-level backup performs no special operation on transaction log files; therefore, the circular logging setting has no effect on file-level backups. Full file-level backups clear the archive flag after backing up the file.

6. **A**   Public Folder Resources is a status object that provides detailed information about the public folders, including disk space used by each folder.

7. **C**   Servers belonging to an Exchange Server group are searched first when a member client attempts to connect to a public folder.

8. **C**   The word *affinity* means exactly that: the tendency for a user to connect to a given public folder. The affinity cost is exactly that: a cost. Given a choice, the user is more likely to attach to the lower-cost public folder instance.

9. **B**   Directory replication occurs automatically between servers belonging to the same site. There is no configuration.

10. **A**   The site connector is the communication link between sites; the replication connector is the high-level replication data manager.

11. **D**   Because of the speed of the LAN, it is practical to configure replication connectors for sites on a single network.

Explanation for the Exercise

If you actually attempted a full server restore as described in this exercise rather than reading through the steps, you learned firsthand that there is a lot of planning and work behind those six simple steps. In terms of the real world, it is important that you have a tested process in place for performing a full server restore at your company. It terms of the MSCE exam, it is important to know the general process described in the exercise and to know the minimum requirements for a full server restore.

4

TEST DAY
FAST FACTS

Here are a few fast facts about this chapter you may want to know ahead of time. These facts provide great last-minute study material.

- The Exchange Server Monitor is used to determine whether an Exchange or NT service has failed. If the Server Monitor detects a failure, it can send a notification and even attempt to restart the service.

- The Link Monitor is used to monitor whether or not any connections between Exchange Servers, Exchange sites, or foreign mail systems are up and running. If not, Link Monitor can send a notification.

- The Message Tracker can be used to trace messages as they flow through an Exchange site.

- The Performance Optimizer is used to optimize an Exchange Server's performance—after Exchange is first installed, anytime server hardware changes, or whenever any major Exchange software configuration changes are made.

- NT Server's Control Panel | Services dialog box is used to pause, stop, or start Exchange services.

- NT Server's Event Viewer is used to view Exchange error messages and other feedback.

Day 5

Server Management Tools

by Brad M. McGehee

This chapter covers a variety of miscellaneous Exchange Server management tools. It also covers a variety of NT Server tools that can be used to help manage Exchange. Compared to some of the other objectives on the certification exam, the ones in this chapter are not emphasized as much. You should find this chapter easy to read and learn, and the objectives easy to master.

Here is a list of the topics included in Day 5:

Microsoft Exchange Server Tools

- Server Monitor
- Link Monitor
- Message Tracker
- Performance Optimizer

Microsoft Windows NT Server Maintenance Tools

- Control Panel | Services
- Event Viewer
- Registry Editor
- Task Manager
- Server Manager

■ Performance Monitor

■ Exchange Server SNMP Support

Objectives

This chapter addresses the following Microsoft exam objectives:

■ Configure a Link Monitor and a Server Monitor

■ Optimize Exchange Server

■ Monitor and optimize the messaging environment

■ Monitor server performance by using SNMP and MADMAN MIB

5.1. Microsoft Exchange Server Tools

Included with Exchange are a variety of tools you can use to monitor or help optimize its performance. Each of the following tools fulfills a specific need of the Exchange Administrator:

- **Server Monitor:** Used to track whether any service has failed on an Exchange Server.

- **Link Monitor:** Used to track whether any connections between other Exchange Servers, Exchange sites, or foreign mail systems have failed.

- **Message Tracker:** Used to track how messages have moved through an Exchange site.

- **Performance Optimizer:** Used to optimize Exchange's performance after any physical hardware has changed or if any major software configuration changes have been made on an Exchange Server. The Performance Optimizer is also used immediately after installing Exchange for the first time.

The following sections describe each tool's major features and give brief instructions for using them.

When studying this chapter, focus your efforts on learning what each tool does and when you should use it. This is more important than learning the mechanics of how to configure each.

5.1.1. Server Monitor

Whether you manage a single Exchange Server or dozens, one of the most difficult tasks is to track whether or not every Exchange service on every Exchange Server is up and running. Although you can wait until you get a call from an unhappy email user to discover that some service has failed, wouldn't it be better if Exchange could tell you whether a service on any of the Exchange Servers has failed before getting a phone call?

The solution to this problem is to use Exchange's Server Monitor. Although Server Monitor cannot predict the failure of a service, it can notify you that one has failed shortly after it has failed, allowing you to take immediate action to correct the problem.

The Server Monitor performs these tasks:

- Monitors both local and remote Exchange Servers.
- Monitors any service you designate on an Exchange Server, including non-Exchange services.
- Allows one or more people to be notified if a service fails.
- Allows you to configure a service to be automatically restarted should it fail, without any intervention by you. You can also configure a server to automatically reboot.
- Allows you to automatically synchronize the time of all Exchange Servers within a site. This is important because Exchange uses the time in many of its operations.
- Allows you to configure how often each service on each server is checked to see whether it is running.
- If desired, you can create multiple Server Monitors that run simultaneously on the same Exchange management workstation.

Configuring and using a Server Monitor is a two-step process. First, you must create and configure a Server Monitor. Second, you must start it. You run Server Monitors from the Exchange Administrator program, which means that the Exchange Administrator program must be continuously running if you want the Server Monitor to run continuously. The Exchange Administrator program can be running on either an NT Workstation-based computer or any server running NT Server and Exchange Server.

One of the test objectives is to configure a Server Monitor. The following tutorial steps you through the process of creating, configuring, and starting a Server Monitor to track Exchange services on a single Exchange Server. This tutorial assumes that Exchange has been properly loaded and configured and is currently up and running. Although creating a Server Monitor has many options, only the required options are described in this tutorial.

1. Load the Exchange Administrator program and expand the Configuration container in the site where you want to add a Server Monitor. Locate the Monitors container and click it. If you have never created a Server or Link Monitor before, the container will be empty (see Figure 5.1).

5

Figure 5.1.

Server Monitors are created using the Exchange Administrator program.

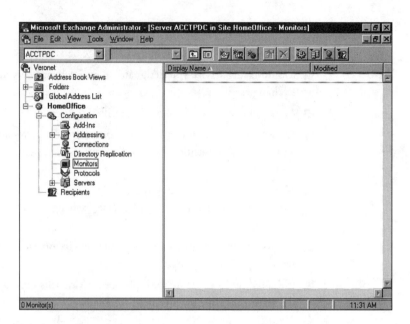

2. To create a new Server Monitor, choose File|New Other|Server Monitor from the menu bar. This action displays the Properties dialog box (see Figure 5.2).

Figure 5.2.

A Server Monitor is created by filling out various options in the Properties dialog box.

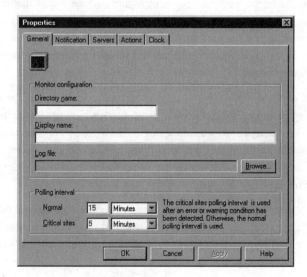

3. The Properties dialog box includes five pages. Each page has a variety of Server Monitor options. To begin, you must enter both a Directory Name and a Display Name for this Server Monitor. The Directory Name is the name (up to 64 characters) used to uniquely identify this particular Server Monitor. The Display Name is the name (up to 256 characters) used to refer to this Server Monitor in the Administrator window.

4. Click the Notification page (see Figure 5.3). One this page, you specify who will be notified—and how they will be notified—should the Server Monitor detect a failed service.

Figure 5.3.

Use the Notification page to tell Exchange who should be notified should a service fail.

5. To tell Exchange who should be notified, click the New button. This action displays the New Notification dialog box (see Figure 5.4).

6. The New Notification dialog box allows you to choose how an administrator can be notified. You can select the Launch a Process option, which runs a program or .bat file. Use the Mail Message option if you want to send an email message through Exchange. Use the Windows NT Alert option to send an NT broadcast message over the network. For this example, select the Mail Message option and click OK. This action displays the Escalation Editor dialog box (see Figure 5.5).

Figure 5.4.

There are three different ways to notify administrators about service failure.

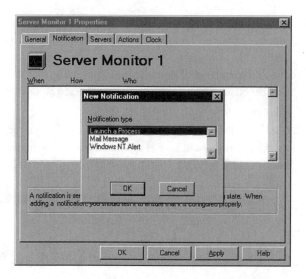

Figure 5.5.

The administrator to be notified is selected from this dialog box.

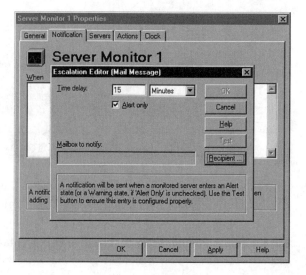

7. From the Escalation Editor dialog box, click the Recipient button. This action displays the Recipient dialog box (see Figure 5.6). From the Recipient dialog box, click the name of the recipient who is to receive the notification, then click OK. The Escalation Editor dialog box reappears. After adding a recipient, click OK to return to the Server Monitor dialog box.

Figure 5.6.

Select the recipient to be notified from this dialog box.

8. Click the Servers page of the Properties dialog box. This page is used to specify the Exchange Servers you want to monitor as well as which services on each server you want to monitor. In the left pane is a list of all the Exchange Servers in the current Exchange site (see Figure 5.7).

Figure 5.7.

Select the Exchange Servers you want to monitor from this screen.

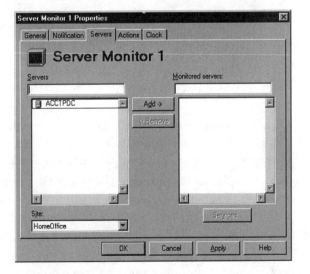

9. Click one of the Exchange Servers in the left pane and then click the Add button. This action moves the selected server from the left pane to the right pane. Servers in the right pane are the ones whose services are to be monitored.

10. Now tell Exchange which services on the selected Exchange Server are to be monitored. To do this, click the Services button. This action displays the Services screen (see Figure 5.8). The top pane shows all the services on the Exchange Server; the bottom pane lists the services to be monitored. Use the Add and Remove buttons to change which services are monitored. For this exercise, leave the services as they are and click OK. This action returns you to the Servers page of the Properties dialog box.

Figure 5.8.

Choose which services you want to monitor from this page.

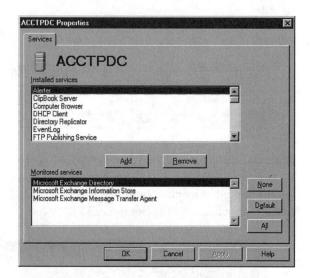

11. Click the Actions page (see Figure 5.9). From this page, you can choose what Exchange should automatically do if a service you specified in the previous step should fail. For this exercise, leave this screen as-is.

12. Click the Clock page (see Figure 5.10). You can use this page to configure how the Service Monitor can be used to automatically synchronize the time of all the Exchange Servers in a site. For this exercise, leave this screen as-is.

13. To save this Service Monitor, click OK. This action saves the Server Monitor and returns you to the Administrator window, where the newly created Server Monitor is displayed in the Monitor container.

14. Now start the Service Monitor. To start it, click the newly created Server Monitor and then choose Tools|Start Monitor from the menu bar. Once the service is started, the Server Monitor screen is displayed (see Figure 5.11). You can minimize this screen if you want so that the Administrator window can again be viewed.

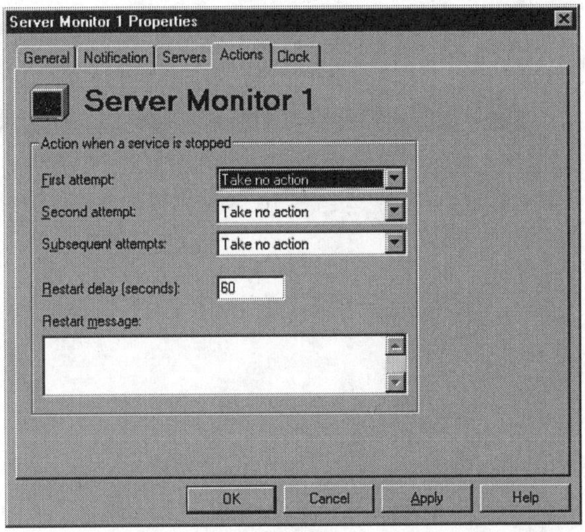

Figure 5.9.

Server Monitors are created using the Exchange Administrator program.

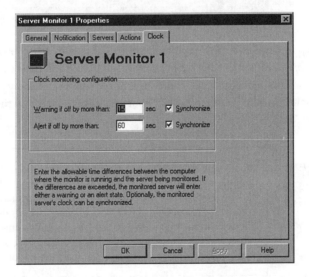

Figure 5.10.

You can automatically synchronize the time between Exchange Servers from this page.

This tutorial showed you how to create a Server Monitor for a single Exchange Server, along with how to start it. You now know how to create a Server Monitor and should be able to answer any questions related to this topic on the certification test.

Figure 5.11.

Server Monitors are monitored from this screen.

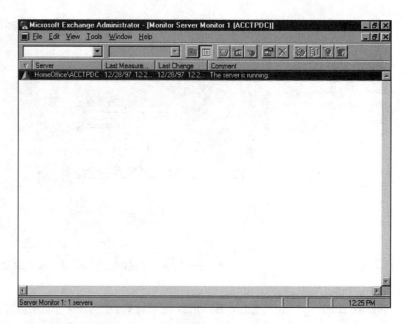

Keep in mind that the Server Monitor is used only to monitor services on Exchange Servers. It cannot predict when a service will fail. It can only tell you that a service *did* fail and perhaps try to restart the service. You should always use the Service Monitor to help you keep tabs on your Exchange Servers and to minimize potential downtime.

Warning

Should you ever have to configure the Polling Interval (located on the General tab) when creating a Server Monitor, don't set it too low. If you do, you may receive notification of service failures every time you have to reboot an Exchange Server. This happens because some Exchange services can take up to five minutes to start. Also, the more often polling occurs, the more work the server has to do, creating an even larger load on the server, which can negatively impact the performance of the server.

5.1.2. Link Monitor

The Link Monitor is similar to the Server Monitor. Instead of verifying that services are working, however, the Link Monitor's goal is to regularly test all the message transports between servers to see whether they are still operating. If they are not, Link Monitor can notify you, allowing you to correct the problem before mail service is interrupted for too long.

The Link Monitor works by sending regular messages between servers to see whether the connection between them is functioning. This task is performed by the Message Transfer Agent (MTA), with a little help from the Information Store (IS). Depending on how the Link Monitor is configured, a successful reply or a non-delivery report (NDR) is used to confirm that the connection is working. When testing a link between Exchange Servers or sites, a successful reply indicates a working link. When testing a link between an Exchange Server and a foreign mail system, an NDR indicates a working link.

The Link Monitor performs these tasks:

- Monitors both local and remote Exchange Servers
- Monitors any connectors or gateways between Exchange sites or between an Exchange Server and a foreign mail system
- Measures the round-trip time of mail messages for communications links
- Allows one or more people to be notified if a communications link fails
- Allows you to configure how often each communications link is checked to see whether it is functional
- Allows you to create multiple Link Monitors that run simultaneously on the same Exchange management workstation

Setting up and configuring a Link Monitor is very similar to setting up a Server Monitor. First, you must create and configure a Link Monitor. Second, you must start it. Link Monitors run from the Exchange Administrator program, which means that the Exchange Administrator program must be continuously running if you want the Link Monitor to run continuously.

Another test objective is to be able to configure a Link Monitor. The following exercise steps you through the basics of creating, configuring, and starting a simple Link Monitor on a single Exchange Server. Because many of the screens for creating and configuring a Link Monitor are similar to those used to create a Server Monitor, this exercise does not repeat any of the screens seen in the preceding section, "Server Monitor." For this exercise, it is assumed that Exchange has been loaded and configured correctly.

1. Load the Exchange Administrator program and expand the Configuration container in the site where you want to add a Link Monitor. Locate the Monitors container and click it. If you have never created a Server or Link Monitor before, the container will be empty. If you performed the preceding exercise, the Monitors container will contain the Server Monitor you created.

5

2. To create a new LinkMonitor, choose File|New Other|Link Monitor from the menu bar. This action displays the Properties dialog box (see Figure 5.12), which is very similar to the Properties dialog box used to create a Server Monitor.

Figure 5.12.

Create a Link Monitor by filling out various options in the Properties dialog box.

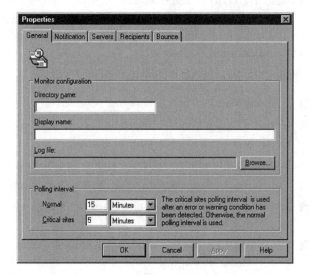

3. The Properties dialog box includes five pages. Each page has a variety of Link Monitor options. To begin, you must enter both a Directory Name and Display Name for this Link Monitor. The Directory Name is a name (up to 64 characters) used to uniquely identify this particular Link Monitor. The Display Name is the name (up to 256 characters) used to refer to this Link Monitor in the Administrator window.

4. Click the Notification page. You use this page to specify who will be notified—and how they will be notified—should the Link Monitor detect a failed mail provider. This screen is virtually identical to the Notification page used when you create a Server Monitor.

5. To tell Exchange who should be notified, click the New button. This action displays the New Notification dialog box.

6. Use the New Notification dialog box to specify how an administrator can be notified. You can select the Launch a Process option if you want to run a program or .bat file. Use the Mail Message option if you want to send an email message through Exchange. Use the Windows NT Alert option to send an NT

broadcast message over the network. For this exercise, select the Mail Message option and click OK. This action displays the Escalation Editor dialog box.

7. From the Escalation Editor dialog box, click the Recipient button. This action displays the Recipient dialog box. From this dialog box, first click the name of the recipient who is to receive the notification and then click OK. You return to the Escalation Editor dialog box. After you add a recipient, click OK to return to the Link Monitor dialog box.

8. Click the Servers page. This page is used to specify the Exchange Servers you want to monitor. The Servers page for the Link Monitor is the same as for the Server Monitor: In the left pane is a list of all the Exchange Servers in the current Exchange site.

9. Click one of the Exchange Servers in the left pane and then click the Add button. This action moves the selected server from the left pane to the right pane. Any Exchange Server listed in the right pane is monitored by this Link Monitor.

10. Click the Recipients page (see Figure 5.13). Use this page only if you want to test a link to a foreign mail system. For this exercise, leave this screen as-is.

Figure 5.13.

The Recipients page is only used to test links to foreign mail systems.

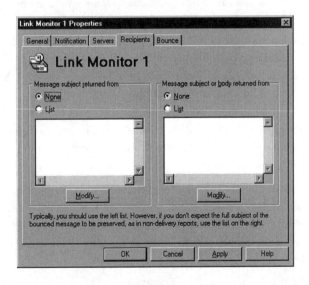

11. Click the Bounce page (see Figure 5.14). This page is used to configure the amount of time that is acceptable for bounced messages (NDRs) sent to foreign mail systems. If a bounced message is not received within the specified time, Link Monitor assumes the link to the foreign mail system is down. For this exercise, leave this screen as-is.

Figure 5.14.

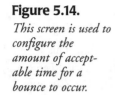

This screen is used to configure the amount of acceptable time for a bounce to occur.

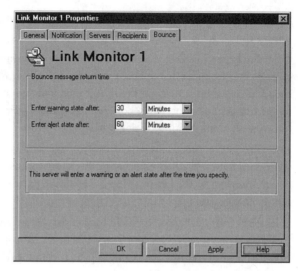

12. To save this Link Monitor, click OK. This action saves the Link Monitor and returns you to the Administrator window, where the newly created Link Monitor is displayed in the Monitors container.

13. Now start the Link Monitor. To start it, click the Link Monitor you created and then choose Tools|Start Monitor from the menu bar. Once the service is started, the Link Monitor screen is displayed. The Link Monitor screen is similar to the screen used to monitor Server Monitors.

In this exercise, you learned the basics of creating and configuring a Link Monitor. You now have enough knowledge to answer questions on the certification exam regarding this subject.

Keep in mind that the Link Monitor is used only to *monitor* communications links in your Exchange organization. It cannot predict link failures, it can only tell you when a failure has occurred. You must determine what is causing the problem and how to correct it. You should always use the Link Monitor to help you keep tabs on all the communications links in your Exchange organization.

5.1.3. Message Tracker

As an Exchange administrator, you will no doubt hear one or more complaints about email messages being lost. In most cases, the problem is user related. For example, a departmental supervisor claims that a memo sent to him by a team member never got to him. Most likely, the team member lied about sending the message and wants to blame the email system for the missing message. Occasionally, however, Exchange can be the culprit.

By default, Exchange does not track the many messages that flow through a site. If it did, it would put an undue processing load on the server and use up valuable hard disk space. But if your site warrants the monitoring, you can turn on message tracking for short periods, allowing the administrator to track the exact flow of every message passing through a site.

Enabling message tracking, and then tracking it with the Message Tracker, allows an administrator to do the following:

- Find slow or stuck messages.
- Trace the path and find the final location of any message.
- Identify the various delays a message may experience as it flows through an Exchange site.
- Audit messages as they flow through an Exchange site, allowing the administrator to identify (and remove if desired) unauthorized messages.

Although enabling message tracking traces the path of a message, Message Tracker cannot be used to read mail messages. In addition, messages cannot be tracked unless message tracking has been turned on. In other words, you cannot go back to trace a problem if message tracking was not turned on. You can only track messages that have been logged by Exchange.

Tracking a message involves two steps: First, message tracking must be turned on. Second, once message tracking has been turned on, you can trace a message using the Message Tracker.

Turning On Message Tracking

Message tracking is enabled at the site level. This means that once message tracking is turned on for a site, all Exchange Servers within that site begin logging mail messages. Each server tracks the messages that flow through it, recording the data in a local log file.

Unfortunately, there is no one single switch used to turn on message tracking for an entire Exchange site. Message tracking must be turned on at several different places if you want to completely track a message's flow. Following are the areas where message tracking can be turned on:

- **Public and Private Information Stores:** Turning on message tracking here allows you to track both private email messages and messages posted to public folders. To turn message tracking on for both the Information Stores, select the Enable Message Tracking option from the Information Store Site Configurations Properties dialog box.

- **MTA:** Turning on message tracking here allows you to track any messages sent between MTAs on the various Exchange Servers in your site. To turn message tracking on for the MTA, select the Enable Message Tracking option from the MTA Site Configuration Properties dialog box.

- **Connectors:** Most Exchange connectors allow you to track any messages that flow through them. You only have to turn on message tracking for those connectors relevant to the task at hand. To turn on message tracking for a particular connector, select the Enable Message Tracking option from the General Properties page for the relevant connector.

Once you turn message tracking for any of the preceding options, you must stop and then restart the relevant services for message tracking to begin. Alternatively, you can reboot the Exchange Server.

When turning on message tracking, don't forget to turn it on for every component (Information Store, MTA, connector) you want to monitor. If you forget to turn message tracking on at one of these locations, you may not get all the data you need to completely track a message as it moves through your Exchange site. Once you are done tracking messages, don't forget to turn message tracking off everywhere you turned it on; otherwise, you will use valuable server resources that can be better used elsewhere by Exchange.

By default, message tracking logs are kept for only seven days. If you want to change this default value, you can do so from the System Attendant Properties dialog box, located in your Exchange Server's container (see Figure 5.15).

Tracking a Message Using the Message Tracker

Once message tracking has been enabled and log files have begin begun to fill up, you are ready to search the logs to track messages. This is accomplished by using the Track Message command, found on the Tools menu in the Exchange Administrator program. This menu option brings up the Message Tracker (see Figure 5.16).

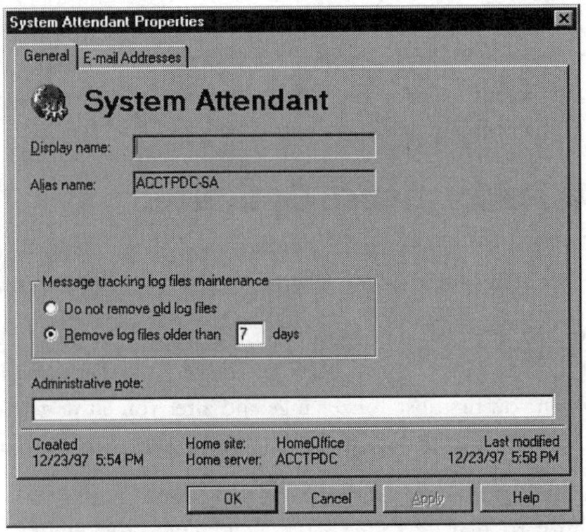

Figure 5.15.

You can configure how long message logs are kept by Exchange from the System Attendant Properties dialog box.

Figure 5.16.

The Message Tracker is used to trace mail messages through a site.

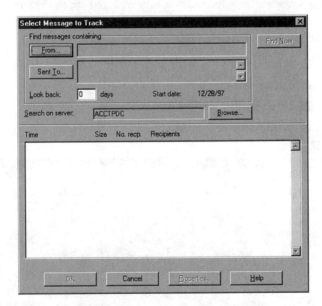

The Message Tracker allows you to search for messages sent from a particular person, sent to a particular person, or both. You can also select how many days back to look for messages. If any messages are found, they are displayed at the bottom of the screen. Once you identify the message or messages you are looking for, you can have the Message Tracker trace its flow through the site.

Keep in mind that the main purpose of the Message Tracker is to identify problems with message flow through your Exchange site. It cannot be used to correct problems or locate messages if message tracking has not been turned on. It is up to you to identify the problem and correct it.

5.1.4. Performance Optimizer

The Performance Optimizer is a wizard used to automatically analyze and optimize key server hardware to help Exchange run at its peak performance.

Unlike the three Exchange tools described in the first part of this chapter (Server Monitor, Link Monitor, and Message Tracker), the Performance Optimizer is used only when you first install Exchange and after you either change the hardware in the Exchange Server or make a major Exchange configuration change.

When the Performance Optimizer wizard begins, it asks you several questions about how this particular Exchange Server will be used (see Figure 5.17). Using this information as well as information it gathers directly from the server hardware, Performance Optimizer makes specific recommendations about where to store the following Exchange data files:

■ Information Store database files (both public and private)

■ Transaction log files

■ Directory database files

■ Message transfer queues

Figure 5.17.

The Performance Optimizer is used to help tune and optimize Exchange.

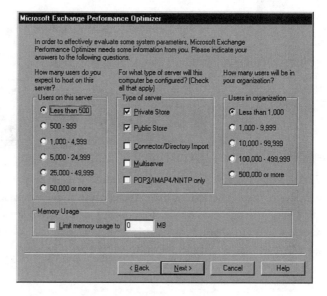

If you agree to its recommendations, the wizard automatically moves the preceding files to the physical locations it has recommended.

Here is how the Performance Optimizer works. First, it analyzes the server's logical drives. It identifies the logical drive with the fastest sequential access and recommends that the transaction log files be stored there. Next, it identifies the logical drive with the fastest random access and recommends that the files that will be used most by this server be located there. For example, if the server is a dedicated Public Information Store server, Performance Optimizer will recommend that you store these files here. If the server is a dedicated backbone server used to move messages to other sites, Performance Optimizer will recommend that the MTA queues be located here. The Performance Optimizer also determines the amount of RAM that is in the server and uses this information to determine the amount of memory to be used by the directory and information stores.

Note that only logical, not physical drives, are analyzed. If your Exchange Server has multiple logical drives on a single physical drive, or if you are using a RAID array, the Performance Optimizer's recommendations for locating files may be meaningless. In this case, you must use your own personal knowledge of the server's performance to determine the ideal locations in which to store these data files.

Exactly when should you run the Performance Optimizer? Although there is no cut-and-dried answer, here are the most common recommendations:

- Always run the Performance Optimizer after you first load Exchange onto any server.
- Whenever an Exchange Server's hardware is upgraded (or downgraded).
- Whenever you add or remove a connector.
- Whenever you change the major role of the Exchange Server. For example, if you dedicate an Exchange Server to the Public or Private Information Store, run the Performance Optimizer.

When preparing for the certification exam, be sure that you thoroughly understand what the Performance Optimizer does and when it should be used.

Performance Optimizer is not part of the Exchange Administrator program. It is a separate program run from the Exchange program group from the Start menu. When the Performance Optimizer runs, it stops all the Exchange services, which means that people cannot send email. Be sure that you run this tool only during times when people are not using the system.

Keep in mind that the Performance Optimizer's capability to increase overall Exchange performance is limited. It is just one tool of many that you can use to optimize performance. Another powerful tool to help optimize Exchange performance is the NT Performance Monitor, discussed later in this chapter.

5.2. Microsoft Windows NT Server Maintenance Tools

One of the best benefits of selecting Exchange for an enterprise mail system is that it is well integrated with NT Server. This means that many of the administrative tools included with NT Server can also be used to help manage Exchange. The next sections take a look at how the following NT Server tools can be used to help administer Exchange:

- Control Panel|Services
- Event Viewer
- Registry Editor
- Task Manager
- Server Manager
- Performance Monitor

Most of these nextsections is dedicated to using the Performance Monitor to help optimize Exchange because Performance Monitor is the tool emphasized over the others on the certification exam.

Note

If you are an experienced NT Server administrator, you can skip this section if you want.

5.2.1. Control Panel|Services

Exchange is made up of many services that run in the background on NT Server. Should any of these services fail to start when NT Server is booted, or should any of the services fail after initial startup, one or more functions of Exchange will fail.

Although you can use the Server Monitor (described earlier in this chapter) to let you know whether a particular service on a particular Exchange Server has failed, Server Monitor may not be able to restart the service. In that case, you need another way to work with the failed service—enter the Control Panel|Services dialog box.

The Services dialog box, which is displayed by double-clicking the Services icon in the Control Panel, allows you to view every NT service, including all Exchange services (see Figure 5.18). The Services dialog box not only allows you to readily see whether or not a service is running, it also allows you to pause, stop, or start any service. If necessary, you can also change a service's login account and password from this screen.

Figure 5.18.

Exchange services can be paused, stopped, or started from the Services dialog box.

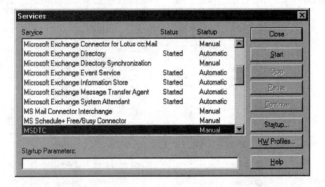

If an Exchange service stops for no apparent reason, try stopping and then restarting the service. This troubleshooting tip often corrects many problems with Exchange.

5

If you are not familiar with the Control Panel|Services, take the time to learn about it so that you can take full advantage of its many features.

5.2.2. Event Viewer

The NT Server Event Viewer (shown in Figure 5.19) not only displays events produced by NT Server, it also displays many Exchange events, helping you to troubleshoot many Exchange-related problems. The Event Viewer is divided into three sections: System, Security, and Application events. Each separate log can be used to track what is happening with Exchange. Although the System log is normally used to track NT-specific events, some of the events that show up in this log directly affect Exchange. For example, if any Exchange services fail to start when NT Server boots, these events are logged in the System log. The Security log can be used if you want to track authorized or unauthorized access to Exchange objects and files. To capture these events, you must turn on Security Auditing using NT Server's User Manager for Domains and Explorer. Of the three logs, the Application log is where most of Exchange's messages will be logged.

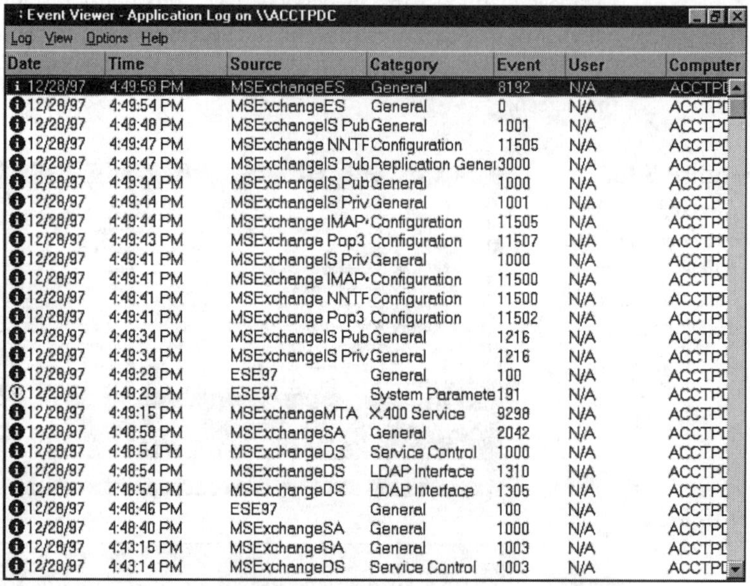

Event Viewer - Application Log on \\ACCTPDC

Log View Options Help

Date	Time	Source	Category	Event	User	Computer
12/28/97	4:49:58 PM	MSExchangeES	General	8192	N/A	ACCTPI
12/28/97	4:49:54 PM	MSExchangeES	General	0	N/A	ACCTPI
12/28/97	4:49:48 PM	MSExchangeIS Pub	General	1001	N/A	ACCTPI
12/28/97	4:49:47 PM	MSExchange NNTF	Configuration	11505	N/A	ACCTPI
12/28/97	4:49:47 PM	MSExchangeIS Pub	Replication Gene	3000	N/A	ACCTPI
12/28/97	4:49:44 PM	MSExchangeIS Pub	General	1000	N/A	ACCTPI
12/28/97	4:49:44 PM	MSExchangeIS Priv	General	1001	N/A	ACCTPI
12/28/97	4:49:44 PM	MSExchange IMAP	Configuration	11505	N/A	ACCTPI
12/28/97	4:49:43 PM	MSExchange Pop3	Configuration	11507	N/A	ACCTPI
12/28/97	4:49:41 PM	MSExchangeIS Priv	General	1000	N/A	ACCTPI
12/28/97	4:49:41 PM	MSExchange IMAP	Configuration	11500	N/A	ACCTPI
12/28/97	4:49:41 PM	MSExchange NNTF	Configuration	11500	N/A	ACCTPI
12/28/97	4:49:41 PM	MSExchange Pop3	Configuration	11502	N/A	ACCTPI
12/28/97	4:49:34 PM	MSExchangeIS Pub	General	1216	N/A	ACCTPI
12/28/97	4:49:34 PM	MSExchangeIS Priv	General	1216	N/A	ACCTPI
12/28/97	4:49:29 PM	ESE97	General	100	N/A	ACCTPI
12/28/97	4:49:29 PM	ESE97	System Paramete	191	N/A	ACCTPI
12/28/97	4:49:15 PM	MSExchangeMTA	X.400 Service	9298	N/A	ACCTPI
12/28/97	4:48:58 PM	MSExchangeSA	General	2042	N/A	ACCTPI
12/28/97	4:48:54 PM	MSExchangeDS	Service Control	1000	N/A	ACCTPI
12/28/97	4:48:54 PM	MSExchangeDS	LDAP Interface	1310	N/A	ACCTPI
12/28/97	4:48:54 PM	MSExchangeDS	LDAP Interface	1305	N/A	ACCTPI
12/28/97	4:48:46 PM	ESE97	General	100	N/A	ACCTPI
12/28/97	4:48:40 PM	MSExchangeSA	General	1000	N/A	ACCTPI
12/28/97	4:43:15 PM	MSExchangeSA	General	1003	N/A	ACCTPI
12/28/97	4:43:14 PM	MSExchangeDS	Service Control	1003	N/A	ACCTPI

Figure 5.19.

The NT Event Viewer is a powerful tool used to diagnose potential Exchange problems.

Both the System and Application logs include the following events:

- **Information events.** Information events (blue in color) describe significant events that have occurred. These are normal events and do not indicate a problem.
- **Caution events.** Caution events (yellow in color) describe a potential problem, but an actual failure has probably not occurred in Exchange's functionality.
- **Warning events.** Warning events (red in color) describe actual problems that may very well describe a failure in Exchange functionality.

Although some of the events described in the Event Viewer are self-evident, many are not. To find out what a particular event message means, you may have to search for a description of the message in the Exchange Books Online or in Microsoft's TechNet.

Some administrators tend to ignore the Event Viewer because it sometimes gives false warnings or because the messages are hard to understand. Don't fall into this trap. Whenever you suspect that you have a problem with Exchange, your first thought should be to check out the event logs to see whether they provide a clue about what the problem is.

5.2.3. Registry Editor

Digging into NT Server's Registry is never fun—and is even dangerous if you don't know what you are doing. Unfortunately, you sometimes have to make changes to the Registry, although Exchange rarely requires you to do this.

When Exchange is loaded onto an NT Server, new Registry keys are added that are used to store Exchange configuration information. If required, you can use NT Server's Registry Editor (regedt32.exe) to view Exchange's Registry settings and make any required changes.

As you probably are aware, you should never make a change in the Registry unless you know exactly what you are doing.

5.2.4. Task Manager

Although it is not common, NT services can malfunction, and you may not be able to stop them from the Control Panel\Services dialog box. Although you can always reboot NT to resolve this problem, rebooting can cause even more problems because you have to take the Exchange Server out of production temporarily. So how do you stop a service that won't respond to actions taken from the Control Panel\Services dialog box? The answer is to use NT Server's Task Manager.

The Task Manager allows you to view the status of, and to stop, any NT process. You can also use the Task Manager to stop any unresponding user programs, such as the Exchange Administrator program or an Exchange or Outlook client.

In addition to being able to view and stop application programs and NT services, you can use the Task Manager (select the Performance page) to provide a snapshot of the server's memory and CPU performance. If Exchange seems to be acting a little slow, a quick check of the Performance page may tell you quickly whether or not you really have a performance problem. If it appears that you do, you can use the Performance Monitor (described later in this chapter) to narrow down the search for the problem.

5

5.2.5. Server Manager

NT Server's Server Manager program is often overlooked by Exchange administrators because they don't know what it can do for them. Specifically, Server manager allows the Exchange administrator to monitor and modify services and network shares of remote Exchange Servers.

If you are like many Exchange administrators, you have probably loaded the Exchange Administrator program onto an NT Workstation at your desk so that you can control Exchange Servers locked in a server room far from your office. If this is the case, you can stay at your desk and use the Server Manager to view all the services on any remote Exchange Server to determine whether they are running. And if need be, you can pause, stop, or restart any service remotely using the Server Manager. If you think that one of Exchange's default shares has been modified accidentally by someone, you can remotely view all shares and, if needed, make changes to them, including making any changes to the share's permissions.

Warning

> Using an NT Workstation to remotely manage an Exchange Server does not work successfully unless the NT Server's tools have been loaded onto the same NT Workstation.

5.2.6. Performance Monitor

One of the most powerful, but underused, tools included with NT Server is the Performance Monitor. Performance Monitor allows you to monitor hundreds of server measurements, letting you know exactly how the server is performing. You can use this information to help identify performance problems, allowing you to optimize a server's performance.

The Performance Monitor can measure hundreds of different server measurements. These measurements are called *counters* in Performance Monitor lingo. To make it easier to keep track of all these counters, Performance Monitor groups them into similar categories of counters called *objects*. Each object has one or more related counters. For example, one of the most used Performance Monitor objects is the Processor object. This object consists of many separate counters that measure specific server events, such as how busy the CPU is. Other objects have counters that measure disk usage, memory usage, and even network performance (see Figure 5.20).

Figure 5.20.

NT Server's Performance Monitor can be use to track the performance of NT Server and Exchange.

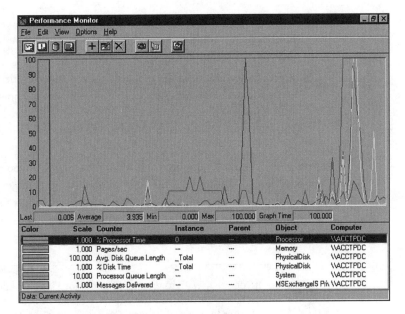

By default, when NT Server is loaded onto a server, the only objects the Performance Monitor can work with are objects specific to NT Server. But when Exchange is loaded onto an NT Server, additional objects are added to the Performance Monitor, allowing you to monitor many specific Exchange events in addition to the NT Server events. You can use the information provided by the Performance Monitor to optimize not only NT Server's performance, but Exchange's performance as well.

The study of the Performance Monitor can take days if you want to master all its nuances. The next several sections focus on only a small part of how you can use Performance Monitor to optimize your Exchange Servers. If you have never used the Performance Monitor, and you find this tool interesting, you will want to dedicate some of your time to learning more about this powerful tool.

The Four Performance Monitor Functions

The Performance Monitor provides the following four distinct functions:

- **Graph Mode.** Both real-time and historical data can be displayed as a line chart or histogram. This mode is best for identifying trends over a period of time.

- **Report Mode.** Both real-time and historical data can be viewed in a tabular report format. This mode is best for viewing summary information.

- **Logging Mode.** This mode allows you to collect data over a period of time (24 hours, one week, one month). This mode allows you to collect and then analyze long-term trends.

- **Alert Mode.** This powerful mode allows you to be notified when a particular event you define occurs. For example, if you want to know when disk space on your Exchange Server is more than 90 percent full, Alert Mode can let you know about this potential problem before it becomes a real problem.

In most cases, you will take advantage of all these modes as you monitor your Exchange Servers. Ideally, you will want to monitor key counters on each Exchange Server over time so that you can identify trends that can affect future performance. You will also want to track current Exchange Server activity to resolve current performance problems.

If you really want to do a good job of tracking and optimizing your Exchange Servers, you can export the data you collect with Performance Monitor to a spreadsheet or database for more extensive analysis.

When monitoring the performance of an Exchange Server, you will want to monitor both NT Server and Exchange counters. Both sets of counters are important because the performance of NT Server greatly affects Exchange's performance. Although there are over 350 NT Server counters and over 260 Exchange counters, in most cases, you have to track only a few key counters. The following sections describe some of the key counters you will want to track.

Counters Used to Monitor Exchange Server Hardware Performance

Exchange Server hardware monitoring can be divided into five major categories: processor, memory, disk, network, and other. Each of these hardware issues can significantly affect Exchange Server performance. Following is a list of the most common counters to monitor for each of the five hardware areas, along with a brief explanation of how to interpret them. The counters are listed in the format of object: counter.

Processor

- **Processor: % Processor Time.** Measures how busy the CPU is. Generally, if this counter exceeds 75 percent on a sustained basis, the server is experiencing a processor bottleneck.

■ **System: Processor Queue Length.** Measures how many CPU operations are queued up and waiting to be processed by the CPU. If this counter exceeds 2 on a sustained basis, the server is experiencing a processor bottleneck.

If your system is sustaining a processor bottleneck, the only options are to get a faster CPU, add additional CPUs, or reduce the processing load on the server by removing one or more services and moving them to less busy servers.

Memory

■ **Memory: Pages/sec.** Measures the number of memory pages (2K) requested by the CPU that were not immediately available in RAM and had to be read from the pagefile (pagefile.sys). Generally, if this counter exceeds 5 pages per second on a sustained basis, the server is experiencing a memory bottleneck.

■ **Memory: Available Bytes.** Measures the amount of RAM currently not being used by the server. Generally, this counter should not fall below 4M on a sustained basis. If it does, the server is probably experiencing a memory bottleneck.

■ **Memory: Committed Bytes.** Measures the amount of virtual memory allocated to both RAM and the pagefile. Generally, this number should be smaller than the total amount of physical RAM that exists in the server on a sustained basis. If it does not, the server is probably experiencing a memory bottleneck.

If your system is experiencing a memory bottleneck, the best solution is to add more RAM to the server. Of all the possible steps you can take to speed up Exchange's performance, adding more RAM is the most effective.

Disk

■ **Physical Disk: % Disk Time.** Measures the amount of time a physical disk is busy performing read or write operations. Generally, this number should be less than 50 percent on a sustained basis. If not, the server's disk subsystem is probably causing a bottleneck.

■ **Physical Disk: Disk Queue Length.** Measures the number of disk operations that are queued up and waiting to be executed by a physical disk. Generally, if this counter exceeds 2 on a sustained basis, the server's disk subsystem is experiencing a bottleneck.

5

If your system is experiencing a disk subsystem bottleneck, some of your options are to get more controllers (to increase bandwidth), get faster controllers, add more disks (for striping), or get faster hard drives.

> Before using disk counters, make sure that you have run the `diskperf -y` command at the command prompt and have rebooted your server. These actions turn on NT Server's capability to monitor disk objects. If you don't perform these steps, the disk counters will not work.

Network

■ **Network Segment: % Network Utilization.** Measures the percent use of the network segment where your server is connected. If you are running on an Ethernet network, this figure should generally not exceed 40 percent on a sustained basis.

■ **Network Interface: Bytes Total/sec.** Measures how many bytes of data your server is putting on and receiving from the network. There is no absolute best measurement for this counter. Instead, watch it over time, because it is a good indicator of how busy your server is when compared to other Exchange Servers.

If the network segment where your Exchange Server is located is overused, consider adding additional network cards to the server, further segmenting the network, or giving the Exchange Server its own dedicated segment by dedicating one or more switch ports to it.

Before you can use the two network counters, you must have loaded the Network Monitor Agent, which can be added as a service from the Control Panel|Network dialog box.

Other

■ **Paging File: %Usage Peak.** Measures the maximum percentage use of the NT pagefile. Generally, you do not want this value to exceed 80 percent. If it does, expand the maximum size of the pagefile.

■ **LogicalDisk: %Free Space.** Measures how full a disk drive is. Generally, you do not want percent free space to be smaller than 10 to 20 percent. If it is, consider adding more hard disk space to the Exchange Server.

Both of these counters can be monitored using the Logging Mode or the Alert Mode. The advantage of the Alert Mode is that you are automatically notified if a problem arises before it becomes a real problem.

Counters Used to Monitor Exchange Server Software Performance

Although the counters described in the preceding sections are used to measure server hardware performance, the following counters are specific to Exchange. These counters are automatically added to the Performance Monitor when Exchange is installed. Here is a list of some of the counters you will want to watch:

■ **MSExchangeMTA: Messages/sec.** Measures the number of messages per second the MTA receives. This counter gives an indication of how much routing work Exchange must perform to deliver messages.

■ **MSExchangeMTA: Message bytes/sec.** Measures the total number of bytes per second the MTA receives. This counter gives you an idea of how much data Exchange has to route over a given period of time.

■ **MSExchangeISPublic: Rate of Open Message Operations.** Measures the number of messages being opened in the Public Information Store. This counter gives you an idea of how busy the Public Information Store is over time.

■ **MSExchangeDS: Reads/sec.** Measures the amount of traffic generated by Directory Synchronization. This counter gives you an idea of how busy the Directory Synchronization service is.

These are just a few of the Exchange-specific counters available. You will want to investigate the others when you have time. None of these counters has any "correct" answers. It is best to watch them over time so that you can get a good feel for how busy your servers are.

Using Performance Monitor to monitor and optimize Exchange Server is more of an art than a science. It takes lots of practice before you can be an expert at interpreting Performance Monitor results and then determining the appropriate action to take in order to optimize performance.

When trying to optimize Exchange's overall performance running on NT Server, be sure that you have made the following NT Server settings:

continues

- Set the Server Properties found on the Control Panel|Network Services page to Maximize Throughput for Network Applications.

- Set the Application Performance option to None on the Control Panel|System Performance page.

- Set the `pagefile.sys` file to a minimum number at least equal to the amount of RAM in the Exchange Server plus 125. For example, if you have 128M of RAM, the minimum size of the `pagefile.sys` should be at least 253M.

Each of these settings helps ensure that Exchange runs at its optimum performance.

5.3. Configuring Exchange Server to Monitor Server Performance Using SNMP and the MADMAN MIB

Many larger enterprises use SNMP Management workstations (such as HP OpenView) to monitor remote hardware and software that have SNMP Management Agents loaded onto them. For example, an SNMP Management workstation might be used to monitor the well-being of all the NT Servers found on a network.

SNMP stands for the Simple Network Management Protocol. This protocol is part of the TCP/IP protocol suite and is used to transfer information from remote hardware and software to an SNMP Management workstation.

For an SNMP Management workstation to communicate with remote hardware and software, the remote hardware and software must be running a special program called an *SNMP Agent*. This software allows an SNMP Management workstation to query the hardware or software about its current status. An SNMP Agent includes both program code and something called a Management Information Base (MIB). A MIB is a standardized way to describe the types of information that an SNMP Management workstation can request from the SNMP Agent.

Unfortunately, Microsoft does not offer SNMP Management software; you must purchase it from a third party if you want to use it. But Microsoft has included an SNMP Agent and MIB that allow virtually any third-party SNMP Management workstation to access performance information from an Exchange Server. The SNMP Agent software is a part of NT Server and must be loaded from NT Server, as described later in this section. The required MIB is called the MADMAN MIB (Mail and Directory Management), and it comes with Exchange Server. The MADMAN MIB allows all Exchange Server Performance Monitor counters to be accessed from an SNMP Management workstation, similar to the way these same counters can be monitored using NT Server's Performance Monitor tool.

Before an SNMP Management workstation can access performance data from Exchange Server, both NT Server's SNMP Agent and Exchange's MADMAN MIB must be configured. Once they are configured, almost any SNMP Management workstation can be used to remotely monitor Exchange Server's performance.

To take advantage of the capability of an SNMP Management workstation to remotely monitor Exchange Server performance, you must first perform the following steps:

1. Make sure that the TCP/IP transport protocol is in use on both the Exchange Servers to be monitored and the SNMP Management workstation.

2. Install the NT Server SNMP service on all the Exchange services to be monitored. If you have not reinstalled the NT Server Service Pack 3 since loading the SNMP service, reload it.

3. To install the MADMAN MIB so that it works with NT Server's SNMP service, you must properly configure it as described in steps 4 and 5. Step 4 assumes that no other MIBs have been installed on the Exchange Server.

4. On the CD-ROM that comes with Exchange, locate the Support\Snmp\platform folder. This folder contains a batch file named INSTALL.BAT. With the Exchange CD-ROM in the CD-ROM drive of the Exchange Server, run the batch file. This action installs the MADMAN MIB file (actually called EXCHANGE.MIB) so that it can be used by NT Server's SNMP service to fulfill requests from an SNMP Management workstation.

5. Stop and then restart the SNMP service on the Exchange Server. Now the MADMAN MIB file is available to SNMP Management workstations.

If you are a beginner with TCP/IP or SNMP, this topic can be hard to follow. But don't worry about it when preparing for the certification exam; all you have to know for the exam is how SNMP and the MADMAN MIB are used to remotely monitor an Exchange Server's performance. You don't have to know how to install or configure this feature.

5

Lab

This lab consists of review questions pertaining to this chapter and provides an opportunity to apply the knowledge you've gained in this chapter.

Questions

1. You are designing an Exchange Site that will have three Exchange Servers. One will be dedicated to public folders, one will be dedicated to mail messages, and the last one will be dedicated for use by the Internet Mail Connector. Which one of the following tools will help you monitor all the Exchange services on each server to ensure that they are up and running as much as possible? Your goal is to remotely manage all the Exchange Servers from your desk.

    A. Link Monitor

    B. Server Monitor

    C. Control Panel|Services dialog box

    D. Performance Monitor

2. You have created a Service Monitor to monitor the Exchange services running on a single Exchange Server. After a couple of days, you look at the Control Panel|Services dialog box and notice that the MTA service has stopped—but you did not receive a notification from the Service Monitor as you had expected. What is the most likely reason you did not receive a notice?

    A. The Control Panel|Services dialog box is incorrect and the MTA service is actually working.

    B. The Service Monitor can be easily fooled and cannot be considered a reliable way to monitor services.

    C. The MTA service automatically turns on and off as needed by Exchange.

    D. Although you correctly configured the Server Monitor, you later exited the Exchange Administrator program and have not restarted it since then.

3. You have recently been made the Exchange administrator of a multisite Exchange organization. The first day on the job, you hear about how unreliable the Exchange system is and how unhappy the users are about not being able to get their messages from one site to another. To try to diagnose this

problem (and perhaps eliminate it), which one of the following steps can you first take?

   A. Set up multiple Server Monitors.

   B. Set up multiple Link Monitors.

   C. Take a baseline measurement of Exchange Server traffic using the Performance Monitor.

   D. Run the Performance Optimizer on each of the Exchange Servers.

4. You are the administrator of a large multisite Exchange organization. The manager from the marketing department gives you a call. She says that she sent an important message to a distribution list that included recipients from several of your Exchange sites. She claims that only 6 of the 8 people on the list received the message. What three steps would you take to help diagnose this potential problem?

   A. Set up a Link Monitor between the Exchange sites in question.

   B. Set up a Server Monitor for every Exchange Server in every site in question.

   C. Start message tracking for every site in question.

   D. Use the Message Tracker to trace the path of messages sent to the distribution list in question.

   E. Use the Performance Monitor to look for potential bottlenecks in each of the Exchange Servers in question in case they are too busy to process all the messages going their way.

5. You have just installed Exchange onto a new server in an existing Exchange site. Then you run the Performance Optimizer. After it is done running, you notice that it does not make any different recommendations about where to locate the various Exchange files than it did before you ran it. Which two of the following may be the cause of this?

   A. Your server may have too much RAM.

   B. Your server may have too much available hard disk space.

   C. Your server may have a RAID array installed.

   D. Your server may have a single physical disk installed.

5

6. You are an assistant Exchange administrator and your boss has told you to run the Performance Optimizer on all the Exchange Servers because she is worried that they are all slowing down. How would you respond to this request?

   A. You would immediately carry out the request because the Performance Optimizer is the best tool available to diagnose and correct performance problems on an Exchange Server.

   B. You would, very nicely, suggest that the Performance Monitor tool is a better choice than the Performance Optimizer tool.

   C. You would, very nicely, suggest that the Server and Link Monitors would be a better choice than the Performance Optimizer tool.

   D. You would, very nicely, suggest that the Performance Optimizer is appropriate to use only when Exchange is first installed, not after it is installed and has been up and running. You would then suggest another, more appropriate tool.

7. After rebooting your Exchange Server, you get a message onscreen telling you that one or more services did not start. What is the fastest way to diagnose the possible cause of this error message?

   A. Go to the NT Server's Event Viewer and take a look at the system log.

   B. Use NT Server's Diagnostic program to run a diagnostic check.

   C. Use the Control Panel|Services to diagnose the problem.

   D. Use the Registry Editor to view the SQL Server keys in the Registry to diagnose the problem.

8. You are using the Exchange Administrator program to manage an Exchange Server. The Administrator program is running on the Exchange Server you are managing. Suddenly, the Administrator program stops responding. Even after several minutes of waiting, the program is unresponsive. What do you do next?

   A. Reboot the server.

   B. Stop and then restart the System Attendant service.

   C. Edit the SQL Server key in the Registry.

   D. Kill the Exchange Administrator process using the Task Manager.

9. Using the Performance Monitor, you have monitored one particular Exchange Server over a typical 24-hour day. You have noticed over the past month that it

has been running more slowly than usual. You export the data to Microsoft Excel and calculate the average of the following counters:

% Processor Time = 67%

Processor Queue Length = .65

Pages/sec = 38

% Disk Time = 61%

Message Bytes/sec = 18,998

Given this information, what is the most likely cause of the slowdown?

   A. Disk subsystem is too slow.

   B. CPU is overused.

   C. RAM is too low.

   D. Network card is too slow.

10. Over the past quarter, you have used the Logging Mode of the Performance Monitor to track the performance of an Exchange Server. It is your only Exchange Server in your Exchange organization, and it has room to add more RAM and disk space. Here is the average of several key counters you measure:

Counter	1 Qtr.	2 Qtr.	3 Qtr.
% Processor Time	22%	24%	27%
Processor Queue Length	.45	.47	.48
Pages/sec	3.6	3.9	3.9
% Disk Time	18%	25%	31%
% Disk Space Used	14%	28%	46%

Given this data, do you foresee the need to add a second Exchange Server in the upcoming quarter?

   A. Yes. Given the growth in most of the counters over time, it would be a good idea to purchase a second Exchange Server during the upcoming quarter.

   B. Yes. It appears that the increase in disk space may be a result of an increasing pagefile. This means that the server is too busy to handle the current load and should be distributed between two Exchange Servers.

5

C. No. The indicators clearly indicate no problem at all.

D. No. But you may want to watch these figures closely, and if things change, you may want to add more RAM and hard disks to the current server. The current CPU is more than adequate to meet the demand for the upcoming quarter as indicated by the counters.

11. Your company's Senior Network Designer gives you a call. He is thinking about purchasing an SNMP Management workstation to help manage the ever-growing network. He wants to know whether Exchange can be monitored using SNMP, and if so, do you think it is worth the effort? What do you tell him?

   A. You tell him that Exchange does not support SNMP.

   B. You tell him that Exchange does support SNMP, but only those SNMP Management workstations that run on NT; UNIX-based Management workstations are incompatible.

   C. You tell him that Exchange does support SNMP and that it would be a great way to remotely manage Exchange.

   D. You tell him that Exchange does support SNMP, but that you think Exchange comes with plenty of built-in tools and that an SNMP Management workstation will not help you in your job. But if he wants to install one, you will configure Exchange to work with it.

12. You have been asked by your boss to configure an Exchange Server to be remotely monitored by a recently installed SNMP Management workstation. What are two key steps you must take to make this work?

   A. You must turn on the Performance Monitor counters in NT Server.

   B. You must configure NT Server's SNMP service.

   C. You must install the MADMAN MIB on the Exchange Server.

   D. You must install the MADMAN MIB on the SNMP Management workstation.

Exercises

Exercise 1: Turning on Message Tracking

Note | This exercise addresses the following certification exam objective:
■ Configure message tracking

This exercise shows you how to turn on message tracking for the Information Store and MTA.

1. Load the Exchange Administrator program and open a site's container. Then click the Configuration container so that it is highlighted.

2. To turn on message tracking for the Information Store, click the Information Store Site Configuration leaf object so that it is highlighted.

3. Select the File|Properties option from the menu bar; the Information Store Site Configuration Properties dialog box appears.

4. Select the Enable Message Tracking checkbox and then click OK to return to the Administrator window.

5. To turn on message tracking for the MTA, click the MTA Site Configuration leaf object so that it is highlighted.

6. Select the File|Properties option from the drop-down menu; the MTA Site Configuration Properties dialog box appears.

7. Select the Enable Message Tracking checkbox and then click OK to return to the Administrator window.

8. Either stop and restart the appropriate services or reboot the Exchange Server. At this point, message tracking is turned on for the Information Store and MTA.

Exercise 2: Running the Performance Optimizer

Note | This exercise addresses the following certification exam objective:
■ Optimize Exchange Server

5

This exercise shows you how to load and run the Performance Optimizer. The tasks include both hardware and operating system optimization.

1. Load the Microsoft Exchange Performance Optimizer by selecting it from the Microsoft Exchange program group in the Start menu. This action starts the wizard.

2. The first screen is mostly informational. It reminds you that all the Exchange services must be stopped before you can continue. Be sure that you run the Performance Optimizer only when you can take the Exchange Server offline. Click the Next button to stop all the Exchange services and move to the next screen.

3. The next screen asks some questions about how this particular Exchange Server will be used. Answer the questions appropriately and click the Next button.

4. When the next screen appears, Performance Optimizer begins analyzing your hardware. Depending on your Exchange Server's hardware features, this test can take a long time. Once the tests are complete, a new screen appears, telling you that Performance Optimizer is done. Click the Next button to continue.

5. The next screen shows you the recommendations Performance Optimizer makes for the physical locations of various Exchange files. If you don't like one or more recommendations, you can change the file locations by directly altering the recommendations on the screen. Once you have made any changes, click the Next button.

6. The next screen reminds you to back up all data before you continue. To automatically move the files, click the Next button.

7. The wizard automatically moves all the files. When the wizard is done moving the files, it displays a new screen telling you that it has completed all its work and asking whether you want it to automatically restart all the Exchange services. If you are done and want all the services to be restarted, click the Finish button. The services are now started, and the Performance Optimizer automatically unloads.

Exercise 3: Using the Performance Monitor

Note

This exercise addresses the following certification exam objective:

■ Monitor and optimize the messaging environment

This exercise shows you how to use the Performance Monitor to track key NT Server and Exchangecounters in real-time using the Performance Monitor's Graph mode.

1. Load the NT Performance Monitor by selecting it from the Administrative Tools program group from the Start menu. This action loads the Performance Monitor program. By default, the Performance Monitor is in the real-time Graph mode when it is first loaded.

2. To load key NT Server and Exchange counters, begin by clicking the plus (+) sign in the tool bar. This action displays the Add to Chart dialog box.

3. To load a counter, first choose the counter's object from the Object drop-down box. Then choose the counter from the Counter list box. And last, click the Add button. These actions add the counter to the graph. Using this procedure, add the following counters:

Object Name	Counter Name
Processor	% Processor Time
Memory	Pages/sec
MSExchangeMTA	Messages/sec

If you want, add some additional counters to your graph.

4. Once you have added various counters, click the Done button. This action removes the Add to Chart dialog box and displays the real-time Graph mode. Immediately, you will see each of the counters you added create a line chart, displaying the measurements of each counter in real time.

5. When you are done, exit Performance Monitor by selecting File|Exit from the menu bar.

Answers to Questions

1. **B** The Service Monitor is used to remotely monitor services running on Exchange Servers.

2. **D** For the Service Monitor to run, the Exchange Monitor program must be running.

3. **B** The Link Monitor is one of the best tools you can use to troubleshoot site-to-site connectivity problems.

4. **A, C, D** Set up the Link Monitor to track potential link problems between

the problem sites. Turn on message tracking to begin keeping a log of the messages that cross each site. Then send a test message to the distribution list and track the message to see what is happening to it. Other options, not listed in the available answers, are also possible.

5. **C, D**   The Performance Optimizer can analyze only logical disk partitions, and it can recommend moving data files only if there is more than one logical drive available.

6. **B**   The Performance Monitor is the best tool to use to track Exchange Server optimization problems.

7. **A**   Although there are several different approaches to identifying why an Exchange Service may have failed, the first place you should look is in the Event Viewer. Generally, any failed service is identified in the System log along with the possible cause.

8. **D**   Your first choice is to try to kill the process, which may have become unresponsive. The easiest way to stop any process is to use NT Server's Task Manager.

9. **C**   The pages/sec counter is very high (over the recommended 5). This means that the server is having to use the pagefile instead of RAM to store data. This problem also causes unnecessary CPU and hard disk use. The server needs more RAM.

10. **D**   Don't you hate question like this? Get used to them, because many of the questions on the certification exam are judgment calls. Based on the data available, and assuming that there are no major changes, the current server should be adequate for at least the next quarter. But because assuming is not always a good thing, you must continuously monitor these counters, and if necessary, bump up the power of the current server. There is no clear need for a new machine within the next quarter.

11. **D**   Again, another subjective answer. SNMP Management workstations can only gather data, they cannot be used to actively manage an Exchange Server. Essentially, they duplicate the tools that Exchange already has, such as the Performance Monitor.

12. **B, C**   Two major steps are involved in preparing an Exchange Server to be remotely monitored by an SNMP Management workstation. First, NT Server's SNMP Service must be loaded and configured on the Exchange Server. Second, the MADMAN MIB must also be installed on the Exchange Server.

TEST DAY FAST FACTS

Here are a few fast facts about this chapter you may want to know ahead of time. These facts provide great last-minute study material.

- Exchange client applications are MAPI (Messaging Application Programming Interface) compliant.

- Windows messaging provides the MAPI for the Windows platform.

- Windows messaging profiles define the connectivity for a client to a messaging service such as Exchange Server.

- Exchange Server can be configured for access by Internet browsers.

- Exchange Server supports SMTP/POP3 mail clients.

- The various Exchange clients available (such as Exchange Client, Schedule+, and Outlook) differ in the Exchange Server features they can use.

- Outlook installations can be automated by using a combination of SETUP command-line options and the Network Installation wizard.

- Network installation points are a common way to distribute Exchange client applications.

Day 6

Microsoft Exchange Clients: Connectivity and Configuration

by William Matsoukas

Microsoft Exchange Server can be accessed by a number of clients. These clients vary in features, functionality, native platforms, and computer equipment requirements. To effectively create an Exchange environment, it is important to understand the differences between these various clients and how they work together in a mixed environment.

This chapter describes these clients in terms of general features and interoperability. You will most likely be tested on three areas of Exchange clients: installation, connectivity configuration, and interoperability.

Objectives

This chapter addresses the following Microsoft exam objectives:

- Choose Microsoft Exchange client installation and integration strategies
- Install and configure Exchange Server client computers

6.1. Understanding MAPI Compliance, Windows Messaging, and Profiles

The configuration of all Exchange clients is based on messaging profiles. Messaging profiles, in turn, are used to connect an application to Windows messaging, which is a MAPI- (Messaging Application Programming Interface) compliant messaging subsystem. The following sections describe each of these components.

6.1.1. Understanding MAPI Compliance

The Windows messaging system, which is the core of Exchange Server's communications, uses the Messaging Application Programming Interface (MAPI) standard for connectivity with Exchange clients. Client applications developed by using the MAPI standard work with Exchange Server as well as with other email systems.

Outlook, for example, is shipped with MAPI-compliant drivers for the following mail systems:

- Microsoft Mail 3.x
- Microsoft Exchange Server
- Internet Mail

These drivers, or *services*, facilitate communication between the client and the messaging server. Other vendors also have services available to provide connectivity with other electronic messaging servers such as Lotus cc:Mail and Lotus Notes.

The core component for message communications for 32-bit Windows products is Windows messaging. Microsoft Outlook, Microsoft Exchange, and Exchange Inbox use Windows *messaging profiles*. The messaging profile controls the way that the Exchange client communicates with Exchange Server as well as the manner in which messages are handled on the client side. A messaging profile is usually associated with a user.

6.1.2. Windows Messaging Profile Configuration Options

A messaging profile defines configuration of the Exchange client for three areas:

- **Services.** Windows messaging services and their associated properties. Service properties vary depending on the service.

■ **Delivery.** Message delivery options such as mail location, name checking, and default email addresses.

■ **Addressing.** Message addressing options such as address list order.

Windows messaging services control the way in which messages are addressed, sent, and received. A Windows messaging profile can be configured with any number of services, including more than one email service. A user can, for example, use Outlook to connect to his or her company Exchange server, CompuServe account, and POP3 Internet mailbox.

6.1.3. Outlook and Default Windows Messaging Profiles

When a user starts Outlook on a computer that does not have a Windows messaging profile, a default profile is created automatically. The profile contains only services for personal folders and an Address Book. To connect to a mail server, the appropriate email service must be added to the profile. The default profile for Outlook can be modified using the Mail and Fax icon in the Control Panel.

As just stated, when a user starts Outlook on a computer that has no profile, a minimal profile is created automatically. You can modify the behavior of this profile: A program separate from Outlook, NEWPROF.EXE, can generate new profiles based on configuration information stored in an Outlook profile information file (*.PRF). When Outlook starts, it looks for a default profile. If Outlook cannot find a profile, it looks in the Windows directory for OUTLOOK.PRF. If Outlook finds OUTLOOK.PRF, it executes NEWPROF.EXE, which creates the new profile based on the information in OUTLOOK.PRF. If Outlook does not find OUTLOOK.PRF, it creates the default profile.

6.1.4. Profiles and Roaming Users

Roaming users should not be confused with remote users. A *roaming user* is a user in an organization who logs on to the network using more than one workstation. A *remote user* logs on to the network using dial-up access; note that a remote user can also be a roaming user.

Because MAPI clients use Windows messaging profiles to connect to mail services, and NEWPROF.EXE can generate a profile based on a configuration file (OUTLOOK.PRF), roaming users can be supported more effectively.

Logon scripts can be written so that a roaming user's profile is automatically created when he or she logs on using a computer that does not already have a profile. The

6

logon script should check to see whether the workstation has a profile for the roaming user. If not, the logon script can execute NEWPROF.EXE to create a profile using the OUTLOOK.PRF stored in the user's home directory.

The best way to manage personal address lists, personal folders, views, and other service files for roaming users is to store them in the user's home directory so that they are accessible from any workstation on the network and so that messages are not distributed across several computers.

6.2. Understanding Exchange Server Clients

Windows messaging supports the MAPI standard; Windows messaging is the underlying messaging transport for Exchange Server and its clients. This means that third-party software companies can create applications that take advantage of Exchange Server's advanced capabilities. The following sections describe the most popular MAPI client applications that work with Exchange Server.

For the purposes of the MSCE exam, it is a good idea to know the general features of Outlook. You will probably encounter questions concerning installation, configuration, and troubleshooting.

6.2.1. Microsoft Outlook

Outlook is the flagship client for Exchange Server. Its underlying functionality is inherited from the email features of the Exchange client and the collaborative features of Schedule+. Outlook is actually the integration of email, collaborative messaging, and a personal information manager. Of all the currently available Exchange Server clients, Outlook makes the most of Exchange Server capabilities. Outlook is available for the 16-bit and 32-bit Windows platforms and for Macintosh. Outlook features differ for these three clients.

For more information about Outlook, see "Installing and Configuring 32-Bit Outlook" and "Outlook Installation Options," later in this chapter."

6.2.2. Microsoft Exchange Inbox and Exchange Client

Inbox is a basic email application that uses Windows messaging; it is shipped with 32-bit Windows operating systems. Inbox can be viewed as the messaging side of Outlook. Although Inbox supports Exchange Server's contact list, all the other specialized folders (such as task lists, calendar, and journal) are treated as email messages. In short, Inbox facilitates minimal functional access to Exchange Server features.

Exchange Client is shipped with Exchange Server. As is true with Exchange Inbox, Exchange Client includes email services, Schedule+, and contact lists. Exchange Client is the upgrade from Inbox.

In terms of the MSCE exam, you should know that an important consideration for Exchange Inbox and Exchange Client is that they are both MAPI applications that use the same Windows messaging profiles that Outlook does. All three of these clients can coexist on the same computer.

6.2.3. Outlook Web Access for Microsoft Exchange Server

Outlook Web Access is not actually a client application but a web-enabled application. Exchange Server can be configured to provide messaging access to any web browser that supports frames, Java controls, and Java scripts. Microsoft Internet Explorer 3.0 and Netscape Navigator 3.0 (and higher) have been tested with Exchange Server.

Outlook Web Access is useful for providing basic email, calendar, public folder, and collaboration services to computers that do not support other Exchange Server client applications, such as older Macintosh or UNIX computers.

6.2.4. SMTP/POP3 Clients

Any standard SMTP/POP3 (Simple Mail Transfer Protocol/Post Office Protocol 3) client can work with Exchange Server. Exchange Server's mailbox can be configured as a POP3 mailbox, which is particularly useful for non-Windows computers such as UNIX machines. Because it is POP3 compliant, Exchange Server can be easily integrated into heterogeneous network environments.

6

6.2.5. Exchange DOS Clients

For some reason, Exchange Server still comes with a DOS/Windows 3.x client. The functionality of this client is limited to sending and receiving email messages. Do not expect to see a DOS/Windows 3.x question on the exam; you should know, however, that the product is still around.

6.3. Understanding Client Interoperability

When implementing an Exchange messaging system, you will probably encounter environments that require more than one Exchange client. It is important for you to understand the way that different clients can interoperate using the features of Exchange Server. The following sections describe client interoperability for Exchange Inbox, Exchange Client, Schedule+, 16-bit Outlook, Outlook for Macintosh, and Microsoft Mail 3.x client in terms of Outlook.

6.3.1. Understanding Exchange Inbox Interoperability

Because Inbox is a MAPI application, it completely supports the email functionality of Outlook. The common mail messaging interface means that Inbox supports the same message and message store format Outlook does.

Inbox also has limited support for most of the standard features of Outlook, such as public and private folders, contact list, task list, and calendar. "Limited support" here means that Inbox manages items in these folders as email messages.

6.3.2. Understanding Exchange Client Interoperability

Exchange Client is an advanced version of Exchange Inbox that also includes Schedule+. Exchange Client interoperability with Outlook is seamless except for two key areas: custom views and Schedule+. Custom view interoperability is discussed in this section. Schedule+ is a more complex interoperability issue, and is discussed in the next section.

Outlook is backward compatible with Exchange Client folder views. Although Outlook can use any view created by Exchange Client, Exchange Client can interpret only table views created by Outlook.

6.3.3. Understanding Schedule+ Interoperability

Outlook and Schedule+ offer a high degree of interoperability. They share two critical scheduling features:

- **Meeting requests.** Both Schedule+ and Outlook have a meeting request feature, a specialized email message that notifies recipients of a planned meeting. Recipients who are using Outlook or Schedule+ can respond to the meeting request by clicking an Accept or Decline button on the request form. The response to the request is returned to the sender, and the time allocated for the meeting is marked "busy" for recipients who accept the meeting request.

- **Free/busy status.** Both Outlook and Schedule+ can access and allocate time on Exchange Server calendars. Free/busy status should not be confused with free/busy details. Free/busy *status* indicates whether or not a given time period is allocated for a particular user; free/busy *details* includes information concerning the nature of the time allocation such as meeting attendees and locations.

Outlook has additional calendar features that cannot be processed by Schedule+ clients.

 The Schedule+ clients discussed in this section are 16-bit versions 1.0 and 2.0, and 32-bit versions 7.0 and 7.0a.

Outlook meeting request messages have more features available than 16-bit Schedule+. Although Outlook recognizes all features of 16-bit Schedule+, 16-bit Schedule+ does not recognize Outlook's attachments, meeting locations, and recurring meeting features. Sixteen-bit Schedule+ ignores attachments and meeting locations and interprets recurring meetings as a single meeting. Thirty-two bit Schedule+ recognizes these features.

Assuming that all users have appropriate permissions, Schedule+ and Outlook can view each other's free/busy status. Outlook has a more detailed implementation of the free/busy status. Outlook can designate busy time blocks, out-of-office time blocks, and tentative time blocks. When published, the free/busy status for an Outlook client is viewed by a Schedule+ client; out-of-office time blocks appear as busy blocks; tentative time blocks appear as free blocks. Schedule+ clients can view

6

unpublished Outlook free/busy status. Outlook clients cannot read unpublished free/busy status unless they open the target user's calendar.

 Note For Schedule+ clients to access the Outlook client's free/busy status, Outlook Driver for Schedule+ must be installed on the Schedule+ client.

Free/busy details are the information associated with scheduled time blocks. They are the information about the planned appointment, meeting, or out-of-office time. Outlook clients can view the free/busy details of Schedule+ users on Exchange Server, but not on Microsoft Mail. Schedule+ clients can view the free/busy details only when all users use Exchange as their mail server.

Schedule+ has a direct booking feature. With appropriate permissions, a Schedule+ user can enter appointments and meetings directly into another Schedule+ user's calendar. To encourage the use of meeting messages, this feature is not available with Outlook. As a result, Schedule+ users cannot directly book to Outlook calendars, nor can an Outlook user directly book to either a Schedule+ or an Outlook calendar.

6.3.4. Understanding Outlook for Windows 3.1x and Outlook for Macintosh Interoperability

The Windows 3.1x and Macintosh Outlook clients support most of the features of the 32-bit Outlook client. Because the interoperability for these clients and 32-bit Outlook is very good, it is more expedient to describe 32-bit Outlook features *not* supported by the Windows 3.1x and Macintosh Outlook clients. The major features *not* supported are listed here:

- **Forms.** Custom forms supported must be either HTML or CDO script format forms. Neither the Windows 3.1x nor the Macintosh Outlook client can design or display Outlook 97 (or higher) compatible forms.

- **Voting messages.** Windows 3.1x and Macintosh Outlook clients can respond to voting messages but cannot send them. A *voting message* is a specialized email message that includes option buttons from which the recipient can choose; selections are reported back to the sender.

- **MIME message format.** The Windows 3.1x Outlook client supports MIME format messages; the Macintosh client supports S/MIME.

- **Internet mail.** SMTP/POP3 mail services are not supported by either client.
- **Calendar details.** The Macintosh Outlook client cannot read 32-bit Outlook calendar details.

As is often the case withMicrosoft products for the Macintosh, the functionality is a bit behind the 32-bit Windows product. With the maturation of the Exchange Server product and Outlook, you can expect that the disparity between the two clients will be short lived.

6.3.5. Understanding Microsoft Mail 3.x Interoperability

Microsoft Mail 3.x clients support only two features of Outlook: message exchange and public folders. Both of these features, however, are severely restricted.

Messaging exchange between Microsoft Mail 3.x and Outlook is minimal. Although Outlook recognizes all Mail 3.x message features, Mail 3.x clients cannot process many Outlook message features, including the following:

- Rich text formats
- Custom forms
- Embedded links

Outlook message sizes are also limited with Microsoft Mail 3.x. The largest single text message Mail 3.x can handle is 32K; the largest attachment is limited to 100M.

Mail 3.x and Outlook use different message stores. For Outlook to read information from a Mail 3.x message store, the store must be imported using the Migration wizard utility, included with Exchange Server.

Mail 3.x clients cannot access Outlook public folders. Outlook clients have full read, write, create, and delete access to Mail 3.x public folders. Because of changes in machine-level code embedded in forms, those forms stored in Mail 3.x public folders may not be accessible to Outlook.

6

6.4. Installing and Configuring 32-Bit Outlook

The process of installing Outlook from a network share point or a CD-ROM is the same as any other Microsoft application installation, therefore it is not useful to walk through such an installation. Instead, the following sections cover the details of attaining connectivity by configuring profiles and setting up installation processes such as network share point installations and custom installations.

6.4.1. Configuring Exchange Server Connectivity Using the Outlook Setup Wizard

The following exercise demonstrates how to create an exchange client profile using the Outlook Setup wizard:

1. Open the Control Panel by selecting Settings from the Start menu and then choosing Control Panel.

2. Double-click the Mail and Fax icon. The Microsoft Outlook Properties dialog box appears as shown in Figure 6.1.

Figure 6.1.

The Outlook Properties dialog box includes profile configuration options.

3. To create a new profile, click Show Profiles; from the Mail and Fax dialog box that appears next, click Add. The Microsoft Outlook Setup wizard appears (see Figure 6.2).

Figure 6.2.

The Microsoft Outlook Setup wizard is used to perform a simplified configuration for the most common mail connection types.

4. Confirm that the only service checked in the list box is Microsoft Exchange Server and click Next. You are offered an opportunity to change (from the default of Microsoft Exchange Settings) the name of the profile you are creating.

5. Change the name of the new profile to Test Profile and click Next. The next dialog box prompts for the name of the Exchange Server and your mailbox name.

6. Enter the appropriate information and click Next. You are asked whether you travel with the computer.

7. Choose the No radio button then click Next. You are prompted for a location for your personal Address Book.

8. Accept the default location by clicking Next. You are asked whether to add Outlook to your startup group so that it runs automatically when you log on to your computer.

9. Choose the No radio button and then click Next. You are informed that a profile with Exchange Server Client and a personal Address Book has been successfully created.

10. Click Finish. You are returned to the Mail and Fax dialog box. Note that Test Profile has been added to the profiles list.

At the conclusion of this exercise, you should be ready to connect to the Exchange server, assuming that the server and mailbox name you entered are valid. This method for creating profiles affords a simple way to create simple, default-based profiles. To create more complex profiles—that is, profiles that use more than the Exchange Server and personal Address Book services, or that use other custom settings—you should either create profiles manually or modify profiles created with the Outlook Setup wizard.

6

6.4.2. Creating an Outlook Client Profile Manually

The following exercise demonstrates how to create a profile manually. This profile is configured with the same services as the profile created in the previous exercise.

1. From the Control Panel, double-click the Mail and Fax icon. The Mail and Fax dialog box appears.

2. Click Add. The Outlook Setup wizard appears.

3. Choose the Manually Configure Information Services radio button and then click Next. You are prompted for a profile name.

4. Enter the profile name Second Test Profile and then click Next. The Properties dialog box for the new profile appears as shown in Figure 6.3.

Figure 6.3.

The Properties dialog box for profiles appears when you select manual configuration in the Outlook Setup wizard.

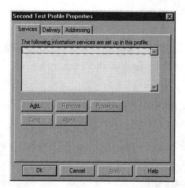

5. Add the Exchange Server service to the profile and click Add. The Add Service to Profiles dialog box appears (see Figure 6.4). Table 6.1 describes each of the standard services available for Outlook.

Figure 6.4.

The Add Services to Profile dialog box displays a list of standard services available for the Outlook client.

Table 6.1. Standard services for Outlook.

Service	Description
Internet Mail	Provides connectivity to SMTP/POP3 mail servers.
Microsoft Exchange Server	Provides connectivity to Microsoft Exchange Server.
Microsoft Mail	Provides connectivity to Microsoft Mail servers.
Microsoft Fax	Sets up Windows messaging to send and receive faxes.
Outlook Address Book	Facilitates an Outlook Address Book, which can be used instead of a personal Address Book.
Personal Address Book	Facilitates a personal Address Book.
Personal Folders	Facilitates personal folders.

6. Add the Microsoft Exchange Server service to the new profile by selecting Microsoft Exchange Server from the Available Information Services list box and then click OK. The configuration dialog box for the Microsoft Exchange Server dialog box appears as shown in Figure 6.5.

Figure 6.5.

Before the Exchange Server client service can be configured, it should be connected to an existing Exchange mailbox.

7. If you are connected to the network where the target Exchange Server is located, you should confirm the connection to a valid Exchange mailbox. Enter the name of the Exchange Server and the mailbox name, then click Check Name. Your computer attempts to connect to the Exchange Server and confirm the mailbox name. If the name check is successful, the mailbox name changes to the mailbox name as displayed in the Global Address List, usually Lastname, Firstname.

6

> **Note**
>
> Remember that there are usually two names associated with an Exchange Server mailbox. One name is the NT user ID associated with the mailbox, and the other is the "formal" name. Both of these names are searched when a name check is run. If you do not know the mailbox name as shown in the Global Address List, you can perform a name check using the NT user ID associated with the mailbox.

8. Configure the rest of the options for the General properties page. To use the local network to access the Exchange mailbox, choose the Connect with the Network radio button. To access an Exchange Server using a RAS connection, choose the Work Offline and Use Dial-up Networking radio button. To allow the user to select either dial-up or local network access when Outlook is started, check the Choose the Connection type when Starting checkbox.

9. Choose the Advanced properties page (see Figure 6.6). If you have delegated access permission to an additional mailbox, you can configure Outlook to open that mailbox in addition to the primary mailbox. Click Add, enter the name of the second mailbox, and then click OK.

Figure 6.6.

The Advanced property page includes security configuration settings and delegated mailboxes.

10. The Encrypt Information options determine whether information sent and received over the local network and information sent over a dial-up connection are encrypted. Leave these settings deselected.

11. Confirm that the Logon Network Security field is set to NT Network Authentication.

12. Configure the offline folders. Click Offline Folder File Settings. The Offline Folder File Settings dialog box appears (see Figure 6.7). The default setting for

offline folder settings are usually adequate for most Exchange Server implementations. The details for the configuration settings are described in Table 6.2 at the end of this exercise. Click OK to return to the Advanced properties page.

Figure 6.7.

Offline folders allow you to synchronize your local computer with your Exchange Server-based folders and then work offline.

13. Review the Dial-Up Networking properties page (see Figure 6.8). The two general settings on this page define whether Outlook will dial up automatically when you start Outlook or use an existing dial-up connection that was made before you started Outlook.

Figure 6.8.

The Dial-Up Networking properties page allows you to configure automatic RAS connections when Outlook starts.

14. Select the Remote Mail properties page (see Figure 6.9). The settings on the Remote Mail properties page define how Outlook processes remote mail and can be used to schedule automatic mail retrieval. Leave the default settings for this properties page.

6

Figure 6.9.

The Remote Mail properties page includes rules for retrieving mail.

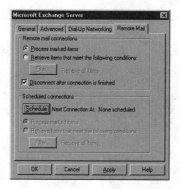

15. Click OK to add the Exchange Server service to the profile. You return to the Profile Properties dialog box.

16. Add a Personal Address Book to the profile. Choose the General properties page and then click Add. The Add Service to Profile dialog box appears.

17. Select Personal Address Book from the Available Information Services list and click OK. The Personal Address Book dialog box appears (see Figure 6.10).

Figure 6.10.

Personal Address Book settings include the name and location of the PAB file as well as the sort order for the names in the book.

18. Confirm the setting for Name, Path, and Show Names By for the Personal Address Book and then click OK to add it to the profile.

19. You are notified that the Personal Address Book service will not work until the next time you start Outlook. Click OK.

20. Click OK to return to the Outlook Setup wizard. You are prompted to add Outlook to the startup group. Choose the No radio button and click Next.

21. Click Finish to return to the Mail and Fax dialog box.

22. Click OK to exit.

Table 6.2. Exchange Server Service configuration settings.

Properties Page	Setting	Description
General	Microsoft Exchange Server	Name of the home server for the target mailbox.
	Mailbox	Name of the Exchange mailbox.
	When Starting Connect with the Network	Uses the local network to connect to the target Exchange server.
	Work Offline and Use Dial-up Networking	Client does not attempt to connect to an Exchange server, then connects to the target Exchange server to send and receive mail using dial-up networking.
	Choose Connection Type when Starting	User is prompted to use the local network, a dial-up connection, or to work offline.
Advanced	Open These Additional Mailboxes	Client will open additional mailboxes if the user is a delegate for those mailboxes.
	Encryption Information When Using the Network	Both incoming and outgoing messages are encrypted.
	When Using Dial-up Networking	Outgoing messages are encrypted.
Logon Network Security	None	User is prompted for ID and password to log on to his or her mailbox.
	NT Network Authentication	User is logged on to his or her mailbox using his or her Windows Network ID and password.
	Distributed Password Authentication	Enables Internet browsers to log on to Exchange servers using MCIS Membership Distributed Password Authentication.
	Offline Folder File Settings	Location and name of offline folder file; Encryption and compression of the offline folder file; Compaction of existing offline folder file; Enable/disable offline folders.
Dial-up Networking	Dial Using Following Connection	RAS connection for dial-up access; Exchange Server logon ID; Password; Domain.

continues

6

Table 6.2. continued

Properties Page	Setting	Description
	Do Not Dial, Use Existing Connection	Uses RAS connection started before client is started.
Remote Mail Connections	Process Marked Items	Remote mail processes all mail items marked for retrieval or deletion.
	Retrieve All Items that Meet the Following Conditions	Remote mail retrieves items based on user-defined rules.
	Disconnect After Connection is Finished	Dial-up connection is closed after messages are processed.
	Scheduled Connections	Remote mail can be scheduled to retrieve or send messages. User-defined rules may be applied to scheduled sessions.

6.4.3. Adding Internet Mail Service to a Profile

In the following exercise, the Internet Mail service is added to the profile that was created in the previous exercise. This exercise demonstrates configuring a profile from within Outlook.

1. Start Outlook using the profile created in the previous exercise. This profile should be named `Second Test Profile`.

2. Choose the Services Option from the Tools menu. The Services dialog box appears.

3. Click Add on the Services properties page; in the Available Information Services list, double-click Internet Mail. The Internet Mail dialog box appears (see Figure 6.11).

4. Complete the General properties page as shown in Table 6.3.

Table 6.3. Settings for Internet Mail General properties page.

Setting	Description	mple
Full Name	Display name for electronic mail messages	`Bill Matsoukas`
E-mail address	POP3 mailbox address	`bmatsoukas@wor-let.att.net`

Setting	Description	mple
Internet Mail Server	DNS name for mail server that holds the POP3 mail	`postoffice.att.t`
Account Name	Mail server account	`bmatsoukas`
Password	Password for mail server account	This is *not* the mailbox password.
Message Format	MIME or plain text; US-ASCII character set for plain text; optional extended character sets N/A	
Advanced Options	Name of the outgoing (SMTP) mail server if different from the Internet mail server	`outserver.att.n`

Figure 6.11.

The Internet Mail service supports SMTP/POP3 mail servers.

5. Complete the Connection properties page. This page is similar to the Remote Mail properties page for the Exchange Server service. The Internet Mail service can be configured to use a local network connection or dial-up networking to connect to the POP3 mail server. Mail collection can be scheduled, and rules for mail collection can be defined. The Internet mail service also facilitates logging mail sessions.

6. Click OK to add the Internet Mail service to the profile.

7. You are notified that this service will not work until you have logged off and then restarted Windows messaging. Click OK. You are returned to the Services dialog box.

6

POP3 mailboxes, commonly referred to as *Internet mailboxes*, are one of the most common types of email repositories available. Do not be surprised if you are asked to solve a connectivity problem or two for Internet Mail service on the Exchange exam.

6.5. Outlook Installation Options

Most network administrators manage application distribution by providing users with a way to install these applications from a file server. Microsoft product installations usually allow administrators to configure that installation in a number of different ways. The following sections describe some of the methods for creating custom installations and the details behind them.

6.5.1. Understanding Setup Files

Setup installs Outlook based on the information in three files normally located in the Outlook install folder:

- The information file (`*.INF`)
- The list file (`*.LST`)
- The setup table (`*.STF`)

You can customize the manner in which Outlook is installed by modifying one or more of these files. These files can be modified by using the Network Installation wizard (shipped with Outlook) or by running Setup with command-line options.

Note

Microsoft does not recommend manually modifying the `*.INF` or `*.STF` files; instead, you should use the Network Installation wizard or Setup command-line switches. This might be a question on the test.

The `*.INF` file details all the files used during an installation. The name of the `*.INF` file used depends on the type of installation:

- **OUTLOOK.INF**: Used for all installation modes except network.
- **ADMIN.INF**: Used when Outlook is installed from a network share (network mode).

By default, the Setup table file (*.STF) is named OUTLOOK.STF. OUTLOOK.STF controls the following aspects of an Outlook installation:

- The installation procedure for each installation mode
- The required user input
- The responses to user input
- The options to install
- The installation location(s)

The *.STF file defines a logical tree structure through which Setup processes the installation based on the installation environment and user input. In other words, Setup uses the information in the *.STF file to follow an installation path.

Note

Because Setup does not know beforehand the path that it will follow through the *.STF file, Setup will not know precisely the disk space required for a given installation.

The default name of the *.LST file is SETUP.LST. It contains, among other things, the command-line parameters for Setup, banner message text, and files to be used for Setup. Table 6.4 describes the Setup command-line options. Most importantly, SETUP.LST points to the *.STF to be used for the installation.

Table 6.4. Setup command-line options.

Option	Description
/a	Runs Setup in administrative mode to create an installation point. This option can only be run from a CD-ROM.
/b <number>	Tells Setup to skip the dialog box that selects the type of installation; <number> should be one of the following: 1 Typical 2 Custom 3 Run from CD-ROM or network share point
/c "number"	Specifies the Product ID so that Setup can skip the Product ID dialog box.
/f	Disables use of long filenames for installation on machines that do not support long filenames.

continues

Table 6.4. continued

Option	Description
/g "file"	Generates a log file to "file". If "file" already exists, it is overwritten.
/g+ "file"	Generates a log file to "file". If "file" already exists, it is appended.
/k "number"	Provides Setup with the CD key so that this dialog box is skipped.
/l "file"	Tells Setup to ignore the default SETUP.LST and instead use "file".
/m <number>	Sets the number of installs for the Microsoft License Pack.
/n ""	Tells Setup to prompt for a user name if none is found in the Windows Registry.
/n "name"	Specifies a user name if a default user name is not found in the Windows Registry.
/o ""	Tells Setup to prompt for an organization name if none exists in the Windows Registry.
/o "organization"	Specifies an organization name if a default organization name is not found in the Windows Registry.
/q <option>	Specifies level of user participation in the installation process; <option> should be one of the following:
	0 Suppresses all dialog boxes except the last. This option has the same effect as not using the /q option at all.
	1 Suppresses all dialog boxes.
	T Suppresses all user interfaces including progress and informational messages.
/qn <option>	Works the same as /q except that Setup does not restart the system. 0 is not a valid option: use /qn with no argument instead.
/r	Reinstalls an application when used in maintenance mode.
/s "folder"	Replaces the default location of SETUP.EXE or the location specified in the maintenance-mode *.STF file.
/u <a>	Tells Setup to uninstall. The optional <a> parameter tells Setup to remove any shared applications without prompting, otherwise the user is prompted before shared applications are removed. This option must be used only in maintenance mode.
/x "file"	Tells setup to create a network installation log file that tracks the number of installations run from a network installation point.
/y	Setup runs normally, but no files are copied to the hard disk. This option modifies Registry settings.

The following options cannot be used together on the same command line:

Illegal Combination	Description
/a, /q	Cannot be used together or an error message is generated and Setup stops.
/a, /n	If used together, the /n option is ignored.
/u, /r	Cannot be used together or an error message is generated and Setup stops.
/u, /q	The prompt to uninstall is suppressed and the shared components are not removed.

6.5.2. Creating a Customized Setup Script with the Network Installation Wizard

Using the Network Installation wizard to create a custom installation is a three-step process:

1. Create a network installation point.
2. Install the Network Installation wizard.
3. Configure a customized installation.

For the exercises that follow, you will create a network installation point, install the Network Installation wizard on a local hard drive, and then configure a customized installation that will install Outlook on a local hard drive.

Creating a Network Installation Point

There are two methods for creating a network installation point: you can run the Outlook Setup program from the target file server, or you can run Setup from a workstation and install to a shared drive on the target server.

The following exercise demonstrates how to run Setup from a workstation and install to a shared folder on the target file server.

1. Create a shared folder on the computer that will contain the installation share point for Outlook. Optionally, create a drive map to that share on your local workstation.
2. Insert the Office or Outlook CD-ROM in the drive and run SETUP.EXE /a located in the 32-bit Outlook folder.
3. Work through the initial copyright, company information, and CD-ROM key screens. You are then prompted for the target installation folder.

6

4. Select the share you created in step 1 and click OK. Click OK again to confirm the target folder. You are then prompted for the name of a folder in which to install shared files. Click OK to accept the default MSAPPS folder.

5. Setup prompts you to confirm the server name and folder for shared files. Accept the default by clicking Continue.

6. Setup asks whether you want shared files to be installed on a user's local drive, the server, or user's choice during client installation. Because you will be changing the setup using the Network Installation Wizard later, the response here is moot. Accept the default Server setting by clicking OK.

7. You are prompted to choose a paper size and language. Choose US Letter, US English dictionaries, and then click OK.

8. Setup copies files to the installation share point and then informs you that Outlook has been installed successfully. Click OK to exit Setup.

9. Setup copies the necessaryfiles to the network share point. Finally, Setup completes by displaying a message box that provides some information concerning language installations. Click OK. A success message box appears. Click OK.

Network-based installations facilitate simple software distribution for many network administrators of small-to-medium-sized networks. Larger networks usually require more sophisticated software distribution methods such as SMS. Using a network share point for Exchange client installation may be an option for a scenario on the Exchange exam.

Installing the Network Installation Wizard

The Network Installation wizard comes with the Back Office Resource Kit. It is also available on the Microsoft web site. To install the Network Installation wizard, complete the following steps:

1. Run the install program SETUPNIW.EXE. You are prompted to continue with the installation. Click Yes.

2. You are prompted to accept the licensing agreement. Read the agreement and then click Yes.

3. You are prompted to close any open applications. Confirm that the Network Installation wizard setup is the only application running and then click Continue.

4. Setup prompts you for the folder in which to install the wizard. Accept the default folder by clicking OK.

5. You are prompted for the installation type. The only option is a Complete Installation. Click Complete to finish the installation.

6. Confirm that the Network Installation wizard has been added to your Start menu.

This quick exercise was a warm-up for the next section. You should know that the Network Installation wizard is shipped with the Resource Kit and is available from Technet or Microsoft's web site.

Creating a Customized Installation Using the Network Installation Wizard

The Network Installation wizard is a tool that customizes Back Office client installations. It accomplishes this by modifying *.INF, *.LST, and *.STF files. Using the Network Installation wizard is the procedure Microsoft recommends for creating custom installations.

The following exercise steps through customizing the network installation point created in an exercise earlier in this chapter. Performing this exercise is a good way to learn the customization features available for Outlook Setup.

1. Start the Network Installation wizard. A Welcome screen appears (see Figure 6.12). Click Next.

Figure 6.12.

The Network Installation wizard can be used to customize installation of any Office product.

2. You are prompted to specify either a *.LST or a *.STF file associated with your installation image. As noted on this screen, if your installation has both *.LST and *.STF files, you should choose a *.LST file. Browse to the network

installation share point you created in an exercise earlier in this chapter and then drill down to the OUTLOOK.W32 folder. Select the SETUP.LST file and click Open.

3. You return to the Open LST or STF File screen. Click Next. The Network Installation wizard reads the OUTLOOK.STF file.

4. The Primary Location screen appears. This is where the primary target folder for client installations is specified. Accept the default <ProgramFilesFolder>\ Microsoft Office folder by clicking Next.

5. The Documents Folder screen lets you determine where all Office documents, including Outlook documents, will be stored by default. Accept the default C:\My Documents by clicking Next.

6. The next screen prompts you to specify where shared Office files are located. Specify the local hard drive and click Next.

> If you specify User's Choice or Server for the shared files location, the Network Installation wizard prompts you for the server location.

7. You are prompted to specify an installation log file. If you enter a log filename, each time a client installation is run, a record is appended to the log file. This record contains the following data:

- Date and time of installation
- User name
- Computer name
- Application name and version number
- Type of operation (install, update, or uninstall)

Skip the log file entry by clicking Next with the Log File Name field blank.

> If you decide to use a log file, consider its location on a file server. Remember that users running Setup probably do not have write permission to the installation share folder, therefore Setup will not be able to make a log entry if the installation log file is located in that folder.

8. Setup prompts you for an installation type. The installation type affects which default components are installed during a client installation. If the client installation is run in interactive mode, the components selected here are presented as default settings to the user. If the client installation is run in batch mode, the selected components are installed automatically. Choose the Custom installation option and click Next.

9. The Network Installation Wizard Components screen appears (see Figure 6.13). Select the components you want to install on client computers and then click Next.

Figure 6.13.

The components selected in the Network Installation wizard become defaults during client installation.

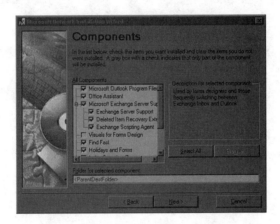

10. The Network Installation wizard displays the Yes/No Answers screen. Each question displayed is a potential prompt to the user during client installation. You can set the default answer to each of these questions by clicking the question to toggle the answer. If the client installation is run in interactive mode, the questions are displayed with the default answer. If the client installation is run in batch mode, the prompts are answered automatically and not displayed to the user. Review the questions, set the default answers, and then click Next.

Note

You may see the same question displayed more than once on this screen. This is because the program-like logic of the `*.STF` file can have several branches that require the same question. Answers to duplicate questions must be the same or unpredictable results may occur at client installation time.

6

11. The Program Manager Items screen lets you select which icons will be added to the Windows NT 3.51 Program Manager and Startup windows. Note that you can also restrict a user from changing these settings at client install time. Leave the default setting on this screen and click Next.

12. The next screen displayed is the Start Menu and Desktop Items screen (see Figure 6.14). You can specify the shortcuts to be added to the Windows 95 and Windows NT 4.0 Start menu and desktop. Note that you can also modify the names and location of each shortcut. Modify these settings to your satisfaction and then click Next.

Figure 6.14.

Start menu and desktop items can be customized for client installations.

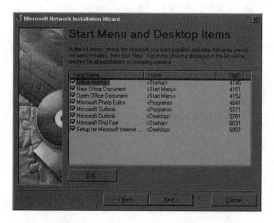

13. The Network Installation wizard prompts you to select a setup files subfolder. This is the folder in which the setup files will be stored along with any new files you add to the installation. Keep the default setting by clicking Next.

14. The Add Files screen lets you specify additional files you may want to copy during client installation. An example of an additional file is a bitmap of your company logo. If you want to try this feature, add a file or two to the list on this screen and then click Next.

15. The Add Registry Entries screen allows you to specify custom Registry entries. Click Next.

16. The Select Quiet Mode screen lets you specify the level of user interaction during client installation. The levels listed on this screen are self-explanatory. Choose a quiet level and then click Next.

17. The Network Installation wizard prompts you to save changes to the setup files with the option to change the setup filenames. Note that these files are written to the custom files folder specified earlier in this exercise. Make any desired changes to the filenames and then click Finish.

18. The final screen displays the Setup command-line options that must be used for the customization just completed to work correctly. Note this command-line text and then click Exit to close the Network Installation wizard.

19. Run a client installation to test the customization.

The Network Installation wizard automates the drudgery that must otherwise be endured when modifying the various setup control files. In fact, Microsoft recommends that you not modify any setup files manually. In preparation for the Exchange exam, be aware of the setup options available for Network Installation wizard as well as the command-line switches used in conjunction with the wizard-generated configuration.

6

Lab

This lab consists of review questions pertaining to this chapter and provides an opportunity to apply the knowledge you've gained in this chapter.

Questions

1. Sheryl has Outlook installed on her workstation and is connected to the company's Exchange messaging system. She also has a personal SMTP/POP3 mailbox on the Internet. Sheryl has asked you to set up Outlook to allow her to access her Internet mailbox. What service would you add to Sheryl's profile to facilitate access to her personal mailbox?

    A. SMTP/POP3 Mail Connector

    B. Internet Mail

    C. TCP/IP Mail Service

    D. None of the above; Outlook does not support SMTP/POP3 mail

2. Which Exchange Client service would you use to access a Microsoft Mail 3.x post office?

    A. Microsoft Exchange Server: Both Exchange Server and Microsoft Mail 3.x are MAPI compliant, therefore the Exchange Server service is backward compatible with Microsoft Mail 3.x

    B. Internet Mail: Microsoft Mail 3.x mailboxes are SMTP/POP3 compliant

    C. Microsoft Mail: The Microsoft Mail connector is provided with Exchange Client specifically for connecting to Microsoft Mail 3.x mail servers

    D. None of the above: You must use Exchange Inbox to connect to a Microsoft Mail 3.x mailbox

3. Your company has several salespersons that travel extensively. Your boss has asked you to provide them with email clients for their laptops and home computers so that they can connect to the company Exchange Server. Each of the 12 users has at least one home computer and one laptop. These computers are

of all types and configurations including Macintosh, Windows 3.1x, Windows NT, and UNIX platforms. These users are already connecting to the Internet to download files from your company's web server.

Your boss wants these users to have basic electronic mail services on the company's Exchange Server. Your boss is also pressed for time and wants the email implemented as quickly as possible. Training time is limited for these salespeople, so a simple, uniform solution would work best. What client/server configuration might you select for this situation?

A. Outlook with a RAS connection to the office so that all users have a secure connection to the Exchange server and a common mail client.

B. Exchange Inbox with a RAS connection to each user's Internet Service Provider. Inbox provides a simple mail interface and the Internet connection is already in place.

C. Set up these users with a POP3 mailbox and let them access the Exchange Server through the company's Internet connection. All users already have an Internet account and browsers, therefore they can access a POP3 mailbox.

D. Set up your Exchange server with Exchange Web Client Access. All users already access the network using Internet browsers, so they are already configured, and the Web Client provides all users with a simple, uniform client.

4. Before installing Exchange Client from the Exchange Server CD-ROM, what must be installed on a Windows 95 workstation?

A. Windows Messaging, which is installed from the Windows 95 CD-ROM

B. Remote Access Services, so that Exchange Client can connect to the mail server

C. The TCP/IP protocol suite, which is used by Exchange Client to communicate with the Exchange Server

D. None of the above

6

5. Why can't you run Exchange Inbox and Exchange Client on the same computer?

   A. The Exchange Client profile format conflicts with the Exchange Inbox profile format. Exchange Inbox will not run when Exchange Client is installed on the same computer.

   B. Exchange Client and Exchange Inbox can run on the same computer because they store profiles in different directories.

   C. Exchange Client and Exchange Inbox can run on the same computer because they are both MAPI applications, and therefore use the same profile(s).

   D. The Exchange Inbox profile format conflicts with the Exchange Client profile format. Exchange Client will not run on the same computer where Exchange Inbox is installed.

6. About half the users in your office use Exchange Client; the other half use Outlook. The accounting department has decided to take advantage of the Exchange Server scheduling features you have been lauding for the last six months. However, the Exchange Client users in that department are not able to view free/busy status for Outlook users. There are no error messages, and the Exchange Server is otherwise working perfectly. What is wrong?

   A. Nothing is wrong. Exchange Clients cannot view Outlook free/busy status information.

   B. The scheduling component in Exchange Client is Schedule+. You must install Outlook Driver for Schedule+ on all Exchange Servers in your organization.

   C. The scheduling component in Exchange Client is Schedule+. You must install Outlook Driver for Schedule+ on each workstation running Exchange Client that wants to access Outlook free/busy status information.

   D. The scheduling component in Exchange Client is Schedule+. You must install Outlook Driver for Schedule+ on each workstation running Outlook that wants to provide free/busy status information to Exchange Client users.

7. When using Outlook for Windows 3.1x, what limitation is imposed on voting messages?

    A. You can send and collect voting messages, but you cannot respond to voting messages.

    B. You can respond to voting messages, but you cannot send voting messages.

    C. You can both respond to and send voting messages.

    D. Voting messages are not supported for this platform.

8. Your company is in the process of migrating from Microsoft Mail 3.x to Exchange Server. At this point, about half the users have been moved to Exchange Server. You are asked to set up a company-wide public folder that all users can access. What might be your best option?

    A. Place the public folder on Exchange Server so that both Exchange users and Microsoft Mail users can access it.

    B. Place the public folder on the Exchange Server and replicate it to the Microsoft Mail post office so that all users can share the information.

    C. Place the folder on the Microsoft Mail server so that Exchange users can access the public folder.

    D. Forget it. Access between Exchange public folders and Microsoft Mail public folders is mutually exclusive. Create a shared directory on a file server and grant users appropriate permissions.

9. Most of the users on your growing network have a difficult time spelling *PC* much less installing an application from a file server. You have decided that the user population has reached a point at which applications should be installed from the network, unassisted by the overworked IS staff. You have just installed your first Exchange Server and it is time to distribute Outlook to the desktop. It would be nice to use SMS, but that's your next project, so you decide to create an automated installation. What method should you use to configure the Outlook installation?

    A. Create a network share installation point, then use Notepad to edit the installation configuration files (*.LST, *.INS, *.PRF).

    B. Place the Outlook CD-ROM in a server and share the CD-ROM drive, then distribute instructions to the users.

6

     C. Create a network share installation point for Outlook, then use the Network Installation wizard to create an automated installation.

     D. Create a network share installation point for Outlook, then modify the OUTLOOK.PDF file to automate the installation.

10. You are creating a custom installation using the Network Installation wizard. When you get to the Yes/No Questions screen, you notice that one of the questions appears three times on the list. What did you do wrong?

     A. Nothing. The structure of the *.LST file sometimes requires that a particular question appear in the file more than once.

     B. You probably specified a shared installation, then specified that shared files be located on the local hard drive.

     C. You probably specified the wrong *.LST file to configure.

     D. Nothing. The structure of the *.STF file sometimes requires that a particular question appear in the file more than once.

11. Which Setup command-line switch is used to create a network share installation point?

     A. /s

     B. /a

     C. /share

     D. -share

Exercise: Setting Up an Outlook Automatic Upgrade

 Note

This exercise addresses the following Microsoft exam objectives:

- Choose Microsoft Exchange Client installation and integration strategies
- Install and configure Exchange Server client computers

Version management should be a major consideration when choosing a client software deployment strategy. One option available with Outlook is network-based installation with automatic version upgrades. This configuration might be used on a small network where a version management system such as Microsoft SMS is not in place.

Microsoft Outlook Versions 8.01 and higher can be configured to automatically upgrade when a newer version is installed in the network installation share point. This brief exercise walks you through the configuration of Outlook for automatic upgrade.

This feature takes advantage of an Outlook configuration file, `OUTLOOK.SRG`. `OUTLOOK.SRG` contains Registry setting information and is run against the Registry when Outlook is started. Any entries in the Registry that do not match the entries in `OUTLOOK.SRG` are applied to the Registry.

1. Install Outlook on the workstation using the network installation share directory.

2. Using a plain text editor, open the `OUTLOOK.SRG` file located in the (default) `\Program Files\Microsoft Office\Office` folder and append the following line to the file:

```
[HKEY_LOCAL_MACHINE\software\microsoft\office\8.0\outlook\upgradepath]"serverpath
➥"=<\\\\servername\\sharename\\subdir
```

In this syntax, `\\\\servername\\sharename\\subdir` is the path to the network installation point.

Each time Outlook is started on the workstation, it checks the network installation share directory to determine whether a newer version of Outlook has been installed there. If so, the user is prompted to upgrade. If the user accepts the upgrade, Setup is executed.

6

Answers to Questions

1. **B**   The Internet Mail service supports SMTP/POP3 mail. Note that in this situation, the computer must be able to access the remote POP3 mailbox through the company's Internet connection or through dial-up networking.

2. **C**   The Microsoft Mail connector is available with Outlook, Exchange Client, and Exchange Inbox.

3. **D**   The keys to this answer are simplicity and uniformity. The RAS-connected clients described in answers A and B are not available across all the platforms mentioned. The POP3 solution in answer C will work, but clients will vary a lot between platforms. All users are already browsing the Internet, and although there may be some browser upgrades required, the Web Client offers a simple mail client that will work the same for all users.

4. **A**   Windows Messaging is in part the MAPI component used by MAPI-compliant applications such as Exchange Client to communicate with messaging servers.

5. **C**   Outlook, Exchange Client, and Exchange Inbox are MAPI-compliant applications. They all use Windows Messaging to connect to a mail server and therefore use the same profile format—and, in most cases, the same profile files.

6. **C**   The Outlook Driver for Schedule+ is shipped with Exchange Server and is installed on Schedule+ clients so that they can access Outlook free/busy status information.

7. **B**   Both Outlook for Windows 3.1x and Outlook for Macintosh support responding to voting messages, but not sending them.

8. **C**   There is not a really *great* answer to this question, only a *best* answer. The question asks about client interoperability of public folders. Exchange clients can read, write, create, and delete Microsoft Mail public folders. Microsoft Mail clients cannot access Exchange public folders. Note that answer D is probably the best solution to the problem in this situation, but a false statement is made in the answer.

9. **C**   Although answers A, B, and C will all work, Microsoft does not recommend editing the `*.INF` or `*.STF` file. Answer B would be chaos at best. The Network Installation wizard is the best tool for this job.

10. **D**   The `*.STF` file contains the logic that Setup follows at installation time.

11. **B**   The `/a` (administrative installation) switch is used to create a network share installation point.

6

Day 7

Exchange Connectivity

One of the strengths of Microsoft Exchange Server 5.5 is its capability to include many servers and many users as well as to communicate with other mail system efficiently. This chapter takes a look at how to connect groups of Exchange Servers to expand an organization; the chapter continues with a look at how Exchange Server can be used to communicate with other mail systems.

Objectives

This chapter addresses the following objectives:

- Configure connectivity to a mail system other than Exchange Server.
- Optimize foreign connections and site-to-site connections.

7.1. Connecting Exchange Sites

To maximize the use of bandwidth, Microsoft designed Exchange Server to group servers together into sites. Sites give the administrator the ability to manage which servers are talking to each other and how often they talk to each other. Sites are a powerful tool for managing the flow of data through the enterprise.

7.1.1. Exchange Sites—A Review

A group of Exchange Servers can be organized into a site. A *site* is a group of servers that have a constant, high-bandwidth RPC (remote procedure call) connection and have a shared security context. The site to which an Exchange Server belongs is determined when the Exchange Server software is installed and cannot be changed without reinstalling the software, resulting in the loss of any mailboxes on that server.

Let's take a closer look at the qualifications of servers in the same site. They must have a constant, high-bandwidth RPC connection. To clarify the adjectives in that sentence, "constant" means an uninterrupted connection (periodic dial-up connections don't qualify). The servers have to be "high bandwidth," which Microsoft defines as Exchange-dedicated 128 Kbps (Bonded ISDN) or faster. "RPC" means that the servers have to use a common network protocol that supports RPC; this requirement includes NetBEUI, IPX/SPX, and TCP/IP but does not include protocols such as DLC.

In addition, the servers have to share a security context. That means that one user account, the Exchange service account, has to be a valid account in the local domain of all Exchange Servers in the same site. In other words, either all the servers have to exist in the same Windows NT domain, or the service account has to be in a domain trusted by all the domains the Exchange Servers are in. Suppose that there is a domain called ACCOUNT, a domain called MAIL, and another domain called MAIL2; MAIL and MAIL2 trust the ACCOUNT domain. In this example, the service account must exist in the ACCOUNT domain in order to have Exchange Servers in the same site that are in both the MAIL and MAIL2 domains (see Figure 7.1).

Figure 7.1.

The trust relation-ships that must exist between domains to maintain an intra-site connection.

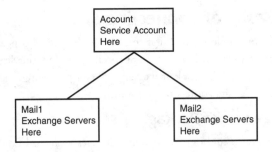

Note

It is probably best to place all the Windows NT Servers that will be hosting Exchange Server into the same domain, and to make that domain trust the central account domain. If there is a security breach with Exchange, the rest of the network will remain protected because of the trust relationship. This arrangement also makes the addition of new Exchange Servers easier because they will all be the same.

Sites play an important role in the use of bandwidth. The servers in the same site all communicate changes to each other as they happen. Servers within the same site can use a lot of bandwidth and communicate to each other using RPCs, which are server-to-server connections that allow for efficient data transfer. When sites have to communicate, they must use a site connector. Without a site connector, there is no way for one site to communicate with another.

Note

The phrase *site connector* is used two different ways. A "site connector" (all lowercase letters) is used to connect two sites together so that they can transfer mail. A "Site Connector" (initial caps) is a type of site connector.

There are many different ways to connect sites together—the site connector is just one of them. Also, keep in mind that directory information does not pass through a site connector unless the directory replication connector has also been set up. First, the site connector must be set up, then the directory replication connector can be set up. Adding a site to an organization does not propagate any user information between the sites, it simply provides an address for such propagation to occur.

• Directory replication is covered in Day 8, "Message Routing and Management."

7

7.1.2. Basics of Connecting Sites

In the following sections, we'll first consider some general concepts of how all the site connectors work; then we'll look at specifics on how the Site Connector is created and configured. We'll look at Exchange Server packaging, the function of a site connector, and at site addressing and routing.

Exchange Server Packaging

Exchange Server is sold in two different packages: Standard Edition and Enterprise Edition. The Enterprise Edition comes with the X.400 Connector and the Site Connector; the Standard Edition does not have these connectors. If it is necessary to install either of the two missing connectors on a server that was installed with Standard Edition, you can purchase the connectors separately.

The Function of the Site Connector

There must be at least one site connector between two sites that have to communicate. That doesn't mean that every site has to have a site connector to all other sites in the organization, however. For example, if there are three sites called A, B, and C, you can set up site connectors between all three sites, or just from A to B and from B to C. Messages that have to flow from A to C flow through site B. The System Attendant service is responsible for generating the routing table used to determine how to get mail from the local site to all other sites. To create the routing table, Exchange Server allows different "costs" to be associated with different connectors. To find a path from one site to another, the System Attendant adds the total cost of each possible path from the current site to the destination, and then chooses the path with the lowest cost. The Message Transfer Agent (MTA) does not perform load balance across connections; it always chooses the lowest-cost connection.

All the site connectors support the concept of a "bridgehead" server. A bridgehead server serves as the endpoint for communication between two sites (just as a bridgehead on a physical bridge is the point at which the bridge touches land on either side of a river). A bridgehead server is configured in each site, and that server is the only server to which the other end of the connector will send mail. Suppose that we have a site called ALPHA, with servers SRVA, SRVB, and SRVC; we have another site called NUMERIC, with servers SRV1, SRV2, and SRV3. If no bridgehead server exists and a mailbox on server SRVC has to send mail to a mailbox on server SRV3, SRVC's MTA opens an RPC connection with SRV3's MTA, and the message is transferred. Figure 7.2 shows the ALPHA/NUMERIC site combination with a bridgehead server; Figure 7.3 shows the ALPHA/NUMERIC site combination without a bridgehead.

Figure 7.2.

The intersite message flow between two sites ALPHA and NUMERIC, using servers SRV3 and SRVC as bridgehead servers.

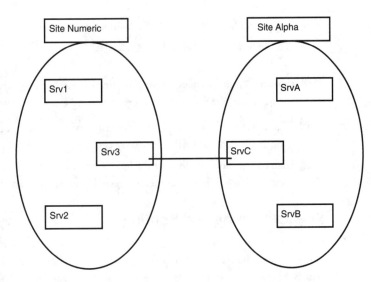

Figure 7.3.

The intersite message flow between two sites ALPHA and NUMERIC, without a bridgehead server.

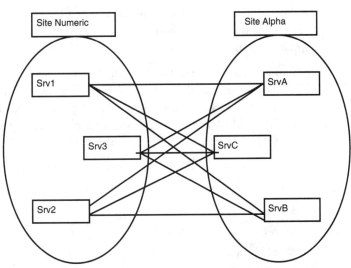

If SRV1 and SRVA are used as bridgehead servers, however, the following occurs when a mailbox on server SRVC has to send mail to a mailbox on server SRV3:

1. SRVC's MTA opens an RPC connection with SRVA.

2. SRVA receives the message.

3. SRVA's MTA opens up an RPC connection with SRV1.

7

4. SRV1's MTA opens up an RPC connection with SRV3.

5. The message is transferred to SRV3.

Under normal circumstances, there is no need to use a bridgehead server when implementing the Site Connector. However, there are some exceptions:

- There is restricted access between the two sites, such as a router's Access Control List, which will allow only certain computers to talk to each other.

- The connection between bridgehead servers is through a high-speed connection available only on one server in each site, such as an ISDN adapter.

Site Addressing and Routing

Every site in an Exchange hierarchy has a site address. The site address can be thought of as the basis for the addresses of all the other objects in the site. In other words, every object in the site has as part of its address, the address of the site. A site address is similar to the share name portion of a UNC name. The site address identifies what part of the organization the object is part of, but does not identify a specific object.

Site addressing is used extensively by the System Attendant service and the MTA service. The System Attendant service configures the routing table for the organization on a scheduled basis. The routing table specifies which site addresses use which connectors. The MTA service uses this routing table to actually figure out where the messages go and then sends them according to the instructions in the routing table.

A site has a series of addresses, one for each type of connector it supports. By default, a site has the following addresses:

- X.400 address
- Microsoft Mail address
- SMTP address
- cc:Mail address

To configure site addressing, perform the following steps:

1. Start the Exchange Administrator tool.

2. Expand the site with the address that you want to adjust.

3. Select the Configuration container.

4. Choose the Site Addressing object and select Properties from the File menu.

5. The General Properties page is displayed (see Figure 7.4). Notice that on the General page, the Display Name of the Site Addressing object can be changed, although it is unclear why you would ever have to do so. More importantly, notice that you can choose the routing calculation server from the General page. The routing calculation server is the server to be used by the System Attendant service to calculate routes.

6. Click the Site Addressing tab to display the site addressing options. To change an address, double-click the address type to change, and change it.

7. Click the Routing Calculation Schedule tab to choose the schedule by which the routing table is calculated (see Figure 7.5).

8. Click the Routing tab of the Properties dialog box to view the routing table. This page shows which addresses will be routed at what cost, and what type of connector will be used.

Figure 7.4.

Choose the routing calculation server from the General page of the Site Addressing Properties dialog box.

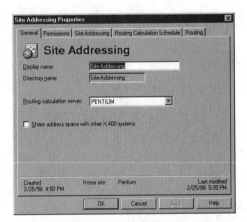

Figure 7.5.

From the Routing Calculation Schedule page, pick times for routing tables to be rescheduled.

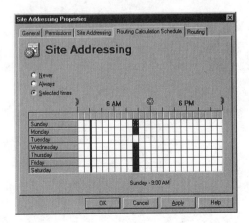

7

That's all there is to it. Most of the time, the only change you have to make to the Site Addressing Properties dialog box is the organization's SMTP name, because this name determines how incoming Internet mail is addressed. After configuring the site addressing, it's time to examine how sites are connected together with the Site Connector.

7.1.3. The Site Connector

The Site Connector works by creating an RPC connection between the sending server and the receiving server. An RPC connection requires that a Windows NT security context be established to validate that the incoming connection is from a trusted source. This increases the security of the site from incoming counterfeit messages. By default, the Site Connector will use the service account, but part of the Site Connector configuration is the Override page, which allows the administrator to enter the domain name and account name of an account with appropriate permissions in the target site. The account that is specified has to have service account rights on the MTA object in the target site. Essentially, the Override page allows two sites that don't necessarily trust each other to perform administrative tasks to still share information.

Configuring the Site Connector

To configure the Site Connector, perform the following steps:

1. Ensure that the Site Connector is installed. Start the Exchange Administrator and connect to the server on which you want to install the connector. Do this by choosing New Other from the File menu. If there is a Site Connector option available in the submenu, as shown in Figure 7.6, the Site Connector is installed on the server and you can skip to step 3.

Figure 7.6.

The File\New Other menu; notice that Site Connector is present in the menu.

2. Insert the Exchange Connector disk or Enterprise Edition CD-ROM into the drive and run Setup. If you are using the Enterprise Edition CD-ROM, choose Add/Remove Components and add the Site Connector.

3. From the Exchange Administrator program, choose File|New Other|Site Connector. This action displays a dialog box that asks for the name of a server in the target site. Type the name of an Exchange Server in the target site and click OK. The server attempts to create a connection with the server in the remote site.

4. On the General page of the Site Connector Properties dialog box, type the display name for the Site Connector. The default is usually good enough (it is the words `Site Connector` followed by the name of the site being connected to in parentheses).

5. Specify a messaging bridgehead server in the local site, if necessary.

6. The Target Servers page (see Figure 7.7) shows which servers in the target sites can have messages delivered directly to them from the local site. If a bridgehead architecture is being used, choose the bridgehead server in the target site; otherwise, choose all servers in the target site that will receive messages from the local site.

Figure 7.7.

The Target Servers page; because there is only one server in this site, it defaults to the Target Servers pane.

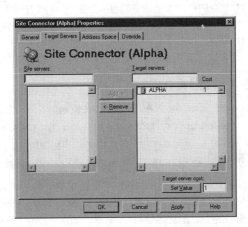

7. On the Override page, enter the username and password of a Windows NT account in the target site. This information is required only if the service account in the local site cannot be validated by the remote site. This is necessary if there is no trust relationship between the domain used by the local site and the domain used at the target site. Usually, the service account used at the remote site is put in on this page.

7

8. Choose OK to establish the connector.

9. Because the remote site must be available using RPC, and because there must be a security context (or the Site Connector couldn't be used), it is possible to create the Site Connector in the remote site at this time. After clicking OK to establish the connector, a dialog box appears asking, Should a site connector be created in the remote site 'SiteName'? If you click Yes, the remote site is set up for you. Otherwise, the remote site must be configured separately, using the preceding eight steps.

When to Use the Site Connector

The Site Connector should be used in the following situations:

- The endpoint of communications is another Exchange Server. The Site Connector works only from one Exchange Server to another.

- There is a constant, RPC-supporting network protocol available between the two servers.

- There is an NT account that can be used to handle message transfer on each side.

- There are no restrictions on when messages can be transferred. Time constraints cannot be placed on this connector, so it sends messages to the other sites all the time.

7.1.4. The X.400 Connector

The X.400 Connector uses the X.400 standard to move mail between sites. The X.400 standard specifies the different parts of a message and how the addresses will be formed. The X.400 Connector has two uses in Exchange Server: The X.400 Connector can be used as a site connector or it can be used to connect to outside X.400 systems.

Regardless of whether or not the X.400 Connector is being used in an organization, every entity in the organization has an X.400 address. This address is in this format:

```
c=US;a= ;p=Book;o=KC;s=KC-1;
```

In this syntax, the following elements are used:

Element	Definition
c=US;	Country code

a= ;	The administrative domain, which is usually a space but is never blank
p=Book;	The name of the organization
o=KC;	The name of the site
s=KC-1;	The name of the mailbox

Notice that all the elements of the address are separated by semicolons, and that no elements are allowed to be blank.

The X.400 standard is implemented in systems that need reliable and efficient delivery of electronic mail. An adaptation of X.400 is used by Microsoft Exchange Server to handle routing and addressing of messages, but it is seldom seen by users unless they specifically look at the addresses in the Address Book.

The X.400 Connector requires a bridgehead server to operate. All communications flow through the bridgehead servers. The X.400 Connector also requires the address and name of thedestination computer. For most uses, the address is the TCP/IP address of the destination. X.400 is also designed to run on a network protocol called TP4, which is part of the true OSI protocol stack. TP4 is very rarely used but is included on the Exchange Server CD-ROM. The X.400 Connector can only be configured to talk to other servers using TCP/IP or the TP4 protocols.

These restrictions notwithstanding, the X.400 Connector is the most flexible and configurable site connector. It allows you to set size limits between organizations as well as to set operation times. That means you can set up the connector to operate only at certain hours, such as late in the evening or early in the morning, reducing the impact on other network traffic. This arrangement provides the administrator with a very high level of control over the use of network bandwidth.

The X.400 Connector works by sending messages to the target site's bridgehead server. The validation is done by including an MTA password during configuration. The MTA password helps reduce the possibility that counterfeit mail is being sent to the connector.

Both the X.400 Connector and the Dynamic RAS Connector, described later in this chapter, use an object called a Remote MTA Transport Stack. The Remote MTA Transport Stack is used to encapsulate some of the communications settings. The stack must be set up before the connector is created.

7

Configuring the X.400 Connector

To configure the X.400 Connector, perform the following steps:

1. Ensure that the necessary network protocols are installed on the server. At least one of the following must be installed:

   - Windows NT TCP/IP
   - TP4/CLNP (the two parts of the TP4 OSI stack)
   - An Eicon X.25 adapter and software (this can be used by the X.400 Connector as a protocol stack)

2. Create the MTA Transport Stack. Choose File|New Other|MTA Transport Stack from the Exchange Administrator program.

3. Choose the server on which the stack is to be created and then choose the type of transport stack.

4. Type the name of the transport stack on the General page of the MTA Transport Stack Properties dialog box. Usually, the type of connection and name of the server are used to create the name (for example, TCP Omaha for a TCP/IP stack on a server called Omaha).

5. In the OSI Address Information section of the General page, type the T, S, and P selector information in the boxes provided (see Figure 7.8). This information is required only if multiple X.400 services use the same TCP/IP address.

Figure 7.8.

The X.400 MTA Transport Stack Properties dialog box with the T, S, and P selector information boxes.

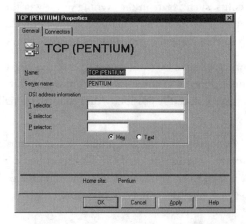

6. Click the Connectors page of the Properties dialog box and look at the list of all the connectors that currently use this protocol stack. Because this is a new

stack, the list is blank, but after the X.400 Connector is created, that connector will be listed in this box.

7. Click OK to create the MTA Transport Stack.

8. Now that you have created the transport stack, it's time to create the X.400 Connector. Choose File|New Other|X.400 Connector from the menu in the Exchange Administrator program.

9. A dialog box appears, asking for the name of a Transport Stack to use. Choose the transport stack you just created and click OK.

10. The X.400 Connector Properties dialog box appears. On the General page, enter the name of the connector; in the Remote MTA Name section, fill in the information for the server to which you will be connecting. For example, if Omaha X400 is the entry in the local server's Display Name field, and you are building the Kansas City side of the connection, the Kansas City connector would have Omaha X400 in the Remote MTA Name field. The Omaha X400 connector would have Kansas City's name in its Remote MTA Name field.

11. On the Schedule page, configure the times at which the connector can transfer messages. There are four selections:

   - **Remote Initiated.** The Remote Initiated selection means the connector will not send mail out until an MTA contacts it asking for mail.

   - **Never.** The Never selection disables the capability of this connector to send messages.

   - **Always.** The Always selection means the connector sends mail out as it arrives.

   - **Selected Times.** The Selected Times selection means the server will initiate connections when selected on the grid.

12. On the Stack page, enter the name of the remote server or a TCP/IP address of the server. This is how the connection to the remote MTA is established. Usually, the Remote Host Name option is selected and the name of the server is entered in the Address field. Otherwise, you can select the IP Address field, and the Address field would contain an IP address. If the remote site specified any OSI address information, enter that information here.

13. On the Connected Sites page, click New and then enter the name of the organization and site to which this connector is being used to connect.

14. On the Delivery Restrictions page, set up permissions for which class of users is allowed to send messages using this connector. If you enter user names in the Accept Messages From box, only users listed in the box can use this

7

connector. If you enter user names in the Reject Messages From box, all messages that originate from the given list of users will be rejected.

15. If you are using a third-party X.400 provider, you may have to adjust options on the Advanced page of the Properties dialog box (see Figure 7.9) to match their settings.

Figure 7.9.

The Advanced page in the Properties dialog box for the X.400 connector.

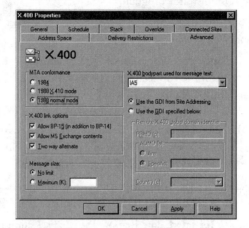

16. Click OK to create the connector.

You must create the connector in the destination site as well. Use the Exchange Administrator tool to connect to the destination site and follow steps 1 through 15 to complete the connection.

When to Use the X.400 Connector

The X.400 Connector should be used in the following situations:

■ You are connecting to a foreign X.400 mail system.

■ It is necessary to transfer messages during administrator-specified time intervals.

■ You can use either TCP/IP or TP4 to connect the two sites.

■ It is desirable to use a password for an MTA instead of allowing an administrator at the other site to know an NT account in your domain.

Both the Site Connector and the X.400 Connector work very well when there is an existing LAN or WAN connection between two sites. The following section looks at the Dynamic RAS Connector, which can be used when there is no existing connection between sites.

7.1.5. The Dynamic RAS Connector

The Dynamic RAS Connector is used to connect two Exchange Servers using Remote Access Service (RAS), which is part of Windows NT. The Dynamic RAS Connector allows the transmission of messages to another site over a telephone line. The Dynamic RAS Connector requires that RAS be installed on both servers (one in each site), which in turn requires a modem at each site. Use the Dynamic RAS Connector as a last-ditch effort if nothing else is logistically possible to connect to a remote site.

Configuring the Dynamic RAS Connector

To configure the Dynamic RAS Connector, perform the following steps:

1. Ensure that RAS is installed on both Windows NT Servers to be used. (Follow the instructions in the Windows NT Help file for more information.) Also ensure that there is a phone book entry on the server that will enable the server to call the remote site.

2. Create an MTA Transport Stack on the server with RAS installed. Do this by starting the Exchange Administrator program, connecting to that server, and choosing File|New Other|MTA Transport Stack. Choose RAS MTA Transport Stack and then choose the server on which RAS is installed. Finally, click OK (see Figure 7.10).

Figure 7.10.

From the Transport Stack dialog box, choose the server and the transport stack to use and click OK to create the transport stack.

3. On the General page of the transport stack Properties dialog box, specify a name and a callback number for the transport stack. A good example of a name is RAS ON OMAHA. The callback number is optional; it is the phone number of the modem on the server. It is used if the remote server has dialback turned on.

4. Click OK to create the transport stack.

5. Choose File|New Other|Dynamic RAS Connector.

7

6. On the General page, type the display name for the server. The display name should be something like RAS Connector on Omaha. In the Remote Server Name box, type the name of the server at the remote site that will be answering the modem. Choose the MTA Transport Stack and then choose the phone book entry (see Figure 7.11). You may want to place a size limit on the messages traveling through this connector because the RAS link is very slow—one user sending a huge PowerPoint presentation can stop mail delivery for a long time.

Figure 7.11.

The General page contains a Message Size box, which is very important for the Dynamic RAS Connector because of its low bandwidth constraints.

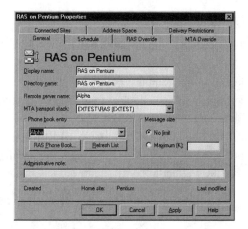

7. On the Schedule page, specify when the connector will be used.
8. You can use the RAS Override page if the service account in the local site is not the same as the service account in the remote site. Specify the username, password, and domain of the service account in the remote site.
9. Click OK to create the connector.

The connector must also be created at the remote site using the preceding nine steps. Simply connect to a server in the remote site with the Exchange Administrator tool and follow the same steps.

When to Use the Dynamic RAS Connector

The Dynamic RAS Connector should be used only if there is no other way to connect two sites. Remember that the transmission media used with the Dynamic RAS Connector is probably a 28.8 Kbps modem—if it is really fancy, the connector may use a 128 Kbps ISDN line—neither of which provides enough bandwidth to move large volumes of message traffic.

7.2. Connecting Exchange Server to Other Mail Systems

Microsoft Exchange Server can connect to other mail systems to enhance its value as a communications system. Currently, Exchange supports message transfer to the following systems:

- The Internet
- X.400 mail systems
- Microsoft Mail
- cc:Mail
- Lotus Notes
- OfficeVision/VM
- SNADS

7.2.1. Connecting Exchange Server to the Internet

Probably the most popular external connection used by Microsoft Exchange Server is the Internet Mail Connector.

• Day 9, "Internet Connectivity Strategies," contains an entire lesson dedicated to connecting Exchange Server to the Internet.

7.2.2. Connecting Exchange Server to X.400 Mail Systems

You can use the X.400 Connector to connect Exchange Server to outside X.400 mail systems. You must collect a lot of details for the connection to be reliable. Usually, the data-gathering process involves acquiring information on the setup of the foreign mail system, including the following:

- The remote MTA name and address information
- The address space
- The options on the Advanced page of the Properties dialog box, including body-part mapping, X.400 version, and message timing

The *remote MTA name* is the name of the MTA service running on the foreign system. Other required information is the TCP/IP or TP4 address for the server, including the T, S, and P selectors.

7

The *address space* information specifies to Exchange Server which addresses are handled by the connector. The address space must specify all the X.400 addresses that should go through that system. All or part of the address from the top down are specified. For example, if the Exchange Server is communicating to an X.400 system in another department, the system may have an address like this:

```
c=US;a= ;p=BigCompany;o=Engineering;
```

Placing that information in the Address Space box allows all messages with that address to go through, including messages to addresses such as this one (in which UserName can be any user at that server):

```
c=US;a= ;p=BigCompany;o=Engineering;s=UserName
```

The Advanced page on the X.400 configuration contains many options that manage how the X.400 Connector communicates with other X.400 systems on the network. Here are some of the options of the Advanced page with which you should be concerned:

- **MTA Conformance:** The X.400 Connector can use the 1984 and 1988 X.400 standards, or the 1988 X.410 standard for communication. It will probably be necessary to consult with the vendor of the other mail system to determine which standard that system adheres to.

- **Body Part:** In X.400 parlance, a message is made up of *body parts*. There are several types of body parts, each containing different types of content, such as mail messages or binary files. Choose the body part that Exchange should consider the message text.

- **X.400 Link options:** The first option, Allow BP-15, determines which body part is used to transmit attachments to email messages. If this box is cleared, body part 14 is used. Use the Allow MS Exchange Contents checkbox to determine whether plain text messages are to be sent (box cleared) or rich text format is to be sent (box selected). The Two Way Alternate option specifies that when two X.400 MTAs connect, they will transfer messages by taking turns (instead of one server transferring all messages and then the other server transmitting all messages).

- **Message Size Limit:** This option allows you to set the maximum size of a message. This option is important because body parts are limited to 64K each. If a commercial X.400 service is being used, there is a charge per body part on each message sent.

After configuring these options to match the settings on the foreign system, test out the connection by building a custom recipient with a valid address in the foreign system and then sending messages to that recipient using the Microsoft Exchange client. Be sure to test the connection's capability to send and receive binary file attachments.

7.2.3. Connecting Exchange Server to Microsoft Mail

The Microsoft Mail Connector and the Schedule Plus Free/Busy Connector are very complex pieces of software that allow messages to be transferred from Exchange to a Microsoft Mail system or back. This software works by using a "shadow" post office on the Exchange Server that emulates a Microsoft Mail post office. The key thing to remember about this connector is that as far as Microsoft Mail is concerned, the entire Exchange organization is just another Microsoft Mail post office. The following sections first go over how Microsoft Mail works, then how the Microsoft Mail Connector works, and then how the Schedule Plus Free/Busy Connector works.

Microsoft Mail Post Offices and the Microsoft Mail MTA

Microsoft Mail has a much simpler hierarchy than Exchange does. The basic unit of Microsoft Mail is the post office. A *post office* is nothing more than a collection of files in a standard directory structure. There is no active service that moves mail inside a post office. When users of Microsoft Mail send a message, theyare actually writing files on a file server in the directory structure that the recipient then reads as mail. All the brains of sending and receiving messages resides on the users' computers in the Microsoft Mail client software.

A Microsoft Mail post office can realistically hold about 200 users before problems with file concurrency start to arise. At that point, it becomes necessary to build another Microsoft Mail post office and connect it back to the first Microsoft Mail post office. This is done using a Microsoft Mail Message Transfer Agent (MTA). The MTA, in most cases, is a program called EXTERNAL.EXE that simply polls file structures for messages that are bound for another Microsoft Mail post office and then copies the messages to the destination Microsoft Mail post office. MTA requires a dedicated computer that simply runs the EXTERNAL.EXE program to move messages around. It is not uncommon to have a cubicle or a nook in every computer room that has several small computers with old monitors sitting in a corner, running EXTERNAL.EXE, and transferring mail. This arrangement makes for a very difficult to configure but relatively solid electronic mail system.

7

How the Microsoft Mail Connector Works

The Microsoft Mail Connector consists of two services in Microsoft Exchange and the shadow post office. The first service is called the Microsoft Mail Connector Interchange. The Interchange service moves mail that has to come into Exchange from the shadow post office into the Exchange Server. The Interchange service also takes mail that has to go from the Exchange Server to the Microsoft Mail system and moves it to the shadow post office.

The other service is the actual Microsoft Mail MTA service, which moves messages from the shadow post office to other Microsoft Mail post offices. The MTA service is essentially a high-powered, multitasking, multithreaded version of the EXTERNAL.EXE from the bad-old-days of Microsoft Mail. MTA is much easier to configure but serves the same function. The MS Mail MTA service simply polls each post office it knows about (this information is configured with the Exchange Administrator tool, explained in the following section) and moves mail around. Fortunately, one of the post offices that the MS Mail MTA service knows about is the shadow post office.

Note

With MTA, all this hoopla is required just to move messages around from Exchange to Microsoft Mail. There is a another service dedicated to replicating directory information (addresses) to Microsoft Mail, which is covered in Day 8, "Message Routing and Management."

Configuring the Microsoft Mail Connector

To configure the Microsoft Mail Connector, perform the following steps:

1. From the Exchange Administrator program, expand the Site and the Configuration containers. Choose the Connections container and then choose the MS Mail Connector. Open the Properties dialog box for the MS Mail Connector (Server), where *(Server)* is the name of the server on which you want to run the service.

2. Set up the administrator's mailbox. This is the mailbox to which diagnostic and troubleshooting messages will be sent. Click the Change button and choose the mailbox that the Exchange administrator uses.

3. Verify that the Primary Language for Clients option is correct. Also verify that the Maximize MS Mail 3.x Compatibility option is turned on; this option allows OLE objects to be correctly viewed by MS Mail clients.

4. Select the Connections page, which defines the Microsoft Mail post offices with which the MS Mail MTA service should exchange messages (see Figure 7.12). The post office listed in the figure, BOOK/PENTIUM, is the shadow post office. Its name is derived from the organization name (Book) and the site name (Pentium).

Figure 7.12.

The Connections page of the MS Mail Connector Properties dialog box.

5. Click the Create button to add a Microsoft Mail post office. This action displays the dialog box shown in Figure 7.13. Click the Change button to choose the Microsoft Mail post office to which you want to connect. The Exchange Administrator program then connects to the Microsoft Mail post office and fills in the Network and Postoffice fields. For post offices that use dial-up connections, choose Async. This action changes the Connection Parameters frame to include Sign-On ID, Password, Network, Postoffice, and Phone Number options. If the Microsoft Mail post office is connected with an X.25 link, follow the same steps used for Async, but fill in an X.121 address instead of a phone number.

Figure 7.13.

From the Create Connection dialog box, click the Change button to enter a post office path.

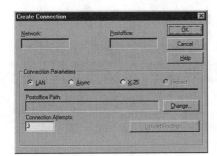

7

> **Note** The Async and X.25 options are for connections between the MS Mail MTA service and a copy of the EXTERNAL.EXE program. In addition to being able to poll network drives and copy messages, the EXTERNAL.EXE program can also dial up a copy of EXTERNAL.EXE running on another post office and exchange messages with it.

6. On the Connector MTAs tab, choose New to build a Connector MTA. A dialog box appears, asking for the post offices to be serviced by this connector and for the name of the Connector MTA. This is the actual service that will run under Windows NT. Multiple services can run on one Exchange Server, and each instance can communicate with multiple Microsoft Mail post offices. The Service Name dialog box is actually the name of the service as it will appear in Control Panel's Services application. Set the options on this page and click OK.

7. Also from the Connector MTAs page of the Properties dialog box, click the Edit button and select which Microsoft Mail post offices the current Connector MTA is to service. Each post office should be serviced by one Connector MTA.

8. Click OK to create the services and update the routing tables.

9. Go to Control Panel|Services and start the Microsoft Mail Connector Interchange service created by Exchange Setup; also start the Connector MTA service created in step 6.

10. Create a custom recipient for the Microsoft Mail post office and send mail to that recipient. Also make sure that binary attachments can be sent.

That completes the connection of Exchange to Microsoft Mail. Be sure that you allow between 10 and 20 minutes for messages to flow from a Microsoft Mail post office to an Exchange mailbox.

Sharing Schedule Plus Information

Schedule Plus is Microsoft's scheduling tool. One of its features is to allow a user to determine when other users are busy and schedule meetings around that information. Free and busy information is stored in Microsoft Mail as a file that can be opened and read by the clients. When a user makes an appointment, new information is written into the file to reflect the change.

When users in multiple post offices have to share free and busy information, a Microsoft Mail Schedule Plus Free/Busy program is run. Similar to the way EXTERNAL.EXE works, the Free/Busy program runs on a computer and polls the free/busy file on the server. If the program detects any changes to the file, it creates a message with the contents of the changes and sends it to the other post offices. If the program receives a message with free and busy information, it updates the file so that the clients in the local post office can see the information from users on other post offices.

On Exchange Server, the free and busy information is stored in a hidden public folder. This information is sent out to the Microsoft Mail post offices by the Microsoft Schedule Plus Free/Busy Connector. It also receives messages from Microsoft Mail post offices running the Microsoft Mail version of the Free/Busy Connector and puts the information into the public folder.

7.2.4. Connecting Exchange Server to Lotus cc:Mail

Lotus cc:Mail is a popular electronic mail package similar in design and capabilities to Microsoft Mail. Lotus cc:Mail has the same basic architecture as Microsoft Mail in that no active services run on the cc:Mail post office, and that there is an external program, called the cc:Mail Router, that moves messages between post offices. The connector for cc:Mail requires one of the following:

- Lotus cc:Mail Post Office Database Version 6, cc:Mail Import Version 5.15, and cc:Mail Export Version 5.14
- Lotus cc:Mail Post Office Database Version 8 and cc:Mail Import/Export Version 6.0

How the Connector for cc:Mail Works

Similar to the connector for MS Mail, the cc:Mail Connector relies on a service in the Exchange Server that copies data from the Exchange Information Store to a temporary holding area (similar to the shadow post office). In cc:Mail, this area is called the *Connector Store*. The Import/Export process on the cc:Mail message route copies messages to and from the store. Each Exchange site looks like a cc:Mail post office from the cc:Mail perspective.

One unique caveat to this process is that the import and export programs must be installed on the Microsoft Exchange Server computer that is running the connector service. These programs are used to write data into and read data from the cc:Mail Connector Store. The Import and Export programs must be in the system path on

7

the Exchange Server. These utilities must be purchased and licensed from Lotus (they are not part of the Exchange Server package). Also, note that there is a version of the Import and Export utilities that works with OS/2, but these versions are not compatible with the Exchange Server cc:Mail Connector.

Configuring the cc:Mail Connector

Follow these steps to configure the cc:Mail Connector:

1. Make sure that the Import/Export utilities are installed on the Exchange Server and that they are in the path.

2. From the Exchange Administrator program, expand the Site and the Configuration containers; then open the Properties dialog box for the cc:Mail Connector.

3. On the Post Office page of the Properties dialog box, select the administrator's mailbox (see Figure 7.14). This mailbox is the one that will receive messages from the system concerning failures and problems.

Figure 7.14.

The Post Office page. Notice that no other tab can be selected until a path is entered in the Path box, and that the version of Import/Export must be selected on this page.

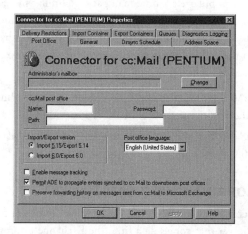

4. Use the Import Container and Export Containers pages to configure these containers. The Import Container contains all the addresses from Lotus cc:Mail; the Export Container contains all the addresses that cc:Mail should know about.

5. Configure the Address Space property page. Add the name of each post office that this connector should service.

6. Click Apply to create the connector.

7. From Control Panel|Services, start the cc:Mail Connector service.

8. From the Exchange Administrator, select the Import Connector page. Click the Run Dirsych Now button to start directory synchronization between cc:Mail and Exchange.

9. Send mail to a cc:Mail recipient from Exchange, and from cc:Mail to Exchange. Make sure that binary attachments are included in the mail.

The connection between cc:Mail and Exchange should now be working. Once again, be sure to allow enough time (say 10 to 20 minutes) between sending a message and receiving it over the connector.

7.2.5. Connecting Microsoft Exchange Server to Lotus Notes

Lotus Notes is a groupware package that includes the capability to send and receive electronic mail messages. The Exchange Server Connector for Lotus Notes allows messages to be transferred between Lotus Notes and Exchange. The connector also allows OLE objects to be transferred between Lotus Notes and Exchange. Because there is a lot of OLE activity on the Exchange Server running the Lotus Notes Connector, it is advised that the Exchange Server not host any user mailboxes; however, you can use the same server for other connections, such as site connections or Internet connections.

The Lotus Notes Connector requires that the Lotus Notes client software be installed on the Exchange Server computer. The client software should be Version 4.52. The client should be able to connect to a server—either a Lotus Notes server Version 3 or 4 or a Domino server Version 4.5. If the server is going to host user accounts in addition to this connector, the server should have at least 64M of RAM. If there are to be no usermailboxes on the server, a standard 32M of RAM is acceptable.

Normally, the service runs on a single computer in the Exchange enterprise. To get messages from all Exchange Servers to Lotus Notes, you have to install the Lotus Notes Email Address generator. At this time, the connector will not run on Digital Alpha hardware, so be sure that the connector is installed on a server with Intel processors.

Configuring the Lotus Notes Connector

The Connector Setup program runs in several phases. First, the Notes Connector mailbox is created on the Notes server. Then the Notes client is installed. The Lotus

7

Notes Connector software is then installed, and then the Notes server is configured. After that, the directory objects for the connector are added, the connector is configured, and you are done.

To configure the connector for Lotus Notes, perform the following steps:

1. Using the Lotus Notes Administrator program, create a user account. Make sure that the user account is not included in the Address Book and make sure that the user account has a blank password.

2. Install the Lotus Notes client software on the Exchange Server. Use the Standard Installation option.

3. Install the Lotus Notes Connector from the Exchange Server CD-ROM. Make sure that all other applications are closed. If SQL Server is running on the Exchange Server computer, close it. Choose Server Setup and then select Install the Connector for Lotus Notes.

4. At the prompt, `Generate e-mail addresses for existing Microsoft Exchange users`, click Yes. This action ensures that all current users have Lotus Notes addresses.

5. Now configure the Lotus Notes server. A NotesScript application is used to configure the Lotus Notes server so that it will queue up messages for Exchange. The user account that runs this script must have full control of the Address Book and the router's mailbox—in addition to the capability to create new databases and access into all existing databases. Choose Start|Programs| Microsoft Exchange Connectivity|Notes Configuration Utility to start the script.

6. When prompted, type the User ID for the user who will configure the Lotus Notes server.

7. On the Configuration page, set the following options:

   ■ The *Notes bridgehead server* is the Notes server the connector will use. The *Exchange side of the bridgehead* is the server on which the Notes client is installed.

   ■ The *connector's Notes user name* is the user account set up in step 1.

   ■ Selecting the Allow Connector to Be Administrator option ensures that the connector has all the rights it should have. Make sure this checkbox stays selected.

   ■ Set the path for the `Notes.INI` file to the location on the local system (the Exchange Server) where the `Notes.INI` file can be found.

- The *foreign domain name* for Exchange is the name the Exchange organization is known by. This is the name the Notes users see in the Address Book for the Exchange mailboxes. Usually, leave this option set to `Exchange`, the default.

- The *connector mail filename* is the name of the file where the connector will store mail that is in transit. Leave this filename set to `Exchange.BOX`.

- The Source Address Book option specifies which address book will be exported to Exchange. The Target Address Book option specifies which address book will receive all the addresses from Exchange. Set both of these options to `Names.NSF`, the default address book, to simplify directory synchronization.

8. Run the script. The connector is set up properly if the following conditions are true:

   - The connector account is listed in the Access Control List for the server router's mailbox with depositor access. This arrangement allows the connector to communicate with the Lotus Notes server.

   - The connectoraccount has access to the address books.

   - The `Exchange.BOX` and `Exchange.BAD` files have been created on the Notes server.

   - There is an entry in the address book for the Exchange network.

9. Configure the Connector for Lotus Notes by running Start|Programs| Exchange Connectivity|Exchange Connectivity Setup. Choose Configure Lotus Notes Connector.

10. Verify that the Server box contains the name of the Lotus Notes server to which Exchange should connect.

11. Verify that the path to `Notes.INI` is correct.

12. Verify that the Notes mailbox is `Exchange.BOX`.

13. In the Poll Delay box, keep the default of 15 minutes.

14. Click Next.

15. Click OK to verify that all the options were set.

16. Choose Exit Setup and then click Next to get out of the Connectivity Setup program.

17. From the Exchange Administrator program, choose the Site container, then select Configuration, and then select Connections.

7

18. Choose the Lotus Notes Connector.

19. On the Export Containers page of the Properties dialog box, select the recipient containers to be exported to Notes. On the Import Containers page, select the containers that will contain addresses imported from Notes.

20. If it is necessary to propagate distribution lists to or from the Notes server, select the Advanced page and select the Propagate Distribution Lists checkbox.

21. Click OK.

22. Start the connector from Control Panel|Services.

Test the connector fromboth sides and make sure that binary attachments can get through.

> Any of the connectors that have to be installed after Exchange Server is installed (Lotus Notes, OfficeVision/VM, or SNADS) must have their address proxy DLLs installed in the other sites. Do this by running the connector setup on one server in each site, and choosing to install the address proxy files.

7.2.6. Connecting Exchange Server to OfficeVision/VM

The Exchange Server connector for OfficeVision/VM provides transparent delivery between Exchange Server the and OfficeVision/VM. The connector resides on a computer running Microsoft's SNA Server and communicates with the OfficeVision mainframe using SNA. Alternatively, the computer may only have the Windows NT client for SNA Server installed.

For host-based connectors, we'll take a look at the system requirements for both sides and the concepts of how the connector works.

> So what is this PROFS thing, anyway, and how about OfficeVision/VM? These packages are available on IBM mainframes; they handle electronic mail, scheduling, and other office automation tasks such as word processing.

The system requirements on the OfficeVision side are as follows:

- IBM PROFS Version 2 Release 2 Modification Level 3 or IBM OfficeVision Release 2 Modification Level 0
- RSCS Version RSCS Version 2.3.0 or 3.1.0 at PUT level 9202 or later
- ACF/VTAM Version 3 for VM/SP or later
- A network connection to an SNA front-end processor running a version of ACF/VTAM that is compatible with ACF/VTAM Version 3, or a Token-Ring connection to a 3174 controller that is correctly configured

On the connector computer, you will need:

- One of the following:
    - SNA Server 3.0
    - SNA Server 2.11 with Service Pack 3
    - Windows NT Client for SNA Server if the computer is connected to an SNA Server with a LAN connection
- Exchange Server 5.5
- Necessary hardware for SNA Server, including a Token Ring, SDLC, or Ethernet controller attached to an ACF/VTAM that is properly configured (a Token Ring adapter can also be attached to a 3174 controller that is appropriately configured)

To configure the connector, first install and configure the necessary SNA components on the NT Server and on the mainframe. That means either install SNA Server on the Exchange Server, or install the SNA Server client software on the Exchange Server. Confirm that the connections are working using the Windows NT SNA client. Then install and configure the connector. The connector for PROFS does not install by default; it must be installed from the CD-ROM, similar to the way the Lotus Notes Connector is installed.

One of the more difficult jobs of any connector is the translation of binary file attachments. This is made even more difficult when working with PROFS because the characters are encoded using EBCDIC instead of ASCII. Attachments that are sent from PROFS to Exchange are sent as follows:

- All normal messages are translated into Microsoft Exchange messages.
- Files of type PC-ASCII are sent as an attachment to the message. The system appends a TXT extension to the file.

7

- Any files of type PC-BINARY are stored as binary attachments.
- Any RFT file is saved as an attachment with an extension RFT and can be viewed by a PC-based RFT file viewer.
- DCF final and draft documents are translated to ASCII text.
- CMS fixed-length or variable-length record files are saved as binary files. All record length information is preserved.
- Any other file type is saved as a binary file.

For files being transmitted from PROFS/OV to Exchange, here's how the conversion happens:

- Message bodies are converted to EBCDIC and will have word-wrap applied so that they are readable on the host system.
- ASCII files sent as attachments are translated to EBCDIC.
- Binary files, such as embedded OLE objects, are translated to variable-length record files. When they arrive on the host system, the files are checked for an RFT header; if they have an RFT header, they are converted to RFT.
- Any softcopy file is translated as a binary file.
- Any CMS file that has the appropriate CMS header is translated into a variable-length or fixed-length CMS file.

As is true with the Lotus Notes Connector, the address proxy DLL files are needed on all servers that have to send mail to the PROFS/OV system. This arrangement allows the addresses to be accepted by the Exchange Server.

7.2.7. Connecting Exchange Server to SNADS

IBM's SNADS system is usedto transfer messages between a variety of packages. SNADS is a set of protocols used to interchange messages. The Exchange Server-to-SNADS gateway can connect to a variety of SNADS-compliant systems, such as the following:

- IBM OfficeVision/MVS
- IBM OfficeVision/400
- IBM JustMail/400
- ICOM OfficePath
- Fischer International EMC2 TAO
- Verimation Memo

- Soft-Switch Central and LMS
- NB Systems TOSS
- Software AG Connect

The configuration process is similar to that of the PROFS/OV gateway. The Exchange Server running the connector to SNADS must have either SNA Server installed (the same version requirements are in effect as for the PROFS/OV gateway) or the Windows NT SNA Server client. The configuration steps are the same. The host system must be configured first, then the SNA Server, and then the host SNADS system. Finally, the Connector is installed and configured.

Messages from SNADS to Exchange are translated as follows:

- EBCDIC attachments or note objects are converted to ASCII.
- RFT documents are sent as attachments and are not changed.
- FFT documents are sent as attachments and converted to ASCII.
- Any other types are sent as binary attachments and are not changed.

For documents going from Exchange to SNADS, the following translations occur:

- Any note is translated to EBCDIC.
- PC files are sent as binary attachments.
- Any PC file that contains RTF information is translated into FFT format.
- Any file with a TXT or ASC extension is converted to FFT format.
- All other files are not converted and are saved as PC binary files.

As with the other connectors, the address proxy DLLs must be added to all the downstream servers.

7.3. Optimizing Connections

Site connectors and connectors to foreign mail systems can be adversely impacted by a variety of conditions. The following sections explain how to monitor conditions present on connectors and cover methods you can use to alleviate performance shortfalls in connectors.

The first step in any performance tuning is to run the Microsoft Exchange Performance Optimizer. The Optimizer determines the correct number of threads for each service to run based on the number of users in the environment and the

7

role of the server. Two very key settings in the Optimizer are the number of users on the server and the server type. For the Number of Users on This Server option, specify the number of user mailboxes present on the local server. If there will be no users on the server, choose 1-25.

The next key setting is the Server Type. For this option, choose all the types that apply to this server—but don't choose types that won't apply. If this server is only going to host connectors and not users, choose Connectors. If the server is going to host users and connectors, choose the Private Folder, Connectors, and Multiserver options.

7.3.1. Monitoring Connector Performance

The key to monitoring performance on any system is to establish realistic baselines for acceptable performance. If it is necessary to send 1M files over an X.400 connection, and you have only a 128K connection between the source and the target, a realistic guideline is about 5 minutes for the file to be transmitted. If the connector has to go faster than that, either limit the message size or increase the available bandwidth on the connection.

Establish performance baselines for all connectors based on the available bandwidth on the connection and a nebulous figure called *acceptable latency*. Acceptable latency is how long you can wait for a message to leave your mailbox before it arrives at the destination. That figure depends on the users and how patient or impatient they are.

Monitoring available bandwidth is critical to monitoring connector performance. If there is not enough bandwidth to transmit messages, it is a waste of time to look for configuration problems on the server.

For the Microsoft Mail Connector, you can watch certain objects in Performance Monitor, including the number of messages and directory synchronizations performed per second. For the Microsoft Mail Connector, if the connector is not transferring messages fast enough, watch the MSExchangeMSMI and MSExchangePCMTA objects. Both objects have counters for Messages Received/hr and Messages Sent/hr. If these counters are low, consider putting message size limits in place or increasing bandwidth to the post offices. For the cc:Mail Connector, examine the Properties pages for the connector and view the message queues to see the message sizes being transferred.

7.3.2. Improving Connector Performance

The key to improving connector performance is to determine the factor that is limiting performance. The limiting factor is one of the following:

- Not enough available memory on the Exchange Server
- Not enough available processor time on the Exchange Server
- Not enough throughput to the disk subsystem on the Exchange Server
- Not enough available bandwidth on the network connection to the target site
- A problem with the server on the other side of the connection

To determine the limiting factor being experienced by the server, use Performance Manager; monitor the Memory/Pages per Second, the Processor/% Processor Time, and the Physical Disk/% Disk Time options. Remember that to monitor disk time, you must make sure that the DISKPERF command has been run on the server. If pages are consistently being written to disk, there is a memory problem. Occasional spikes happen on all servers; any constant level of paging, however, is detrimental to performance. If the % Processor Time or % Disk Time are constantly above 60 percent, add another processor.

Monitoring bandwidth is more difficult to do. The key is acquiring the correct hardware or software to do the job. If the connection between the Exchange Server and the target is only used by the Exchange Server (as is the case with a modem or ISDN connection), use the RAS counters on the Exchange Server to monitor the throughput. If the communication is occurring over a TCP/IP connection, monitor the bandwidth the Exchange Server is using with the Network Interface object in Performance Monitor (which is available only if the SNMP service is installed).

Keep in mind that all the queues are stored in the MTADATA directory. That means that all the messages waiting in queue are actually stored on disk. If access to the MTADATA directory is slow, the connector will take a little more time to read the messages from disk and transmit them.

Use these techniques to monitor the bandwidth being used by the Exchange Server. The bandwidth being used by the other computers on the network is also critical. If there is a 1 Mbps connection between two sites, and users are consuming .99 Mbps, there isn't much left for Exchange. Use a tool such as a Network General Sniffer or the Network Monitor tool included with Microsoft Systems Management Server (SMS). Because the Network Monitor that comes with Windows NT Server can only monitor traffic being transmitted to or from the server, it is necessary to use a

7

different package to perform this diagnostic. You can also use router software to monitor the usage of different connections.

Problems on the other side of the system can include server congestion or bandwidth problems on the other side of the connector. Sometimes, you can alleviate these problems by reducing the message size or by increasing the amount of available bandwidth (work with your ISP if it is an Internet connection).

7.3.3. Other Common Solutions to Performance Problems

The Lotus Notes, PROFS, and SNADS connectors both use client software to connect to another system. As a result, the processor time on these servers is at a premium. In most cases, it is a good idea to place these connectors on a server that has no user activity. This arrangement provides the connectors with more resources and also makes performance problems easier to spot. In addition, from a maintenance perspective, if there are no user mailboxes on the connector server, the users usually don't notice if that server has to go down for a reconfiguration.

For any connector that has a high-bandwidth connection to the target site, ensure that there is adequate space available on the drive with the MTADATA subdirectory and that the MTADATA subdirectory is on a disk with a fast access time and a lot of throughput. Because the MTADATA directory is used to hold the message queues, fast access to this directory is crucial to the performance of site connectors.

In most cases, the easiest way to increase connector throughput is to reduce the maximum message size to a manageable number. Start with 1M and work with that. If users complain too much, up the value; otherwise, close the gap until performance is at desired levels. Although limiting message size is sometimes not a popular decision with users, doing so increases throughput if the users insist on sending large files such as PowerPoint slides across the Internet.

Lab

This lab consists of review questions pertaining to this chapter and provides an opportunity to apply the knowledge you've gained in this chapter.

Questions

1. An administrator wants to connect two Exchange sites together. The sites have a constant 56K frame relay connection that uses TCP/IP. During business hours, the link is saturated with traffic from users running a database application, so the connector should only be active during off hours. Which site connector should the administrator use to connect the two sites?

   A. Site Connector

   B. Dynamic RAS Connector

   C. X.400 Connector

   D. Internet Mail Connector

2. An administrator wants to connect two Exchange sites together. The two sites are on the same LAN: a 100 Mbps Ethernet connection. Which site connector should the administrator use?

   A. Site Connector

   B. Dynamic RAS Connector

   C. X.400 Connector

   D. Internet Mail Connector

3. An administrator is using an Exchange Server to host public folders, an Internet Mail Connector, and a Site Connector. What options should be chosen in the Server Type box in the Performance Optimizer?

   A. POP3/IMAP/NNTP Only

   B. Public Store

   C. Connector/Directory Import

   D. Multiserver

7

4. During a performance monitoring session, the administrator notices that the Memory Pages per Second option is spiking, that processor time on the single-processor server is averaging 98percent, and that the % Disk Time value is at 50 percent. What is the best upgrade for the administrator to pursue?

    A. Add memory

    B. Add another processor

    C. Add a faster disk I/O card

    D. Add a faster network card

5. An administrator wants to install the SNADS connector on a server. The server is not running SNA Server, but does have a TCP/IP connection to an SNA Server. What is the minimum that must be installed on the Exchange Server in order to run the SNADS connector?

    A. SNA Server 3.0

    B. SNA Server 2.11 Service Pack 3

    C. The SNA Server client

    D. Attachmate Extra! client

6. After installing the connector for Lotus Notes, the administrator starts receiving complaints of very slow performance from users with mailboxes on that server. What can the administrator to do alleviate the problem with the least impact on the users?

    A. Move the users to a different server

    B. Add more memory to the server

    C. Increase the size of the page file on the server

    D. Move the connector to a different server

7. After correctly installing the X.400 Connector between two sites, the administrator cannot find the addresses for the users in the remote site on the server. What should the administrator do?

    A. Wait; the addresses will show up, but it can take up to 8 hours

    B. Create a directory replication connector

    C. Reconfigure the X.400 Connector to start directory replication

    D. From the File|New menu, create a new Dirsync Server object

8. An administrator wants to connect two sites together. Right now, there is no connection between any of the computers in either site. The remote site has 50 users. What is the best connector to use?

   A. Site Connector

   B. Internet Mail Connector

   C. X.400 Connector

   D. Dynamic RAS Connector

9. After successfully installing the PROFS/OV connector in one site, the administrator notices that although the site at which the connector is located can see the users on PROFS/OV, the rest of the sites in the organization cannot. Directory replication is working between all sites in the organization. What can the administrator do to alleviate this problem?

   A. Remove the connector and reinstall it

   B. Wait; it can take up to 3 days for the addresses to propagate through directory replication

   C. Install the address proxy files on one server in each site

   D. Remove the cc:Mail address type from the directory

10. The cc:Mail connector is being installed in a new site. Which components must be installed with it to enable communications between Exchange and cc:Mail?

   A. The Lotus cc:Mail Client for Windows NT

   B. The Lotus cc:Mail database must reside on the Exchange Server

   C. The Lotus cc:Mail Import and Export utilities must reside in a directory in the path on the Exchange Server

   D. The Connector for Lotus cc:Mail must be installed on the computer with the Lotus cc:Mail database

7

Exercises

Exercise 1: Using the Site Addressing Properties to Modify SMTP Addresses

 This exercise addresses the following Microsoft exam objective:
- Configure connectivity to a mail system other than Exchange Server

Part of how Exchange interoperates with other messaging systems is by managing its routing table. A key part of that process is manipulating the internal addresses that Exchange uses. Here's how to change the SMTP site address for all recipients in a site:

1. Start the Exchange Administrator tool.

2. Expand the site with which you want to work.

3. Click the Configuration object in the left window pane.

4. Double-click Site Addressing in the right window pane. This action brings up the Site Addressing Properties dialog box.

5. Select the Site Addressing page. Notice that you can enable or disable particular addresses by deselecting the checkboxes. For now, select SMTP and click the Edit button.

6. The SMTP Properties dialog box pops up. Change the address to @*<organi-zation>*.com, where *<organization>* is the name of the organization. This process should involve just removing the name of the site from the box.

7. Click OK. You return to the Site Addressing Properties dialog box.

8. Click OK on the Site Addressing Properties dialog box. A message box prompts you to update all recipients within the site to the new address. Click Yes to reset all the existing addresses in the site to the new standard you specified in step 6.

9. A message box pops up, telling you that the address change process has started. Click OK. The address changes start immediately. It may take a while for the changes to complete if you have a lot of recipients.

Exercise 2: Setting Up and Configuring the Dynamic RAS Connector

Note | This exercise addresses the following Microsoft exam objective:
■ Optimize foreign connections and site-to-site connections

1. Start the Exchange Administrator tool.

2. Choose File|New Other|MTA Transport Stack.

3. From the Server list, choose a server in the site that has RAS installed and click OK. The Properties dialog box for the new connector appears. Click OK to create the transport stack.

4. Choose File|New Other|Dynamic RAS Connector. The Properties dialog box for the new connection displays.

5. Type a name for the connector. The name should describe the connection, such as RAS Connection to Site B. This name must go in the Display Name and Directory Name fields on the General page.

6. In the Remote Server Name box, enter the name of the server to which you want to connect.

7. From the Phone Book Entry drop-down box, choose a phone book entry to dial. If you don't have a phone book entry on the server, you are guided through the creation of a phone book entry.

8. Also on the General page, make sure that you set the message size limit to a reasonable number. For Dynamic RAS connections running over normal phone lines, this value should be very low (about 300K or so), or mail messages may not transmit in a timely manner.

9. Select the Schedule page and choose when the RAS connection can be made. For this example, leave this option set to Always.

10. On the RAS Override page, enter the Windows NT account information to use to dial in to the remote server. Usually, the service account information is entered here.

11. On the Connected Sites page, click the New button and enter the name of the site to which you are connecting.

12. Click OK to create the Dynamic RAS connection.

7

Answers to Questions

1. **C**   Use the X.400 connector in this situation because it can be scheduled to queue up messages during the day and move the messages all at night, making the best use of the bandwidth available.

2. **A**   Use the Site Connector in this case because it is easiest to configure and provides the lowest message latency on the high-speed connection.

3. **B, C, D**   Choose all that apply. In this case, any option that says "only" shouldn't be chosen because the server is hosting a large variety of services.

4. **B**   If the processor time is that high, it's time to add another processor. Adding memory or a disk I/O card or a network card would probably only aggravate the problem by giving the processor more to do.

5. **C**   The SNA Server client is the minimum required. Installing SNA Server 3.0 will also work, but requires more steps.

6. **B**   Adding more memory to the servers has the least impact on the users. The best solution, however, is to move the users to another server.

7. **B**   Addresses are never moved without Directory Replication being installed. There is no automatic replication between sites.

8. **D**   With only 50 users, a Dynamic RAS connector can probably handle the load with the least expense.

9. **C**   Without the address proxy files, the other sites don't know how to deal with PROFS addresses, so it is important to install those proxy DLL files.

10. **C, D**   The only required components are the connector software and the import/export utilities. The NT client isn't required, and the database can reside anywhere on the network.

TEST DAY FAST FACTS

Here are a few fast facts about this chapter that you may want to know ahead of time. These facts provide great last-minute study material.

- Microsoft Exchange Server public folders are an efficient way of sharing and distributing information.

- Public folder affinity allows the administrator to set public folder access to different sites based on cost.

- Public folder replication allows administrators to create and maintain regularly updated copies of public folders across multiple servers.

- Directory replication between Microsoft Exchange Servers throughout an organization ensures that directory information is current and accurate.

- Directory synchronization provides a way to share directory information between Microsoft Exchange and other messaging systems.

- The Message Transfer Agent (MTA) component of Microsoft Exchange Server moves messages between servers using cost-based routing paths.

Day 8

Message Routing and Management

by Syed Hussain

Microsoft Exchange Server stores information in a variety of ways. This chapter first discusses the Server's Public Information Store and how to create and manage public folders within the Public Information Store. You'll also learn about directory replication and directory synchronization between Exchange and other email systems. Finally, this chapter shows you how to configure the Message Transfer Agent within a site and also between sites.

Objectives

This chapter addresses the following Microsoft exam objectives:

- Configure synchronization of directory information between Exchange Server and other mail systems
- Configure directory replication
- Configure the Message Transfer Agent within a site
- Configure the Message Transfer Agent among sites
- Configure message tracking
- Manage Public Information Stores

8.1. Overview of Public Folders

A *public folder* holds information that can be shared by a group of users. Public folders can contain different types of information, from simple messages to complex notes containing multimedia clips and custom forms. Information in a public folder is presented as follows:

- **Views**. The presentation of information in a public folder is specified by defining which columns of data are displayed and how data is grouped, sorted, and filtered. A view is a specific combination of these settings. Public folders can have predefined views, and users can create custom views.
- **Forms**. Forms define the format by which individual items in a public folder are viewed. Custom forms can be associated with items in a public folder.

8.1.1. Public Folder Setup

You use the Microsoft Exchange Client and Administrator programs to set up public folders.

Use the Administrator program to do the following:

- Set up the public folder hierarchy
- Set up public folder size limits, storage warnings, and age limits
- Set up access to public folders

Use the Client program to do the following:

- Create public folders
- Set public folder permissions
- Create rules and views

8.1.2. Public Folder Creation and Design

You can create and design public folders using the Microsoft Exchange Client. Once you have created a public folder, you can design its properties by setting permissions, rules, and views. The Administrator program allows you only to modify properties for existing folders.

Advanced Properties for a Public Folder

The Advanced property page of the public folder is used to provide a simple display name, set a trust level for directory synchronization, and determine whether the mailbox or public folder appears in the Address Book (see Figure 8.1).

Figure 8.1.

The Public Folder Advanced property page.

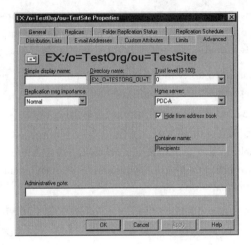

To get to the Advanced page of the public folder Properties dialog box, perform the following step:

1. From the Administrator window, choose Public Folders.
2. Double-click the public folder you want to configure.
3. Select the Advanced tab.

The following procedure uses the Advanced property page for the public folder to create a display name, set a trust level for the public folder, and select whether or not the public folder is displayed in the Address Book.

1. Select the Advanced tab of the public folder Properties dialog box.
2. In the Simple Display Name field, enter a name that will be used by systems that cannot read all the characters in the normal display name.

    If the name of the public folder contains non-ANSI characters, you can specify a simple display name to be used for the Address Book. The simple display name allows only those characters that can be read and displayed by any computer.

3. In the Trust Level field, select a trust level. The trust level determines whether a recipient is sent during directory synchronization. If the trust level exceeds the trust level you specified when you set up the directory synchronization requestor, the recipient will not be sent.

The next exercise uses the Limits tab of the public folders property page to set storage limits (optional) on public folders to control how much space is occupied in a server's Public Information Store.

1. In the Administrator window, highlight a public folder, right-click it, and select Properties from the pop-up menu.

2. Select the Limits tab from the Properties dialog box.

3. Select Use Information Store Defaults for the Information Store Storage Limits field to set the storage limit to be the default limit used by the Public Information Store. This default value is set in the General property page of the Public Information Store.

4. Select Issue Warning (K) and enter a number representing the largest amount of space this public folder can occupy before a warning message is sent.

When a public folder exceeds the storage limit, a warning message is sent to the public folder contacts. Configuring storage warnings allows administrators to delegate the task of monitoring public folder disk use to the public folder contacts.

8.1.3. Public Folder Replication

There are two parts to public folders:

- **Public folder hierarchy:** The structure of the public folders as they are displayed in the Microsoft Exchange Client or Administrator program.
- **Public folder content:** The information contained in the public folder.

During public folder replication, the hierarchy is replicated to every public folder server, but the content is replicated only to servers on which replicas have been set up by an administrator. When a user or administrator creates a public folder, its location in the hierarchy is replicated to every public folder server. If the new public folder is a top-level public folder, the contents of the new folder are on the user's public folder server (specified in the General property page of the user's Private Information Store). If the new public folder is not a top-level public folder, the contents are located on every public folder server on which the parent's contents reside.

Administering public folder replication involves the following tasks:

1. Deciding which public folder replicas each public folder server will have.
2. Setting replication schedules for public folders on a per-server or per-folder basis.
3. Setting up public folder affinities between sites.

A public folder can beconfigured to have replicas on multiple public folder servers. Each public folder server in the organization can have zero or one replica of each public folder. Each replica of a public folder is equivalent, that is, there is no "master" replica. Public folder replication is the process of keeping these replicas up to date. The principal advantage offered by public folder replication is to balance user load on servers. However, public folder replication can also serve as a way to back up public folder data.

Creating Public Folder Replicas

You can create replicas of public folders from any site in your organization. During replication, changes made to the contents in the replica are sent out to all other replicas of the public folder throughout the organization. Changes made to the folder properties or the public folder hierarchy are replicated to all public folder servers (even to servers that do not contain replicas of this folder).

When more thanone replica of a public folder exists, connections users make are distributed automatically across all replicas that exist in a site. If a replica of the public folder exists on the user's default public folder server, the first attempted connection is to that replica. If the replica cannot be connected, a connection to a different replica in that site is attempted. Each replica in the site is attempted in turn. If none can be connected to in the site, and if public folder affinities are set up, replicas in different sites are attempted.

You can use the Instances property page to create a replica of a public folder that exists on another server's Public Information Store (see Figure 8.2).

The following procedure creates and removes a replica of a public folder.

1. From the Public Information Store Properties dialog box, select the Instances tab.
2. From the Public Folders list box, select one of the public folders in your organization.

Figure 8.2.

The Public Information Store Instances property page.

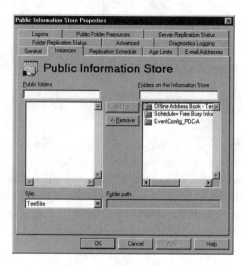

3. Click Add to create an instance of the public folder in the Public Information Store of the current server.

4. To remove an instance of a public folder, select a public folder from the Folders on this Information Store list box and click Remove.

The Exchange Server will now maintain the replica of the public folder according to the public folder replication schedule.

Viewing the Replication Status

You can use the Replication Status property pages for different views of replication status and to see whether the replicas are up to date.

To view the replication status of all servers on which a particular public folder is replicated, and to see whether the replicas are up to date, perform the following steps:

1. From the Administrator window, choose Public Folders.

2. Select the public folder you want to configure and then choose File|Properties.

3. Select the Folder Replication Status tab.

To view the replication status of all public folders on a specific server, and to see whether the replicas are up to date, perform the following steps:

8

1. From the Administrator window, choose Servers and then select a server.
2. Double-click Public Information Store.
3. Select the Folder Replication Status tab.

To view the replication status of all servers with which a specific server replicates public folders, and to see whether the replicas are up to date, perform the following steps:

1. From the Administrator window, choose Servers and then select a server.
2. Double-click Public Information Store.
3. Select the Folder Replication Status tab.

8.1.4. Public Folder Replication Schedule

You can set up a replication schedule to determine how often changes to public folders are replicated to other servers and sites. You can set the schedule for all public folders on a server or for a specific public folder.

To check the replication schedules for public folders, you must use the Public Folder Replication Schedule property page, as follows:

1. In the Administrator window, choose Public Folders.
2. Select the public folder you want to configure and then choose File|Properties.
3. Select the Replication Schedule tab (see Figure 8.3).

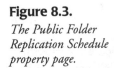

Figure 8.3.

The Public Folder Replication Schedule property page.

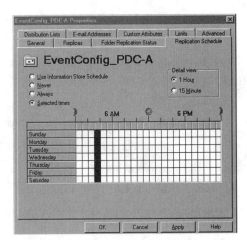

Setting the Replication Schedule for a Specific Public Folder

Use the Replication Schedule property page to determine when changes to the selected folder are distributed to replicas of the public folder on other servers.

If the folder contains time-critical information that is updated frequently, you can set up more frequent replication to ensure that all replicas remain current.

 Note It is important to note that a schedule set for a specific public folder overrides the schedule set for a server.

To set the replication schedule for a selected public folder, follow these steps:

1. Select the Replication Schedule tab.
2. In the Detail View area, select an appropriate view of the schedule grid.
3. Select one of the following options to set the times for public folder replication:

   ■ **Use Information Store Schedule.** The public folder uses the replication schedule set for the Public Information Store.

   ■ **Never.** Disables public folder replication for this public folder.

   ■ **Always.** Runs replication every 15 minutes.

   ■ **Selected Times**. Assigns specific replication times in the schedule grid.

Setting the Replication Schedule for All Public Folders on a Server

You can use the Replication Schedule property page to determine when changes to all public folders on a server are distributed to replicas of the public folder on other servers.

To set the replication schedule for all public folders on a server, follow these steps:

1. In the Administrator window, choose Servers and then select a server.
2. Double-click Public Information Store.
3. Select the Replication Schedule tab.
4. In the Detail View area, select a view of the schedule grid.

5. Select one of the following options to set the times for public folder replication:

   ■ **Use Information Store Schedule.** The public folder uses the replication schedule set for the Public Information Store.

   ■ **Never.** Disables public folder replication for this server.

   ■ **Always.** Runs replication at the interval specified in the Replicate Always Interval box in the Public Information Store property page.

   ■ **Selected Times.** Assigns specific replication times in the schedule grid.

8.1.5. Public Information Store Advanced Properties

You can use the Public Information Store Advanced property page to set replication message size and the frequency for Public Information Store replication.

To get to the Public Information Store Advanced property page, perform the following steps:

1. In the Administrator window, choose Servers and then select a server.

2. Double-click Public Information Store.

3. Select the Advanced tab (see Figure 8.4).

Figure 8.4.

The Public Information Store Advanced property page.

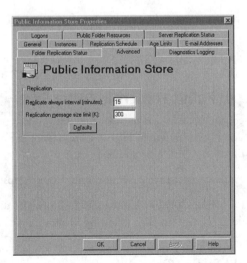

Setting the Frequency and Message Size for Public Information Store Replication

During replication, public folders communicate changes between replicas by sending messages. You can limit the size of these messages by setting a *replication message size* limit on the Public Information Store Advanced property page. This limit is useful if you are replicating across a connector or gateway that has a restriction on the size of messages that can flow through it. The *replication interval* is the frequency at which replication of the Public Information Store occurs; the default interval is 15 minutes.

8.1.6. Public Folder Affinity

Use the Information Store Site Configuration Properties Public Folder Affinity property page to configure Microsoft Exchange Server so that clients in your site can connect to public folders in other sites. This arrangement allows users to access information in other sites without replicating the public folders to their current site.

By associating a *cost* with each site, you can determine the order in which the client will attempt to connect to other sites. For example, if a client attempts to connect to a public folder that has multiple replicas in other sites, a connection will be made to the site with the lowest cost first. Typically, sites with higher bandwidth connections are set up with lower costs.

To access the InformationStore Site Configuration Properties Public Folder Affinity property page, perform the following steps:

1. In the Administrator window, choose Configuration.
2. Double-click Information Store Site Configuration.
3. Select the Public Folder Affinity tab (see Figure 8.5).

Connecting to Public Folders in Other Sites

Users can connect to public folders in other sites within your organization. This allows them to access information in different sites (assuming network connectivity) without replicating the public folders to their current site.

To connect to a public folder in another site, follow these steps:

1. In the Information Store Site Configuration Properties dialog box, select the Public Folder Affinity tab. The following fields are available:
   - **Sites**: A list of all sites in your organization.
   - **Public Folder Affinity:** A list of all sites to which connections can be established when a client attempts to connect to a public folder outside the site.

8

■ **Connected Site Cost:** A number that determines the preference between sites if a public folder replica is available in more than one site.

2. From the Sites field, select the site to which you want to connect and click Add.

Figure 8.5.

The Information Store Site Configuration Properties Public Folder Affinity property page.

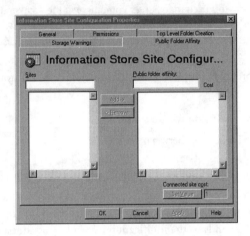

Changing the Connected Site Cost

The *connected site cost* determines the public folder to which your client tries to connect if there are multiple copies of that public folder.

To change the connected site cost, perform the following steps:

1. In the Information Store Site Configuration Properties dialog box, select the Public Folder Affinity tab.

2. Select the site for which you want to set up a cost.

3. In the Connected Site Cost box, enter the cost for the site and click Set Value.

   Remember: The lower the cost, the higher the preference for connecting to that particular site.

8.2. Configuring Directory Replication

The Microsoft Exchange Server directory provides detailed information about an organization's resources and recipients. One of the key features of Microsoft Exchange Server is its ability to share up-to-date directory information between Microsoft Exchange Server sites. Replicating directory information from one server in a site to other servers throughout the organization guarantees every user that his or her data is current and accurate. Within a site, directory replication is automatic.

> Before attempting to set up directory replication, verify that the Microsoft Exchange Server computers in the local and remote sites are installed and can exchange messages between sites.

Two different processes keep directory information current throughout an organization:

- Directory replication within a site
- Directory replication between sites

Within a site, directory replication is automatic and starts five minutes after a change is made to a directory object. The directory to which the change was made notifies all other directories, one directory at a time, with a Remote Procedure Call (RPC). Each directory responds to the notification by sending a request for updates. After receiving the updates, all directories are current.

A directory replication connector connects directories at different sites. To set up directory replication between sites, you must create and configure a directory replication connector. This connector describes a bidirectional replication link between two sites. A server at each site must be designated for requesting updated directory information from the other site and the specific times at which directory replication is to occur must be specified.

At the scheduled times, the directory in the local site sends a request for directory updates to the remote site. The remote directory packages any directory updates in a message and sends them back to the requesting site. After receipt of the updated messages, the directory at the local site is updated with current information, and replication to all other servers within the local site is initiated.

8.2.1. Directory Replication Between Sites on the Same Network

You can share directory information between two Microsoft Exchange Server sites on the same local area network. Before this can be configured, make sure that the following are true:

8

- A messaging connection exists between the two sites. This is important because all directory replication updates are sent using email. A Site Connector is often used to connect two sites on the same LAN.

- You know the name of the server in the remote site that will be in charge of processing and responding to requests for updated directory information. In a large organization, the Microsoft Exchange Server dedicated to this task is known as the *bridgehead server.*

- You have Administrator permissions for the sites where you are establishing the directory replication.

To set up directory replication between sites on the same LAN, you must do the following:

1. Create a directory replication connector in both sites.

2. For each site, indicate the bridgehead server that will be in charge of processing and responding to requests for updated directory information.

3. Establish a schedule to determine when requests for updated directory information are issued. Because processing and responding to directory updates places a load on the server, schedule a time when the server is likely to be least busy.

4. Specify the remote site where replication will take place.

Because both sites are on the same LAN, you can create and configure both directory replication connectors at the same time. This saves time and reduces the chance of configuration errors.

8.2.2. Directory Replication Between Sites on Different Networks

To share directory information between two sites that do not have network connectivity, make sure that the following are true:

- A messaging connection exists between the two sites so that replication messages can be exchanged. This connectivity can be established using an X.400 Connector or Internet Mail Connector.

- An entry for the remote site exists in the Connected Sites property page.

- You know the name of the bridgehead server in the remote site.

To set up directory replication between sites that do not have LAN connectivity, you must do the following:

1. Create a directory replication connector in both sites. Because the sites do not have LAN connectivity, you must do this individually on each site.

2. Indicate the server in both the local and remote sites that will be acting as the bridgehead server.

3. Establish a schedule for directory replication.

Setting Up Bridgehead Servers

A *bridgehead server* is a Microsoft Exchange Server computer that acts as the end-point of a messaging connection between two sites configured as an X.400 Connector. Changing a bridgehead server causes all replication information to be rewritten and re-replicated.

To set up the bridgehead servers, follow these steps:

1. Select the General tab of the Directory Replication Connector property page.

2. From the Local Bridgehead Server list box, choose the local server that will process incoming and outgoing requests for directory updates. The *default server* is the server to which you are currently logged on.

3. From the Remote Bridgehead Server list box, choose the server in the remote site from which the local bridgehead server will request and receive directory updates.

Inbound and Outbound Sites

Inbound sites are all sites from which the local site receives directory updates through the directory replication connector. *Outbound sites* are sites to which the local bridge-head server sends directory updates through the directory replication connector. Once a directory replication relationship between two sites is configured and a replication successfully completes for the first time, the lists of inbound and outbound sites in the Directory Replication Connector Sites property page are populated.

8.2.3. Setting the Directory Replication Schedule

The directory replication schedule determines when requests are sent from a local bridgehead server to a remote bridgehead server for directory updates. In situations where directory information in the remote site is updated often, you should schedule more frequent requests to ensure that the most current information is replicated. Doing so, however, increases the amount of message traffic between the two sites.

8

To set the directory replication schedule, perform the following steps:

1. From the Administrator window, choose Directory Replication.
2. Double-click the Directory Replication Connector option.
3. Select the Schedule tab.
4. Select Never, Always, or Selected Times to set times for directory replication.
5. From the Detail View area, select a view for the schedule grid.

8.2.4. Synchronizing Directories with Other Email Systems

Microsoft Exchange Server uses directory synchronization to share address information with other messaging systems. *Directory synchronization* is the process of exchanging address information between your Exchange organization and any system that uses the MS Mail directory synchronization protocol.

Microsoft Exchange Server can be configured to function in two roles:

- **Dirsync requestor.** The dirsync requestor periodically queries the Microsoft Exchange Server directory for changes to address information. When address entries are added, deleted, or modified, the directory synchronization agent sends (according to schedule) an update message to the MS Mail directory server post office. It also requests MS Mail address updates from the MS Mail directory server post office.

- **Dirsync server.** The dirsync server processes incoming update messages from one or more MS Mail directory requestors and incorporates the updates in the directory as custom addresses. It also sends updates on Microsoft Exchange Server recipient addresses in response to an update request from an MS Mail directory requestor. There can be only one directory synchronization server per site.

A Microsoft Exchange Server computer can be either a directory synchronization server or a directory synchronization requestor. It cannot be configured to function in both roles. Thus, a single Microsoft Exchange Server computer cannot participate in more than one directory synchronization process at the same time.

Installing Microsoft Exchange Server as a Dirsync Requestor

You can set up Microsoft Exchange Server as a dirsync requestor to one MS Mail (PC) directory synchronization server. The dirsync requestor functions similarly to an MS Mail directory requestor. Address updates are sent from the dirsync requestor to the MS Mail (PC) directory server. The MS Mail directory server compiles a master list of all changes since the last update to the global address list and sends it to the Microsoft Exchange Server dirsync requestor. The new entries are added to the Microsoft Exchange Server global address list.

To set up a Microsoft Exchange Server dirsync requestor to an MS Mail (PC) directory server, you must do the following:

- Define and configure a dirsync requestor.
- Configure the MS Mail (PC) directory synchronization server to recognize the new requestor.

Creating the Dirsync Requestor

The basic requirements for creating a dirsync requestor object include specifying a display name for the dirsync requestor object and choosing a recipient container from the Import Container property page.

1. From the Administrator window, choose Connections.
2. From the File menu, choose New Other, and then choose Dirsync Requestor.
3. Select the directory synchronization server from the list of MS Mail post offices.

Setting General Requestor Properties

When you configure the General property page for a dirsync requestor, you must specify a dirsync server mailbox for sending and receiving system messages. By default, a hidden mailbox on the dirsync server is chosen. Typically, you should not specify a different mailbox for processing dirsync messages.

1. In the Administrator window, choose Connections.
2. Double-click the dirsync requestor.

8

3. Select the General tab. The General property page presents the following options:

- **Name.** A unique name for this requestor. This name appears in the Connections container.
- **Append to Imported User's Display Name.** If selected, puts the requestor's name after each custom recipient created by the dirsync process.
- **Dirsync Address.** The hidden recipient mailbox on the MS Mail (PC) directory server. Directory syncronization messages are sent to this mailbox.
- **Address Types.** MS Mail (PC) addresses are sent and received by default. Select other address types that this requestor will receive and request. You can select foreign address types such as PROFS and SNADS.
- **Requestor Language.** The primary language in your MS Mail (PC) system. English is the default language.
- **Server.** The Microsoft Exchange Server in your site that will act as the dirsync requestor. The default is the server to which you are currently connected in the Administrator program.

Import Containers

Import containers are used to store imported addresses sent from the MS Mail directory server to the Microsoft Exchange dirsync requestor. Use the Import Container property page to specify which recipient container receives imported address information. You cannot select another directory import container once one has been specified. If you want to modify the import container, you must delete the existing requestor and configure a new one.

To make address information from more than one directory server available to Microsoft Exchange Server recipients without combining information between directory synchronization servers, you must create a separate container for each group of imported recipients.

Export Containers

Export containers are used to specify the Microsoft Exchange Server recipients that will be exported to the MS Mail directory server. Use the Export Containers property page to specify containers to use when exporting directory information. You can also assign a trust level for the connection so that only recipients with a trust level equal to or less than the connection will be exported.

Settings Properties

Use the Settings properties page to specify whether the Microsoft Exchange Server dirsync requestor will send address updates, receive address updates, or both from the MS Mail directory server. You can also use the Settings page to specify whether to send and receive address template information during directory synchronization.

Setting the Requestor Schedule

Use the Schedule property page to set the time when directory update messages are sent to the MS Mail directory synchronization server. The default is to send an update message at midnight. Messages received from the directory synchronization server are handled automatically as they are received by the dirsync requestor.

Dirsync Server Installation

You can configure a Microsoft Exchange Server acting as a dirsync server to update and distribute address information to remote dirsync requestors.

To set up adirsync server, perform the following steps:

1. Create and configure a dirsync server for the local Microsoft Exchange Server site.
2. Specify remote directory Exchange requestor objects.
3. Configure a requestor on each system that will use this server.

General Properties

To use the General tab to set dirsync server properties, perform the following steps:

1. In the Administrator, choose Connections.
2. Double-click the dirsync server.
3. Select the General tab.
4. In the Name field, enter a name for this directory synchronization server.
5. Choose Dirsync Administrator. Select the mailbox you want to receive directory synchronization messages.
6. Select Copy Administrator on Outgoing Messages to send an update message to each requestor. This option can be used as a troubleshooting tool.

7. Select Forward Incoming Dirsync Messages to Administrator to view each message from each requestor. This option can also be used as a valuable troubleshooting tool.

8. Under Server, select a Microsoft Exchange Server in your site that will act as a dirsync server.

9. Click OK to exit the General tab and complete the configuration.

8

Schedule Properties

The Schedule property page is used to specify when a Microsoft Exchange Server dirsync server sends address list updates to remote dirsync requestors. You should schedule your remote dirsync requestors to send local address list updates before your dirsync server's scheduled process time.

Installing a Remote Dirsync Requestor

Each requestor to a Microsoft Exchange Server dirsync server must be defined in the Microsoft Exchange Server directory as a dirsync requestor. To set up a remote dirsync requestor, you must do the following:

- Define a remote directory Exchange requestor object in the Microsoft Exchange Server directory.

- Specify which directory containers to use when importing and exporting address information from the remote dirsync requestor.

After you have defined Microsoft Exchange Server remote dirsync requestor objects on the dirsync server, you must configure the MS Mail directory synchronization requestor computers. These requestor computers can be MS Mail (PC), MS Mail (AppleTalk), or any foreign system that supports the MS Mail (PC) directory synchronization protocol.

Diagnostics Logging

You can use the Diagnostics Logging property page of the directory synchronization object to control how logging information for the dirsync server is written to the Windows NT Event log. You can also specify a logging level for the directory synchronization service.

8.3. The Message Transfer Agent

The Message Transfer Agent (MTA) delivers messages to their destinations by moving them from one server to another. Connector and gateway messages (except the Microsoft Mail Connector) are processed by the MTA for security and routing purposes. Queues for each connector and gateway are displayed along with other MTA queues in the Administrator program.

8.3.1. Configuring the MTA Within a Single Site

Within a single site, the MTA delivers messages to their destination by moving them from one server to another. The routing table for the MTA is rebuilt automatically once a day. You can also manually update the MTA routing table after a change has been made. Changes to address space information force a rebuild of the MTA routing table.

Rebuilding the Routing Table

When you make changes to message routing, the changes are incorporated into the routing table for the MTA. To manually update the routing table, perform the following steps:

1. From the Administrator window, choose a server.

2. Double-click Message Transfer Agent.

3. Select the General tab.

4. Choose Recalculate Routing.

The routing table is rebuilt on the selected server and is replicated to all other servers in the site. It can take several minutes for the new routing information to reach all servers in the site.

Diagnostics Logging for the MTA

The logs provided in the MTA are a valuable resource for troubleshooting message routing problems. You can view the Event log to see the status of the MTA and message transfers. You can also change the logging level to provide the desired level of logging by using the Diagnostics Logging property page. You can vary the logging level of the services independently (choose between a logging level of None or Maximum). Setting the level to None disables any logging; setting the level to Maximum provides the most amount of information for troubleshooting.

Test Tip

Setting the logging level to Maximum increases the overhead on the Exchange Server and may affect performance. Use maximum logging only when troubleshooting and remember to set it back to a level that does not adversely effect performance.

8

8.3.2. Configuring the MTA Between Multiple Sites

Each of the Microsoft Exchange Server connectors—such as the Site Connector, X.400 Connector, MS Mail Connector, and Internet Mail Connector—must have an MTA configured to route messages between sites. Configuring an MTA involves setting up and configuring an appropriate MTA transport stack.

Before you install a RAS MTA transport stack, the network hardware and software the MTA transport stack will use must be installed on the Microsoft Exchange Server. For communications over public telephone, X.25 PAD, or ISDN networks, one RAS transport stack can be installed on the Microsoft Exchange Server. That is, multiple connectors can be configured to use a single MTA transport stack.

MTA Transport Stack Installation for an X.400 Connector

Before you install the X.400 Connector, you must do the following:

1. Determine which type of MTA transport stack you will use to connect to the site or foreign system. The MTA transport stack can be X.25, TCP/IP, or TP4/CLNP.

2. Install the network transport protocols that will be used by the MTA transport stack and test the connection.

3. Obtain the address of the site or foreign system.

Multiple MTA transport stacks and X.400 Connectors can be installed on other servers in the same site to provide load balancing and fault-tolerant connections for the remote site.

Configuring the MTA for Connecting to MS Mail Post Offices

You must define and configure Microsoft Mail Connector (PC) MTAs for transferring messages between the connector and one or more MS Mail post offices. Each connector MTA defined in the Connector MTAs property page of the MS Mail Connector becomes a separate Windows NT service. The connector MTA can be started or stopped using the Windows NT Control Panel.

Connector MTAs can service MS Mail post offices for three connection configurations:

- LAN-only connections
- Asynchronous and LAN connections
- X.25 and LAN connections

Installing an MS Mail Connector MTA for LAN-Only Connections

To exchange messages between the MS Mail Connector and one or more MS Mail post offices, you must configure an MS Mail Connector MTA. To create a Microsoft Mail Connector MTA for LAN-connected post offices, complete the following steps:

1. Select the Connector MTAs tab from the MS Mail Connector property page.
2. Choose New to create a new connector MTA.
3. Enter the service name. This is the name that will be visible in the Control Panel.
4. Specify the logging options.
5. Specify the polling frequency.
6. Click the Options button to configure the connector MTA options. These options include setting the maximum LAN message size, closing the post office if the minimum disk space is below the specified space, and notifying MS Mail users about new mail immediately.

To set up service to LAN-connected MS Mail post offices, follow these steps:

1. Select the Connector MTAs tab on the MS Mail Connector property page.
2. From the Microsoft Mail Connector MTA services box, select a connector MTA.
3. Choose List.
4. From the Available LAN Post Offices list, select a post office.
5. Click Add to add the service to the post office.
6. Click OK to return to the Connector MTAs property page.

Configuring an MTA for an Asynchronous Connection

A connector MTA set up to provide asynchronous or X.25 message transfer can also service MS Mail post offices available over a LAN connection. To optimize performance, however, each instance of the connector MTA should be configured to service one primary type of connection (such as LAN, asynchronous, or X.25).

Before configuring an MTA service for an asynchronous connection, confirm that a modem is installed and functioning on the Microsoft Exchange Server computer and on the external MS Mail post office.

1. Select the Connector MTAs tab of the MS Mail Connector property page.
2. Click New to create a new connector MTA.
3. From the Connection Parameters list, select Async and LAN.
4. Click Options to define the communications port configured for asynchronous communication, the modem script provided by the MS Mail Connector, the modem timeout, and either two-way mail transfer or one-way mail transfer. If the MTA is configured for one-way mail transfer, you have the option of selecting whether the MTA is set to transfer incoming or outgoing mail only.

Configuring an MTA for an X.25 Connection

The X.25 adapter must be installed and configured on the Microsoft Exchange Server computer before you can set up an MTA instance to service an X.25 Connector.

1. Select the Connector MTAs tab.
2. Click New to create a new connector MTA.
3. From the Connection Parameters list, select X.25 and LAN.
4. Specify the X.121 Address, Port Number, and X.25 Listen User Data and X.25 Listen User Facilities as specified by your X.25 service provider.

With proper configuration of the MTA between sites, mail messages can be routed efficiently between sites.

8.4. Tracking Messages

The Track Message command automates the process of tracing a message through the network. Many daily tracking logs are searched for any events that may have been generated when the components of each server handled the message. The Track

Message command follows the message through the logs of all Microsoft Exchange Server computers on the same physical network.

8.4.1. Using Message Tracking

Tracking is a two-step process:

1. Finding and selecting the message you want to track in a Select Message to Track dialog box.
2. Tracking the message in the Message Tracking Center.

The Message Tracking Center includes an Advanced Search button that lets you search for a message by its message ID, for messages from or to gateways, or for messages involving a sender or recipient that does not appear in the global address list.

The first step in message tracking is to connect to a server to locate the message to be tracked. Select a server that has the sender or recipient of the message in its global address list. If the sender and recipient are only in your personal Address Book or are Microsoft Exchange Server components, connect to any server in the site. From the Tools menu in the Administrator window, choose Track Message. In the Connect to Server dialog box, type or select a server.

8.4.2. Finding a Message to Track

Messages are found by searching the logs on one server for messages by the sender or recipient. Once a message is found, the logs of all servers in the site are searched to follow the path of the message through the network.

Note
> Message Tracking must be enabled (select the Enable Message Tracking checkbox in both the Information Store Site Configuration Properties dialog box and the MTA Site Configuration Properties General tab) if message tracking logs are to be generated.

Exercise 2, "Tracking a Message" at the end of this chapter leads you through the process of tracking a message from the sender's server to the recipient's server.

Lab

8

This section consists of review questions that pertain to this chapter and provides an opportunity to apply the knowledge you acquired in the course of this chapter.

Questions

1. Which connector allows concurrent configuration of directory replication between two Microsoft Exchange Server sites?

   A. Site Connector

   B. Internet Mail Connector

   C. X.400 Connector

   D. Dynamic RAS Connector

2. Where can you specify storage limits on a per-folder basis for public folders?

   A. In the Public Information Store General Property page

   B. In the Public Folder Limits Property Page

   C. In the Public Information Store Public Folder Resources property page

   D. You cannot specify a storage limit on a per-folder basis

3. Where can you verify the replication status of a particular public folder?

   A. In the Server Replication Status property page of the Public Information Store

   B. In the Replication Schedule property page of the Public Information Store

   C. In the Folder Replication Status property page of the Public Information Store

   D. In the Age Limits property page of the Public Information Store

4. You assign public folder permissions using what?

   A. The Microsoft Exchange Server Administrator program

   B. The Microsoft Exchange Client

   C. Windows NT Server Manager

   D. The General property page of the public folder

5. To set up directory replication between sites on the same LAN, you must ___.

   A. Create a directory replication connector in the master site

   B. Create a directory replication connector in the slave site

   C. Create a replication connector in both sites

   D. Do nothing; directory replication is automatic between sites on the same LAN

6. Which of the following statements is true?

   A. Microsoft Exchange Server can only serve as a dirsync server.

   B. Microsoft Exchange Server can only serve as a dirsync requestor.

   C. Microsoft Exchange Server cannot serve as either a dirsync server or a dirsync requestor.

   D. Microsoft Exchange Server can serve as either a dirsync server or a dirsync requestor.

7. You set up the public folder size limits, storage warnings, and age limits using ___.

   A. Microsoft Exchange Client

   B. Microsoft Exchange Administrator

   C. Windows NT Server Manager

   D. Microsoft Outlook

8. Messages received from the directory synchronization server are handled automatically as they are received by the dirsync requestor.

   A. True

   B. False

9. You use the Public Folder Affinity property page to configure Microsoft Exchange clients in your site to ___.

   A. Access public folders in other sites.

   B. Access public folders in other mail systems.

   C. Access public folders on servers in your site.

   D. Replicate public folders to your site.

10. Which of the following protocols can you use for the X.400 Connector MTA transport stack?

   A. X.25

   B. TCP/IP

   C. TP4/CLNP

   D. All of the above

8

Exercises

Exercise 1: Configuring Directory Replication

 Note This exercise addresses the following Microsoft exam objective:
- Configure directory replication

In the following steps, we will configure directory replication between two Microsoft Exchange Server sites on different networks. This will enable you to share directory information between the two sites.

1. In the Exchange Administrator window, click the Configuration container and choose Directory Replication from the right pane.

2. From the File menu, choose New Other, and then choose Directory Replication Connector.

3. Select No, The Remote Site Is Not Available on This Network.

4. From the Remote Site Name field, select the name of the remote site.

5. In the Server in Remote Site field, type the name of the bridgehead server in the remote site. A replication bridgehead server processes requests from other bridgehead servers for updated directory information.

6. Choose OK to display the Directory Replication Connector property pages. Use these pages to complete the configuration process and create the directory replication connector.

Exercise 2: Tracking a Message

 Note This exercise addresses the following Microsoft exam objective:
- Configure message tracking

This exercise leads you through the process of tracking a message using the Track Message command within the Microsoft Exchange Server Administrator program.

1. Verify that message tracking is enabled: Double-click the Information Store Site Configuration object within the Configuration container and make sure that the Enable Message Tracking checkbox is selected.

8

2. Verify that the Enable Message Tracking checkbox is enabled in the MTA Site Configuration Properties General tab.

3. From the Tools menu in the Administrator window, choose Track Message.

4. In the Connect to Server dialog box, type or select a server.

5. In the Select Message to Track dialog box, click From and select the sender's name from the address list.

6. Click the Sent To button and select the recipient's name from the address list.

7. Click the Find Now button. The server searches the message tracking logs starting at the sender's server and following it through to the recipient's server. the server returns delivery information about messages that meet the search criteria.

Answers to Questions

1. **A**   When two Exchange Servers are connected with a Site Connector, Exchange allows concurrent configuration of directory replication between the two sites. This saves time and reduces the chance of configuration errors.

2. **B**   Any settings that affect a particular public folder must be specified in the property pages of that public folder.

3. **C**   The Replication Schedule page simply gives the schedule for replication and does not give the status of the replication.

4. **B**   Public folders can be created and managed by an owner from the Exchange Client software.

5. **C**   In a directory replication connector, both sites operate as equals; there is no "master" site.

6. **D**   Microsoft Exchange Server can serve as either a dirsync server or a dirsync requestor.

7. **B**   Management of public folder resources is done through the Exchange Administrator program. Content and access management of individual public folders can be done using the Exchange Client software.

8. **A**   The dirsync requestor automatically handles messages received from the dirsync server.

9. **A**   The Public Folder Affinity property page is used to configure Exchange clients in your site to access public folders in other sites. Public folder affinity allows the administrator to set the order in which connections to various sites are made when accessing public folders in other sites.

10. **D**   All X.25, TCP/IP, TP4/CLNP protocols can be used for an X.400 Connector MTA transport stack.

Day 9

Internet Connectivity Strategies

by Brad McGehee

As you probably know, in the past two years Microsoft has made great inroads in adding Internet connectivity to all its products. This is especially true for Exchange. Each new version of Exchange has become more and more Internet compatible because Microsoft has incorporated virtually every significant industry-standard Internet protocol in Exchange.

This chapter takes a look at how Exchange works with the Internet; it is a very important chapter for you to master. For the most part, this chapter assumes that you are familiar with the Internet and Internet terminology. If you are not familiar with the Internet, you may want to read up on the subject before attempting the certification exam. Just as this chapter makes some assumptions about your Internet knowledge, so does the certification exam.

In this chapter, you will specifically learn how to install and configure the Internet Mail Service as well as learn how to configure and use the many Internet protocols included with Exchange.

Objectives

This chapter addresses the following Microsoft exam objective:

■ Configure Internet protocols and services

9.1. The Internet Mail Service

One of the most important aspects of Exchange is its capability to send and receive messages over the Internet using the Simple Mail Transfer Protocol (SMTP). This capability is performed by the Internet Mail Service (also referred to as the Internet Mail Service Connector), which is integrated directly into Exchange. The Internet Mail Service runs as an NT Server service, along with the many other Exchange services.

The next two sections discuss what the Internet Mail Service can do, along with how it works. Later in the chapter, you will learn how to plan an Internet Mail Service implementation, and then you will learn how to use the Internet Mail wizard to install and configure the Internet Mail Service.

9.1.1. Internet Mail Service Features

The Internet Mail Service can perform many functions, including the following:

- Send or receive SMTP mail from one Exchange Server to another Exchange Server over the Internet. These Exchange Servers may be in the same Exchange organization or in different organizations.

- Act as the message transport to link Exchange sites within an Exchange organization. Not only can mail messages be sent back and forth, but so can directory synchronization and folder replication messages. The Internet Mail Service can be either a primary message transport or a backup message transport.

- Send or receive mail from an Exchange Server to any SMTP-based mail server over the Internet. The SMTP-based mail server can run virtually any operating system as long as it is running SMTP over TCP/IP and can connect to the Internet.

The Internet Mail Service can send mail over the Internet because it uses the industry-standard SMTP protocol, which is designed for sending messages over the Internet. SMTP is discussed in more detail later in this chapter.

9.1.2. How the Internet Mail Service Works

One of the best ways to understand how the Internet Mail Service works is to follow the flow of a message from an Exchange client to its final destination at an SMTP-based mail server located on the Internet. Here's what happens:

1. A Microsoft Outlook user creates and sends an email message addressed to another user who has an Internet-based email address. This message is sent from the user's workstation immediately to the user's default Exchange Server.

2. At the Exchange Server, the message is received by the Information Store. The Information Store then queries the Directory Service to find out what to do with the message. Once the Information Store finds out that the address is for a nonlocal recipient, it passes the message to the Message Transfer Agent (MTA).

3. When the MTA receives the message, it compares the recipient's address with its Gateway Address Routing Table (GWART) for every Exchange Server running in the local site that has the Internet Mail Service running on it. In most cases, only one Exchange Server will be running the Internet Mail Service in any given Exchange site. But depending on how the site is designed, there may be more than one. The MTA determines which Exchange Server running the Internet Mail Service to use (assuming there is more than one).

4. After the MTA determines which Internet Mail Service to use, it must route the message to it. The Internet Mail Service can be on the same Exchange Server as the MTA; if this is the case, the MTA places the message into a folder in the local Information Store designated for use by the Internet Mail Service. If the Internet Mail Service is located on another Exchange Server, the MTA routes the message to the MTA of the correct Exchange Server. There, the MTA places the message in the local folder designated for use by the Internet Mail Service.

5. The Internet Mail Service then retrieves the message from the holding folder and asks the Information Store to convert the message (and any attachments) from the internal Exchange format to the SMTP format. When the conversion is done, the Internet Mail Service puts the message into the data directory, which is a temporary storage area for all outgoing and incoming Internet mail messages.

6. While the message is waiting in the data directory, the Internet Mail Service asks the Directory Service for the SMTP address of the recipient. When the Internet Mail Service receives the address, the address is substituted for the distinguished (DN) recipient name used internally by Exchange.

7. Finally, the Internet Mail Service uses TCP/IP to make a physical connection to the SMTP-based mail server to which the message is to be delivered and delivers the message. This process also requires the Internet Mail Service to use a Domain Name Server (DNS) during this process. This process is discussed in the section, "Configuring DNS," later in this chapter.

9

After the message is received by the SMTP-based mail server, it can then be delivered to the appropriate user using the POP3 or IMAP4 protocols, as discussed later in this chapter.

9.2. Planning Internet Access

Before you install the Internet Mail Service, you will want to prepare a plan that includes a variety of steps that should be taken before the service is installed. If you don't make these preparatory steps, you will not be able to successfully install the Internet Mail Service. In fact, most of the troubleshooting regarding the Internet Mail Service can be traced back to poor planning. The following sections take a brief look at four basic planning steps:

- Making the connection to the Internet
- Configuring DNS
- Evaluating security issues
- Determining the proper number and location of Internet Mail Service connectors

9.2.1. Making the Connection to the Internet

Before you can use the Internet Mail Service to communicate over the Internet, you must have a physical connection to the Internet. Every Exchange Server running the Internet Mail Service must have access to the Internet. The Internet Mail Service is not picky about how you make the connection, all it wants to hear is a *webtone* (Internet dial-tone).

The connection can be a leased line or a dial-up line. It can run at T-1 speeds or at 28,800bps. It can use NT Server's Remote Access Service (RAS) or some other communication's software. It doesn't make any difference.

What you have to do is ensure that the connection to the Internet is up and running and that it has enough bandwidth to support the expected amount of Internet mail traffic. Don't even think about installing the Internet Mail Service until your Internet Connection is up and running successfully.

9.2.2. Configuring DNS for the Internet Mail Service

To make a connection over the Internet to an SMTP-based mail server, the Internet Mail Service must be able to resolve the email address to an IP address. This means your Exchange Server must have access to a Domain Name Server (DNS). This can be a DNS server provided by your Internet Service Provider (ISP) or an internal DNS server, such as the one provided with NT Server. However you get access to a DNS server, this access must be set up and running successfully before you install the Internet Mail Service.

A related issue is to ensure that your domain name is properly registered with InterNIC (the group responsible for domain name registration) and that your Exchange Server has the appropriate MX (mail exchanger) and A (host address) records in the DNS server you use so that other SMTP-based mail servers can resolve your email addresses and connect to the Internet Mail Service to deliver mail to your users.

9.2.3. Evaluating Security Issues

Because the Exchange Server running the Internet Mail Service is connected to the Internet, it is subject to unauthorized access from the Internet. You will need some sort of firewall or proxy software, such as Microsoft's Proxy Server, to help prevent unwanted access.

Although you will have to rely on special software to prevent most unauthorized access, the Internet Mail Service does have several configuration options that can affect email security. For example, you can configure message size limits for messages, disable delivery of certain messages sent to recipients on the Internet, or prevent messages from specific SMTP-mail servers from connecting and delivering mail to your system.

Although you don't have to have your security measures in place before installing the Internet Mail Service, doing so is a good idea. You never know when your system might be "attacked" from the outside.

9.2.4. Determining the Proper Number and Location of Internet Mail Service Connectors

Most Exchange sites need only a single Internet Mail Service Connector; some very busy sites may need two or more. One of the things you have to evaluate during the planning stage is the expected amount of Internet mail that will run through the connector.

If you find that your Internet mail needs are heavy, you may have to install the Internet Mail Service on two or more Exchange Servers. Each Exchange Server can support only one Internet Mail Service Connector. Other design issues to consider are where to locate the Exchange Servers within your Exchange site, and whether each Internet Mail Connector should share a common Internet connection or each have its own Internet connection for greater fault tolerance.

If you add one Internet Mail Service Connector now, and your use of Internet mail grows more than you expected, you can always add another connector later; you don't have to install them all now.

9.3. How to Implement the Internet Mail Service

The following sections describe how to install and configure the Internet Mail Service. First, we will take a look at how to use the Internet Mail Wizard to install the Internet Mail Service. Second, we will take a look at some of the most common Internet Mail Service configuration options.

9.3.1. Installing the Internet Mail Service with the Internet Mail Wizard

Installing an Internet Mail Service Connector is easy with the Internet Mail Wizard, which steps you through the process of installing and configuring a basic setup for the Internet Mail Service. After the service is installed using the Internet Mail Wizard, you can change any of the configuration options as needed.

Although it is not a specific exam objective, it is important to know how to use the Internet Mail Wizard to install the Internet Mail Service. It is important because so many of the exam objectives relate indirectly to the Internet Mail Service and how it works. This tutorial assumes that Exchange has been properly installed and is running correctly. You do not have to be connected to the Internet to run this wizard, although you cannot use the Internet Mail Service unless all the previously described planning steps have been taken and implemented.

1. Load the Exchange Administrator program and expand the Connections container in the site where you want to add an Internet Mail Service Connector. Locate the Connectionscontainer and click it. Depending on how your Exchange Server is configured, you may see other connectors in the Connections container (see Figure 9.1).

Figure 9.1.

The Internet Mail Service Connector is created from the Exchange Administrator program.

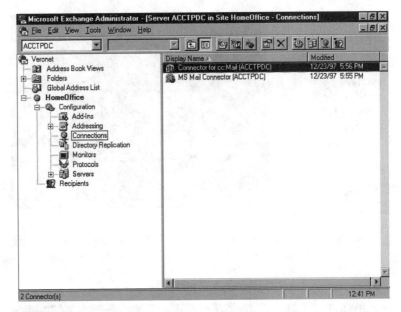

2. From the menu bar, select File|New Other|Internet Mail Service. This action starts the Internet Mail Wizard and displays the Welcome page (see Figure 9.2).

Figure 9.2.

The Internet Mail Wizard begins with the Welcome page.

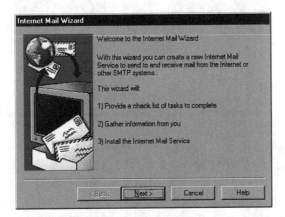

3. Click the Next button; the wizard displays another page that reminds you of all the steps you have to take before installing the Internet Mail Service (see Figure 9.3).

Figure 9.3.

The Internet Mail Wizard reminds you of all the steps you must take before installing the Internet Mail Service.

4. Click the Next button to display the first of several pages in which you have to answer questions about the Internet Mail Service's configuration (see Figure 9.4).

Figure 9.4.

You must select the Exchange Server on which to load the Internet Mail Service.

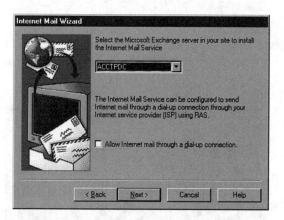

5. From this screen, you must make two choices. First, you must select the Exchange Server on which you want to install the Internet Mail Service. You can install it on the current Exchange Server (the default option) or specify another Exchange Server within the Exchange site. Second, you have to let the wizard know whether you will be using a dial-up line to reach the Internet. If so, check the appropriate box. If you will be using a dedicated Internet connection, leave the checkbox empty. Click the Next button to continue.

6. Use the next wizard screen (see Figure 9.5) to tell the Internet Mail Service whether it should use DNS to resolve email addresses or not to resolve email addresses to IP addresses. Normally, the first option is the one you use. Some organizations use a central SMTP receiver server to gather outgoing mail from multiple SMTP mail servers. Once an SMTP receiver receives a message, it is used to resolve the email address and make the actual connection to a remote SMTP host to transfer mail, relieving the Internet Mail Service of this task. Leave this screen as is. Click the Next button to continue.

Figure 9.5.

The Internet Mail Service needs to know whether or not it should use DNS.

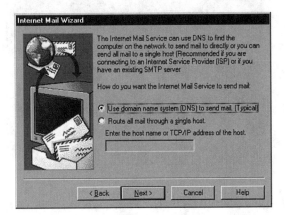

7. Use the next screen (see Figure 9.6) to configure the Internet Mail Service to allow mail to be sent to any Internet address or to restrict delivery to only limited Internet addresses. Leave the screen as is. Click the Next button to continue.

Figure 9.6.

You can choose to restrict who can be sent Internet mail.

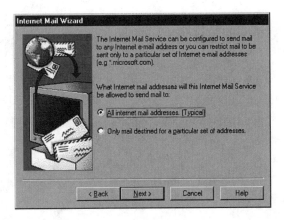

8. Use the next screen (see Figure 9.7) to specify how your internal recipient's Internet mail address will look. All you enter is the @ sign along with the domain name you have registered with InterNIC. Exchange will automatically use this format, along with each recipient's mailbox name, to generate an Internet mail address for all your users. Leave this screen as it is. Click the Next button to continue.

Figure 9.7.

You must tell Exchange the format you use for your Internet email addresses.

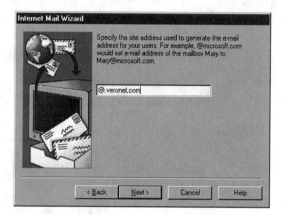

9. Use the next screen (see Figure 9.8) to tell the Internet Mail Service who is to receive any nondelivery reports sent to it from SMTP hosts that received a mail message from the Internet Mail Service, but could not be delivered because of a bad Internet mail address. You can use the administrator's account or designate any email account you want. Leave this screen as it is. Click the Next button to continue.

Figure 9.8.

You must tell the Internet Mail Service who is to receive nondelivery reports.

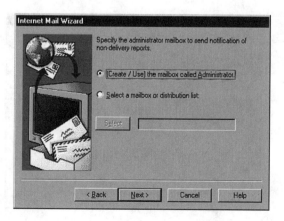

10. The next screen (see Figure 9.9) requires you to enter the password of the service account being used by the Exchange Server on which the Internet Mail Service will be running. This requirement prevents just anyone from creating an Internet Mail Service Connector. Enter the appropriate password and click the Next button to continue.

Figure 9.9.

You must enter the Exchange service account's password.

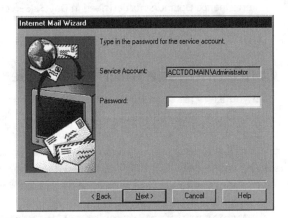

11. We have reached the last screen (see Figure 9.10). This screen notifies you that you are done. Click the Finish button to create the new Internet Mail Service Connector. Once the connector is created, the wizard disappears and you return to the administrator's screen.

Figure 9.10.

The final screen of the Internet Mail Service Connector setup wizard.

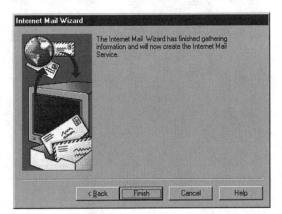

After the Internet Mail Service Connector has been created, it appears in the Connectors container with any other connectors you have loaded on your Exchange Server.

> **Note**
>
> Any time you add or remove a connector, you should run the Performance Optimizer, as described in Day 5, "Server Management Tools."

9.3.2. Configuring the Internet Mail Service

Any time after you have created an Internet Mail Service Connector, you can change any of its configuration options. To make a change, first click the Internet Mail Service Connector from the Connectors container so that it is highlighted. From the menu bar, select File|Properties. This action displays the Internet Mail Service Properties dialog box (see Figure 9.11). This tabbed dialog box offers many different configuration options you can change as dictated by your particular circumstances.

Figure 9.11.

The Internet Mail Service Connector is configured from this dialog box.

If you make any configuration changes to this dialog box, you must stop and then restart the Internet Mail Service before the changes go into effect. The easiest way to do this is to use the Control Panel|Services option, which is described in more detail in Day 5, "Server Management Tools."

The exam does not ask any specific questions about the configuration options found in the Internet Mail Service dialog box, so you may want to focus your study time on other areas of more importance.

9.4. Internet Messaging Protocols

9

For Exchange to communicate over the Internet, it has to adhere to a variety of industry-standard protocols. Up to this point, we have focused only on the SMTP protocol because SMTP is the protocol required to send and receive messages over the Internet. In addition to sending and receiving messages over the Internet using SMTP, Exchange offers related capabilities, each of which adheres to one or more industry-standard Internet protocols.

The following sections review the various Internet protocols supported by Exchange, explaining what they do and how to configure them. Exchange supports the following protocols:

- SMTP
- POP3
- NNTP
- HTTP
- LDAP
- IMAP4

Before taking the certification exam, make sure that you have a thorough understanding of what each of the Internet protocols does. Study and understand them well.

9.5. SMTP

As you know, SMTP is used by the Internet Mail Service to send and receive messages from other SMTP-based mail servers. SMTP is part of the TCP/IP protocol suite and runs at the Application level. SMTP is an industry standard; as long as two hosts understand SMTP, mail can be exchanged between them.

9.5.1. How SMTP Works

The best way to understand how SMTP works is to follow a message being sent from an Exchange Server running the Internet Mail Service to another SMTP-based mail server:

1. The Internet Mail Service has a message waiting in the data directory, waiting to be delivered to another SMTP host.

2. The Internet Mail Service uses DNS to resolve the host name of the remote SMTP-based mail server to an IP address. Next, a physical connection is created between the two SMTP hosts using the TCP protocol and port 25. After this is done, it is time for SMTP to begin its work.

3. Using SMTP, the Exchange Server sends a HELO message to the remote host. The HELO command is used to tell the remote host that another SMTP host wants to begin a mail session with it. After the receiving SMTP host receives the HELO message, it returns an OK message, telling the sending SMTP host that it is ready.

4. The sending SMTP host sends a MAIL FROM command. This command is used to tell the receiving host which SMTP server is initiating the connection. The receiving SMTP host acknowledges the command with another OK message.

5. The sending SMTP host sends one or more RCPT TO commands. Each command, if there is more than one, includes the person who is to receive the mail message. The receiving SMTP host acknowledges each command with a separate OK message.

6. The sending SMTP host sends a DATA command, which contains the body of the message being sent. The receiving SMTP host acknowledges the command with an OK message.

7. After all the data has been sent from the sending SMTP host to the receiving SMTP host, the sending host sends a QUIT command to end this particular SMTP session. The receiving SMTP host acknowledges the command with a CLOSING message, and the connection is broken.

This series of steps is repeated for every message that must be sent to remote SMTP hosts.

9.5.2. How to Configure SMTP

Unlike the other protocols discussed below, there is no specific place where SMTP is configured. SMTP is automatically configured when the Internet Mail Service is installed and configured.

9.6. The Protocols Container

Except for the SMTP protocol, the remaining Internet protocols are all configured from the Protocols container (see Figure 9.12). The Protocols container is located under the Configuration container at the site level.

9

Figure 9.12.

The Protocols container is where most Internet protocols are configured.

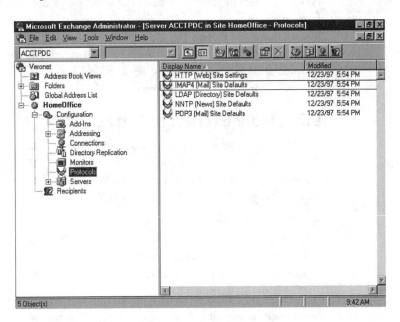

Although the Internet protocols are located in the Protocols container, this is not the only place from which they can be configured. All the protocols—except for SMTP and HTTP—can be configured from three levels: the site level (the Protocols container), the server level, and the mailbox level. The HTTP protocol can be configured only from the site and mailbox levels.

This means you have a great deal of control over who is affected when you configure a protocol. For example, if you configure a protocol at the site level, that protocol affects all servers and recipients for that entire site. If you configure a protocol at the server level, the changes affect only that single server and all the recipients who have mailboxes on that server. If you configure a protocol at the recipient level, it affects only a single recipient at a time. As the protocols are discussed in the next several sections, we will focus solely on the site level because this is the most common place to change a protocol's configuration.

9.7. POP3

You already know that SMTP is used to send and receive messages between SMTP-based mail hosts. SMTP is also used to send mail from a mail client to an SMTP host for delivery by the SMTP host. But what SMTP does not do is move messages from an SMTP host to a mail client. SMTP cannot be used by a mail client to check its mail on an SMTP host. To accomplish this task, you can add the Post Office Protocol 3 (POP3) to both the SMTP-based mail host and the mail client. POP3 is designed to allow a mail client to check and retrieve mail stored on an SMTP host that is also running the POP3 protocol.

9.7.1. How Exchange Implements POP3 Support

The POP3 protocol is built into Exchange's Information Store and is turned on by default. In other words, you don't have to configure POP3 to get it working; it is automatically configured and turned on when Exchange is first installed. By definition, Exchange Server is both a POP3 and STMP server.

Any POP3 mail client (even non-Microsoft mail clients) can connect to an Exchange Server and retrieve mail. A limitation of the POP3 protocol is that only a recipient's inbox can be checked. Users cannot check the contents of personal or public folders or access their schedules using POP3.

For a POP3 mail client to access a mailbox on an Exchange Server, the Exchange Server must be accessible from the Internet. This generally means that at least one server in the Exchange site must be running the Internet Mail Service and be connected to the Internet. If a person's mailbox is on a server other than the Exchange Server with the Internet Mail Service, there is no problem because the MTA is used to route the mail appropriately.

When a POP3 client accesses an Exchange Server, it must provide both the correct mailbox name and password. This arrangement prevents anyone from checking another user's mailbox.

9.7.2. How POP3 Works

Whenever a POP3 mail client wants to retrieve its mail from an POP3/SMTP-based mail host, it follows these steps:

1. The POP3 client opens a TCP connection to the POP3 host using port 110. In return, the POP3 host sends a GREETING message to the POP3 client.

2. The POP3 client enters the AUTHORIZATION state in which it identifies itself to the POP3 server by sending a message. If the POP3 client is successfully identified, a message is sent back to the POP3 client from the POP3 host, acknowledging this fact. In addition, the POP3 server enters the TRANSACTION state, in which it is ready to accept requests from the POP3 client.

3. The POP3 client makes the necessary request to retrieve its mail from the POP3 server. The POP3 server responds by sending the mail to the POP3 client.

4. When the POP3 client has retrieved its mail, it issues a QUIT command. When the POP3 server receives the QUIT command, it enters the UPDATE state and responds with a CLOSING statement. The TCP connection between the two hosts is then closed.

This sequence of steps is repeated every time a POP3 client checks and retrieves its mail from a POP3 server.

9.7.3. How to Configure POP3

Because the POP3 protocol is automatically installed and configured for you, there is little you can configure yourself. To make what configuration changes you can, click POP3 from the Protocols container and choose File|Properties from the menu bar. The POP3 (Mail) Site Defaults Properties dialog appears (see Figure 9.13).

The dialog box has four tabs. The General tab allows you to change the display name of the protocol—and, more importantly, to turn POP3 support off and on.

The Authentication tab (see Figure 9.14) allows you to control how POP3 clients access the POP3 server.

Figure 9.13.

POP3 is configured from this dialog box.

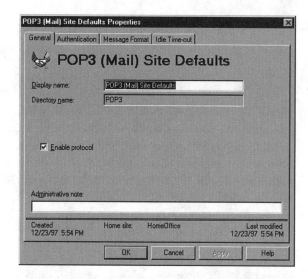

Figure 9.14.

You can control the level of security for POP3 client access from the Authentication tab.

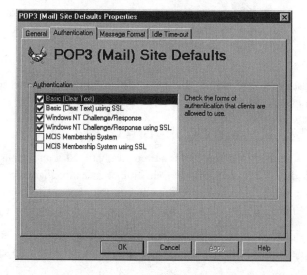

From the Authentication tab, you can control how a POP3 client must be authenticated so that it can connect and retrieve mail. Here is how each option works:

■ **Basic (Clear Text):** Allows a user at a POP3 client to enter his or her mailbox name and password and to pass this information to the POP3 server without using encryption. Virtually any POP3 client supports this authentication method. It is also the least secure method.

■ **Basic (Clear Text) using SSL:** Allows a POP3 client to use SSL encryption to pass the mailbox name and password to a POP3 server. Both the client and server must support SSL for this to work.

■ **Windows NT Challenge/Response:** Allows a POP3 client to use NT Server's integrated security, which is encrypted, to log into a POP3 server. The client must be able to support Windows NT Challenge/Response security for this to work.

■ **Windows NT Challenge/Response using SSL:** This option works the same as the preceding option except that it also uses SSL encryption. This option is currently supported only by the Outlook Express POP3 client.

■ **MCIS Membership System:** Allows a POP3 client to be authenticated using Windows NT network security using the Microsoft Commercial Internet Server (MCIS) Membership System.

■ **MCIS Membership System using SSL:** This option works the same as the preceding option except that it also uses SSL encryption.

You must decide on the level of POP3 security you want to support and make the appropriate choices.

The Message Format tab (see Figure 9.15) allows you to select how messages are encoded. You can choose between MIME and UUENCODE.

Figure 9.15.

You can control how POP3 messages are encoded from the Message Format tab.

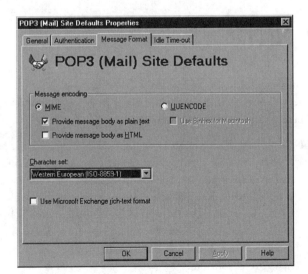

The last tab, Idle Time-out (see Figure 9.16), allows you to determine how long a POP3 server should wait before it automatically disconnects from a POP3 client (if it does not receive a QUIT command from the POP3 client).

Figure 9.16.

You can control how long a POP3 server waits until it automatically disconnects from the Idle Time-out tab.

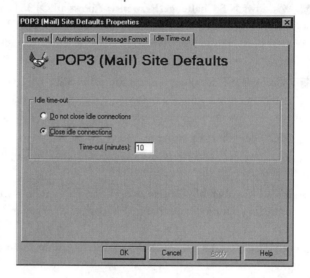

After you have made any changes, click the OK button; any changes you made are automatically saved.

9.8. NNTP

The Network News Transport Protocol (NNTP) and the Internet News Service, working together, allow an Exchange Server to provide the same functionality as Usenet newsgroup servers available on the Internet, and more. Here's how Exchange can take advantage of this feature:

■ An Exchange Server can be configured to receive Usenet newsfeeds from Usenet nodes on the Internet. *Usenet nodes* are servers on the Internet that maintain newsgroups on a worldwide basis. For example, if your organization is interested in seeing all the newsgroup postings on the subject of computers, the organization can subscribe to these newsgroups. "Subscribing" means that the postings are sent from a Usenet node to the Exchange Server, where they can either be published in public folders or be accessed using conventional news reader software.

- If desired, Exchange can be configured to participate in newsgroups. When so configured, you can send postings originating from the Exchange Server to a Usenet node to be published worldwide.

- By taking advantage of NNTP, Exchange can publish public folders as if they were newsgroups. This means that anyone with news reader software—and permission—can read and post messages to an Exchange public folder.

The focus of this part of the chapter is specifically on the NNTP protocol, not on the Internet News Service or public folders. Because of this focus, you will only learn how NNTP works and how it is configured, not how to set up Exchange to participate in Usenet nodes or how to publish public folders as newsgroups.

9.8.1. How Exchange Implements NNTP Support

The NNTP protocol works hand in hand with the Internet News Service. By default, the NNTP protocol is installed when Exchange is installed. But the protocol by itself is not enough. To take advantage of the NNTP protocol, the Internet News Service must be installed and configured. This is done through a wizard found in the Exchange Administrator program main menu (select File|New Other|Newsfeed). How to use the wizard is beyond the scope of this chapter.

After the Internet New Service is installed and configured, the NNTP protocol is active and can be configured, as discussed in "How to Configure NNTP," later in this chapter.

9.8.2. How NNTP Works

NNTP is an industry-standard Internet protocol used by Usenet nodes to allow users to both read and post messages to specific newsgroups supported on Usenet nodes. Currently, there are over 18,000 newsgroups available worldwide, each covering a specific topic. To read and post messages, users must use news reader software that supports NNTP.

When NNTP is implemented on Exchange, it allows Exchange itself to become a Usenet node, participating in the worldwide exchange of newsgroup messages. In addition, NNTP allows any user with a NNTP-based news reader to view newsgroups published by Exchange. The newsgroups published by Exchange can be either conventional newsgroups or information from public folders stored on Exchange.

Although Exchange supports many different NNTP and Usenet options, there are basically two main reasons you may consider setting up Exchange to use NNTP:

■ To receive newsfeeds of interest to the company; you can then publish that news as public folders, which can be accessed by Exchange clients from within the organization.

■ To publish public folder information that can be read by employees using news reader software instead of the Microsoft Exchange or Outlook client software. With this arrangement, an employee on the road or at home can view public folder data using a news reader instead of another client. You can control access by news readers to public folders by changing NNTP configuration properties, as described in the following section.

9.8.3. How to Configure NNTP

To configure the NNTP protocol, click NNTP from the Protocols container and choose File|Properties from the menu bar. The NNTP (News) Site Defaults Properties dialog appears (see Figure 9.17).

Figure 9.17.

NNTP is configured from this dialog box.

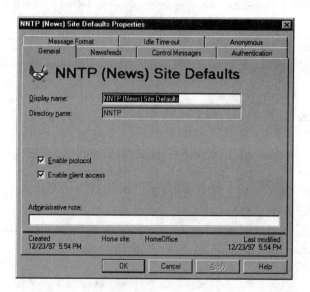

This dialog box has seven tabs, from which you can make various configuration changes. The Authentication tab, Message Format tab, and Idle Time-out tab are all virtually the same as the tabs of the same name in the POP3 properties dialog box. Their explanations are not repeated here.

You can use the General tab to change the display name, but more importantly, to turn the protocol off and on (enabling or disabling Exchange's ability to act as a Usenet node). An additional option is whether or not you want NNTP clients to access Exchange. If you do, leave the option enabled. If not, disable the option so that clients cannot access your Exchange Server. Even though this option is disabled, assuming the protocol is enabled, Exchange can still exchange newsfeeds with Usenet nodes.

The Newsfeeds tab (see Figure 9.18) is used to show any newsfeeds that have been already added with the Internet News Service. You can also use this tab to change some of the newsfeed properties. This screen is empty (as it is in Figure 9.18) if the Internet News Service has not been installed or configured.

Figure 9.18.

You can change newsfeeds from the Newsfeeds tab.

The Control Messages tab (see Figure 9.19) is used to accept or delete control message from Usenet nodes. Use this screen only if you have set up Exchange to automatically receive newsfeeds from Usenet nodes. Periodically, Usenet nodes can send control messages to your Exchange Server; these messages queue up on this tab until you decide to accept or delete them. You may want to delete a control message from a Usenet node you don't trust.

Figure 9.19.

Control messages from Usenet nodes can be accepted or deleted from the Control Messages tab.

The Anonymous tab (see Figure 9.20) is used to determine whether or not you want to accept anonymous logons from news reader clients. The default is to accept them. To turn this option off, remove the checkmark from the checkbox.

Figure 9.20.

You control whether people can anonymously access your Exchange Server using NNTP from the Anonymous tab.

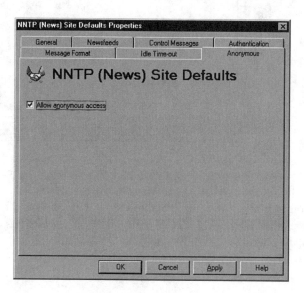

If you want a better understanding of NNTP, you will have to spend some time learning about the Internet News Service. Both are closely integrated and should be studied together. On the other hand, the certification exam does not cover how to configure the Internet News Service, so you may be better off spending your study time on more important topics that *are* covered on the exam.

9

9.9. HTTP

The Hypertext Transport Protocol (HTTP), along with the Exchange Active Server components running on Microsoft's Internet Information Server (IIS), allows any user running an HTTP client (web browser) to access his or her mailbox, schedule, and even public for which he or she has permission. In other words, virtually any web browser can be used to access a user's mailbox on an Exchange Server from anywhere in the world the user can access the Internet.

9.9.1. How Exchange Implements HTTP Support

HTTP is not automatically installed with Exchange unless the optional Active Server components are also installed. If the Exchange Active Server components are properly installed, then the HTTP protocol is automatically working, allowing anyone with a web browser to access his or her mail from an Exchange Server.

For a web client to access mail on an Exchange Server, the following must be in place:

- Within the Exchange site, there must be at least one NT Server running Internet Information Server (IIS) version 3.0 or greater, and this IIS server must have installed on it the IIS Active Server components. These components are not the same as the Exchange Active Server components. The IIS Active Server components come with IIS. In addition to these IIS Active Server components, the Exchange Active Server components must also be loaded. You can install these components when Exchange is first installed or anytime after.
- The Exchange Active Server components must be installed on each of the Exchange Servers within the site.

Assuming that all the preceding elements are in place, a web browser can be used to access a user's mailbox, schedule, private folders, and public folders. Here's how a web browser can be used to access an Exchange Server:

1. At the web browser, the URL for the IIS server that is running the Exchange Active Server components is entered. Using HTTP, the web browser accesses the Active Server Page (ASP) designated in the URL on the IIS server running the Exchange Active Server components. An ASP includes server-based code that automatically runs when required. For a web browser to be able to access Exchange, it must support JavaScript and Windows.

2. After the ASP is called by the web browser, it fires off the code that is part of that ASP page and creates a connection to an Exchange Server. In addition, the ASP sends the web browser a combination of HTML and JavaScript, which is used to create a special page on the web browser that allows the user to access Exchange. The initial screen received by the web browser allows the user to enter his or her mailbox username and password (see Figure 9.21).

Figure 9.21.

Almost any web browser can act as a mail client to Exchange.

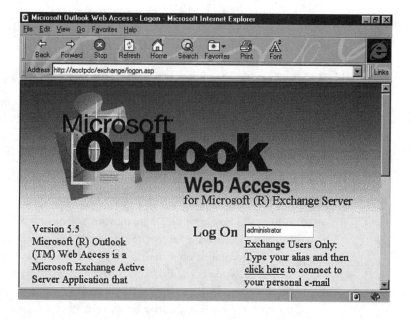

3. After the username and password are passed from the web browser to an ASP on IIS, the request is authenticated. After the request is authenticated, the user's mailbox information is automatically sent to the web browser where the user can read or send messages, check his or her schedule, or access any private or public folders to which he or she has permission (see Figure 9.22).

Figure 9.22.

The Microsoft Outlook Web Access client running in a web browser.

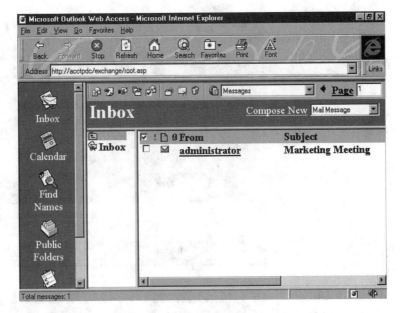

4. Every time the user wants to perform some task such as read a message, the web browser sends a message to IIS. At IIS, the appropriate ASP page takes over, retrieving the information from the Exchange Server. Once the data is formatted for display, IIS sends it to the user's web browser for display.

9.9.2. How to Configure HTTP

To configure the HTTP protocol, click it from the Protocols container and choose File|Properties from the menu bar. The HTTP (Web) Site Settings Properties dialog box appears (see Figure 9.23).

Use the General tab to change the display name and, most importantly, to enable or disable the protocol for the site. In addition, you can specify whether or not users can anonymously access public folders or the global address list on your Exchange Servers.

Use the Folder Shortcuts tab (see Figure 9.24) to create optional folder shortcuts that will appear on the Web Outlook Client when accessed by anonymous users. These shortcuts can be used to gain access to any public folder or folders you want made available to anonymous users.

Figure 9.23.

HTTP is configured from this dialog box.

Figure 9.24.

Create optional folder shortcuts from this dialog box.

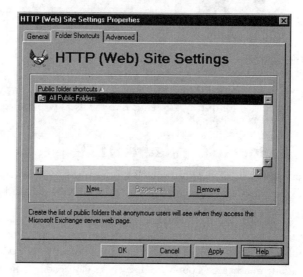

Use the Advanced tab (see Figure 9.25) to determine how many entries in the global address list are automatically sent to the user when an address search is conducted from the web client. If the number of positive hits is greater than the allowed number, the user is told to refine the search.

To save any changes made to the HTTP protocol, click the OK button; any changes you made are automatically implemented.

Figure 9.25.

Use the Advanced tab to specify how many global address listings can be downloaded at once.

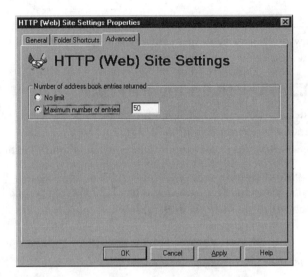

9

9.10. LDAP

The Lightweight Directory Access Protocol (LDAP) is an industry-standard Internet protocol that allows LDAP clients to access Exchange's global address list. For example, I might want to send a message to Franklin Telling at XYZ Company, but I don't know his email address. If I had an LDAP client (assuming that XYZ Company uses Exchange and is connected to the Internet), I could access XYZ Company's global address list using the LDAP client and look up Franklin's email address.

Currently, the versions of the Exchange Client and Outlook that come with Exchange 5.5 do not support LDAP. Instead, they use a proprietary method of accessing Exchange's global address list. The current version of Outlook Express supports LDAP, and future versions of Outlook will also support LDAP at the client level.

9.10.1. How Exchange Implements LDAP Support

LDAP has been made a part of Exchange's Directory Service, which allows LDAP clients to easily gain access to Exchange's global address list.

Whenever an LDAP client, with access to the Internet, wants to view the global address list on your Exchange Server, all the client has to do is enter the name of your server. Assuming that your server allows anonymous access, that user can view directory information from your Exchange Server. As you might imagine, you may not want just anyone to view your Exchange global address list. The next section shows you how to configure security for LDAP.

9.10.2. How to Configure LDAP

By default, LDAP is installed and turned on when Exchange is first installed, so configuration is not required. Be definition, Exchange is an LDAP server. But there are several settings you may want to change—such as security settings.

To configure the LDAP protocol, click it from the Protocols container and choose File|Properties from the menu bar. The LDAP (Directory) Site Defaults Properties dialog box appears (see Figure 9.26).

Figure 9.26.

LDAP is configured from this dialog box.

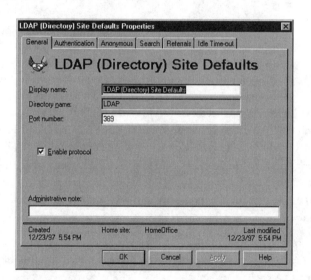

The General, Authentication, Anonymous, and Idle Time-out tabs are virtually identical to ones you have seen before. Only the tabs unique to LDAP—Search and Referrals—are described here.

The Search tab (see Figure 9.27) is used to control how searches are made by LDAP clients of Exchange's global address list.

Figure 9.27.

LDAP search settings are controlled from the Search tab.

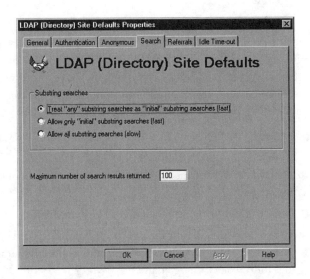

The Referrals tab (see Figure 9.28) is used to optionally configure Referral LDAP servers. If this option is configured, what happens is that when an LDAP client makes a request of an LDAP server, and the requested information is not available, the LDAP server provides the name of Referral LDAP servers within the scope of the search initiated by the client.

Figure 9.28.

LDAP referrals are configured from the Referrals tab.

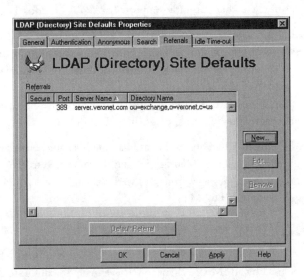

After all configuration changes are made, click the OK button to automatically save any changes.

9.11. IMAP4

The Internet Mail Access Protocol, Version 4 (IMAP4), is very similar in functionality to the POP3 protocol. It does everything the POP3 protocol does and a few new things, too. POP3 is considered an older protocol and will eventually be replaced by the more fully featured IMAP4 protocol. Here is what IMAP4 can provide:

- It allows IMAP4 clients to retrieve mail from IMAP4/SMTP-based mail servers.
- It allows IMAP4 clients to read and post messages to public folders on Exchange.
- It allows IMAP4 clients to connect to Exchange mailboxes that are not their own, assuming they have permission to access the other mailboxes.
- It supports HTML as a message format, which allows messages to contain various fonts, colors, and graphics.

9.11.1. How Exchange Implements IMAP4 Support

IMAP4 allows an IMAP4 client to access mail and other resources on an IMAP4 server such as Exchange. Currently, the versions of the Exchange Client and the Outlook client included with Exchange 5.5 do not support IMAP4. The only Microsoft client that currently supports IMAP4 is Outlook Express.

IMAP4 works in a way very similar to POP3. Whenever an IMAP4 client wants to access mail or other resources on an Exchange Server, it must first make a TCP connection. After the connection is established, the client is authenticated; then mail can be retrieved, messages can be posted or read from public folders, and other mailboxes can be accessed. IMAP4 is a richer, more complete protocol than POP3, and provides many more internal commands than POP3.

Like POP3, IMAP4 requires that at least one Exchange Server in an Exchange site be running the Internet Mail Service and be connected to the Internet. IMAP4 is not used to send messages from an IMAP4 client to an IMAP4 server; this task can be performed only by SMTP.

9.11.2. How to Configure IMAP4

By default, when Exchange is first loaded, IMAP4 is automatically configured and can be used by an IMAP4 client to retrieve mail. To configure the IMAP4 protocol, click it from the Protocols container and choose File|Properties from the menu bar. The IMAP4 (Mail) Site Defaults Properties dialog box appears (see Figure 9.29).

Figure 9.29.

IMAP4 is configured from this dialog box.

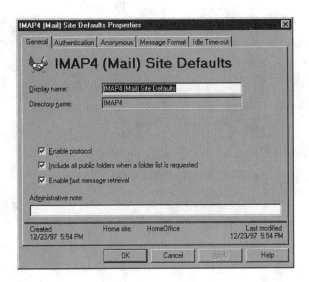

9

The Authentication, Anonymous, and Idle Time-out tabs are virtually identical to tabs of the same name for protocols described in preceding sections. Because the General and Message Format tabs are somewhat different, they are discussed here.

In the General tab, you can of course disable or enable the protocol at any time. What is new to this tab is that you can control whether or not all public folders are automatically included when an IMAP4 client requests a list of folders from Exchange. Also, you can choose something called *fast message retrieval*. This option controls how messages are downloaded from the server to the client. Most IMAP4 clients support fast message retrieval, but some don't. If your IMAP4 client does not support fast message retrieval, you may have to turn off fast message retrieval for the client to work with Exchange.

The Message Format tab (see Figure 9.30) allows you to control the format of messages. You can choose plain text, or HTML for more colorful messages. Note that IMAP4 supports only MIME encoding, not UUENCODE.

After you have made any changes to IMAP4 properties, you can save them by clicking the OK button.

When preparing for the certification exam, be sure to take the necessary time to experiment with a copy of Exchange to see how it works. Although you may not be able to test every feature discussed in this chapter, you can at least see the screens and examine all the various options.

Figure 9.30.

IMAP4 message format is configured from the Message Format tab.

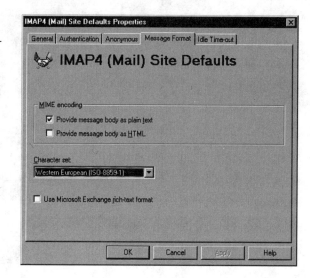

Lab

This section consists of review questions that pertain to this chapter and provides an opportunity to apply the knowledge you acquired in the course of this chapter.

Questions

1. A company is considering purchasing Microsoft Exchange to connect their business's many regional offices. One of the key deciding factors when choosing Exchange over other products is whether it works well over the Internet. You are a consultant who has been hired to evaluate Exchange for the business, and you tell company officials about Exchange's Internet Mail Service. When describing the features of the Internet Mail Service, you mention many. Which of the following three are features of Exchange's Internet Mail Service?

    A. Exchange can send SMTP mail from one Exchange Server to another over the Internet.

    B. Exchange can use the Internet to publish public folders to another SMTP-based host.

    C. Exchange can use the Internet to not only send mail messages but also to perform directory synchronization and folder replication.

    D. Exchange can send SMTP mail to an SMTP-based UNIX host over the Internet.

2. You have installed the Internet Mail Service onto an Exchange Server that has a direct connection to the Internet. Although you can send mail successfully to SMTP-based hosts, you apparently cannot receive any mail because you have not received the many messages you are positive have been sent to your Exchange Server over the Internet. What is the most likely cause of this problem?

    A. The DNS server, which is running under NT Server, is not properly installed.

    B. Your WINS server(s) is not working properly.

    C. Your ISP is having routing problems.

    D. You have not registered your domain name with InterNIC.

3. As your organization's Internet expert, the Exchange administrator has asked you to plan an upcoming Exchange Internet connection. Which one of the following planning issues will you *not* be concerned about?

    A. Arranging an Internet connection with an ISP.

    B. Configuring DNS access for your Exchange Server.

    C. Establishing the distinguished name naming convention.

    D. Registering your domain name with InterNIC.

4. You have just connected your Exchange Server to the Internet for the very first time. Currently, only your Exchange Server communicates over the Internet. No other servers on your local network communicate over the Internet. Later that week, you learn from your network administrator that one of the file and print servers was hacked into, causing it to crash. Which of the following options could you have implemented to help prevent your organization's network from being attacked by hackers on the Internet?

    A. You could have installed Microsoft's Proxy server on one of the NT Servers in your network to act as a firewall between your network and the Internet.

    B. You could have turned on PPTP filtering for the Exchange Server.

    C. You could have unbound the TCP/IP protocol from your Exchange Server's Server service.

    D. You could have installed two network cards in your Exchange Server. One of the cards would be connected only to the local network, and one of the cards would be connected to the router used to make the Internet connection. Then, on the Exchange Server, you would have enabled TCP/IP routing.

5. You want to install the Internet Mail Service Connector in one of the Exchange Servers in your Exchange site. Someone else has already arranged for the Internet connection and it appears to be working properly. What is the first step required to install the Internet Mail Service Connector?

    A. Configure the MTA to recognize the Internet Mail Service Connector.

    B. Configure the Information Store to route messages to the Internet Mail Service Connector.

    C. Reboot the Exchange Server.

    D. Start the Internet Mail Wizard.

6. You are using NT Server's Network Monitor to analyze the packets flowing between your Exchange Server and the Internet. Which of the following application-level TCP/IP protocols will you be the most interested in examining?

   A. SMTP

   B. POP3

   C. ARP

   D. IP

   E. IMAP4

9

7. You want your organization's employees to be able to access their inboxes from the Internet. Which of the following protocols would you want to be running and properly configured for the employees to *check* their mail with the widest possible number of mail clients?

   A. HTTP

   B. POP3

   C. IMAP4

   D. NNTP

   E. SMTP

   F. LDAP

8. Many of your organization's employees use the Internet to check mail on the company's Exchange Server. But some of the employees are complaining that they cannot view public folders. What is the most likely cause of this problem?

   A. The employees are using a POP3 mail client.

   B. The employees are using an IMAP4 mail client.

   C. The employees are using an SMTP mail client.

   D. The employees are using an HTTP mail client.

9. As the Exchange administrator, you want to make it easy for employees working at home to access the various public folders used throughout the company. At the same time, it is critical that no unauthorized users have access to the public folders. How would you implement this?

   A. Configure the IMAP4 protocol to allow only company employees to view public folders.

    B. Configure the NNTP protocol to allow only company employees to view public folders.

    C. Configure SMTP and NNTP to allow only company employees to view public folders.

    D. Configure POP3 and SMTP to allow only company employees to view public folders.

10. You want to configure Exchange to allow employees to use their web browsers to check mail and view schedules. When you go to the Protocols container, you notice that the HTTP protocol is not displayed. What is the mostly likely reason it is not there?

    A. You haven't yet loaded the Internet Mail Service Connector.

    B. HTTP is not used for web access, so that is why it is not shown.

    C. Your Internet connection is probably down, but when it comes back up, the HTTP protocol will again be displayed.

    D. You forgot to install the Exchange Active Server components when you installed Exchange.

11. You want to make it easier for anyone who has access to Internet email to be able to send messages to your organization's staff. To help accomplish this goal, you want to somehow publish your organization's global address list so that it can be viewed by people connected to the Internet. How can you best produce this result using Exchange?

    A. Publish the Exchange global address list as a public folder

    B. Use HTTP

    C. Use LDAP

    D. Use IMAP4

Exercise: Viewing Internet Protocol Settings

 Note This exercise addresses the following Microsoft exam objective:

■ Configure Internet protocols and services

9

This exercise steps through the process of viewing all the various configuration settings for the Internet protocols found in the Protocols container. You do not make any changes; you only become familiar with the various options available. It is very important not only to know where to change the various Internet protocol configuration settings, but to be familiar with the various options and what they can do for you.

This exercise assumes that you have Exchange properly loaded along with the Exchange Active Server components. If the Exchange Active Server components have not been loaded, you cannot view the HTTP configuration settings.

1. Load the Exchange Administrator program. Click the name of your Exchange site in the container pane (left window) to display the Configuration container. Then click the Protocols container in the container pane to display the Internet protocols in the contents pane (right window).

2. First, you will examine the settings for the HTTP protocol (assuming that you have the Exchange Active Server Components loaded). To examine the HTTP configuration properties, double-click the HTTP protocol in the contents pane. This action displays the HTTP (Web) Site Settings Properties dialog box.

3. Take a look at the General tab and notice the various settings. If you want, you can click the Help button for specific information about each tab. Select the Folder Shortcuts and Advanced tabs to view their settings. Once you have examined each setting and become familiar with it, exit the dialog box by clicking the Cancel button.

4. Next, you will look at the settings for the IMAP4 protocol. Double-click the IMAP4 protocol in the contents pane. This action displays the IMAP4 (Mail) Site Defaults Properties dialog box.

5. For each of the tabs (General, Authentication, Anonymous, Message Format, and Idle Time-out), take the time to become familiar with all the options and their default settings. When you are done, click the Cancel button to exit the dialog box.

6. Next, you will examine the settings for the LDAP protocol. Double-click the LDAP protocol in the contents pane. This action displays the LDAP (Directory) Site Defaults dialog box.

7. For each of the tabs (General, Authentication, Anonymous, Search, Referrals, and Idle Time-out), take the time to become familiar with all the options and their default settings. When you are done, click the Cancel button to exit the dialog box.

8. Next, you will take a look at the settings for the NNTP protocol. Double-click the NNTP protocol in the contents pane. This action displays the NNTP (News) Site Defaults Properties dialog box.

9. For each of the tabs (General, Newsfeeds, Control Messages, Authentication, Message Format, Idle Time-out, and Anonymous), take the time to become familiar with all the options and their default settings. When you are done, click the Cancel button to exit the dialog box.

10. Next, you will examine the settings for the POP3 protocol. Double-click the POP3 protocol in the contents pane. This action displays the POP3 (Mail) Site Defaults dialog box.

11. For each of the tabs (General, Authentication, Message Format, and Idle Time-out), take the time to become familiar with all the options and their default settings. When youare done, click the Cancel button to exit the dialog box.

Answers to Questions

1. **A, C, D**   Exchange does not have the capability to publish public folders to SMTP-based hosts over the Internet, but it can publish public folders using NNTP, which can then be read by NNTP-based news readers.

2. **D**   Although there could be many reasons you are not receiving your Internet mail, the most likely is that you have not registered your domain name with the InterNIC. If you don't register, any message sent to your domain cannot be resolved to an IP address, and thus cannot be routed to your Exchange Server.

3. **C** Establishing the distinguished name naming convention has nothing to do with configuring Exchange for the Internet. The remaining steps are critical to a successful Exchange Internet connection.

4. **A** Only the first option will do you any good. Microsoft's Proxy server, if installed properly, acts as a firewall, which can help block unauthorized access to your network.

5. **D** Assuming that your Exchange Server is configured properly, and assuming that the Internet Connection is up and running, the next logical step is to load and configure the Internet Mail Service Connector by starting the Internet Mail wizard.

6. **A, B, E** SMTP, POP3, and IMAP4 are all mail-related protocols, so they are of the most interest to you. The other protocols are not mail related.

7. **A, B, C** HTTP is used by the Outlook Web client; POP3 can be used by any POP3 mail client; and IMAP4 can be used by any IMAP4 mail client. NNTP is used for news readers, and SMTP is used to send, not receive, mail.

8. **A** POP3 mail clients do not support the capability to view messages stored in public folders, although IMAP4 and HTTP do. SMTP is used to send messages, not to receive them.

9. **B** The NNTP protocol must be properly configured to allow employees-only access to public folders.

10. **D** If the Exchange Active Server components have not been installed, the HTTP protocol does not appear in the Protocols container.

11. **C** LDAP is the industry-standard protocol used by Exchange to allow LDAP-enabled clients to access your Exchange Server's global address list over the Internet.

9

TEST DAY
FAST FACTS

Here are a few fast facts about this chapter that you may want to know ahead of time. These facts provide great last-minute study material.

- You can leverage Microsoft Exchange Server's single-instance storage capability by setting up mailboxes to use the Private Information Store on the server.

- Microsoft Exchange Server performs online maintenance on a scheduled basis. You can use the IS Maintenance property page to schedule this maintenance for each server.

- Because expanding distribution lists can be processor-intensive, you can force a distribution list to be expanded on a specific server.

- You can delegate distribution list management to the distribution list owner.

- The directory stores all information available about an organization's resources and users such as mailboxes, servers, and public folders.

- Replication of directory information between servers in the same site is an automatic process that occurs in the background.

Day 10

Exchange Resource Access Management

by Syed Hussain

This chapter is designed to help you achieve proficiency in managing Microsoft Exchange Server resources such as the directory, Private Information Store, and mailboxes. It also introduces you to maintenance tasks such as managing distribution lists, site security, and connectivity. After completing this chapter, you should understand the processes involved in maintaining a Microsoft Exchange Server site.

Objectives

This chapter addresses the following Microsoft exam objectives:

- Manage Private Information Stores
- Manage users
- Manage the directory
- Manage distribution lists
- Manage connectivity
- Manage site security

10.1. The Information Store

The Information Store is the central repository of all folders on a server. Each server can have two Information Stores: the *Public Information Store*, which holds all public folders and their information, and the *Private Information Store*, which holds all private folders and their information. You can configure all Information Stores in your site by using the Information Store Site Configuration property pages.

10.1.1. Information Store Site Configuration

The Information Store Site Configuration container contains site-wide Information Store configuration properties. To set up the Information Store, you must specify the name of the container in which the public folders are located and who will have permissions to create top-level folders. You can specify that messages are automatically sent to mailbox owners who have mailboxes over the maximum allowed size. You can also use the Information Store Site Configuration property pages to specify the cost associated with connecting to public folders in other sites.

You use the General tab of the Information Store Site Configuration property page to define the display name for the Information Store, choose a public folder container, and enable message tracking. To access General tab, perform the following steps:

1. From the Administrator window, choose Configuration.

2. Double-click Information Store Site Configuration.

3. Select the General tab. You use the General tab to define the following:

   ■ **Display name.** This required field has a maximum of 256 alphanumeric characters, which can include spaces and special characters.

   ■ **Directory name.** This name is defined during installation and cannot be changed.

10.1.2. The Public Folder Container

A *public folder* container is the receptacle for all newly created public folders. You can change this container to be any Recipients container in the site. Note, however, that changing the public folder container changes the location in which all new public folders are stored. The change does not affect the public folders that have already been created. If no container is specified, the default is the Recipients container for the site.

Top-Level Folder Creation

Use the Top Level Folder Creation property page to specify which users have the right to create top-level public folders in the Microsoft Exchange Client. Limiting the number of people who can create top-level public folders allows you more control of the public folder hierarchy. Once a top-level folder is created, the owner of that folder can set permissions that allow other users to create subordinate folders below the top-level folder.

You can specify that only certain people have the right to create top-level folders. You can select individuals or distribution lists. If you use a distribution list, you can specify that certain people in that list cannot create top-level folders by entering their names in the Not Allowed to Create Top Level Folders box in the Top Level Folder Creation tab within the Information Store Site Configuration property pages.

You can prevent general users from creating top-level folders in two ways. By default, if you have any name listed in the Allowed to Create Top Level Folders box, all other users are prevented from creating top-level folders. Likewise, if you have any name listed in the Not Allowed to Create Top Level Folders box, all other users can create top-level folders.

The second way to prevent general users from creating top-level folders is that if you specify a distribution list in the Allowed to Create Top Level Folders box, you can specify individuals from the distribution list and prevent them from creating top level folders by entering their names in the Not Allowed to Create Top Level Folders box.

Note | When both the Allowed to Create Top Level Folders list and the Not Allowed to Create Top Level Folders list are empty, everyone in the global address list can create top-level folders.

Storage Warnings

Use the Storage Warnings property page to set the times at which notification messages are sent to mailbox owners or public folder contacts who have exceeded the maximum amount of space allotted for their mailbox or public folder. Storage limits can be defined in the Advanced property page for mailboxes and public folders.

To get to the Information Store Site Configuration Storage Warnings property page, perform the following steps:

1. From the Administrator window, choose Configuration.

2. Double-click Information Store Site Configuration.

3. Select the Storage Warnings tab (see Figure 10.1).

Figure 10.1.

The Storage Warnings tab of the Information Store Site Configuration Properties page.

Use the Storage Warnings property page to set the times at which notification messages are sent to mailbox owners or public folder contacts who have exceeded the maximum amount of space allotted for their mailbox or public folder.

1. Select the Storage Warnings tab from the Information Store Site Configuration property page.

2. Select Never, Always, or Selected Times.

3. From the Detail View area, select a view for the schedule grid.

Rather than manually monitoring the disk usage of each mailbox or public folder, an administrator using the Storage Warnings page can automatically alert mailbox owners or public folder contacts.

Moving a Public Folder

You can move a public folder (an action also known as *re-homing*) to optimize performance based on the location and number of connected users.

Use replication to move a public folder to another server in the same site when you want to continue uninterrupted access to the folder. Multiple replicas are also good for redundancy. If one server fails, the other is still available to service requests.

To move a public folder using the Replicas tab, follow these steps:

1. In theAdministrator window, double-click Public Information Store.

2. Double-click on Public Folder Resources.

3. Double-click the public folder you want to move.

4. Select the Replicas tab (see Figure 10.2).

5. From the Servers box, select the server you want to host the public folder and choose Add.

6. From the Replicate Folders To box, select the server or servers you want to remove and then choose Remove.

Figure 10.2.

The Public Folder Replicas property page.

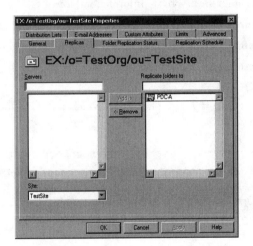

10

10.1.3. The Private Information Store

The Private Information Store contains all mailboxes for users who have the Microsoft Exchange Server 5.5 computer as their home server. The Private Information Store holds messages belonging to individual mailboxes on the server. The Private Information Store uses single-instance storage to minimize disk usage on the server.

Statistics for the Private Information Store

Use the Mailbox Resources property page to periodically view statistics for a Private Information Store. You can determine how mailboxes are being used and whether the present resources are sufficient. The columns in the Mailbox Resources property page are selectable and can be rearranged to suit your viewing needs. Columns can also be sorted by clicking them.

To find out who is using the mailbox resources on a server, use the Mailbox Resources property page:

1. From the Administrator window, choose Servers and then choose a server.

2. Double-click Private Information Store.

3. Select the Mailbox Resources tab. The following columns are displayed:

   - **Mailbox:** Displays the full email address of this mailbox.

   - **Windows NT Account**: Displays the Windows NT account name of the user who last logged on to this mailbox.

   - **Total K**: The total amount of disk space in kilobytes that this mailbox occupies in the Private Information Store.

   - **Storage Limits:** The storage limit assigned to this mailbox.

   - **Total No. of Items**: The total number of items stored in the mailbox.

   - **Last Logon Time**: The time at which a user last logged on to this mailbox.

   - **Last Logoff Time**: The time at which a user last logged off this mailbox.

You can customize the view that provides the information you want on the Mailbox Resources tab of the Private Information Store property page: Choose Columns in the Mailbox Resources tab to select the columns you want to view and omit columns you do not want to view.

10.1.4. Maintenance Schedule for the Information Store

Microsoft Exchange Server 5.5 performs online maintenance on a scheduled basis. You can use the IS Maintenance property page to schedule the online maintenance for each server. Note that there is a degradation in Information Store response times while maintenance tasks are being performed. Set the Information Store maintenance schedule for the least busy time of day. Maintenance should be run at least once a day because infrequent maintenance for a large or heavily used Information Store can cause performance deterioration.

To set the maintenance schedule, perform the following steps:

1. From the Administrator window, choose Servers and then choose the server you want to configure.
2. From the File menu, choose Properties.
3. Select the IS Maintenance tab (see Figure 10.3).
4. From the Detail View area, select a view for the schedule grid.
5. Select Always to perform maintenance tasks every 15 minutes; select Selected Times to perform them at scheduled intervals.
6. Assign specific times in the schedule grid.

Figure 10.3.

The Exchange Server properties IS Maintenance tab.

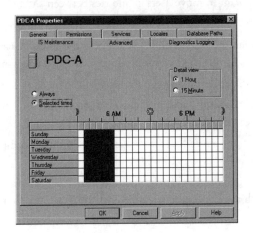

Mailbox Management Within a Site

Mailboxes are the containers for receiving and sending mail to a recipient group. You can move mailboxes from one server to another to provide load balancing between servers, to coordinate with the physical location of users, or to limit downtime when a server must be taken offline.

Moving Mailboxes Using the Tools Menu

You can move mailboxes using the Tools menu in the Microsoft Exchange Administrator program. The Move Mailbox command moves mailboxes only between servers in the same site; it does not move users between sites or between recipient containers.

To move mailboxes between servers in the same site, follow these steps:

1. From the Administrator window, choose Recipients.
2. Select a mailbox or group of mailboxes you want to move.
3. From the Tools menu, choose Move Mailbox.
4. In the Move Mailbox To box, select the server to which you want to move the selected mailboxes.

Moving Mailboxes Between Sites or Between Recipient Containers

The Move Mailbox command moves mailboxes only between servers in the same site. When you want to move users' mailboxes between sites, Microsoft recommends the following steps:

1. In the Microsoft Exchange Client, choose the Inbox Assistant to set up an AutoForward rule that forwards all new mail to the new mailbox.
2. Set up an AutoReply message stating that the mailbox has moved.
3. In the Administrator window, choose a recipient, select the Advanced tab, and then select Hide from Address Book.
4. If the user has server-based messages, the administrator must notify the user to move all mail messages to a .PST file.
5. Use the Directory Export command to export all the user's directory information, such as phone number, title, or distribution list membership.
6. If the mailbox is to be moved to a different recipient container, modify the export file to indicate the new recipient container and use Directory Import to create the user.

Warning

In step 4 of the preceding exercise, be careful if the user decides to protect the .PST file with a password. If the password is lost or forgotten, all data in the .PST file will be lost.

Mailbox Maintenance

When performed regularly, mailbox maintenance can recover space contained in the Private Information Store on the Microsoft Exchange Server. Mailbox maintenance includes activities such as cleaning a mailbox.

The Clean Mailbox command works on a single mailbox or multiple mailboxes but does not work on distribution lists, custom recipients, or public folders. Mailbox cleaning can be performed while the mailbox is open.

To get to the Clean Mailbox dialog box, follow these steps:

1. From the Administrator window, choose Recipients and select a mailbox.

2. From the Tools menu, choose Clean Mailbox. The Clean Mailbox dialog box appears, as shown in Figure 10.4.

Figure 10.4.

The Clean Mailbox dialog box.

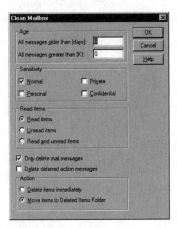

The Clean Mailbox dialog box options are listed in Table 10.1.

Table 10.1. The Clean Mailbox dialog box options.

Group	Option	Description
Age	All Messages Older Than (Days)	All messages older than the specified number of days will be deleted.
	All Messages Greater Than (K)	All messages larger than the specified number of kilobytes will be deleted.
Sensitivity	Normal	Leaves the item header blank and sends messages with no sensitivity.
	Personal	A personal message containing non-business-related information.

continues

Table 10.1. continued

Group	Option	Description
	Private	A private message prohibits any recipient from modifying your original message when it is replied to or forwarded.
	Confidential	A confidential message should be treated according to the policies on confidentiality for your organization.
Read Items	Read Items	Deletes all messages that have been read.
	Unread Items	Deletes all messages that have not been read.
	Read and Unread Items	Deletes all messages that have been read and those that have not been read.
Action	Delete Items Immediately	Immediately deletes all messages that meet the specified criteria. After messages are deleted, they cannot be retrieved.
	Move Items to Deleted Items Folder	Deleted messages are moved into the user's Deleted Items folder. Messages in the Deleted Items folder can be viewed, retrieved, and moved to other folders.

Mailbox Templates

When you create a mailbox, you use the Mailbox dialog box to define the properties. However, you can create mailbox templates to set default values for many of the new mailbox properties. A *mailbox template* is a generic mailbox whose configuration is copied to new mailboxes as they are created with the Migration wizard, the Directory Import command, and the Duplicate File menu command.

You can use templates to do the following:

- Preconfigure properties that a large number of mailboxes share, such as trust level, delivery restrictions, company name, and postal address.

- Create a single mailbox with preconfigured properties by duplicating a template mailbox.

Properties that are unique for each mailbox, such as telephone number, location, pager, and display name, can be filled after migration using the Directory Import command.

You create a new mailbox to add someone to your organization. Creating mailbox templates for new mailboxes can greatly ease the process of creating mailboxes consistently.

Creating a Template for New Mailboxes

Mailbox templates can automatically set default values for mailbox properties. The mailbox configuration is copied to new mailboxes as they are created with the Migration wizard, the Directory Import command, or the Duplicate command. All template mailbox properties except first name, last name, alias name, permissions, and email addresses are copied when you create a new mailbox. This prevents you from entering the same information repetitively for several mailboxes. You can complete the configuration process after the mailboxes are created.

Follow these steps to create a mailbox template:

1. From the Administrator window, choose a site within the organization.
2. Choose the Recipients container in which the new mailbox is to be created.
3. From the File menu, choose New Mailbox.
4. In the Display box, type a name for the new template.
5. Enter any information that is not mailbox-specific.

Using the Template to Create New Mailboxes

A mailbox template can keep you from typing the same information repeatedly. The template lets you preconfigure properties for a single mailbox or a large number of mailboxes. The template also lets you use the Migration wizard, the Duplicate command, or the Directory Import command for bulk creation of mailboxes.

Follow these steps to use a mailbox template to create a mailbox:

1. From the Administrator window, choose a site in your organization.
2. Choose the Recipient container in which the new mailbox is to be created.
3. If the template is hidden from the Address Book, choose Hidden Recipients from the View menu.
4. Select the mailbox template you want to use to create the new mailbox.
5. From the File menu, choose Duplicate.

10

6. Provide any mailbox-specific information; for example, specify the email address by selecting the Email Addresses tab.

Email addresses identify recipients to the connectors and gateways that connect Microsoft Exchange Server to other messaging systems. You can use the Email Addresses property page to create, modify, or remove email addresses. Microsoft Exchange Server automatically generates these email addresses for the server core components and recipients.

10.2. The Microsoft Exchange Server Directory

The Microsoft Exchange Server directory stores all the information available about an organization's resources and users, such as servers, mailboxes, and public folders. In the directory hierarchy in the Administrator window, a directory entry appears for each Microsoft Exchange Server object. An object's directory entry stores all the information you set using the Administrator window.

Synchronizing a directory within a site notifies a server that it should request directory updates from all other servers within the site.

Directory knowledge consistency checks look for the existence of other connected servers within a site and for the existence of new sites within the organization.

10.2.1. Synchronizing Server Directories Within a Site

Microsoft Exchange Server 5.5 synchronizes directory information within a site every five minutes. You can synchronize directory information manually if you have made changes to directory information on this server and don't want to wait for automatic synchronization.

Directory Replication Knowledge Consistency

Directory replication tables contain information that describes the replication connections between servers in a site. For example, when a new server is added to a site, the directory replication tables on all existing servers are updated to reflect the addition of the new server. The next time replication occurs, the new server is included in the process and can both send and receive directory updates to all other servers in the site.

Directory replication tables also describe the connections between servers in a site and the *bridgehead server* (the designated single server in a site that receives updated directory information from remote sites).

By default, directory replication tables are synchronized between sites once every three hours.

10.2.2. Directory Import and Export

The Microsoft Exchange Server directory contains information about mailboxes, custom recipients, and other objects. Using the Directory Export command, you can write information about mailboxes, custom recipients, and distribution lists to a text file. Using the Directory Import command, you can create or modify most objects in the directory based on the contents of a text file.

The Directory Export and Directory Import commands can be valuable when you're doing the following tasks:

- Making modifications to multiple objects of the same type.
- Creating multiple objects in a batch fashion.
- Deleting multiple custom recipients before migrating their mailboxes.
- Exporting configuration or template information.

Directory Export

You can use the Directory Export command to export directory information to another email system and to create a text file of all properties for mailboxes, custom recipients, or distribution lists. Directory Export does not require an existing export file. If no export file exists to specify which properties are to be exported, Directory Export exports a default set of properties.

To export the directory, follow these steps:

1. From the Tools menu in the Administrator window, choose Directory Export.
2. Select a directory server and a home server.
3. Select an export file.
4. Select a directoryexport container.
5. Select the Exchange Server object types you want to export.
6. Select a logging level.

10

7. Select the column, quote, and property field separators by clicking the Separators button.

8. Choose Export to start the export process.

Directory Import

Directory Import requires an import file with the modifications for the directory. The format of the information in import and export text files is the same.

To initiate the directory import process, follow these steps:

1. From the Administrator window, choose Directory Import from the Tools menu.

2. Select a Windows NT domain and a server.

3. Select a container.

4. Choose an import file.

5. Select a logging level.

6. Select the appropriate separators for the column, quote, and property fields by clicking the Separator button.

10.2.3. Directory Maintenance

Maintaining the directory on each Microsoft Exchange Server includes periodically viewing and clearing the event logs to verify that the directory, directory replication, and synchronization processes are working correctly.

Information about the Microsoft Exchange Server directory and the directory replication process are stored in the Windows NT application Event log using the source label MSExchangeDS. Directory synchronization events are logged using the label MSExchangeDX. You view these events using the Windows NT Event Viewer.

Directory maintenance also includes periodically verifying that the replicated directory information is correct. Use the Directory Service General property page to update the directory from within the site or to check knowledge consistency.

Verifying Directory Consistency

Replication of directory information between servers in the same site is an automatic process that occurs in the background. Replication between sites is a scheduled process you set up using the Directory Replication Connector. You can initiate a consistency check of all directories in your organization if servers or sites were added while a server was not operating or if you suspect an error may have occurred during the directory replication process.

To initiate the directory consistency check, follow these steps:

1. Select the General tab.

2. Choose Check Now to check the consistency of all directories in your organization.

Resynchronizing Replicated Directory Information

You can resynchronize the directory replication process with other servers in the same site if a server has been added to your site or was temporarily offline. You can also initiate an immediate directory replication request to other sites in your organization if a site has recently been added or the connection between sites was temporarily offline.

Setting Import and Export Requests

Import and export requests are processed during the next scheduled directory synchronization cycle.

To set these options, perform the following steps:

1. From the Administrator window, choose Connections.

2. Double-click Dirsync-Requestor.

3. Select the Settings tab.

4. Under Dirsync Information, specify whether you want to import or export directory entries:

   - **Import on Next Cycle:** Requests available directory entries in the directory synchronization server.

   - **Export on Next Cycle:** Sends all local directory entries to the directory synchronization server.

10.3. Distribution Lists

A *distribution list* is a group of recipients created to facilitate mass mailing of messages. When a message is sent to a distribution list, all members in the distribution list receive a copy of the message.

10.3.1. Creating a Distribution List

You can create a new distribution list whenever you want to send the same information to a group of recipients rather than addressing each individual separately.

To create a new distribution list, follow these steps:

1. From the Administrator window, choose Recipients.
2. From the File menu, choose New Distribution List.

Use the Distribution List General property page to specify a new distribution list or modify the distribution list display name.

To enter or modify the name of a distribution list, follow these steps:

1. From the Administrator window, choose Recipients.
2. Double-click the distribution list you want to configure.
3. Select the General tab.
4. Type the Display Name and Alias for the distribution list.

10.3.2. Choosing an Expansion Server for the Distribution List

An *expansion server* is a server in your site on which the distribution list is always expanded. When a user sends a message to a distribution list, Microsoft Exchange Server expands the list, resolves the names of all recipients in the list, and determines the most efficient routing solution for the message. For large distribution lists, this expansion can be processor-intensive. To allow for greater administrative control, you can use the Distribution List General property page to force the distribution list to be expanded on a specific server.

Distribution List Owners

The *owner* of a distribution list is the primary contact person for that list. The owner can edit the distribution list in the Microsoft Exchange Client.

To select a distribution list owner for an existing distribution list, follow these steps:

1. Select the General tab of the Distribution List Property pages.
2. In the Owner box, choose Modify.
3. Select a recipient to be the owner of the distribution list and then choose OK.

Advanced Properties for Distribution Lists

The Advanced property page for the distribution list allows the administrator to control how the list behaves when it is used. Some of the options available under the Advanced tab of the Distribution List property pages are listed here:

- **Report to Distribution List Owner:** Sends a message to the distribution list owner whenever there is a problem sending to the distribution list. For example, the owner of the distribution list would receive notification if a message cannot be delivered.

- **Report to Message Originator:** Sends a message to the message originator when a message is sent to the distribution list.

- **Allow Out of Office Messages to Originator:** Responds with an out-of-office message for any user who is a member of the distribution list. If this option is not selected, members of the distribution list do not receive an out-of-office reply from the selected mailbox.

- **Hide from Address Book:** Indicates whether or not the distribution list should appear in the Address Book.

- **Hide Membership from the Address Book:** Indicates that you do not want the names of recipients who are members of the distribution list to appear in the Address Book.

10

10.4. Managing Connectivity

The Microsoft Exchange Server 5.5 Administrator program provides a powerful and flexible environment for administering the services and components of your messaging organization. The Microsoft Exchange Administrator program is a Windows NT application that lets you view and manipulate the structure of your organization and perform a variety of administrative tasks.

To open the Administrator window, you must have logon rights for the site at which the server is located.

Initially, the only accounts with Administrator permissions for the Microsoft Exchange computer are the service account provided during setup and those accounts that were logged on to the Exchange Server during setup. You can add other users with Administrator permissions using the Administrator program.

If a remote site is connected over the network connection that supports Remote Procedure Call (RPC) communication, the remote site can be administered from the local site if appropriate permissions have been granted in the remote site. With the Microsoft Exchange Server Administrator program, you can connect and modify objects on multiple servers.

Microsoft Exchange Server provides several connectors to link sites in your organization. Each connector uses different transport protocols for message exchange. Managing these connectors and their transport protocols is part of routine administration.

10.4.1. Assigning a Routing Cost

Routing costs determine the preference between multiple routes to a remote site. The cost associated with each address space is used to optimize message routing to the foreign system but does not affect message reception. All mail is sent using the address with the lowest cost. If two or more routes are available with the same cost, the load placed on the routes is roughly equal. Address space costs range from 1 to 100.

Follow these steps to assign a routing cost for the Site Connector:

1. From the Exchange Administrator program, highlight the Exchange Server site and double-click the Site Connector.
2. Select the Address Space tab in the Site Connector property pages.
3. Select the address for which you want to assign a cost.
4. In the Cost box, type a routing cost for messages transferred using this address. Type a cost between 1 and 100. The lowest cost of the active connections is chosen when routing a message.

Assigning a Cost to Target Servers

Target server costs determine the preference between servers in a remote site. If two or more servers are available with the same cost, the load placed on these servers is roughly equal.

You can assign a cost to target servers by selecting the Target Servers tab from the Site Connector property page and assigning a cost in the Target Server Cost box.

Setting a Schedule for Connectors

The Dynamic RAS Connector and the X.400 Connector can be configured to establish a connection with the remote server at specified times. This is useful to reduce the costs for connections where telephone charges apply.

10.5. Overall Site Security and Management

An administrator has many options when creating and maintaining standards that promote security within the Microsoft Exchange Server 5.5 organization. Proper enforcement of these standards enhances performance and ensures overall site security.

The following is a list of the options available in setting up and managing site security:

- **Protect the MTA**: Configure passwords to provide security for the MTA. Microsoft Exchange Servers in the same site do not require passwords because they use Windows NT security within the RPC environment. Passwords can be required when a foreign X.400 system is configured to use the MTA.

- **Protect the Internet Mail Connector**: The IMC can be set to reject incoming SMTP connections from a single IP address or a range of IP addresses. By default, the Internet Mail Connector accepts incoming SMTP connections from all hosts. You can specify a range of IP addresses to reject and have a list within that range that should be excluded from the restriction. You can also set the IMC to accept SMTP connections for a single host and refuse connections from all other hosts.

- **Protect the mailboxes**: Try to eliminate or minimize assigning multiple users to a single mailbox. Mailboxes should be set up with the most restrictive permissions.

- **Protect the Exchange service account**: Because the Exchange Server service account carries inherent permissions that make the site vulnerable, disclose the service account password to only those who need it.

- **Protect the backup media:** In case of disaster (such as a fire that destroys your servers and backup tapes), you should plan on storing tape backups at a secure off-site location.

Note Changing an established MTA password can break connections to other sites or foreign X.400 systems. If you change an MTA password, be sure to notify administrators of all connected sites so that they can update their connection information.

10

Lab

This section consists of review questions that pertain to this chapter and provides an opportunity to apply the knowledge you acquired in the course of this chapter.

Questions

1. For each target server in a site connector, a cost can be associated with the connection to that server. What cost assignment causes that connector to be used 100 percent of the time?

    A. 0

    B. 1

    C. 100

    D. 50

2. What happens if a user attempts to protect his or her personal folder file (.PST) with a password, but later forgets the password?

    A. The administrator can reset the password.

    B. A decryption utility can be used to recover the file.

    C. The data in the .PST file is permanently lost.

    D. The owner of the .PST file can reset the password.

3. What is the procedure for setting the times at which notification messages are sent to mailbox owners or public folder contacts when those folders have exceeded the maximum amount of space allocated?

    A. Adjust the public folder object in the Servers container.

    B. Adjust the public folder object in the Configuration container.

    C. Adjust the Information Store site configuration object in the Configuration container.

    D. Adjust the Information Store site configuration object in the Servers container.

4. What is the default interval of the Exchange public folder hierarchy replication?

   A. 30 seconds

   B. 60 seconds

   C. 30 minutes

   D. 60 minutes

5. What is required to configure a public folder for use when operating offline?

   A. Create a .PST file.

   B. Create an .OST file.

   C. Designate the public folder as a favorite folder.

   D. Create an .OST file and designate the folder as a favorite folder.

6. The Internet News Service uses which protocol to replicate the Usenet newsgroups into Microsoft Exchange and represent these newsgroups as public folders?

   A. LDAP

   B. NNTP

   C. HTTP

   D. SMTP

7. The MTA transfers all messages to other Exchange Server MTAs. What two formats are supported by the MTA?

   A. X.500 IPM and X.400 IPM

   B. Microsoft Exchange mail message and X.500 IPM

   C. Microsoft Mail message and X.400 IPM

   D. Microsoft Exchange mail message and X.400 IPM

8. Which predefined role should be assigned to a user who has to create items in a public folder?

   A. Owner

   B. Author

        C. Publishing Editor

        D. Contributor

9. Which option on the Advanced property page of a distribution list is used to determine whether a distribution list is replicated to other mail systems during directory synchronization?

        A. Hidden Distribution Lists

        B. Trust Levels

        C. Disable Dir. Sync

        D. Distribution List size

10. When configuring public folder replication from the information store level, which property page is used to pull replicas of a specified public folder into the public information store?

        A. Instances

        B. Public folder Resources

        C. Scheduling Replication

        D. Folder Replication status

Exercises

Exercise 1: Using Directory Import to Create Mailboxes

 Note This exercise addresses the following Microsoft exam objective:
- Manage the directory

In this exercise, we will extract user accounts from a Windows NT domain and use the Directory Import command to create mailboxes. Using these tools together provides you with a powerful way to eliminate manual data entry when creating Exchange Server mailboxes in large numbers.

1. From the Exchange Server Administrator window, click the Tools menu and select Extract Windows NT Account List. The Windows NT User Extraction dialog box pops up.

2. Select the Windows NT domain from which you want to extract the accounts.

3. Select the Windows NT domain controller for the selected domain.

4. Enter the path and name of the output file. This file contains the NT user account information in a comma-separated format.

5. After the Windows NT account extraction is complete, click the Tools menu and select Directory Import. The Directory Import dialog box pops up.

6. Verify the entries in the Windows NT Domain and MS Exchange Server boxes. Click the Import File button and enter the path and filename where the NT account file was created.

7. Click the Import button to start creating Exchange Server mailboxes.

Exercise 2: Managing the Private Information Store

 Note This exercise addresses the following Microsoft exam objective:
- Manage the Private Information Store

In the course of administering Microsoft Exchange Server, you will have to maintain one of its most critical resources, the Private Information Store. In this exercise, you learn how to monitor the Private Information Store and manage its maintenance schedule.

1. From the Exchange Server Administrator window, highlight the Exchange server and double-click the Private Information Store.

2. From the Private Information Store property page, select the Mailbox Resources tab. Use this tab to find who is using the mailbox resources. The Mailbox Resources tab displays the full email address of the mailbox, total number of messages associated with this mailbox, the mailbox's Windows NT account, and the total amount of disk space the mailbox occupies in the Private Information Store.

   The Mailbox Resources tab also displays the storage limit assigned to a mailbox as well as the last logon and logoff time for that mailbox.

3. Select the IS Maintenance tab from the Private Information Store property page. Microsoft Exchange Server performs online maintenance on a scheduled basis. You use the IS maintenance tab to schedule this maintenance for each server.

4. Assign the specific times in the grid at which you want Exchange Server to perform maintenance on the Private Information Store. If you do not schedule maintenance or schedule infrequent maintenance for a large or heavily used Information Store, performance will deteriorate.

   Selecting maintenance times that are too frequent can result in poor performance because the store response times are slower while maintenance tasks are being performed.

Answers to Questions

1. **A**   A cost assignment of 0 sets the target server as a default. The higher the cost of a connection, the lower the probability of that connection being used.

2. **C**   All data will be lost because a .PST file secured by a password can only be used with that password.

3. **C**   All notification times can be set site-wide through the Information Store Site Configuration object.

4. **B**   The default interval for Public Folder hierarchy replication is 60 seconds.

5. **D**   Creating an .OST file enables a user to work offline; designating a public folder as a favorite causes it to be replicated to the .OST file each time a connection is made to the Microsoft Exchange Server.

6. **B** The Internet News Service uses the Network News Transfer Protocol (NNTP), which is the standard protocol for Internet news services.

7. **D** The MTA supports the Microsoft Exchange mail message and the X.400 IPM.

8. **D** The Contributor predefined role is sufficient for a user who needs to create items in a public folder.

9. **B** Trust levels are used to determine which objects are replicated to other mail systems during directory synchronization.

10. **A** The Instances property page can be used to pull replicas of a specified public folder into a Public Information Store.

10

TEST DAY FAST FACTS

Here are a few fast facts about this chapter you may want to know ahead of time. These facts provide great last-minute study material.

- Exchange's security is closely intertwined with NT Server's security. All Exchange mailbox users must also have an NT Server user account.

- Most Exchange objects can be assigned permissions based on NT user accounts or groups.

- Exchange must use an NT Server-based service account to start its various services.

- Exchange offers five administrative roles—Permissions Admin, Admin, Service Account Admin, View Only Admin, and the Key Manager Administrator. An administrative *role* specifies the set of rights that define how much and what type of access an administrator has on a particular object.

- The Internet Mail Connector has its own security options that affect STMP-based communications between Exchange Servers over the Internet.

- Exchange supports SSL and S/MIME.

- Each of the Internet protocols supported by Exchange has its own security settings.

Day 11

Security

by Brad M. McGehee

Although everyone claims that protecting their data from unauthorized access is important, it often seems that data security is a low priority for most organizations when it comes to devoting resources to it. Most people think that a security breach will never happen to them. This is a dangerous belief—especially if you connect your Exchange Server to the Internet, where your valuable data is exposed to the entire world for possible attack.

Because of the potential for attack, Microsoft has included many security features in Exchange to make an attack more difficult. But that is not enough; a good security policy also includes using additional software, such as firewalls, to provide protection against attack. Although non-Exchange security measures are important, they are beyond the scope of this chapter. This chapter focuses on the features built in to Exchange to increase security. This chapter covers the following topics:

- How Exchange uses NT security for data protection

- How to use Exchange's built-in security features

- How to install and implement Exchange Advanced Security

Studying for the security-related objectives of the certification exam is tough because most of the questions you will see on the exam are situational. In other words, the question presents a scenario and you have to resolve it appropriately. This means that you must learn how to apply what you learn in this chapter to answer the questions on the certification exam.

Objectives

This chapter addresses the following Microsoft exam objectives:

- Develop security strategies
- Configure security
- Manage site security
- Diagnose organization security problems

11.1. How Exchange Uses NT Security for Data Protection

One of the advantages of using Exchange instead of competing products is its tight integration with Windows NT Server. One of the ways Exchange is integrated with NT Server is that Exchange uses NT Server's security for many purposes. The first part of this chapter looks at how Exchange takes advantage of the various security features of NT Server, including the following specifics:

- How Exchange uses NT Server's login security
- How Exchange uses NT Server's NTFS file system for security
- How Exchange uses NT Server's security auditing capability

 Before you can fully understand Exchange security, you need a good understanding of how NT security works. If you don't have a good understanding of NT security, read up on NT security before taking the certification exam.

11.2. NT Server Login Security and Authentication

Exchange security and NT Server security are closely intertwined, as you will see in the next few sections. Specifically, you will learn the following:

- How Exchange uses NT Server logon authentication
- How Exchange takes advantage of NT Server users and groups
- How Exchange uses an NT Server user account for its services
- When Exchange ignores NT Server security

11.2.1. How Exchange Uses NT Server Logon Authentication

Normally, before any user can access an Exchange Server, he or she must first log on to NT Server with a unique user name and password. Assuming that Exchange is running in a standard NT server domain environment, what happens next is that the user is authenticated as a legal user by a domain controller (the Primary Domain

Controller or Backup Domain Controller) in the accounts domain where the account exists.

Once authenticated by NT Server, the user is assigned an Access Token, which defines the user's security context. In other words, an *Access Token* is a key that unlocks the doors in NT Server and Exchange that the user is permitted to open. Whenever a user attempts to access an object within Exchange (for example, a mailbox), the Access Token is compared with the object's Access Control List (a list of users who have permission to access an object) of the object he or she is trying to access. If the user's Access Token and the object's Access Control List "fit," the user is given access to the object. If there is "not a fit," access is denied.

As you learned in Day 3, "Exchange Server Installation and Configuration," whenever a new mailbox is created in Exchange, it must be associated with an NT Server user account. This task can be performed from either the Exchange Administrator or NT Server's User Manager for Domains. This is the step that tells Exchange who the legal users are and ties Exchange and NT Server security together.

Another important benefit of Exchange using NT Server's security is that users have to log on only once to the system and have to remember only one user name and password. This approach is in contrast to other mail systems that require a user to log on to both the network and the mail system using different user names and passwords.

11.2.2. How Exchange Takes Advantage of NT Server Users and Groups

Up to this point, all we have been concerned about with Exchange security is how a user can access his or her mailbox. By default, normal users cannot access any object in Exchange other than their mailboxes or the public folders for which they have been given explicit permission. But there are some times when you may want a regular user to directly access objects in Exchange. For example, you may want to allow a user to use the Exchange Administrator program to perform some minor administration task. With Exchange, this is possible by explicitly giving this user the necessary permission to access the object.

How this permission is given is explained in "How to Modify Exchange Object Permissions" later in this chapter; what is important to understand now is that you assign permissions to specific Exchange objects much the same way an NT administrator assigns file, directory, and printer permissions to NT users: by specifying which user or group of users has permission. In other words, Exchange can directly use NT Server's user accounts and groups to assign permissions on Exchange objects. This is just one more example of Exchange's tight integration with NT Server.

11.2.3. How Exchange Uses an NT Server User Account for Its Services

Another way Exchange uses NT Server's security is that each of Exchange's services must be started and logged on using an Exchange Site Services Account. As described earlier in Day 3, "Exchange Server Installation and Configuration," you have to create a Site Services Account before you install Exchange for the first time. When Exchange is installed, it uses this account as the logon account for each of the Exchange services instead of the built-in LocalSystem account. The benefit of logging on with an NT Server user account for services instead of the LocalSystem account is that the user account allows a service to cross over to other Exchange Servers. This happens because the services use an NT Server domain user account which, of course, can be used anywhere in a domain. The LocalSystem account is limited to the security context of the local server and cannot be used to cross over to other servers in a domain.

11.2.4. When Exchange Ignores NT Server Security

If a user attempts to access Exchange using a network, the security scenarios described in the preceding sections always play out. But if a user attempts to access Exchange over the Internet, the way the user is authenticated varies, depending on the client used to access Exchange resources, the protocol used to access Exchange, and how Exchange security is configured. For example, if a user is using Microsoft's Internet Explorer 4.0 to access his or her Exchange mailbox, the user has the option to be authenticated using NT's built-in authentication method. But if the user accesses his or her Exchange mailbox with a non-Microsoft web browser, NT authentication cannot be used. Instead, basic authentication is used, which is not as secure.

Exchange supports a variety of authentication methods, depending on the protocol and mail client used. These authentication methods are discussed in "Built-In Internet Protocol Security," later in this chapter.

11.3. Using NT Server's NTFS File System

NT Server supports two file systems—FAT and NTFS. Although either can be used on an Exchange Server, NTFS is recommended because it supports much better security than FAT, which offers no file-level security. NTFS security allows the NT administrator to prevent anyone without permission from accessing any files located on an NT Server, including any Exchange files.

Using NTFS is especially critical when your network is connected to the Internet. NTFS prevents hackers who get into your system from accessing files on your servers.

> **Warning**
>
> Keep in mind that the default NTFS file permission is to give all permissions on files to the Everyone group. Be sure that you don't forget to change the NTFS permissions for any new directories or files created on an NT Server, or you may accidentally open your system up for unauthorized access.

When Exchange is installed, it assigns specific share-level permissions to some of the directories it creates to store its program and data files, but it does not automatically create NTFS permissions on any of them. To ensure greater security, you will also want to set NTFS permissions on these same directories to prevent unauthorized access.

11.4. Using NT Server's Auditing Ability

Because Exchange security is tied to NT Server's security, you can take advantage of NT Server's capability to audit virtually any NT or Exchange object.

For auditing to work, Exchange must be located on an NTFS partition, and auditing must be turned on with the User Manager of Domains. If you want file or direct auditing, you must turn it on using the NT Explorer.

If you turn on auditing for Exchange, you can tell whether anyone is trying to make unauthorized access to any Exchange objects. This is especially important if your Exchange Server is connected to the Internet. By reviewing the security log in the NT Event Viewer on a regular basis, you can determine whether anyone is trying to breach security.

11.5. How to Use Exchange's Built-In Security Features

In addition to the NT Server security features described in the first part of this chapter, Exchange has some of its own built-in security features. The following sections look at what these features do and how you can configure them. The following sections cover these topics:

- Exchange administrative roles
- How to display Exchange object permissions
- Exchange object permissions and context
- How to modify Exchange object permissions

11.5.1. Exchange Administrative Roles

If you are familiar with Windows NT Server, you know that within any given domain there is only one Administrative role. You also know that there is no such role as an assistant administrator. Sure, there are the Server Operators and Account Operator's roles, but these roles are very limited in capability. In NT Server, if you have been given administrative rights, you can do everything. This can be a problem in NT Server if you want to have multiple levels of administrative control. Until NT Server 5.0 comes out, we are stuck with this limitation.

Exchange administration, on the other hand, works differently. Unlike NT Server, which has only one administrative role, Exchange has essentially five administrative roles: Permissions Admin, Admin, Service Account Admin, View Only Admin, and the Key Manager Administrator. An administrative role specifies the set of rights that define how much and what type of access an administrator has on a particular object. Here's what each administrative role provides:

- **Permissions Admin:** This is the administrative role with the most rights. The Permissions Admin can perform any task in Exchange, including changing object permissions. By default, whoever installs Exchange becomes the Permissions Admin. This may or may not be what best suites your security plans, and you may have to change who is the Permissions Admin in your organization.

- **Admin:** This is the next level of Exchange administrator. Users with this role can perform any Exchange administrative task except change object permissions.
- **View Only Admin:** This administrative role allows the user to view Exchange configuration settings, but not to change them.
- **Service Account Admin:** This administrative role is used only by the NT Server user account you specified during installation to be used by the Exchange services. Users are not assigned this role.
- **Key Manager Administrator:** This special administrative role pertains to your Exchange organization only if you install a Key Management Server in your organization. Key Management Servers are discussed later in this chapter. Users with this role can administer Exchange's Advanced Security features, which other administrative roles (including the Permissions Admin) are not permitted to do.

As you can see, you have a lot of flexibility when designating administrative roles in Exchange. The key is to keep things simple by using only those roles you need and assigning the minimum number of people to each of the roles. How you assign NT Server users and groups to these roles is described in "How to Modify Exchange Object Permissions" later in this chapter.

11.5.2. How to Display Exchange Object Permissions

Virtually every object in Exchange can be assigned its own unique set of permissions. Although this is possible, it is rarely done because of the amount of work it takes to do it (plus, it does not really provide much benefit). Instead, it makes more sense to control permissions at a very high level. For example, it is much easier to set the permissions for the entire Configuration container (which includes all objects that fall under this container) than it is to change the permissions for each of the individual objects.

Because of this, the Exchange Administrator program displays object Permissions pages only for container objects, not for every Exchange object. But if you want, you can configure Exchange to display a Permissions page for every object. After you make this change, you can display the Permissions page and change permissions on an object-by-object basis. Unless you intend to change an object's specific permissions, you will probably not want to display the Permissions page for each object because doing so just adds to the confusion on the screen.

11

Here's how to tell Exchange to always display the Permissions page for all Exchange objects:

1. Load the Exchange Administrator program.

2. Select Tools|Options from the menu bar. This action displays the Options dialog box.

3. Select the Permissions page (see Figure 11.1).

Figure 11.1.

From the Options dialog box, you can display the Permissions page for all Exchange objects.

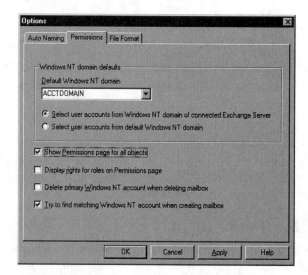

4. Select the Show Permissions Page for All Objects checkbox.

5. Click OK to save the new setting and close the Options dialog box.

Now, every time you display any Exchange object's Properties dialog box, you will see a Permissions page, on which you can change the permissions for that specific object. You can assign permission for a single NT Server user account or for an NT Server group.

Leaving the Show Permissions Page for All Objects option on or off makes no difference to Exchange. Because Exchange already has more than enough tabs in the object Properties dialog boxes, you may want to leave this option off to make it easier to read the page tabs.

11.5.3. Exchange Object Permissions and Context

Exchange defines rights and permissions differently than does NT Server. In Exchange, a *permission* is a set of rights to control Exchange objects; those rights can be granted to one or more NT Server users or groups. Exchange rights include the following:

- Add Child
- Modify User Attribute
- Delete
- Logon
- Modify Permission
- Replication
- Mailbox Owner
- Search
- Send As

Each of these rights to Exchange objects can be assigned to any NT Server user or group.

Permissions are affected by the context of the Exchange object. A *context* is a group of related permissions that have distinct boundaries. This concept is much easier to understand if we relate it directly to Exchange. In Exchange, there are three contexts:

- **Organization.** Any permission given at the organization context level applies only to the Organization container object, which includes all the containers under it. In other words, if I am assigned Permissions Admin for an organization, I am also the Permissions Admin for every site and server in the organization.

- **Site.** Permissions given at the site context level apply only to that site and all its containers. For example, if I am made a Permissions Admin of one site, I am the Permissions Admin for only that site, no others.

- **Configuration.** Permissions given at the configuration context level only apply to the Configuration container and any objects in it. For example, if I am made a Permission Admin for a Configuration container, I am the Permission Admin only for that container; I am not the Permission Admin for any other containers at the same level in the Exchange hierarchy.

11

By default, anyone who is given permission at a higher level has the same permissions for any context levels below it.

By using context levels, you can very finely control who can perform what tasks on Exchange objects. The key to success here is to keep things from being complicated by using the highest possible context to assign permissions when possible.

11.5.4. How to Modify Exchange Object Permissions

Now that you understand the various administrative roles, permissions, and contexts, it's time you learn how to actually change object permissions. In the following exercise, you learn how to change permissions at the container level, and then at the leaf object level. A *leaf object* is an Exchange object that has no objects below it. Both techniques are very similar, but the screens are somewhat different.

The first part of this exercise shows you how to change permissions at the container level:

1. Start the Exchange Administrator program.

2. Click a container that represents an Exchange site, making sure that it is highlighted in the Container pane. Although this is an example of changing permissions at the container level, the same procedure applies to every container that has a Permissions property page.

3. Select File|Properties from the menu bar and then select the Permissions page from the site's Properties dialog box (see Figure 11.2). The Permissions page shows you who has been given permission to this object, along with their assigned role.

4. To give permission to this container object to others, click the Add button. This action displays the Add Users and Groups dialog box (see Figure 11.3). If this screen looks familiar, it's because it is the same screen used to assign permissions within NT. Use this dialog box to select an NT Server user or group to add to the list of users who can access this container object.

5. To add a new user or group, click the user or group in the Names pane and then click the Add button. The user or group moves to the Add Names pane. When you are done adding users or groups, click OK. You return to the site's Properties dialog box.

6. Now you must assign a role to the NT Server user or group. To do this, first select the user or group to which you want to assign a new role and then click the down-arrow of the Roles drop-down list box. This action displays the currently available roles (see Figure 11.4). Select the role you want to assign; the drop-down box closes and the selected role is assigned.

Figure 11.2.

Container permissions can be changed from the Permissions page of the Properties dialog box.

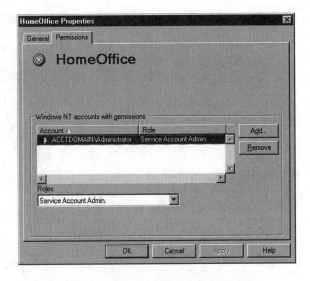

Figure 11.3.

The Add Users and Groups dialog box allows you to add NT Server users or groups to the list of those who can access the object.

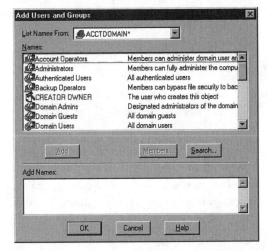

7. When you are done changing roles, click OK to save your change and exit the site's Properties dialog box.

Figure 11.4.

You change the role of a user or group using the Roles from this drop-down list box.

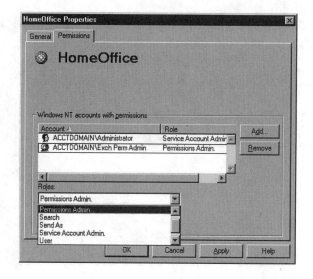

In this next exercise, we take a look at how to change the permissions of a leaf object:

1. From the Exchange Administrator program, open the Configuration container and then open the Protocols container.

2. In the Contents pane of the Protocols container, double-click the LDAP protocol. This action displays the LDAP (Directory) Site Defaults Properties dialog box.

3. Select the Permissions page (see Figure 11.5). This page is divided into two panes: The first pane shows any NT Server users or rights who have inherited permissions for this object. The second pane is used to add or remove any specific users or rights for this specific leaf object. Together, both panes show who has specific permission for this object and what the role of each user is.

4. If you want to add additional NT Server users or groups to the permissions for this leaf object, follow the steps in the preceding exercise to add a new user or group: First click the Add button to display the Add Users and Groups dialog box. From this dialog box, select one or more users or groups and click OK. Then assign the appropriate role to the user or group.

Keep in mind that most permissions are set at the container level, not at the leaf object level. This is true because it is much easier from an administrative point of view to set permissions at higher levels and let them flow down to lower levels.

Figure 11.5.

The screen you use to modify leaf object permissions is different from the one you use to modify container permissions.

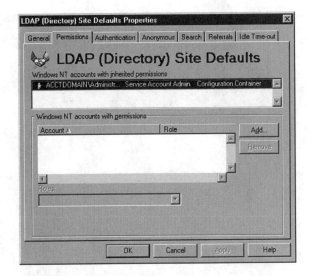

About the only time you would want to set a permission at the leaf object level instead of the container level is when you want to prevent a current Exchange administrator from performing some task that they normally have by default. For example, if you know that a particular administrator likes to modify a configuration parameter that you don't want changed, you can prevent that person from changing that option by restricting his or her access to that one leaf object.

11.6. Internet Mail Connector Security

If you use the Internet Mail Connector to send SMTP-based messages to other Exchange Servers, you will want to configure the Internet Mail Connector security options. The Internet Mail Connector security options are set on the Security page of the Internet Mail Service Properties dialog box (see Figure 11.6), accessed from the Connectors container. To access this option, first select the Internet Mail Connector so that it is highlighted. Then choose Properties from the File drop-down menu in Exchange Administrator. Then select the Security page. You can create a separate security configuration for each Exchange Server to which you connect and send SMTP-based mail.

11

Figure 11.6.

You can create separate security configuration settings for each Exchange site to which you send SMTP-based mail.

To add a new security configuration file, from the Security page, click the Add button; the Edit E-Mail Domain Security Information dialog box appears (see Figure 11.7).

Figure 11.7.

Enter domain security information on the Security page.

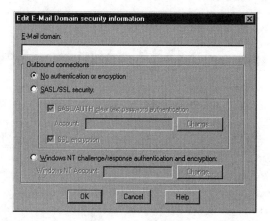

On this page, you must enter the IP address or domain name where the Exchange Server to which you are connecting exists; you must also specify how the sending Exchange Server is authenticated when it sends a message to another Exchange Server. You can choose to use no encryption or authentication, to use SSL encryption, or to use NT Server's Challenge/Response authentication encryption.

Once you have created a security configuration setting for an Exchange Server, you know that your SMTP-based communications between them is more secure.

11.7. Built-In Internet Protocol Security

In addition to the object permissions discussed in the first part of this chapter, Exchange also makes use of a specific level of security that applies only to Exchange's built-in Internet protocols. In Day 9, "Internet Connectivity Strategies," you learned that Exchange supports many different industry-standard Internet protocols. These protocols allow Exchange to communicate with a wide variety of mail clients, making it easier for users to check mail, update schedules, and access public folders.

Because of the security problems associated with being on the Internet, and the different types of user authentication used on the Internet, Microsoft has given these built-in Internet protocols their own special security features. The following sections explain the security features of these built-in Internet protocols:

- HTTP
- SSL
- LDAP
- POP3
- IMAP4
- NNTP

11

11.7.1. HTTP

Exchange uses HTTP to allow users to check mail using a web browser over the Internet. The user's web browser displays the Microsoft Outlook Web client, which is automatically downloaded to the user's system from an Internet Information Server (IIS) that communicates with an Exchange Server. The Microsoft Outlook Web client allows users to perform many of the same tasks the standard Outlook client can perform.

When a user uses the Outlook Web client to access his or her mailbox on Exchange, the user has to pass one of two types of user authentication. If the IIS running the Exchange Active Page Components exists on the same server as Exchange, Windows NT Challenge/Response authentication can be enabled, providing a high level of security. But if Exchange is running on a different Server than the IIS, Windows NT

Challenge/Response authentication cannot be used. Instead, basic authentication must be used. Basic authentication is an Internet standard available with most web browsers and does not offer much security. For example, with basic authentication, passwords are passed over the Internet unencrypted. Basic authentication for HTTP is configured on the IIS server, not with Exchange.

The HTTP protocol in Exchange also allows anonymous users to access public folders or the global address list on Exchange. If you do not want to support anonymous access, be sure to specify this preference on the General page of the HTTP (Web) Site Setting Properties dialog box in the Exchange Administrator.

For the best security when using the Outlook Web client, be sure that both IIS and Exchange run on the same server. If your Exchange site experiences heavy Outlook Web client access, you will probably want to dedicate one of the Exchange Servers in your Exchange site for this sole purpose.

11.7.2. SSL

Exchange supports the use of the Secure Sockets Layer (SSL) security protocol. SSL is an industry-standard protocol that encrypts data that flows over the Internet.

SSL is not built into Exchange. Instead, it is supported by IIS. Whenever an Outlook Web client hits the IIS to access Exchange, the communications between the web browser and the web server exchange all data in an encrypted format. This can be a great advantage if you are using basic authentication for your Outlook Web clients to access Exchange mailboxes. SSL encrypts all data—even the password—sent between the Outlook Web client and Exchange, providing good security.

Not only can you use SSL with basic authentication, you can also use it with NT Challenge/Response Authentication, offering even greater security.

To take advantage of SSL, both the web browser and web server must support it. IIS supports SSL, but before SSL can be used, a security certificate must first be obtained from a supplier of security certificates (such as VeriSign, Inc.). Once a security certificate is obtained, SSL can be used with IIS. For more information on security certificates, see VeriSign's web site at www.verisign.com.

11.7.3. LDAP

LDAP is an industry-standardInternet protocol that allows LDAP-enabled clients to access an Exchange organization's global address list.

LDAP is built into Exchange and is configured from the Exchange Administrator program in the LDAP (Directory) Site Defaults Properties dialog box. Two of the pages in the dialog box allow you to configure LDAP security, Authentication (shown in Figure 11.8) and Anonymous (shown in Figure 11.9).

Figure 11.8.

LDAP user authentication is set on the Authentication page.

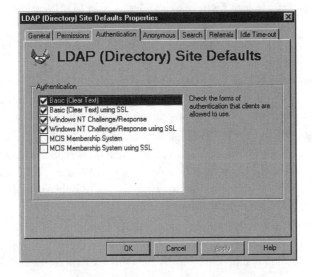

Figure 11.9.

LDAP anonymous access is set on the Anonymous page.

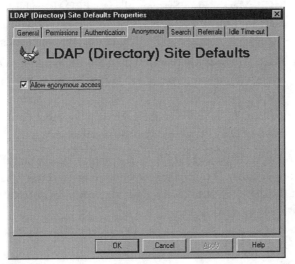

Most of LDAP security is controlled from the Authentication page; you use this page to specify what type of user authentication is permitted when an LDAP client tries to access Exchange's global address list. There are six levels of user authentication available; if you want, you can permit more than one level of authentication at a time. This list defines each user authentication option:

- **Basic (Clear Text):** Allows a user with an LDAP-enabled client to enter his or her Exchange mailbox name and password and to pass this information to the LDAP service without using encryption. Obviously, this option provides poor security.

- **Basic (Clear Text) Using SSL:** Allows an LDAP-enabled client to use SSL encryption to pass the mailbox name and password to the LDAP service. Both the client and server must support SSL for this option to work.

- **Windows NT Challenge/Response:** Allows an LDAP-enabled client to use NT Server's integrated security, which is encrypted, to log into the LDAP service. The client must be able to support Windows NT Challenge/Response security for this option to work. Currently, only Microsoft web clients permit NT Challenge/Response security.

- **Windows NT Challenge/Response Using SSL:** This option is the same as the preceding option except that it also uses SSL encryption. Currently, this option is supported only by the Outlook Express mail client.

- **MCIS Membership System:** Allows an LDAP-enabled client to be authenticated with the Windows NT network security, using the Microsoft Commercial Internet Server (MCIS) Membership System.

- **MCIS Membership System Using SSL:** This option is the same as the preceding option except that it also uses SSL encryption.

The more options you allow at the same time, the more flexible you make it for a wide variety of clients to access Exchange's global address list.

The Anonymous page of the LDAP (Directory) Site Defaults Properties dialog box is self-explanatory. If you want anonymous users to access your global address list, select the checkbox. If you want only your own users to access the list, don't allow anonymous access.

11.7.4. POP3

POP3 is an industry-standard Internet protocol that allows POP3 clients to check their mailboxes on Exchange. Like most of the other Internet protocols supported by Exchange, the POP3 security settings are found on the Authentication page in the POP3 (Mail) Site Defaults Properties dialog box. The Authentication page offers the same user authentication options it does for the LDAP protocol, described in the preceding section.

11.7.5. IMAP4

IMAP4 is an industry-standard Internet protocol that works very similarly to POP3. IMAP4 is designed to allow IMAP4 mail clients to check mailboxes on Exchange (which can act as an IMAP4 server). IMAP4 offers more features than POP3, such as the capability to access public folders.

Security for IMAP4 is controlled through two pages in the IMAP4 (Mail) Site Defaults Properties dialog box—Authentication and Anonymous. These two pages are virtually identical to the pages of the same name in the LDAP Site Defaults Properties dialog box. Use the Authentication page to select the various user authentication methods you want to support; use the Anonymous page to determine whether or not anonymous users can have access to public folders through IMAP4.

11.7.6. NNTP

NNTP is an industry-standard Internet protocol that allows Exchange to participate in Usenet newsfeeds and to publish public folders as newsgroups.

Security for NNTP is controlled through two pages in the NNTP (News) Site Defaults Properties dialog box—Authentication and Anonymous. These two pages are virtually identical to the pages of the same name in the LDAP and IMAP4 Site Defaults Properties dialog boxes. Use the Authentication page to select the various user authentication methods you want to support; use the Anonymous tab to determine whether or not anonymous users can have access to public folders published as newsgroups.

11.8. Exchange Advanced Security

One of the least understood and most underused features of Exchange Advanced Security. By installing an Exchange Key Management (KM) Server in an Exchange organization, email can be both *sealed* (encrypted) and *signed* (digitally signed with a digital signature), providing powerful security. The following sections explain the following:

■ How encryption and digital signatures work

■ How to install a KM Server

■ How to enable Advanced Security

■ How to send signed and sealed mail

11

When studying these sections in preparation for the certification exam, focus on learning the terminology and the major steps required to install and enable Advanced Security. This subject is not extensively covered on the exam, so don't worry about memorizing all the details.

11.8.1. How Encryption and Digital Signatures Work

Exchange's Advanced Security feature uses industry-standard public/private key technology along with secret keys used to protect private keys. Here's how Advanced Security works.

Each mailbox that has been enabled for Advanced Security is assigned two keys. One key is publicly known and is stored in a public area, where it can be accessed by anyone who requires access to it. The other key is a private key, which is kept secret by the mailbox user. The private key itself is protected with a secret key (a password), that prevents anyone other than the owner of the secret key from accessing the private key.

A *key* is a long number, generally 40 characters or longer. Because keys are so long, they are not used directly. To gain access to a key, a password is generally used. It is much easier to remember a password than it is to remember a key of 40 characters or longer.

Key technology can be used to seal (encrypt) messages or to sign (digitally sign) messages. Encrypted messages cannot be read by anyone who intercepts the message as it is being sent between recipients.

Although encryption prevents unauthorized users from reading messages, it does not prevent someone from forging or changing a message. Preventing this type of tampering is what digital signatures are for. A message with a digital signature guarantees that it came from the person who says they sent it. The digital signature also ensures that the message was not somehow altered in transit. When you send a message, you can seal it, sign it, or both. Performing both methods ensures the best security.

When a user wants to send an encrypted message, he or she uses the public key *of the recipient* to encrypt the message. The only person who can decrypt and read the message is the recipient because the only way the message can be decrypted is by using the recipient's private key. The recipient's public key is used to encrypt the message, and the recipient's private key is used to decrypt the message.

When a user wants to send a digitally signed message, he or she uses his or her own private key to sign the message. When the message is received by the recipient, the recipient uses the sender's public key to verify that the message indeed came from that person and was not altered. The sender's private key is used to sign the message, and the sender's public key is used to verify the message.

11.8.2. How to Install a KM Server

When planning to implement a KM Server in your Exchange organization, keep the following points in mind:

- There should be only one KM Server in an Exchange organization.

- The Exchange Server you choose to act as the KM Server should be in the same domain where you centralize administration; it should use the NTFS file system; it should be located in a physically secure location; and it should be backed up often.

- The server you use to install Exchange and the KM Server software must also be a Microsoft Certificate server configured as either a server or a client to another Microsoft Certificate server. The KM Server uses the Certificate server to certify public signing and encryption keys. In addition, the Microsoft Certificate server must also have the Microsoft Exchange Policy Module installed. The Exchange Policy Module enables the Certificate server to evaluate, accept, and issue certificate requests. The Microsoft Certificate server and the Exchange Server Policy Module are available free from Microsoft and are designed to run under IIS 4.0. Be sure that the Certificate server is running properly before installing your KM Server.

Detailed coverage of the Microsoft Certificate server is beyond the scope of this book; for more information, see the documentation that comes with the Certificate server.

Because the steps involved in installing a KM Server are extensive—and because they are not covered on the certification exam—only the highlights are covered here:

- The KM software used to install a KM Server is accessed with Exchange's Setup program.

- During the installation of the software, you must deal with two passwords. One of the passwords is used to start the KM Server service; this password is generated for you. You can display the password on the screen so that you can write it down, or you can automatically write the setup routine to a floppy disk. This password is required every time the KM Server service is started. Keep this password in a secure place.

The second password is for the KM Server administrator. By default, this password is `password`. Once the KM Server is installed, change this password. Only a KM Server administrator can configure Advanced Security. You can create as many KM Server administrators as you deem necessary.

■ Once the KM software has been loaded, you must manually start the KM service. To start the KM service, you need the password, or the disk that contains the password, as mentioned in the preceding item. The KM service never starts automatically. Every time the server is rebooted, the KM service must be restarted manually.

Once a KM server has been installed and the service started, Advanced Security must still be configured. The following sections describe how this is done.

11.8.3. How to Enable Advanced Security

Once a KM Server has been installed and is running in an Exchange organization, Advanced Security can be enabled. Enabling Advanced Security is a four-step process:

1. The KM Manager must configure Advanced Security and configure various security policies.
2. The KM administrator must enable Advanced Security for the various Exchange sites that need it.
3. The KM administrator must enable individual recipients, or recipients in bulk, for Advanced Security.
4. Each user who is to be enabled for Advanced Security must enable Advanced Security on his or her client.

Once all these elements are in place, Advanced Security can be used to seal and sign messages.

The KM Administrator's Role

It is the responsibility of the KM administrator to configure Advanced Security and to enable Advanced Security for recipients. Advanced security configuration is performed using the Properties dialog box of the CA (Certificate Authority) object, located in the Configurations container of the Exchange site where the KM Server is located. The CA Properties dialog box includes the following pages:

- **General:** Shows the current display and directory names for the CA object, along with the name of the Certificate Authority used by the KM Server.

- **Permissions:** The standard Exchange Permissions page used to assign NT user accounts access to Exchange objects.

- **Administrators:** Used to add or remove KM administrators and change KM administrator passwords. You will want to change the default password of password as soon as possible after starting the KM service.

- **Passwords:** Used to set multiple password policies. To prevent a KM manager from making unauthorized security configuration changes, you can require more than one KM administrator to authorize some security tasks, further increasing the overall security of Exchange.

- **Enrollment:** Used to set security policies in regard to how individual or bulk recipients are handled. For example, you can specify whether temporary keys can be sent to recipients using email or whether they must be personally handed to the recipient.

- **Certificate Trust List:** Used to import and revoke certificates from other organizations. The trust list allows Exchange users to send sealed and signed messages to foreign mail systems. The certificates are used to bind a public key from an organization to a particular certification authority.

Only a KM administrator can access these pages of the Properties dialog box to make changes.

Configuring Site Security

Once Advanced Security has been configured, the KM administrator must enable Advanced Security for each site that is to participate in Advanced Security. To do this, use the Site Encryption Configuration Properties dialog box, found in the site's Configuration container. This dialog box includes three pages:

- **General:** The object's display and directory names are shown, as usual. Also, you can specify the site at which the KM Server is located.

- **Permissions:** This is the standard Permissions page that you use to assign NT user accounts to Exchange objects.

- **Algorithms:** This page specifies the type of encryption used by Exchange. You can choose the Preferred Microsoft Exchange 4.0 and 5.0 Encryption Algorithms, the Preferred S/MIME Encryption Algorithms, and the Preferred Security Message Format.

11

Exchange can use any one of the following encryption algorithms to encrypt messages: CAST-64, CAST-40, and DES. In North America, you can choose whichever method you prefer. The CAST-64 algorithm provides the highest degree of security. If your Exchange site is not in North America, you can use only the CAST-40 algorithm, which is the only one of the three algorithms that is allowed to be exported outside the United States.

If the mail clients you are using to access Exchange support the Secure Multipurpose Internet Mail Extensions (S/MIME) format, you can use it to encrypt and digitally sign messages sent between S/MIME-compatible mail clients. S/MIME supports several different algorithms including DES, 3DES, RC2-40, RC2-64, and RC2-128. You can use any of these algorithms with S/MIME.

You can also select the Preferred Security Message Format. You can choose to use Exchange's own propriety format or S/MIME when sending sealed or signed messages.

Once you have configured the appropriate Exchange sites for Advanced Security, it's time for the KM administrator to enable Advanced Security for the recipients who need it.

Enabling Advanced Security for Recipients

Once all Advanced Security settings have been made, it's time for the KM administrator to enable Advanced Security for recipients. This can be done one recipient at a time, or it can be done *en masse*.

Here's how a KM administrator enables a single recipient for Advanced Security.

1. Select the Security page from the user's mailbox Properties dialog box. This page does not appear if a KM Server has not already been installed and configured for the Exchange organization.

2. From the Security page, click the Enable Advanced Security button. This action generates a one-time-use, temporary key that must be given to the recipient so that he or she can turn on Advanced Security at his or her mail client. This key can be either automatically sent to the user with email or hand delivered to the recipient. Your delivery options depend on how you set the security polices earlier in the configuration process.

Now the KM administrator is done. It is up to the recipient to configure security on his or her own mail client using the temporary key. The KM administrator can enable as few or as many recipients as desired, whenever desired.

The Recipient's Role

Once a KM administrator has enabled Advanced Security for a recipient and delivered the temporary key to the recipient, the recipient must perform several steps before Advanced Security is actually enabled. The steps required to enable security vary depending on which mail client is being used. But in essence, the recipient must enter the temporary key when prompted to verify that he or she is participating in Advanced Security. Once the key is entered into the client software, a message is sent to the KM Server, which verifies that the temporary key is legitimate. If the temporary key is correct, a message is returned to the user and a local key is created and secured with a secret password assigned by the user. If the key was entered incorrectly, the recipient can try again.

Finally, Advanced Security has been enabled and the user can send sealed or signed messages to others who are also participating in Advanced Security.

11.8.4. How to Send Signed and Sealed Mail

If a user wants to send a sealed message to another user using Advanced Security, he or she first creates the message and then selects the encryption option at the mail client. The recipient's public key is retrieved from the Certificate server and used to encrypt the message; the message is then sent to the recipient. Once the recipient receives the message and attempts to read the message, he or she is prompted to enter his or her secret password. By entering the secret password, the recipient's private key is extracted and used to decrypt the message, which now can be read.

If a user wants to send a signed message, he or she selects the signing option at the mail client and then enters his or her secret password. This action retrieves the sender's private key, which is used to digitally sign the message; the message is then sent. Once the message is received by the recipient, the recipient can verify the digital signature by selecting the appropriate option at the mail client. This action retrieves the sender's public key from the Certificate server, which is used to validate the digital signature and message.

11.8.5. Troubleshooting Advanced Security

Like other Exchange services, the KM Server logs events to the NT Event log. If you are having problems with the KM Server, your first step should be to view the KM Server events in the NT Event log. This log may give you a clue about what is causing any problem you may be experiencing. But as is true for many NT Event log

11

messages, the messages are often not much help because the explanations provided are either incomprehensible or incomplete. If this is the case, write down the message's event ID and then do a search for this ID using Microsoft TechNet or Microsoft's web site. If the problem is a known problem, you should be able to find out more about what is causing the problem—and hopefully how to fix it.

Lab

This lab consists of review questions pertaining to this chapter. It provides an opportunity to apply the knowledge you've gained in this chapter.

Questions

1. You are planning to install a new Exchange organization. The organization will include several sites, all connected through the Internet. Your boss is concerned about security. You tell your boss that Exchange has many built-in security features. Which of the following security feature will you tell your boss about?

   A. Exchange includes a built-in firewall to prevent unauthorized users from accessing data on the Exchange Server.

   B. Exchange includes an Advanced Security feature that allows users to send encrypted and digitally signed data over the Internet.

   C. Each of Exchange's many built-in Internet protocols has its own security options.

   D. Exchange automatically uses S/MIME to encrypt all email messages sent between all Exchange recipients.

   E. Exchange takes advantage of NT Server's security features, such as Challenge/Response authentication.

2. You have just hired a new assistant who will help you administer Exchange. Unfortunately, she is not familiar with NT security. You tell her about the various NT Server security features that Exchange can take advantage of. Which of the following is *not* a good example of how Exchange takes advantage of NT Server security?

   A. Exchange uses NT Server's DNS server to prevent unauthorized SMTP-based servers from sending Exchange SMTP-based messages.

   B. Exchange uses NT Server's login security.

   C. Exchange can take advantage of NT Server's NTFS partitions for added security.

   D. Exchange can take advantage of NT Server's Security Auditing capabilities.

11

3. A new employee, who already has an NT Server user account, is unable to access his Exchange mailbox. This is the first time the user has ever tried to use his mailbox. He was told by another user that all new employees are automatically given an NT Server user account and an Exchange mailbox. Although he can log on to NT Server, he cannot access his mailbox. Which of the following is the most likely cause of the problem?

   A. The employee used the wrong NT Server user account and password.

   B. The employee's mailbox has yet to be created.

   C. The employee is using the wrong mail client.

   D. The employee is attempting to use the wrong mailbox name.

4. You have just been hired to become the administrator of an Exchange site. The previous Exchange administrator was not very familiar with Exchange and made many mistakes installing and configuring the Exchange organization. One problem you notice right away is that anyone—even average users—can use the Exchange Administrator program to configure Exchange. How did the other administrator ever allow this to happen?

   A. When the other administrator installed the first Exchange Server in the organization, he used his own NT user account for the Exchange service account.

   B. The other administrator did not format with NTFS the hard drives that contain the Exchange files.

   C. The other administrator forgot to assign a password to the Permissions Admin global group.

   D. The other administrator gave the NT Server Everyone group Permission Admin rights.

5. You are designing a new Exchange organization and want to ensure that each site in the organization is administered by only a single administrator. You want to prevent an administrator from one site from making changes in another site. How can you implement this in Exchange?

   A. You can do this only by allowing the correct person to actually install the Exchange site he or she will be administering. By default, the person who installs an Exchange Server is automatically the administrator for that site.

    B. The Permissions Admin can designate additional Permissions Admins for each site, on a site-by-site basis.

    C. The Permissions Admin can designate specific Exchange site administrators by assigning the NT Server user account of each Exchange administrator to the Admin role for each specific site.

    D. This is not possible. Anyone who is designated as an Exchange administrator can always change any Exchange setting in any Exchange site within the same Exchange organization.

6. You want to add Advanced Security to your Exchange organization. However, you don't want every Exchange administrator to be able to configure Advanced Security. How can you accomplish this objective?

    A. By default, the only person who can configure Advanced Security is the Exchange administrator who originally installed it. Unless this person adds additional KM administrators, this person is the only KM administrator.

    B. Only Permissions Admins can configure Advanced Security; Admins or any other Exchange administrative role cannot configure Advanced Security.

    C. This task is not performed using the Exchange Administrator program; instead it is set using NTFS permissions.

    D. This is not possible. All Exchange administrators can configure Advanced Security.

7. You want to change the object permissions for an Exchange object, but when you go to the Properties dialog box for the object, the Permissions page is not there. But you *know* that this object has a Permissions page. What happened to it?

    A. For the Permissions pages to be displayed for Exchange objects, Advanced Security must first be turned on.

    B. The Show Permissions Page for All Objects option on the Permissions page of the Options dialog box must be selected.

    C. You have to be a Permission Admin to see the Permissions page.

    D. The Exchange SA service has not been started.

11

8. You want to maximize the security between two separate Exchange sites that exchange mail using SMTP. Which one of the following steps would you most likely take if you wanted to accomplish this goal?

   A. First, you would turn on PPTP filtering in the Control Panel|Network dialog box. Then you would configure NT Server Challenge/Response security between the two Exchange Servers.

   B. There are no special security configuration options available when you establish a link between two Exchange Servers. The only way to ensure good security is to use a third-party firewall.

   C. You must configure the Security page of the HTTP protocol, which is located in the Protocols container. Once this option is configured, you must stop and then restart the Internet Mail Connector.

   D. You would use the Security page of the Internet Mail Connector Properties dialog box to create a security configuration setting for the two Exchange Servers. This security configuration includes the type of authentication to be used between the two Exchange Servers.

9. You have configured an Exchange site to use the Exchange Active Page Components so that a web browser can be used to access a user's Exchange mailbox over the Internet. Although everything appears to be running correctly, you hear a report that an unauthorized user has somehow gained access to several of your users' mailboxes. How is this possible, and how can you prevent this from happening in the future?

   A. You forgot to turn on HTTP filtering. Once you turn it on, unauthorized users cannot access your users' mailboxes.

   B. When you configured your Exchange site, you placed IIS on one server and Exchange on another server. By doing this, only basic authentication is available, which means that someone with a sniffer program can possibly listen in to a connection between a user's web browser and IIS and find the user's login name and password. One way to prevent this in the future is to incorporate SSL on the IIS server to encrypt any communications between the web browser and IIS server.

   C. Most likely, the reports you have heard are false. You know that any communication between a web browser and IIS are always encrypted.

D. By default, all information sent between IIS and a web browser are sent using clear text. This means that anyone with a sniffer program can listen in and steal user names and passwords. The best way to resolve this problem is to incorporate Advanced Security in your Exchange organization for those users who have to access their mailboxes over the Internet.

10. You want to allow your users to use an LDAP-enabled client to view the global address list of your Exchange organization, but you do not want anyone else to do so. How can you configure Exchange to accomplish this goal?

   A. You configure LDAP for basic authentication.

   B. You configure LDAP for basic authentication using SSL.

   C. You configure HTTP for basic authentication using SSL.

   D. You configure LDAP to not permit anonymous access.

11. You are the administrator of an Exchange organization and your boss has come to you about a possible security breach in the email system. She believes that someone has been forging mail in her name, which has proved to be embarrassing to her. As the Exchange administrator, how can you configure Exchange to prevent someone from forging an email message?

   A. Configure Exchange with NT Server Challenge/Response authentication using SSL.

   B. Configure Exchange with SSL and S/MIME.

   C. Configure Exchange for Advanced Security, then enable your boss's mailbox (and the mailboxes of anyone to whom she sends messages) with Advanced Security. This way, she can encrypt her messages so that no one else can forge her email messages.

   D. Configure Exchange for Advanced Security, then enable your boss's mailbox (and the mailboxes of anyone to whom she sends messages) with Advanced Security. This way, she can sign her messages with a digital signature to guarantee that her messages cannot be forged.

12. Before you can install and configure Advanced Security in Exchange, which of the following must be in place?

   A. Microsoft Certificate Server

   B. Microsoft Exchange Server Policy Module

C. IIS Version 4.0

D. Internet Mail Connector

E. Exchange Active Page Components

Exercises

Exercise 1: Turning On Object Permissions

> **Note**
>
> This exercise addresses the following certification exam objectives:
> - Configure security
> - Manage site security

This exercise steps you through the process of turning on the Permissions page in the Properties dialog boxes of the various Exchange objects. By default, this option is turned off. By turning this option on, you can view the Permissions page for each Exchange object and make any changes you deem appropriate. This exercise assumes that Exchange has been properly loaded and configured.

1. Load the Exchange Administrator program.
2. From the menu bar, select Tools|Options. This action displays the Options dialog box.
3. From the Options dialog box, select the Permissions page.
4. Select the Show Permissions Page for All Objects option so that a check appears in the checkbox.
5. Click OK to save the setting. The Options dialog box disappears.
6. From now on, when you view the Properties dialog box of an Exchange object, the Permissions tab is displayed.
7. To test this now, open the Configuration container for an Exchange site and click the Protocols container. Double-click any of the protocols in the contents screen. This action displays the object's Properties dialog box. Note that the Permissions tab is displayed.

Exercise 2: Adding a New Exchange Administrator to an Exchange Site

> **Note**
>
> This exercise addresses the following Microsoft exam objective:
> - Configure security

11

By default, the person who first loads Exchange Server in an Exchange organization is the Permissions Admin for the organization and the site. If you want to add additional Exchange administrators, you must specifically do so. This exercise shows you how to add a new Exchange administrator to an organization. This exercise assumes that Exchange has been properly loaded and configured, and that you are currently the Permission Admin for the organization.

1. Load the Exchange Administrator program.

2. Click the organization's name in the Container pane. This is the very top object in the hierarchy. Be sure that the organization's name is highlighted.

3. From the menu bar, choose File|Properties. This action displays the organization's Properties dialog box.

4. Select the Permissions tab to display the Permissions page.

5. To add a new Permissions Admin to the organization, click the Add button. This action displays the Add Users and Groups dialog box.

6. From the Names window, click the name of an NT user whom you want to assign as a Permissions Admin for your Exchange organization.

7. Click the Add button to add this NT user account to the Add Names window.

8. Click OK after you have added the NT user account to the Names window; the Add Users and Groups dialog box disappears.

9. From the organization's Properties dialog box, click the NT user account you just added, making sure that it is highlighted.

10. Click the Roles drop-down list box and then select Permissions Admin. The drop-down list box closes; the NT user account you added now appears in the Windows NT Accounts with Permissions pane as a Permissions Admin.

11. Click OK to save your changes and close the dialog box. You return to the Exchange Administrator program.

The user you just added is now a Permissions Admin for your entire Exchange organization.

Exercise 3: Changing LDAP Security

Note

This exercise addresses the following Microsoft exam objective:

■ Configure security

Sometimes, the default Internet protocol security settings are not appropriate for your Exchange site and must be changed. This exercise shows you how to make a change to the LDAP protocol. This exercise assumes that Exchange has been properly loaded and configured.

1. Load the Exchange Administrator program.

2. Open the Configuration container for an Exchange site and then click the Protocols container. Double-click the LDAP protocol in the contents screen. This action displays the LDAP (Directory) Site Defaults Properties dialog box.

3. Select the Authentication tab. This page specifies the various authentication methods Exchange will accept when an LDAP-enabled client tries to access Exchange's global address list. Suppose that you want to prevent anyone from using the basic (clear text) authentication method to be authenticated because you don't want your user account names and passwords to be exposed to the Internet in clear text. To prevent this, deselect this option.

4. Select the Anonymous tab. If you don't want anonymous (non-Exchange users) to access Exchange's global address list, be sure that the Allow Anonymous Access option is deselected.

5. When you are done making any changes to LDAP security, click OK to save your changes. From now on, your changes are in force.

Answers to Questions

1. **B, C, E**   Exchange does not have a built-in firewall, nor is S/MIME used for all message encryption (although it can be turned on for use by S/MIME mail clients).

2. **A**   Although Exchange does use DNS for many tasks, it does not use it to enforce security.

3. **B**   Although there are many possible reasons that a user may not be able to access his or her mailbox, of the available options, the most likely reason is that the mailbox has not been created yet. The other options don't make any sense in the context of the question.

4. **D**   The only way for this to happen is for the NT Server Everyone group to be assigned the Permissions Admin role. This situation is easily remedied by removing this group from this role.

5. **C**   Only a user who has been assigned the Permissions Admin role can change permissions for Exchange objects. People who have been assigned the

11

Admin role cannot change object permissions, but they can perform all other Exchange administrative tasks. Because of this, it is the responsibility of the Permissions Admin to assign the appropriate NT user accounts to the Admin role in each site. After assigning an individual NT user account to a specific role in a specific site, only the assigned people can administer the site to which they are assigned, not any others.

6. **A**   The administrator who installs a KM Server is, by default, the KM administrator and is the only person who can configure Exchange Advanced Security. If additional KM administrators are desired, they must be added by the default KM administrator.

7. **B**   By default, an object's Permissions tab is not shown. If you want the tab displayed with the rest of the tabs when the object's Properties dialog box is displayed, you must turn it on as indicated.

8. **D**   You would use the Security page of the Internet Mail Connector Properties dialog box to create a security configuration setting for the two Exchange Servers. The configuration setting would include the type of authentication to be used between the two Exchange Servers. If you have more than two sites you want to connect this way, you can set up a separate security configuration setting for each site connection.

9. **B**   If Exchange and IIS are on separate servers, basic authentication is the only type of authentication allowed. If Exchange and IIS are on the same server, you can use either basic authentication or NT Server Challenge/Response authentication. By adding SSL support to your IIS server, you can encrypt any communication between a web browser and IIS, preventing sniffer programs from being successful at stealing user names and passwords.

10. **D**   By preventing anonymous access, only users with accounts in Exchange can use LDAP to access Exchange's global address list.

11. **D**   The use of digital signatures is the only way to be absolutely sure that someone is not forging email messages. Encryption only scrambles data, it does not guarantee that a message is from a specific user.

12. **A, B, C**   All three of these components must be installed, configured, and operational before you can install and configure Advanced Security in Exchange.

Here are a few fast facts about
this chapter that you may want
to know ahead of time. These
facts provide great last-minute
study material.

- Upgrading any previous version of Exchange to Exchange 5.5 is performed using the Exchange Setup program.

- Planning the Exchange upgrade process is very important. If you don't plan the upgrade properly, you could turn a working Exchange organization into a non-working Exchange organization.

- Single-phase migration and multiphase migration are two strategies for migrating from a foreign mail system to Exchange.

- Single-phase migration works best in smaller environments where the infrastructure is already in place to support the clients, such as Windows NT servers and domains.

- Multiphase migration is usually done in very large organizations where the network and personnel resources are not large enough to support migrating the entire user base at once.

- The Migration wizard is used to import the files that were exported from the existing mail system.

Day 12

System Migration

This chapter covers two important aspects of migrating to Microsoft Exchange: First, you learn how to migrate from previous versions of Microsoft Exchange to Exchange 5.5. Second, you learn how to migrate non-Microsoft Exchange mail systems to Exchange 5.5. Both of these very powerful features greatly lessen the workload of upgrading to Exchange. This chapter covers the tools and steps needed to perform a migration, the tools included with Exchange, and the steps necessary to migrate from an unsupported system.

Exchange supports migration from the following systems:

- Microsoft Exchange Version 4.0 and Version 5.0
- Microsoft Mail for PC Networks (Version 3.x)
- Microsoft Mail for AppleTalk Networks (Version 3.x)
- Lotus cc:Mail (database Version DB6 and DB8)
- Novell GroupWise (Versions 4.1 and 4.1a)
- Netscape Collabra Share (Versions 1.x and 2.x)
- Digital All-in-1 (Versions 2.3 and later)
- IBM PROFS/OfficeVision (all versions)
- Verimation Memo MVS (Version 3.2.1 and later)

Objectives

This chapter addresses the following Microsoft exam objectives:

- ■ Identify strategies for migration from previous versions of Exchange Server to Exchange Server 5.5
- ■ Import directory, message, and scheduling data from existing mail systems

12.1. Migrating to Microsoft Exchange 5.5

In the more than two years Exchange has been available, tens of thousands of Exchange servers have been installed to serve millions of Exchange clients. Because of this, there is a good chance you will have the opportunity to upgrade one or more Exchange servers to Exchange 5.5.

Fortunately, upgrading to Exchange 5.5 from previous versions is relatively easy. But like any important task, you must take the time to carefully plan the upgrade—especially if your Exchange organization has multiple sites. The following sections cover these important steps:

- Planning the upgrade
- Performing the upgrade
- Following up on the upgrade

12.1.1. Planning the Upgrade

If you are planning to upgrade your current version of Exchange to Exchange 5.5, you probably already realize two important facts. First, your users depend on their email to conduct business, and you want to do your best to minimize the amount of downtime that occurs because of the upgrade. Second, you don't want to do anything to lose anyone's data. Naturally, then, you want to carefully plan your upgrade. Even if you have only a single Exchange Server to upgrade, you should think through the upgrade before you perform it. In large Exchange organizations, you should not only carefully plan the migration, you should commit it to paper for review by others. Although an upgrade is generally easy to perform, simple mistakes can result in lost data and much wasted time.

As part of the upgrade planning process, you will want to consider and plan for the following issues:

- Verify that current servers meet the requirements for Exchange 5.5
- Identify which previous versions of Exchange exist
- Identify directory replication bridgehead Exchange Servers
- Identify the Key Management Server
- Verify that the site services account has the correct user rights
- Back up your data on all servers

■ Plan for lots of down time

■ Make sure that an NT administrator will perform the Exchange upgrade

Verify that Current Servers Meet Requirements for Exchange 5.5

Exchange 5.5 has slightly different minimum hardware and software requirements than did previous versions of Exchange. One of your tasks is to identify the current hardware in your Exchange Servers and upgrade those servers before you begin the migration if you find that the current hardware does not meet the minimum requirements to run Exchange 5.5. You should also do the same for your NT Server software. You can find information about the hardware and software requirements for Exchange 5.5 in Day 3, "Exchange Server Installation and Configuration."

When you begin the upgrade process, you are asked whether you want to perform a Standard Upgrade or a Fault-Tolerant Upgrade. If you choose to perform a Standard Upgrade, the Exchange Server must have free space equal to 15 percent of the current size of the Exchange databases. If you choose to perform a Fault-Tolerant Upgrade, the Exchange server must have an amount of free space equal to the current Exchange databases.

Consider both of these suggestions as *minimum* amounts of required disk space. You should include an extra amount of free disk space above and beyond these recommendations just to play it safe.

Identify Which Previous Versions of Exchange Exist

You must identify the versions of Exchange that are currently running on the existing Exchange Servers. This includes which, if any, Exchange Service Packs are in use on your Exchange Servers. Hopefully, all your Exchange Servers are using the same version.

12

Although you can upgrade from any version of Exchange to version 5.5, Microsoft recommends that your Exchange Servers be running at least Exchange version 4.0, Service Pack 2. This minimum makes the upgrade go much more smoothly. If you don't have a copy of this Service Pack, you can download it free from Microsoft's web site. If you have only a single Exchange site, you can ignore this recommendation because it applies only to Exchange organizations with two or more sites.

If you don't upgrade to at least Service Pack 2 for Exchange version 4.0 as recommended, you must upgrade your Exchange Servers in a specific order—an order that may or may not be convenient. If you don't upgrade the servers in the proper order, any directory replication you have established between sites in your Exchange organization will fail. To prevent this failure, you must upgrade all your directory replication bridgehead servers first. After these bridgehead servers are upgraded, you can upgrade the rest of the Exchange Servers in your organization in any order.

 Note A directory replication bridgehead server is the server in each Exchange site designated to move directory replication messages from site to site.

Identify Directory Replication Bridgehead Exchange Servers

As just mentioned, if you choose to upgrade Exchange Servers that aren't running at least Exchange version 4.0, Service Pack 2, and if you have multiple sites, you must upgrade all the directory replication bridgehead servers before upgrading the other Exchange Servers to Exchange 5.5. Obviously, then, you must identify which Exchange Servers in your organization, if any, are directory replication bridgehead servers. You should make this information an important part of your plan because it determines the order in which you upgrade your Exchange Servers.

Although it is not required, Microsoft also makes the following recommendation about Exchange organizations that have multiple sites: No matter what previous version of Exchange you have—even if it's version 5.0—you should always upgrade your directory replication bridgehead servers first. Not following this recommendation doesn't cause your site's directory replication to fail, but it helps ensure that there will be no problems with directory replication in your site as you upgrade each server. After all thedirectory replication bridgehead servers have been upgraded, you can upgrade the other Exchange Servers in any order.

Identify the KM Server

If your organization uses a Key Management (KM) Server for advanced security, you must also upgrade this server. When it is time to upgrade the Exchange Server running the KM service, the KM administrator must be available to enter his or her KM password.

Verify That the Site Services Account Has the Correct User Rights

If you are upgrading from version 4.0 of Exchange, you must add one additional NT Server User right to your site services account before performing the upgrade.

You must add the Act as Part of the Operating System right. This right is required to take advantage of the POP3 protocol found in version 5.5. If you are upgrading from version 5, you don't have to worry about adding this user right because it has already been set for you.

Back Up the Data on All Servers

It should go without saying that you must back up all your Exchange databases before performing an upgrade. Although there should not be a problem with the upgrade, unexpected events can happen. Even if you decide to perform a Fault-Tolerant Upgrade, you still must make a backup. Although the odds of a Fault-Tolerant Upgrade failing and destroying all your data are slim, don't take the chance. Be sure to back up your Exchange Server databases using either the NT Backup program or a third-party backup program that has an Exchange Server back-up agent.

Plan for Lots of Downtime

You don't want to hear this, but plan for lots of time to perform the upgrade. Although it is difficult to predict the amount of time it will take for the upgrade, you must allocate time for making the original backup and performing the upgrade—and you should include some extra time just in case something goes wrong and you have to restore your backup.

If you are upgrading from version 4.0, plan on some extra time for the upgrade to complete. When Exchange performs the upgrade from version 4.0, it does it in two stages: First, it upgrades to version 5.0 and then to version 5.5. As you can imagine, this process takes extra time.

Although the amount of time the upgrade process takes varies based on the speed of your server and the amount of data stored in Exchange, you should know that it can take as long as 24 hours to upgrade an Exchange server with very large databases. Just before you begin an upgrade, the Setup program provides you with an estimate of the amount of time it will take for the upgrade, helping you to plan your time.

Ensure That an NT Administrator Performs the Exchange Upgrade

As you might expect, whoever performs the upgrade must have NT administrative rights.

12

12.1.2. Performing the Upgrade

There is no separate program used to upgrade to Exchange 5.5. All you have to do is run the Exchange 5.5 Setup program. When the Setup program starts, one of the first things it does is verify whether there is any previous version of Exchange on the server. If there is, you are asked whether you want to perform an upgrade.

If the Setup program determines that you are upgrading from version 4.0, your current Exchange Server is first upgraded to version 5.0. After that process is complete, the Setup program automatically performs an upgrade from version 5.0 to version 5.5. If you are upgrading from version 5.0 to 5.5, the upgrade is a single step.

If you are upgrading from version 5.0, before the upgrade begins, you are asked whether you want to perform a Standard Upgrade or a Fault-Tolerant Upgrade. The Fault-Tolerant Upgrade option is not available if you are upgrading from version 4.0.

If you choose the Standard Upgrade, the current Exchange databases are upgraded in place. Should the upgrade fail, you have to restore your backup before you can try the upgrade again.

If you choose the Fault-Tolerant Upgrade option, the Exchange databases are copied to a temporary area on the server's local hard drives and then the upgrade is performed on the original copies of the databases. Should the upgrade fail, you can reboot and run Setup again. Setup then automatically restores the backed-up files over the bad files and continues with the upgrade normally. The Fault-Tolerant Upgrade option can save you a lot of time should you have any problems with the upgrade. Just keep in mind that your Exchange Server must have an amount of free space equal to or larger than the size of the current Exchange database files for the Fault-Tolerant Upgrade option to work.

After the upgrade has been performed correctly, you are notified with a message on the screen.

12.1.3. Following Up on the Upgrade

When the upgrade has completed, you will want to run the Exchange Performance Optimizer. The Performance Optimizer was described in Day 3, "Exchange Server Installation and Configuration." This tool is used to analyze the hard disks and memory configuration of the server to determine the best location of the Exchange database files and other configuration information.

After you run the Performance Optimizer and the Exchange services have been restarted, take some time to review the NT Event Viewer's Application log to look for any possible errors. You should also review the server's configuration for any possible problems. Assuming that there are no problems, your newly upgraded Exchange 5.5 Server should be able to participate successfully in its current site, coexisting with other Exchange servers that have yet to be upgraded.

12.2. Migration Planning and Strategies for Foreign Mail Systems

The first step of any migration from a foreign mail system is to develop a clear plan that you will follow and to assess the resources required to carry out the plan. The strategy you develop should cover the phases of the migration, such as whether it will occur all at once or in gradual steps. These different strategies are called *single-phase migration* and *multiphase migration.*

12.2.1. Single-Phase Migration

A single-phase migration basically means that you convert your mail system to Exchange all at once (see Figure 12.1). Moving users all at once means that you don't have to configure or maintain connectors between the old mail system and Exchange, and that you can convert foreign addresses (such as Internet gateways) instead of maintaining both a new connection in Exchange and the existing connection. The single-phase migration strategy works best in smaller environments where the infrastructure is already in place to support the clients, such as Windows NT servers and domains. If you already have an NT network and everyone is configured to use it, the migration will go quickly and smoothly because you don't have to create user accounts. A key to deciding whether to use the single-phase or multiphase migration strategy is the amount of data you have to move and the topology of the organization.

12

12.2.2. Multiphase Migration

The multiphase strategy involves moving users in separate steps, for example, by site or by department (see Figure 12.2). The multiphase strategy is usually employed in very large organizations where the network and personnel resources are not largeenough to support migrating the entire user base at once. Some reasons for using the multiphase strategy include hardware availability, allowable system downtime, and financial reasons (such as hardware and licensing costs).

Figure 12.1.

The single-phase migration strategy.

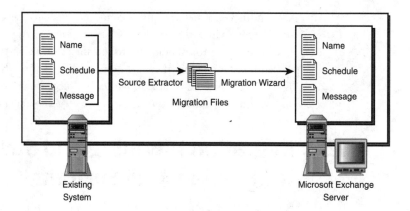

Figure 12.2.

The multiphase migration strategy.

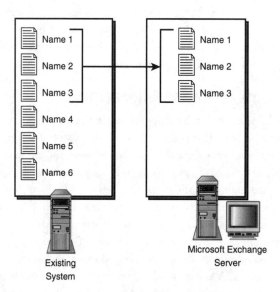

12.2.3. Naming Conventions

Another important planning consideration is creating a naming convention for the organization. The migration process can offer a unique opportunity to implement a new naming scheme. Your naming convention can include mailbox names, aliases, and Exchange directory names. A *directory name* is also known as the *common name* and is used to create the unique name of a mailbox. This name is visible only from the Exchange Administrator program and cannot be changed after it has been created.

12.2.4. Message Considerations

Another facet of the migration process is how messages will be handled during the migration. This is not usually a concern during a single-phase migration because it is assumed that all new messages will be routed to Exchange. In a multiphase migration, however, you must take into account how the new and the old mail systems will communicate with each other. You must arrange for directory synchronization to keep the address lists currentand to enable the existing mail system to forward and reply to the email from the migrated users. If the existing mail system does not have the capability to do this, you have two choices: The migrated users will have to access their old mailboxes, or the administrator will have to periodically run either the Migration wizard or the Source Extractor to transfer the email.

12.2.5. Testing and Maintenance

One of the most important aspects of a migration plan is testing the proposed procedures. Testing can include migrating test users, creating external aliases for forwarding mail, modifying existing addresses, configuring connectors, and determining network throughput. You should also develop a directory maintenance plan for use during the migration and for use after the migration is complete. This plan should include keeping both the Exchange Server directory and the legacy mail systems directory synchronized. You must also remember to modify both systems when a change is made to foreign connectors.

12.3. Using the Migration Wizard

The Exchange Migration Wizard is a tool contained in the Exchange Administrator application. It is installed automatically when the Administrator is installed. The Migration Wizard is used to import the files that were exported from the existing mail system. The exported files include a packing list file and primary and secondary files. The Migration Wizard is also used to create mailboxes and addresses.

12.3.1. Importing Files

All migration files are imported using the same procedure, regardless of the originating system. To get the best performance, it is recommended that the import procedure take place on the destination Exchange Server.

12

To import migration files, perform the following steps:

1. Start the Migration Wizard, which is located in the Microsoft Exchange folder (CY.3).

Figure 12.3.

The Microsoft Exchange Server Migration Wizard.

2. Select Import from Migration Files and click Next.

3. Read the informational screen and click Next.

4. Type the path to the packing list file in the Pathname for Migration Files field and click Next (see Figure 12.4).

Figure 12.4.

Enter a pathname for the migration files in this screen.

5. Type the destination Exchange Server name in the Enter a server name field and click Next (see Figure 12.5).

6. Select the default access permissions if you are importing shared data to a public folder and click Next (see Figure 12.6).

Figure 12.5.

Enter the destination Exchange Server name on this screen.

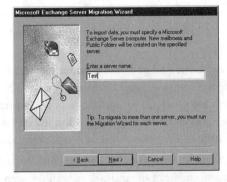

Figure 12.6.

Choose a default access permission when importing shared data to a public folder.

7. From the Choose a Recipients Container list, select the Recipients container in which you want the new mailboxes to be created or in which you have already created existing mailboxes (see Figure 12.7).

   To create custom recipients or mailboxes using a template, enter the template directory name in the Use This Account as a Template field and click Next.

12

Figure 12.7.

Select the Recipients container and account template.

8. From the For users that don't have Windows NT Accounts list box, select an option for creating the Windows NT accounts (see Figure 12.8). The options are listed here:

   ■ **Create accounts and generate random passwords.** Accounts are created using the common name of the migrated mailboxes. Random passwords are generated for each account and written to the Accounts.Password file in the Migration wizard's working directory. You must distribute the passwords so that users can log on to NT.

   ■ **Create accounts and use alias as password.** Accounts are created with the common name of the mailbox as both the account name and password.

   ■ **Don't create Windows NT accounts.** The Migration wizard will associate common name with existing NT accounts. If no NT account exists, the mailbox cannot be accessed until an NT account is associated with the mailbox.

Figure 12.8.
Selecting NT user account options.

9. From the Windows NT Security Domain list box, select the domain in which the user accounts are to be created or are located and click Next to begin the migration process.

12.4. Microsoft Mail for PC Networks

The migration from MS Mail to Exchange is one of the easiest to undertake. This is, in part, because of the support for MS Mail built into Exchange Server and clients. This support includes the MS Mail Service for the Outlook client and the MS Mail connector included in Exchange Server. We will look at two separate scenarios involving MS Mail migration. The first one involves partially migrating a post office; the second scenario involves migrating an entire post office all at once.

12.4.1. Migrating a Partial Post Office

For many reasons, migrating a partial post office is generally not recommended. It is much easier and less intensive to migrate entire post offices because the MS Mail address is not retained in Exchange when the mailbox is migrated.

This can cause the following problems:

- All foreign systems sending mail to the migrated mailboxes have to be modified to send to the new address, one mailbox at a time.
- Replies sent to the old mailbox are returned as undeliverable.
- Routing from other post offices and gateways must be maintained and routing must also be established for the Exchange Server.
- Mail messages migrated to Exchange keep only the display name of the sender; replies will fail unless that display name is in the Global Address Book or a Personal Address Book.

The biggest problem is having to maintain multiple routing configurations and resolving old and new addresses. This can be a nightmare for an administrator and should be avoided.

12.4.2. Migrating an Entire Post Office

Migrating an entire MS Mail post office to Exchange is much easier and simpler to undertake. When an entire post office is migrated, you only have to reconfigure the MTA on the MS Mail side to forward all messages from that post office to Exchange. You can also enable directory synchronization between Exchange and the MS Mail post offices to resolve addresses.

Here are some of the advantages of migrating the entire post office at the same time:

- Replies sent to the old mailbox are routed to the new mailbox on the Exchange Server.
- Any Personal Address Book entries pointing to the migrated post office users are still valid.
- The directories on the rest of the post offices are still valid.

12

■ Foreign systems do not have to be modified. The mail can still be sent to the MS Mail gateway, which will then forward it through the MTA and Exchange MS Mail connector to the new mailboxes.

12.4.3. Replacing Groups with Distribution Lists

MS Mail allows groups to be located on a single post office and also to span multiple post offices. This arrangement is a limitation when you migrate post offices one at a time because the mail sent to the group go only to the mailboxes that still reside on MS Mail. These groups are also not included in the directory synchronization process. It is recommended that you replace all multiple post office groups with Exchange Server distribution lists as soon as possible because Exchange Server does not experience these limitations.

12.4.4. Migrating Shared and Group Folders to Public Folders

The Migration wizard copies shared and group folders to the Exchange Public Information Store. The permissions on the public folder are assigned according to the values entered in the Migration wizard. Once a shared or group folder has been migrated, it cannot be synchronized with the copy on the MS Mail post office. This means that you should migrate all the users of the shared or group folder at the same time.

12.4.5. Using the Migration Wizard to Perform a Single-Step Microsoft Mail Post Office Migration

The following steps walk you through the process of migrating from a Microsoft Mail post office to an Exchange Server using the single-phase migration strategy. This process involves moving all users in one step; once the migration is complete, no further maintenance is required on the Microsoft Mail post office (because there won't be any users left using the post office).

1. Start the Migration Wizard, located in the Microsoft Exchange folder.

2. Select Migrate from MS Mail for PC Networks and click Next.

3. Read the informational screen and click Next.

4. In the Path to MS Mail Postoffice field, type the path to the MS Mail post office and click Next.

5. Enter the MS Mail administrator's mailbox name in the Account Name field; enter the password to that account in the Password filed and click Next.

6. Select One Step Migration and click Next.

7. Select where you want to migrate the data—either to a .pst file or to an Exchange Server—and click Next.

8. Select the desired migration options and click Next. The migration options are listed here:

   - **Information to Create Mailboxes.** Creates mailboxes for users selected in the user list.

   - **Personal Email Messages.** Copies all messages and folders.

   - **Shared Folders.** Copies all shared folders to public folders.

   - **Personal Address Book.** Copies the MMF Personal Address Book to a special message in the new Exchange user's Inbox.

   - **Schedule Information.** Copies calendar entries to a special message in the new Exchange user's Inbox.

9. Select the mailboxes to be migrated or choose Select All and then click Next.

10. In the Enter A Server Name box, type the name of the destination Exchange Server and then click Next.

11. Select the public folder option to set the permissions on the migrated folders and then click Next.

12. Select the Recipients container and the default template (if required) and then click Next.

13. Select the Windows NT Accounts options and click Next. The Accounts options are listed here:

    - **Create Account and Generate Random Passwords.** Accounts are created using the common name of the migrated mailboxes. Random passwords are generated for each account and written to the Accounts.Password file in the Migration Wizard's working directory. You must distribute the passwords for users to be able to log on to NT.

    - **Create Accounts and Use Alias as Password.** Accounts are created with the commonname of the mailbox as both the account name and the password.

12

■ **Don't Create NT Accounts.** The common name is associated with existing NT accounts. If no NT account exists, the mailbox cannot be accessed until an NT account is associated with the mailbox.

14. Select the NT domain name and click Next to start the migration.

When the migration is complete, you should use Exchange Administrator to verify that all users were migrated and that all the data was successfully transferred. It is recommended that you leave the old mail system available for a period of time as an emergency backup, in case some data was not migrated.

12.4.6. Using the Migration Wizard to Perform a Two-Step Microsoft Mail Post Office Migration

A two-step migration from MS Mail to Exchange Server requires that you extract a user list using the Migration Wizard, modify it as needed, and then run the Migration Wizard to extract specific mailboxes using the modified user list. The two-step migration process allows you to rename mailboxes and aliases and also to change user information such as group membership and personal data.

You start a two-step migration the same way you start the one-step migration, as explained in the preceding exercise. In step 6, however, you choose the Two Step Migration option. You can then select the same migration options as were presented in the one-step process.

12.4.7. Upgrading Microsoft Remote Mail Users

Your migration plan should also take into account the need to migrate the mailbox data of remote users. This can add complexity to the plan because remote users must either move their data up to the post office (which can cause problems with system resources such as drive space), or the remote users must be upgraded manually, one machine at a time.

12.5. Microsoft Mail for AppleTalk Networks

Migrating from a Microsoft Mail for AppleTalk Networks post office to an Exchange Server requires the use of the MS Mail (AppleTalk) source extractor. The MS Mail (AppleTalk) extractor can migrate messages, Personal Address Books, and calendar information but cannot migrate groups. To migrate groups, you can use the MS Mail (AppleTalk) Administrator program to create a list of groups and members. You can then import this list into a distribution list using the Directory Import feature. For further information on this, refer to the Microsoft Exchange Books Online.

During the migration, the MS Mail (AppleTalk) server *cannot* be used. For best performance during the migration, the destination Exchange server should not be used either. You have two options when extracting data: You can use a control file if you are migrating only some of the mailboxes, or you can use the default User Interface options if you are migrating an entire post office.

There are two ways to create migrations files on an MS Mail for AppleTalk Networks server. The first way is to specify control file options in a custom control file. This approach gives you greater control over the migration, but is also much more difficult because you have to create a formatted control file before starting the migration process. The control file format can be found in the Microsoft Exchange Server Books Online. Control File formatting is not on the Microsoft Exchange exam.

12.5.1. Specifying Control File Options

Because the Migration Wizard cannot directly access the post office, you must first run a Source Extractor on the MS Mail for AppleTalk server to extract the required migration files. Follow these steps:

1. Log on to MS Mail as Network Manager.
2. Start the source extractor program on the MS Mail (AppleTalk) Migration Source Extractor floppy disk.
3. Choose Control File from the Migrate menu.
4. Select the control file and click OK.
5. Select the account file and click OK.
6. Specify the folder in which you want to create the migration files and then click Save.

12

The source extractor will create the migration files in the specified folder and then display the results.

12.5.2. Using the User Interface

The easier way to migrate an MS Mail for AppleTalk Networks post office is to use the user interface included in the source extractor. Follow these steps:

1. Log on to MS Mail as Network Manager.

2. Start the extractor program on the MS Mail (AppleTalk) Migration Source Extractor floppy disk.

3. Choose Migrate Users from the Migrate menu.

4. Select the desired import options and click Next. The import options are listed here:

   ■ **Mailbox Creation Information.** Creates mailboxes for all users (users are selected in the following screen).

   ■ **Generate First and Last Names.** Parses the mailbox name to resolve first and last names; otherwise, names are left blank. The parsing option is selectable.

   ■ **Email Messages.** Copies messages and folders (you can select either all messages or only those messages within a specified range).

   ■ **Schedule+ Information.** Copies calendar data to a special message in the new mailbox Inbox (you can select either all calendar data or only that data within a specified range).

   ■ **Personal Address Books.** Creates a new PAB in Windows format as an attachment in a message in the new mailbox Inbox. Users must send a message with all PAB entries in the Cc field before the migration. After the migration, users can open the message and add the recipients to a new PAB.

5. From the Available Accounts list box, select the mailboxes to be migrated and click Next.

6. Specify the folder in which you want to create the migration files and click Save.

The source extractor will create the migration files in the chosen folder and then display the results.

To import the files into Exchange Server, you use the Migration Wizard and select the Import Migration Files option.

12.6. Lotus cc:Mail

The Migration Wizard supports migrating entire Lotus cc:Mail post offices in one operation. If you want to modify the migration files before importing them into Exchange Server, you can use the source extractor for Lotus cc:Mail included with Exchange Server. You then use the Migration Wizard to import the files.

The Lotus cc:Mail post office cannot be accessed during the extraction and all users must be logged off. If you have an Exchange Lotus cc:Mail connector configured, you must stop the connector before beginning the migration process. The Migration Wizard cannot migrate archived messages. Users must move the archives to the post office or those messages are not migrated. The Migration Wizard also cannot migrate information from Lotus Organizer. This information must be migrated using the importer included with Microsoft Outlook.

12.6.1. One-Step Migration

Follow these steps to perform a single-phase migration from a Lotus cc:Mail post office to a Microsoft Exchange Server:

1. Start the Migration Wizard, select Migrate from Lotus cc:Mail, and then click Next.
2. Enter the cc:Mail post office path and password and click Next.
3. Select the One Step Migration option and then click Next.
4. Select whether you want to migrate into Exchange Server or to a .pst file and click Next.
5. Select the desired migration options and click Next. The migration options are listed here:

   - **Information to Create Mailboxes.** Creates new mailboxes. Clearing this box imports mailboxes into existing mailboxes.
   - **Personal Email Messages.** Copies all email messages (or those messages within a specified range) and folders from mailboxes.
   - **Bulletin Board Information.** Copies all bulletin boards to public folders.

12

6. Select the account you want to migrate and click Next.

7. Enter the name of the destination Exchange Server and click Next.

8. Select the public folder permissions. Following are the options:

   - **No access.** Creates public folders with access limited to the administrator.

   - **Author Access.** Creates public folders with read and create permissions for everyone and Administrator permissions for the administrator.

   - **Publishing Editor Access.** Adds Subfolder Create permissions to the Author access permissions described in the preceding entry.

9. Select the Recipients container and the default template to be used (not required) and then click Next.

10. Select the Windows NT Accounts options and click Next. Following is a list of the NT Accounts options:

    - **Create Account and Generate Random Passwords.** Accounts are created using the common name of the migrated mailboxes. Random passwords are generated for each account and written to the `Accounts.Password` file in the Migration Wizard's working directory. You must distribute the passwords for users to be able to log on to NT.

    - **Create Accounts and Use Alias as Password.** Accounts are created with the common name of the mailbox as both the account name and the password.

    - **Don't Create NT Accounts.** The common name is associated with an existing NT account. If no NT account exists, the mailbox cannot be accessed until an NT account is associated with the mailbox.

11. Select the NT domain name and click Next to start the migration.

12.6.2. Two-Step Migration

The Migration Wizard can also perform a multiphase migration from Lotus cc:Mail by first creating only the migration files. This allows you to modify the files before you migrate them into the Exchange Server. After the modifications are complete, the migration into Exchange is performed by running the Migration Wizard and choosing the Import from Migration Files option.

Follow these steps to perform a two-step migration from Lotus cc:Mail to Exchange Server:

1. Start the Migration Wizard, select Migrate from Lotus cc:Mail, and then click Next.

2. Enter the post office path and password and click Next.

3. Select the Extract Migration Files Only option, specify the path to store the migration files, and click Next.

4. Select whether you want to migrate into Exchange Server or to a .pst file and click Next.

5. Select the migration options (refer to the option details in the preceding exercise, "One-Step Migration") and click Next.

6. Select the account you want to migrate and click Next.

7. If you are migrating bulletin boards, specify the public folder owner and click Next to start the migration process.

12.6.3. Migrating Public Mailing Lists to Exchange Distribution Lists

To migrate Lotus cc:Mail public mailing lists over to Exchange Server distribution lists, you must perform a separate extract operation using the Lotus cc:Mail extract utility. Then you must modify the file and then use the Exchange Server Directory Import feature to create the distribution lists.

These are the basic steps you follow to migrate Lotus cc:Mail public mailing lists to Exchange Server distribution lists:

1. Export the public mailing lists using the Export utility.

2. Modify the names to reflect the directory names of the migrated mailboxes.

3. Convert the exported file to the Directory Import format and import the file.

Note

Lotus cc:Mail supports mailbox names up to 126 characters. The Exchange Server common name and alias properties support only up to 64 characters. If you are using long mailbox names, you must use the two-step migration process and modify the migration files before importing them into Exchange Server. If you don't do this, the Migration Wizard returns an error.

12

12.7. Novell GroupWise

Exchange Server comes with a Novell GroupWise source extractor that extracts information to migration files.

The source extractor can migrate the following data:

- Email and phone messages
- Attachments
- Notes
- Tasks
- Calendar

It cannot migrate the following data:

- Character formatting
- Message security settings
- Filters
- Rules
- Macros
- External gateway addresses
- Distribution lists
- Group addresses
- Deleted messages

12.7.1. Planning for a Novell GroupWise Migration

You must install the Novell GroupWise client on the NT machine from which the Migration Wizard will run. The GroupWise client should be installed using the Standard installation option. This option installs the conversion tools you need to convert the Novell WordPerfect format to Rich Text format. The GroupWise post office must not be used by anyone during the migration. The GroupWise account you use to access the post office must have read and write access to all mailboxes that are to be migrated.

12.7.2. Migration Steps

Before starting the migration, each user must grant proxy access to his or her mailbox to the account that will be used to perform the migration. The user can do this manually through the GroupWise client or the user can do it using a macro included with Exchange. This macro is located on the Exchange Server CD-ROM in the `Migrate\tools\Gwise` directory.

You must modify the macro file to reflect the correct user ID that will be used. Then the macro must be embedded in a view by creating a view in the GroupWise View Designer. The view must then be sent in a message to each user and executed to set the proxy access. Optional confirmation messages can be enabled to verify that each user to be migrated has executed the macro.

You can perform either a one-step or two-step migration. A one-step migration extracts the information from the post office and imports it into Exchange Server. A two-step migration extracts the data into migration files for modification as necessary and then runs the Migration Wizard to import the migration files.

12.7.3. One-Step Migration

You can perform a single-phase migration from Novell GroupWise by using the Migration Wizard and choosing the Migrate from Novell GroupWise option. The wizard extracts the data directly into Exchange, much as it does for MS Mail for PC Networks and Lotus cc:Mail.

Follow these steps to perform a one-step migration for Novell GroupWise to Exchange Server:

1. Start the Migration Wizard, select Migrate from Novell GroupWise, and click Next.

2. Enter the path to the Novell GroupWise post office and click Next.

3. Enter the user ID and password (if required) to access the post office and click Next.

4. Select whether the Migration Wizard will look in the GroupWise Address Book or the User Group for mailboxes to migrate. Select the users to migrate and click Next.

5. Select the One Step Migration option, enter the path where the migration files will be placed, and click Next.

6. Select whether the data will be migrated to Exchange Server or to a `.pst` folder and click Next.

12

7. Select the desired migration options and click Next. The following options are available:

   - **Information to Create Mailboxes.** Migrates mailbox data. This option creates a new mailbox. Clear this check box to migrate into existing mailboxes.

   - **Mail.** Migrates all email messages.

   - **Phone Messages.** Migrates all phone messages.

   - **All.** Migrates all email data.

   - **Dated.** Migrates all email messages in a specified date range.

   - **Appointments.** Migrates all appointments.

   - **Notes.** Migrates all notes.

   - **Tasks.** Migrates all tasks.

   - **All.** Migrates all calendar data.

   - **Dated.** Migrates all calendar data in a specified date range.

8. In the Enter a Server Name box, enter the name of the destination Exchange Server and click Next.

9. From the Choose a Recipient Container list box, select the directory container; then select the default template (if required) and click Next.

10. Select the required NT account options and click Next. The NT options are listed here:

   - **Create Account and Generate Random Passwords.** Accounts are created using the common name of the migrated mailboxes. Random passwords are generated for each account and written to the `Accounts.Password` file in the Migration Wizard's working directory. You must distribute the passwords for users to be able to log on to NT.

   - **Create Accounts and Use Alias as Password.** Accounts are created with the common name of the mailbox as both the account name and password.

   - **Don't Create NT Accounts.** The common name is associated with an existing NT account. If no NT account exists, the mailbox cannot be accessed until an NT account is associated with the mailbox.

11. From the Choose a Windows NT Domain for Accounts list box, select the Windows NT domain to be used and click Next to begin the migration process.

12.7.4. Two-Step Migration

You can also perform a multiphase migration if necessary. You may have to do this if modifications are needed or desired. To migrate from Novell GroupWise to Exchange Server in more than one step, you first extract the migration files, modify the files, and then use the Migration Wizard to import the files into Exchange.

Follow these steps to perform a multiphase migration from Novell GroupWise to Exchange Server:

1. Start the Migration Wizard, select Migrate from Novell GroupWise, and then click Next.

2. Enter the path to the Novell GroupWise post office and click Next.

3. Enter the user ID and password (if required) to access the post office and click Next.

4. Select whether the Migration Wizard will look in the GroupWise Address Book or the User Group for the list of mailboxes to migrate. Select the users to migrate and click Next.

5. Select the Extract Migration Files Only option and click Next.

6. In the Pathname for Migration Files box, type the destination path for the migration files and click Next.

7. Select whether the data will be migrated to an Exchange Server or a .pst folder and click Next.

8. Select the desired migration options (refer to the preceding exercise, "One-Step Migration," for details) and click Next to start the migration process.

12.7.5. Migration Data Mappings

Tables 12.1 and 12.2 describe how the Novell GroupWise source extractor converts data into Exchange. The GroupWise object is listed in the left column; the corresponding Exchange Server object that is created is listed in the right column.

Table 12.1. Mailbox data.

Novell GroupWise	Exchange Server
Message	Read note
Note request	Text-based read note
Appointment request	Text-based read note

continues

Table 12.1. continued

Novell GroupWise	Exchange Server
Task request	Text-based read note
Phone message	Text-based read note
Routing slip	Text-based read note
Calendar data	Outlook calendar entries

Table 12.2. Folder data.

Novell GroupWise	Exchange Server
Inbox	Inbox
Inbox/user name	Inbox
Inbox/user name/subfolder	Inbox/subfolder
Outbox	Sent Items
Outbox/username	Sent Items
Outbox/user name/subfolder	Sent Items/subfolder
Personal folders	Personal folders
Personal folders/subfolder	Personal folders/subfolder
Week view	Outlook Calendar

12.8. Netscape Collabra Share

Exchange Server includes a source extractor within the Migration Wizard for the Netscape Collabra Share product. All documents in forums are converted to Exchange messages; attached files are migrated with the forum document as a message attachment. Threads are converted into messages with the conversation topic as the message title. Forums are converted to public folders, and Forum Categories are converted to subfolders within the Exchange public folders.

The source extractor cannot migrate encrypted forums or documents. This data must first be decrypted before the migration can begin. Forum membership lists and permissions to the lists are lost during the migration and must be re-created as Exchange distribution lists after the migration is complete. All message drafts and template information are also lost.

The Collabra account used during the migration must have read permission to the entire Collabra directory. You can perform either a one-step or a two-step migration process; you must decide whether to directly import information into Exchange or to first create migration files and then import them into Exchange.

 Note The two-step migration process is the only way to change the default directory name when migrating from Netscape Collabra Share.

12.8.1. One-Step Migration

A single-phase migration from Netscape Collabra Share is available by using the Migration Wizard and choosing the Migrate from Collabra Share option. The wizard extracts the data directly into Exchange.

Follow these steps to migrate data directly from Netscape Collabra Share to Exchange Server:

1. Start the Migration Wizard, select Migrate from Collabra Share, and click Next.
2. Enter the path to the Collabra share files and click Next.
3. Select the forums to be migrated and click Next.
4. Select the One-Step Migration option and click Next.
5. In the Pathname for Migration Files box, type the destination path for the migration files and click Next.
6. Enter the name of the destination Exchange Server and click Next.
7. Select the desired migration options and click Next. The migration options are listed here:
   - ■ **No Access.** Creates public folders with Administrator access only.
   - ■ **Author Access.** Creates public folders with read and create permissions for everyone and Administrator permissions for the administrator.
   - ■ **Publishing Editor Access.** In addition to the Author access permissions described in the preceding entry, adds subfolder create permissions.
8. Enter the account to be used as the public folder owner and click Next to begin the migration process.

12

12.8.2. Two-Step Migration

You can also perform a multiphase migration if necessary. You may have to do this if modifications are needed or desired. To perform a multistep migration from Netscape Collabra Share to Exchange Server, you first extract the migration files, modify the files, and then use the Migration Wizard to import the files into Exchange.

Follow these steps to migrate modified data from Netscape Collabra Share to Exchange Server:

1. Start the Migration Wizard, select Migrate from Collabra Share, and click Next.
2. Enter the path to the Collabra share files and click Next.
3. Select the forums to be migrated and click Next.
4. Select Extract Migration Files Only, enter the destination path for the migration files, and then click Next to begin the migration process.

12.9. Microsoft Exchange Host Migration Tools

The Host Migration Tools provide the capability to create migration files from host-based systems. These tools are not supported by standard Microsoft Support. Documentation on how to customize these tools for specific installations is included with the Host Migration Tools.

12.9.1. Digital All-in-1

The Host Migration Tools for the Digital All-in-1 product support both VAX and Alpha platforms. Objects that can be migrated include messages, pending messages, attachments, shared folders, events, and distribution lists. The source extractor must be used with a special account called the EX_MIGRATE account on the All-in-1 system. This account must be created before the migration can be started. The source extractor cannot extract more than 950 users per batch.

The migration process from a Digital All-in-1 system is very complex and requires the migration team to have a high level of experience with the Digital operating system. The procedure required for this migration is beyond the scope of this book because it involves working with the OpenMVS operating system. Information about the migration from Digital All-in-1 is beyond the knowledge needed to pass the certification exam and is not covered in the exam. More information can be found in the Microsoft Exchange Books Online and from numerous third-party vendors that offer migration support.

12.9.2. IBM PROFS/OfficeVision

The source extractor included with Exchange Server provides support for both the IBM PROFS and the OfficeVision VM product. It provides the capability to copy information to a VM ID, which can then be transferred to a PC for use by the Migration Wizard.

This migration requires a considerable amount of work on the mainframe side. The procedure required for this migration is beyond the scope of this book because it involves working with the IBM mainframe operating systems. Information about the migration from IBM PROFS/OfficeVision is beyond the knowledge needed to pass the certification exam and is not covered in the exam. More information can be found in the Microsoft Exchange Books Online and from numerous third-party vendors that offer migration support.

12.9.3. Verimation Memo

Microsoft Exchange Server provides a Memo source extractor that can migrate users and Memo documents into Exchange. The source extractor creates migration files that can then be transferred to a PC for use by the Migration Wizard.

The migration requires extensive knowledge of the MVS Job Control Language and PC-TSO file transfer programs. The procedure required for this migration is beyond the scope of this book and is not part of the certification exam. More information can be found in the Microsoft Exchange Books Online and from numerous third-party vendors that offer migration support.

12

12.9.4. Custom Source Extractors

Microsoft Exchange Server also allows you to create a custom source extractor for email systems not supported by the included migration tools. Source extractors can be created to extract mailboxes, public folders, personal address books, scheduling data, and other custom information. Creating source extractors involves more programming knowledge than is possible to present here and is not covered on the certification exam. More information can be located in the Microsoft Exchange Books Online.

Lab

This lab consists of review questions pertaining to this chapter. It provides an opportunity to apply the knowledge you've gained in this chapter.

Questions

1. When planning to upgrade any previous version of Exchange to Exchange 5.5, what should you consider during the planning process? Select all that apply.

   A. Whether the Exchange server is a PDC, BDC, or member server.

   B. Which Service Pack version is installed on Exchange Server.

   C. Will the server's hardware run Exchange 5.5?

   D. Will you have enough disk space to perform the upgrade?

   E. Does your Exchange organization have any directory replication bridgehead servers?

   F. The amount of time it will take to perform the upgrade.

   G. The amount of time it will take to perform a backup of the Exchange Server databases.

2. You are the manager of an Exchange organization that has three sites, each with its own directory replication bridgehead server. Currently, all the servers are running Exchange 4.0 with Service Pack 1. You want to perform an upgrade to Exchange 5.5. Given your current situation, do you need to make any special plans in regards to the upgrade process?

   A. You must ensure that each of the Exchange Servers is running NT Server 4.0 with at least Service Pack 2.

   B. Assuming that you don't want to upgrade the current Exchange Servers to Version 4.0, Service Pack 2, you must begin your Exchange upgrade by upgrading all the directory replication bridgehead servers. After the bridgehead servers are upgraded, you can upgrade the rest of the Exchange Servers in any order.

   C. You must first upgrade each of the directory replication bridgehead servers to Exchange Version 5.0, then you can upgrade to Version 5.5.

   D. You must first upgrade each of the Exchange Servers that is running the KM Service. After they are all upgraded, you can upgrade any of the other Exchange Servers in any order.

3. If you want to upgrade an Exchange Server that is currently running Version 4.0 to Version 5.5, what must you consider before performing the upgrade?

   A. Exchange 4.0 musthave at least one Service Pack applied to it before the upgrade can begin.

   B. You are unable to upgrade a directory replication bridgehead server if it is currently running Exchange 4.0.

   C. If you want, you can take advantage of performing a fault-tolerant upgrade.

   D. You should plan for extra time because the Exchange Setup program will first upgrade Version 4.0 to Version 5.0, and then upgrade Version 5.0 to Version 5.5.

4. You want to perform a Fault-Tolerant upgrade of Exchange Server 5.0 to Version 5.5. When you attempt to perform this type of upgrade, the upgrade fails. What could possibly prevent you from performing this type of upgrade?

   A. You can perform a Fault-Tolerant upgrade only from Version 4.0, not from Version 5.0.

   B. You can perform a Fault-Tolerant upgrade only if you first install Service Pack 2.

   C. Your hard disk does not have enough free hard disk space.

   D. You are not an Exchange Permissions Administrator.

5. You have just performed a successful upgrade of your Exchange Server to Version 5.5. Are there any steps you should perform before putting the server back into production?

   A. Run the Performance Monitor.

   B. Run the Performance Optimizer.

   C. Reload Service Pack 2.

   D. Recreate all the Exchange share points on the server.

6. What application is included with Exchange Server that allows migration from other mail systems?

   A. Performance Optimizer

   B. Exchange Administrator

12

      C. Migration Wizard

      D. User Manager

7. What are the different migration strategies called?

      A. One-step migration

      B. Single phase

      C. Multiphase

      D. Connection strategy

8. Choose the files that the Migration Wizard uses:

      A. Packing list

      B. Directory export

      C. Primary

      D. Secondary

      E. Backup

9. What must be loaded on the Exchange Server computer before you begin a Novell GroupWise migration?

      A. File and Print Services for NetWare

      B. Gateway Services for NetWare

      C. Novell GroupWise client

      D. Microsoft Outlook

10. Name the two most important aspects of planning a migration to Exchange Server:

      A. Architecture

      B. Testing

      C. Maintenance

      D. Backup

11. What are the source extractors for mainframe-based networks included in Exchange Server called?

    A. Host Migration Tools

    B. Mainframe Connectors

    C. Host Transfer Agents

    D. Migration Wizard

12. What can you create to migrate from a unsupported mail system to Exchange?

    A. Migration batch files

    B. New Migration Wizard

    C. New Exchange connector

    D. Custom source extractor

13. From which of the following mail systems can you migrate using only the Migration Wizard?

    A. Digital All-in-1

    B. Microsoft Mail for PC Networks

    C. Netscape Collabra

    D. Lotus cc:Mail

Answers to Questions

1. **B, C, D, E, F, G**   With the exception of the answer A, all these are important steps when planning to upgrade an Exchange server to Version 5.5.

2. **B**   If you have two or more Exchange sites and are running a version of Exchange earlier than Exchange 4.0, Service Pack 2, Microsoft recommends that you first upgrade all the directory replication bridgehead servers. After they are upgraded, you can upgrade all the other servers in any order.

3. **D**   If you are running any version of Exchange Version 4.0, it must go through two upgrades. First it must be upgraded to Version 5.0 and then it must be upgraded to Version 5.5. This two-step process is performed automatically by the Exchange Setup program.

12

4. **C**   Your server must have enough free hard disk space to equal or exceed the current size of your Exchange databases or you cannot perform this type of upgrade.

5. **B**   You should run the Exchange Performance Optimizer to ensure that Exchange will perform the best it can, given the current server resources.

6. **C**   The Migration Wizard can be used to migrate from a supported mail system or from import files.

7. **B, C**   A single-phase migration involves migrating all users over at once; a multiphase migration migrates users over time with connectors between the old mail system and Exchange providing a link between the systems.

8. **A, C, D**   The primary, secondary, and packing list files make up the import file set that can be used by Migration Wizard.

9. **C**   The Novell GroupWise client must be loaded on the Exchange Server to provide access to the GroupWise post office before you can perform the migration.

10. **B, C**   Each migration should be tested fully before being implemented. It is important to maintain both the old mail system and Exchange (such as directories, external connectors, and addresses), especially during a multiphase migration.

11. **A**   The Host Migration Tools include the source extractors for Digital All-in-1, IBM PROFS/OfficeVision, and Verimation Memo.

12. **D**   Custom source extractors can be created by programmers to create import files from unsupported mail systems to be used by the Migration Wizard.

13. **B, C, D**   MSMail, Collabra, and cc:Mail are options available from the Migration Wizard. Digital (and other mainframe systems) require the use of the Host Migration Tools to create import files first.

Day 13

Connectivity Diagnostics

by Steve Wiles

You have just finished getting all the Exchange mailboxes built for your clients and have established all the connectors between the sites and foreign mail systems. You go home to get some much-needed rest. Tomorrow should be an easy day. When you come in the next morning, however, the telephone starts to ring. No one is getting mail from the old mail system at the other branch office. Corporate HQ is asking why they have not received the reports someone sent a few hours ago. Somebody down in accounting is upset because the new mail client takes forever to start. Field sales reps are upset because they cannot check their mail remotely over the Internet. Best of all, after you set up and checked your mail at home last night, everything was missing from your Inbox folder. Welcome to another day in paradise.

Exchange connectivity is formal. What I mean by "formal" is that it is not forgiving of little things like misspellings and assumed permissions. Diagnosing connectivity issues is frustrating work. You have to try to isolate the cause of the problem. After you isolate the probable cause, you have to meticulously check each setting. Both sides of the connection must be talking the correct language and have the correct permissions and settings. Without these things, the connections are slow or do not work. Fortunately, Exchange usually leaves a good set of clues. Unfortunately, you have to find them and correctly interpret them. Exchange runs on many different clients: Windows 95 has three different versions currently running (Windows 95, Windows 95 with SP1, and Windows 95 OSR2)—and Windows 98 is coming out soon. (*Windows 9x*, like the older designation *Windows 3.x*, is an abbreviation for the Windows 95 family of operating systems.) Windows 9x, Windows 3.x, Windows NT, MS-DOS, and Macintosh are all operating systems that can use standard Exchange Clients.

Exchange connectivity is at the heart of the Exchange organization. Before we work on anyone's heart, however, we have to understand a little bit about what we are doing. This chapter talks about tools and techniques that can help you troubleshoot Exchange connectivity.

Objectives

This chapter addresses the following Microsoft exam objectives:

- Diagnose and resolve connectivity problems
- Diagnose and resolve problems with client connectivity problems
- Diagnose and resolve message delivery problems
- Diagnose and resolve migration problems

13.1 Connectivity: Checking Things Out

The first thing we do when something breaks depends on our experience with the problem. If the problem is new, some of us jump to conclusions and react. The knee-jerk reaction to rip it out and replace it may be the first thing that happens. What we have to do, however, is overcome that initial knee-jerk reaction and focus on discovering and diagnosing the problem and finding the best way to fix it. We have to check things out. There are many different ways to look at the topics in this chapter. You could skip one or two topics or work through them in a different order. If we skip a step and focus on one machine when the problem is enterprise-wide, we cannot fix the problem (unless we are lucky). You may find yourself hammering away at the Exchange service only to find that the problem is that someone installed a 120-day copy of NT. You have to be quick and careful, and you have to be thorough.

13.1.1. Verify the Scope of the Connectivity Problem

Determine the scope or extent of the connectivity issues. The scope of the problem can often give you a clue or some insight into what is causing the problem. Figuring out the extent helps narrow down the possible causes of the problem.

- **Is it every system or just a group of systems?** If the problem affects every system, it is probably not a simple spelling error on one system. Try to determine the similarities of the affected systems. Are they the same hardware platform? Are they running the same Exchange configuration? Are they in the same NT domain?

- **Is it a total failure or a partial failure?** Is the entire Exchange system down or just one or more services? If it is a messaging failure, is it all messages or just a particular type of message? Is it a 100-percent stoppage or just a slow-down?

- **Which type of systems does the problem affect?** Is it only Exchange Servers? What about the NT version and service packs? Is it the same software or hardware as another affected system?

- **Which sites or servers are affected?** Is it the same domain or network? The same protocol or messaging connectors?

- **What are the exceptions?** Sometimes the systems that are *not* affected tell us more about the problem. This is especially true if there are many systems with problems and only a few without. What makes these exceptions different?

In this chapter, we will look at different tools and techniques for diagnosing and resolving connectivity issues. Day 14, "Troubleshooting," goes into more detail about troubleshooting Exchange problems; this chapter looks just at those areas that really focus on Exchange connectivity. To paraphrase Sherlock Holmes, "When searching for something, eliminate everything. Whatever is left, however improbable, must be the truth."

13.1.2. Verify the Network Connectivity

Exchange is a network-dependent service. Sometimes the problem is not an Exchange issue—it's a network issue. Start with the simple, yet obvious things. Are the physical network connections intact? You can imagine how frustrating it can be to spend hours troubleshooting a connection only to find that the network cable is loose in the back of the server. See whether you can connect to network shares on the remote system. Use the RPC Ping utility to check the RPC connectivity between systems.

13.1.3. Verify the Rights and Permissions

Exchange relies on NT security. Some tasks and connections require site service account access; some require local NT administrator privileges. Exchange does not require NT trust relationships to work. However, if you do not have NT trust relationships established, things such as messaging connectors and public folder access can cause problems because they do not have rights and permissions to local and remote resources and objects.

This list covers the common permissions issues:

- Is this a local NT domain account or is it an NT account from another NT domain?
- Does this account have the correct rights and permissions to perform this task in NT?
- Does this account have the rights and permissions to perform this task inside this Exchange organization, site, server, or mailbox?

13

Remember that you need additional rights and permissions when you are dealing with foreign mail. Although trust relationships between NT 4.0 domains are not transitive, this situation changes with NT 5.0.

13.1.4. Verify the Service

Exchange has many services to offer to its clients. If, for some reason, the services do not start up, they do not work. Check the Event Viewer application and system logs for service failures. The Event Viewer's logs can tell you when an explicit dependent service failed. However, the log may not tell you that an indirectly dependent service's failure is affecting Exchange. Some things such as the POP3 and IMAP clients require an Internet mail service to send their SMTP mail. The Outlook Web clients require an Internet information server to browse with their Web browsers. Did you enable that service or protocol at the appropriate site, server, or client level?

13.1.5. Verify the Spelling

Remember that Exchange is formal. Check the spelling of the connection parameters and then retype them. Because some things must match *exactly*, look for extra values and spaces. X.400 addresses are one example of something that must match exactly. Names, address spaces, account names, domain names, alias names, and server names are not case-sensitive, but they do not work if they are misspelled. MTA passwords and NT account passwords—including the override passwords—are case-sensitive.

13.2. Troubleshooting Connectivity

Exchange has many tools for measuring, testing, and diagnosing problems. Which ones are good for connectivity issues? Resolving general problems correctly means that you need to find the right tools to identify the underlying issues.

Table 13.1 lists tools that come with Exchange or are available with the Exchange Resource Kit. Some are free-standing utilities and some are logs and log viewers you can enable and search for information.

Table 13.1. Exchange tools.

Utility	Description
RPC Ping utility	Checks RPC connectivity.
Performance Optimizer	Configures the physical directory structure of Exchange and the performance settings of Exchange messaging based on physical hardware, OS settings, and network bandwidth. Not a connectivity tool *per se*, but if Exchange Server has not had Performance Optimizer run in a while, you can significantly improve connectivity, speed, and efficiency if you run this tool. Use `Perfwiz -v` to see and set all the settings. The `-v` switch puts Performance Optimizer in verbose mode.

Utility	Description
Crystal Reports	Statistical data and information about NT and Exchange.
Event Viewer	Views NT system, application, and security event logs.
Diagnostic Logging	Various Exchange components such as the IS, MTA, and other connectors and gateways can log events.
Protocol Logging	Exchange can log most of the communication protocols such as POP3, NNTP, and SMTP.

Table 13.2 lists the tools organic to Windows NT. You do not grow "organic tools" outside, without any man-made fertilizers and pesticides. "Organic tools" are the tools that come with NT; you do not add or purchase them separately. However, some assembly and configuration may be required.

Table 13.2. Windows NT tools.

Utility	Description
TCP/IP Ping	Checks TCP/IP connectivity.
Net Use and Net View	NT networking commands to check for NetBIOS connectivity.
Performance Monitor	Collects data from NT and Exchange components.
Rping	Determines RPC connectivity.
Telnet	Checks TCP/IP-based protocol issues and TCP/UDP port connectivity.

The tools and the information we get from them can be useful or useless. When you use a tool, make sure that you use it to gather or verify information from the right system or service. Otherwise, you may end up buried under data you do not really need. Do not just turn on everything you can think of and hope something jumps out to tell you what is wrong. Do some preliminary work to help focus your hypothesis and then use the tools to prove or disprove the idea.

13.3. RPC Methods

Both Exchange Server-to-Server and Exchange Client-to-Server connectivity use RPC methods. Although this discussion uses client-to-server examples, the same examples also apply with server-to-server connectivity.

Without a transport protocol capable of supporting RPC methods, the client will fail to connect to the home server. Fortunately, TCP/IP, IPX/SPX, NetBEUI, Vines IP, and NetBIOS support RPC methods. Native SPX supports RPC methods, and NetBIOS over IPX also supports the RPC methods. The Windows sockets interface for TCP/IP is required to support its RPC methods. Using named pipes is a final option for supporting RPC methods. If the Exchange Client cannot connect to Exchange, verify the network protocol connectivity from the Exchange Client to the Exchange Server. A quick way to check for RPC connectivity is to use the Microsoft Exchange Server property profile. From the Start menu, select Settings, Control Panel, Mail and Fax. Select Microsoft Exchange Server, and click properties. If you retype the Exchange Server name and click the Check Name button, the client uses the RPC methods to connect to the Exchange Server and resolve the mailbox name to a display name. If the client can resolve the mailbox name with that Exchange Server, the client will display both the Exchange Server name and the client name underlined. Figure 13.1 shows the Exchange Client property dialog box.

Figure 13.1.

The Microsoft Exchange Client properties dialog box.

Exchange Server uses ambiguous name resolution to check the name. You can use your Exchange alias, your full name, or your NT user account. Sometimes, you can even use just parts of the name if it is unique to the server.

13.3.1. RPC Connection Order

NDIS supports multiple network adapters connecting with multiple protocols to multiple services. With two network adapters, three protocols, and six or more services, there are 2×3×6 or 36 possible paths a piece of data can follow between a client and a server. If you let the system make its own best guess, the operating system usually uses whichever adapter or protocol was installed first (or last, depending on the operating system) as its first choice for connecting. However, that may not be what we want to happen. The OS uses the network binding order to determine the order in which the protocols and network cards are used. A system administrator configures the network binding order in the network property pages. In addition to the network binding order, the Exchange Client has a client connection order. The RPC binding order is the preferred order in which this system uses the RPC methods. A client using the wrong RPC methods suffers a noticeable delay when connecting to the Exchange Server. It is also possible that the connection could time out before the client tried a valid RPC connection method. The 32-bit clients query a registry entry for the RPC connection order. To check the connection order on a system running Windows NT or Windows 9x, use the Registry Editor to look at the following key:

```
HKLM\Software\Microsoft\Exchange\Exchange Provider
```

Look at the data in the RPC_Binding_Order value. Figure 13.2 shows the RPC_Binding_Order value and data from a Windows 9x system. The RPC binding order for this system is Local Procedure Calls (LPC), Native TCP/IP, Native SPX, Named Pipes, NetBIOS, and Vines IP. This system follows the default RPC binding order shown in Table 13.3.

Figure 13.2.

The RPC binding order for a 32-bit client registry value.

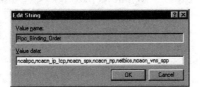

The 16-bit clients search the Exchang.ini file and use the value associated with the RPC_Binding_Order. Although Exchange 5.5 does not come with the old Exchange Clients, it is still backward-compatible with the older Exchange Clients for MS-DOS, Windows 3.x, and the 32-bit Windows messaging clients. The 16-bit and 32-bit Exchange Clients for Windows messaging use the same RPC connection order settings that the Exchange 5.5 Outlook Clients use. The MS-DOS client sets the environmental variable RPC_Binding_Order in the AUTOEXEC.BAT file. At a DOS prompt, use the SET command to examine and set the RPC connection order. Adding or modifying the SET statement in the AUTOEXEC.BAT file permanently changes the MS-DOS client's connection order.

13

Note

You can modify the 16-bit client setup to specify the connection order during the installation of 16-bit clients. Just modify the following line in the EXCHNG.STF file:

```
62 AddIniLine """exchng.ini"". ""Exchange Provider"",
➥""RPC_Binding_Order"",
""ncacn_np,ncacn_spx,ncacn_ip_tcp,netbios""
```

You can modify the connection order for the MS-DOS clients by modifying the MLSETUP.INI file and changing the value for RPC_Binding_Order.

Each operating system has a default RPC methods connection order. Table 13.3 shows the default connection orders. Note that the 32-bit operating systems use Local RPC as the default RPC connection method. Local RPC, or LRPC, works only if the client is on the same system as the server.

Table 13.3. Default RPC connection order by operating system.

Windows NT and Windows 9x	Windows 3.x	MS-DOS
Local RPC	Named Pipes	Local RPC
TCP/IP	SPX	Named Pipes
SPX	TCP/IP	SPX
Named Pipes	NetBIOS	TCP/IP
NetBIOS	Vines IP	NetBIOS
Vines IP		

13.4. Connectivity Protocol Issues

Exchange uses RPC methods to connect systems. RPC methods use protocols to transport the RPC calls. Each of the network protocol suites has additional considerations. TCP/IP, IPX/SPX, and NetBEUI are the three primary protocols Exchange uses. However, foreign mail system and other hardware and OSes use additional network transport protocols. For example, the SNA server connecting to an OfficeVision/VM mail service might use the DLC protocol. Macintosh clients use the AppleTalk protocol to connect to their Exchange Servers.

13.4.1. TCP/IP Connectivity Issues

If TCP/IP is the network protocol, use the Ping utility to verify IP connectivity to the server. If you ping the Exchange Server by name instead of by IP address, you can also see the speed of name resolution. A slow name resolution slows the initial client connection and affects future transactions when the connection is dormant for more than a few minutes. If name resolution is slow or fails, verify the TCP/IP settings for DNS and WINS resolution. If you are not using DNS or WINS, consider putting an entry in the HOSTS or LMHOSTS file for name resolution.

The way we input Exchange Server's name determines just how the name is resolved when TCP/IP is the primary network protocol. If the name is a legal NetBIOS name, the OS uses NetBIOS name resolution to resolve the name to an IP address. If the name is a host name and not a legal NetBIOS name, the OS uses host name resolution to resolve the name to an IP address. A legal NetBIOS name is up to fifteen alphanumeric characters with no spaces. ExchangeServer is an example of a legal NetBIOS name. ExchangeServer.microsoft.com is an example of a legal host name.

If possible, always use host names instead of NetBIOS names to set the Exchange Server name in the profile. You can also substitute the Exchange Server's IP address for the Exchange Server's name in the profile's Microsoft Exchange Server service property. To set the profile properties, go to the Start menu and select Settings, Control Panel, Mail and Fax. Select Microsoft Exchange Server and click Properties. The profile stores the original name, even if it displays an underlined NetBIOS name. If we use an IP address instead of a name, the IP address is resolved and underlined. RPC methods use TCP port 530.

> **Note**
> If you want to connect to the Exchange Server over the Internet using TCP/IP, you have to use host name resolution through the DNS system to resolve the IP address from the Internet. You can also just use the IP address of the target Exchange Server.

13

13.4.2. IPX/SPX and Novell Networking Connectivity Issues

According to Microsoft, the rule of thumb is that when you are dealing with Novell networks, you use an IPX/SPX-compatible protocol. A large number of Novell networks today use TCP/IP instead of IPX/SPX as the primary (if not only) networking protocol. Regardless, the rule of thumb still applies. Windows 9x has a 32-bit Microsoft implementation of the IPX/SPX protocol; Windows NT also has a 32-bit Microsoft implementation of the IPX/SPX protocol called NWLink.

IPX/SPX does not have as many configuration options as TCP/IP does. Therefore, when it comes to diagnosing connectivity problems, IPX/SPX is simpler. One of the configuration issues with IPX/SPX is setting the correct frame type. The client cannot connect to an Exchange Server unless both systems are using the same frame type. In networking environments that use multiple frame types, a system set to Auto Frame Type Detection will select only one of the detected frame types. To check for network connectivity, try to map a drive to a share on the Exchange Server. Remember that RPC requires either SPX or NetBIOS over IPX to connect to the Exchange Server. For a Novell client to connect to an Exchange Server, the Exchange Server must have Gateway Services for NetWare installed and correctly configured to support the NetWare clients attempting to connect with Exchange Clients. The older 16-bit and MS-DOS clients may require a Server Advertising Protocol (SAP) agent to identify and connect to the Exchange Servers. Finally, if an IPX/SPX router separates the Exchange Client and server, verify that the router transports the SAP type 0x640 messages.

13.4.3. NetBEUI Connectivity Issues

NetBEUI is one of thesmallest and easiest protocols to configure. It is self-tuning, provides its own error correction, and is self-configuring. It has a small memory footprint, making it a nice choice as a protocol for MS-DOS clients and Windows 3.x clients. However, it is not routable, does not support Windows Sockets, and relies on broadcasting for most of its connectivity. This makes it a poor choice for a network protocol (except for small networks that don't have a requirement for Windows Sockets support). There is not much to troubleshooting NetBEUI Exchange connectivity. Make sure that the client and the Exchange Server are both running the NetBEUI and ensure that a router does not separate them.

13.5. Foreign Messaging System Connectivity

Exchange 5.5 is not the only messaging system in use today. But with the X.400 connectors and foreign mail system connectors built into the Exchange Developer's Kit, we can connect to these foreign mail systems. When Microsoft released Exchange 4.0, the company included the Microsoft Mail connector and the Internet

Mail connector. Exchange 5.0 came with the Microsoft Mail connector, the renamed Internet Mail Service, and a cc:Mail connector. Exchange 5.5 comes with the Microsoft Mail connector, the cc:Mail connector, a Lotus Notes connector, an OfficeVision/VM/PROFS connector, and a SNADS connector. Where do they all come from? Well, they were there all along, in a third-party form. Developers built the connectors using the Exchange Developer's Kit.

What are the biggest problems of migrating from an existing mail system to a new one? (Okay, after we fight and win the budget battles, the hardware requirements, the software compatibility issues, and the user inertia problems.) How do we get all the old mail into the new mail system? How do we keep everyone communicating as user groups migrate from the old mail system to the new one? Answer: Gateways and connectors. Each connector has its specific switches and requirements.

13.5.1 Troubleshooting Foreign Mail Connectors

Each foreign mail connector has its peculiar issues and settings. Some of them, such as the OfficeVision/VM connector, require an underlying service (such as SNA server) to communicate with the foreign mail system. Troubleshooting each connector requires an understanding of the foreign mail systems as well as an understanding of the Exchange mail system. Troubleshooting the foreign mail systems and the individual connections to each of them is beyond the scope of this book. However, most of the foreign mail connectors share a number of common items that you can quickly troubleshoot from the Exchange side of the connector. When you are troubleshooting problems with the foreign mail connectors, ask yourself these questions:

- Are all the services that support the connector running?
- Are the right network protocols running on the Exchange Server?
- Does the address space of the connector contain an address space that supports the message?
- Does that foreign mail system's address space exist in each of the Gateway Address Routing Tables (GWARTs) throughout the Exchange organization?
- Is the security for the connector current on both sides of the connector? In other words, if the connector requires a password to communicate with Exchange, is it the correct name and password?
- If you enable message tracking on the connector, can you trace the message in question? Can you trace a test message?
- If you enable diagnostic logging at the connector, can you send a test message? What shows up in the log?

13

■ Is that type of message supported by the connector? Some connectors allow only certain types of messages, limit attachments, or addresses.

■ Is the connector connected to the correct foreign post office?

■ Is the schedule property of the connector correct?

13.6. Internet Connectivity

Many organizations today have some kind of Internet presence. Company Web page and Internet email are the most common. Exchange offers more than just a basic Internet email capability. Correctly configuring Exchange's Internet protocols is critical to a stable Internet messaging presence. Using an unsecured or unprotected Internet connection is a problem waiting to happen. Organizations use a proxy, a firewall, packet filtering, or a combination of these methods to protect themselves from unwanted problems. Each additional service we expose to the Internet requires one or more open TCP or UDP ports and pathways to support that service. The trick is to open only the necessary ports and pathways for those services. Double-checking the TCP/IP settings on the server can save you a lot of trouble later. Exchange Servers can in some cases be DHCP clients, but in most cases, it is much more efficient for them to manually configure them for TCP/IP. Make sure that the host name, domain name, DNS, and WINS settings are correct. If your Exchange Server is a DHCP client, you can use the IPCONFIG /ALL command at a command prompt. An incorrect DNS or WINS setting degrades name resolution and potentially disrupts the TCP/IP Exchange services. You can use Ping to test network connectivity. You can use NSLOOKUP to check the DNS entries and use Telnet to test and troubleshoot the Internet protocols and services of an Exchange 5.5 server.

The following sections look more closely at the Internet protocols supported by Exchange 5.5. These protocols include the following:

■ Simple Mail Transfer Protocol (SMTP)

■ Lightweight Directory Access Protocol (LDAP)

■ Post Office Protocol Version 3 (POP3)

■ Internet Mail Access Protocol (IMAP)

■ HyperText Transfer Protocol (HTTP)

■ Network News Transfer Protocol (NNTP)

Of these six protocols, Exchange initiates communication using only two of them: SMTP and NNTP. Clients use the other four to communicate with Exchange either directly or indirectly.

13.6.1. Simple Mail Transfer Protocol (SMTP)

Simple Mail Transfer Protocol is one of the oldest Internet message protocols. The Internet Mail Service (IMS) performs the SMTP services within Exchange. SMTP sends and receives messages between different host systems on a TCP/IP network. SMTP uses TCP port 25 to send and receive messages with basic authentication. SMTP requires a 24-hours-a-day, seven-days-a-week presence. The Internet Mail Service uses SMTP to connect to other SMTP servers to transfer mail. Secure Sockets Layer (SSL) requires a security certificate, and the Exchange service account must be an administrator on the local Exchange Server. Here are a few questions to ask yourself when you are troubleshooting the SMTP protocol and IMS services on an Exchange Server:

- Is the Internet mail service running? Is it installed on the same servers that the DNS servers have listed for your MX records?

- Is TCP/IP installed and working on the Exchange Server?

- Does the address space of the Internet Mail Service contain an address space that supports the message?

- Does an SMTP entry exist in all the GWARTs throughout the Exchange organization that need SMTP access?

- Is the security setting correct? Only other Exchange 5.5 connectors support the SSL and SASL options.

- Telnet to the IMS server; does it respond a Telnet session to the correct TCP port?

- Is the schedule property of the connector correct?

If you still cannot find a problem with the SMTP services, try enabling message tracking and diagnostic logging at the connector and follow a test message through the Exchange system.

13

Note: The SMTP protocol is the only protocol in Exchange that does not have protocol logging enabled using a Registry entry. The IMS property page contains the option that enables SMTP protocol logging.

Remember to stop and restart the Internet Mail Service after any configuration change.

13.6.2. Internet Mail Service as a Messaging Connector

The Internet Mail Service can also be a messaging connector between Exchange sites. Troubleshoot it as you would a foreign mail connector. Exchange sites using IMS as a site connector, or communicating with other trusted Exchange sites, can use SSL or SASL security.

13.6.3. IMS and DNS

Every email domain your organization supports should have at least one Mail Exchange (MX) entry in the DNS system. If you can send email but cannot receive external SMTP mail, make sure that the DNS system has the correct MX records for your domain. Each MX record has a preference value. If the email domain name has more than one MX record, the sending SMTP server tries the record with the lowest preference value first. If it fails, the sender tries the record with the next lowest preference value. To check the DNS records for your email domain, open an NT command prompt and type **NSLOOKUP -QUERYTYPE=MX** *emaildomain.com.* This command returns the DNS entries for a Mail Exchange record (MX) for the *emaildomain.com* domain. If this returns an incorrect SMTP host or nothing at all, contact your DNS provider to correct the MX record. To determine your DNS server's IP address, use the command NSLOOKUP -QUERYTYPE=NS *emaildomain.com.*

13.6.4. Lightweight Directory Access Protocol (LDAP)

Lightweight Directory Access Protocol is a telephone directory for email addresses that can also change and modify some of the recipient properties. At least, that is what most people use it for today. However, it has the potential to be so much more powerful. It has the capability to add, delete, create, and modify recipient objects and object locations. Most client applications do not call the service LDAP; they refer to it as some kind of email, address, or phone number lookup directory. Outlook Express refers to it as Directory Services. The Outlook Client does not use LDAP; it uses the standard simple MAPI commands over RPC to retrieve the global address list and to manipulate the messages and other directory objects.

Remember that Exchange 5.5 supports only six of the eight LDAP requests and five of the eight LDAP responses. Exchange 5.0 supports only three requests and two responses. The older Exchange 5.0 does not support as many of the LDAP commands as does version 5.5; therefore, clients connecting to the older systems can only read the directory.

The specific properties or information available to the LDAP client depends on two things: How they are connected and how many of the Directory Services properties of the site are configured to be available to the LDAP client. If anonymous clients cannot connect to the Exchange Server, check the LDAP properties of the site. If the specific properties available to the LDAP client are not correct, check the Directory Services properties at the site. Exchange also can perform LDAP directory referrals in other Exchange organizations, but you can specify only one server per organization.

LDAP uses TCP port 389 for basic authentication connections. LDAP uses TCP port 636 to support SSL and MCIS authentication connections. You must have at least one of these TCP ports available for an LDAP client to connect to an Exchange Server. Because of the nature of the LDAP connection, you cannot use Telnet to troubleshoot or connect to an LDAP server.

13.6.5. Post Office Protocol Version 3 (POP3)

POP3 is the default mail-reading protocol for most Internet email accounts. RFC 1939 and 1734 definePOP3. However, POP3 is a read and delete only protocol. A typical POP3 client reads mail from its home Exchange Server and sends mail through an IMS on an available Exchange Server. Each POP3 client connects to the Exchange 5.5 Information Store of the user's home server. The more Exchange Servers are used for users' mailboxes, the more we need to expose the network for POP3 clients. This can be a security problem if we allow POP3 access from the Internet. However, we could just allow the necessary TCP ports through the firewall or proxy to each of the Exchange Servers.

POP3 clients connect using TCP port 110 for basic, NTLM, and MCIS authentication. An SSL-capable client can connect using TCP port 993 for SSL connection basic, NTLM, and MCIS authentication. If you are having problems connecting a POP3 client, remember that at one time, only Microsoft POP3 clients supported NTLM-style authentication, but now some third-party clients support it. Exchange is also rather annoying when it comes to setting up the POP3 client. The user account must be in this form:

```
NT_Domain/NT_Username/Exchange_Alias
```

If you have ever used Telnet to test a POP3 connection to Exchange, you know exactly what this means. Any user ID receives the okay from the POP3 server, but only a correctly formatted account can authenticate using the PASS command. If we

13

enter an incorrect user ID, we have to drop and reconnect the Telnet session. Another important thing to remember is that only mail currently in the user's Inbox is available to the POP3 client. If the user has an Inbox Assistant or a Rules wizard that moves mail to other server-based folders, these moved messages are not available to the POP3 client.

If you want to log the POP3 protocol, protocol logging is enabled through these Registry values:

```
HKLM\System\Current Control Set\Services\MSExchangeIS\Parameters\System\
➡POP3_Protocol_LogPath
HKLM\System\Current Control Set\Services\MSExchangeIS\Parameters\System\
➡POP3_Protocol_Logging_Level
```

Depending on just how detailed you set the logging options, you can log all the contents of the POP3 messages as well as the POP3 client actions.

Here are some questions to ask when you are trying to resolve POP3 connection issues:

- Is the Information Store service running? The Information Store is the POP3 server for each Exchange Server. If none of the clients on one server can connect, this might be a cause of the problem.

- Is the POP3 protocol enabled at the site or at the server? This might be the answer if no one on the site or server can connect. If individuals cannot connect, check whether you enabled POP3 at the mailbox level.

- Is TCP/IP installed and working on the Exchange Server and on the client? This may seem like one of those silly things you can overlook, but remember that the clients and servers usually use DNS or WINS for name resolution. If they cannot resolve the names correctly, the IP connection cannot happen.

- Does the client support the SSL, NTLM, or MCIS authentication? Check to see that the Exchange Server supports the authentication method you are using. Only some clients can support the advanced authentication features; if your client is not one of the advanced clients, try basic authentication or non-SSL connections.

- Try to Telnet to the user's home Exchange Server. Does the server respond to the correct TCP port 110? Can you log in using the correct user ID format? Does the server respond to TCP port 993?

13.6.7. Internet Mail Access Protocol (IMAP)

IMAP version 4.0 can connect to any server-based mail folder or Exchange public folder. Exchange 5.5 supports IMAP4 revision 1. RFC 2060, 2088, and 1731 define IMAP. As do POP3 clients, IMAP clients connect to the Information Store on the user's home Exchange Server. Because IMAP is a new mail protocol, fewer clients are available that can use it. Outlook Express and Outlook 98 are IMAP clients.

IMAP connects to TCP port 143 and TCP port 995 for SSL connections. Each client must have access to its home server or it cannot check mail. As is POP3, IMAP is also a potential security problem. IMAP supports basic, NTLM, and MCIS authentication. IMAP supports anonymous client access. If you want anonymous users to have access to a mailbox, you must set up a mailbox with the same alias as the anonymous account. If an anonymous user connects using IMAP, Exchange Server 5.5 does not perform password verification, but it does log the anonymous user's password.

You can enable IMAP protocol logging using these Registry values:

```
HKLM\System\Current Control Set\Services\MSExchangeIS\Parameters\System\
➥IMAP_Protocol_LogPath
HKLM\System\Current Control Set\Services\MSExchangeIS\Parameters\System\
➥IMAP_Protocol_Loggging_Level.
```

Troubleshooting IMAP is a lot like troubleshooting the POP3 client connection. You can see the similarities between the following questions and the questions presented in the preceding POP3 section.

- Is the Information Store service running? The Information Store is the IMAP server for each Exchange Server. If none of the clients on one server can connect, this might be a cause of the problem.

- Is the IMAP protocolenabled at the site or at the server? This might be the answer if no one on the site or server can connect. If individuals cannot connect, check whether you enabled IMAP at the mailbox level.

- Is TCP/IP installed and working on the Exchange Server and on the client? This may seem like one of those silly things you can overlook, but remember that the clients and servers usually use DNS or WINS for name resolution. If they cannot resolve the names correctly, the IP connection cannot happen.

- Does the client support the SSL, NTLM, or MCIS authentication? Check to see that the Exchange Server supports the authentication method you are using. Only some clients can support the advanced authentication features; if your client is not one of the advanced clients, try basic authentication or non-SSL connections.

13

■ Try to Telnet to the user's home Exchange Server. Does the server respond to the correct TCP port 143? Can you log in using the correct user ID format? Does the server respond to TCP port 995?

13.6.8. Outlook Web Access Using HTTP

The Outlook Web client is usually the easiest and most trouble-free of all of the extra clients provided you installed it correctly. Each Exchange Server needs its own web page, but not necessarily its own web server. The IIS server supporting the Exchange Server needs at least Service Pack 2, preferably Service Pack 3. After installing the Exchange ASP, files on the IIS server reapply the NT Service Pack. Otherwise, you will get an error accessing the mailboxes. If the Exchange Server is not running IIS itself, then the IIS server must have RPC connectivity back to the user's home Exchange Server. Exposing an Exchange Server that is also an Internet Information Server to the Internet poses a significant security challenge.

The user connects to the IIS server connected to their Exchange home server. Unless you want to completely rewrite the active server page scripts, the client's browser must support frames and JavaScript. Most browsers use TCP port 80 to connect to the web server. Browsers connecting to servers requiring SSL connection use TCP port 995 instead. Most non-Microsoft web browsers only support basic authentication. Few web browsers other than Internet Explorer support NTLM authentication.

The few configuration settings that support the Outlook Web client are options set at the Site Protocol property page. We can enable anonymous access to both the global address list and public folders. In order to use grant access on specific public folders, we must explicitly list them in the HTTP property settings on the Site Protocol page.

13.6.9. Network News Transfer Protocol (NNTP)

NNTP supports connections to a widely distributed network of bulletins on multiple servers. Here are a few reminders about NNTP:

■ NNTP is a multiple master model of interconnected message servers.

■ The original NNTP servers supported only plain text, but Exchange 5.5 NNTP supports UUENCODE and MIME.

■ Exchange 5.5 also supports S. Barbers' *Common NNTP Extensions*.

■ RFC 977 and 1036 define NNTP.

■ NNTP servers and clients connect using TCP port 119.

Each Exchange Server can support multiple Internet News Services (INS) of both push and pull feeds. Make sure that multiple INS for the organization do not overlap newsgroups, or unnecessary additional copies will download in each of the overlapped newsgroups. The ICS.DAT file contains all the checkpoints for read messages in all the active newsgroups. Deleting the ICS.DAT file resets the checkpoints and forces the reposting of all messages. You can set message-size limits on each INS, but most newsreaders can post and read multipart postings, which usually circumvents most message-size limits. Most NNTP clients merge the multipart messages together to give the appearance that they are one message.

It is possible to configure multiple inbound hosts for push feed INS. If you want to filter inbound newsfeeds, adjust the settings on each INS property page. You can also filter many newsgroups at one time using wildcard characters. The two wildcard characters are the exclamation point (!) and the asterisk (*). The * is used here as it is any other place—as a wildcard. The ! is used to exclude newsgroups. If we set up folder replication between Exchange organizations using NNTP, we cannot use the advanced RTF and Exchange message formatting.

Control messages require the INS administrator to manually accept or delete NNTP control messages using the INS property page. The Exchange 5.5 INS generates only CANCEL control messages.

You can enable protocol logging using these Registry values:

```
HKLM\System\CurrentControlSet\Services\MSExchangeINS\ParametersSystem\
➥ProtocolloggingLevel
HKLM\System\CurrentControlSet\Services\MSExchangeINS\ParametersSystem\
➥ProtocollogPath
```

Remember that each Internet News Service has individual diagnostic logging settings. This can get confusing if you set different logging levels for each INS. Logging the NNTP protocol at high levels also logs all the NNTP contents. If you are not careful, this can use up a lot of disk space fast.

Here are some questions to ask when troubleshooting the Internet News Service and the NNTP client/server issues:

- Is the Internet News Service running? Is the Information Store service running? Not only does the INS have to be running, the Information Store must also be running. The INS stores the NNTP messages in the public folders on the Information Store.

- Is the inbound host sending the correct newsgroups? Are they available from that inbound host? Are the correct newsgroups configured on each INS? You

13

may have to check your active file to see the list of newgroups for each INS. Make sure that you are not filtering out the groups you want to receive.

■ Are you trying to connect anonymously to the INS? Some NNTP clients assume that the NNTP server supports anonymous connections. Exchange 5.5 does not support anonymous NNTP connections. If you want anonymous client access to the NNTP newsgroups, you can configure the Outlook Web client to support anonymous clients and then make the public folders associated with the newsgroups visible to the Outlook Web clients.

■ Is TCP/IP installed and working on the Exchange Server and on the client? This may seem like one of those silly things you can overlook, but remember that the clients and servers usually use DNS or WINS for name resolution. If they cannot resolve the names correctly, the IP connection cannot happen.

■ Do you have TCP/IP network connectivity to the NNTP hosts? Ping the inbound and outbound host names and IP addresses.

■ Is the NNTP protocol enabled on the site or on the server? Is the recipient mailbox enabled for NNTP?

■ Is the INS listening to the correct TCP port? Telnet to TCP port 119; you should be able to log on with basic authentication.

■ Does the clientsupport the SSL or NTLM authentication? Not all clients support these advanced authentication features. Does the Exchange Server have the SSL certificate? If not, try basic authentication or non-SSL connections.

13.7. Site-to-Site Connectivity

Connecting sites together with the various messaging connectors is challenging at times. Trying to decide which tools to use for maintaining and troubleshooting systems is equally challenging. Many of the tools organic to Exchange are really logging and after-the-fact warning systems. Nevertheless, they still are useful to tune and test configurations.

13.7.1. Performance Monitor

Windows NT's Performance Monitor (PM) can measure many things. The trick is to determine what is important and what is not. You can use PM to test for bottlenecks. You can use PM to monitor connectivity, but it has limited use detecting Exchange connectivity-specific issues. It is, however, great for checking out non-Exchange–specific issues. Before using PM, make sure that you have a good idea (or at least a good guess) about what you want to look for. Exchange has several prebuilt PM charts. If you are not looking for something specific to monitor, start with a PM chart with counters that, under ideal circumstances are zero (MTA queues, outstanding directory replication requests, out-of-sync counters, and similar objects, should all be zero at some point). This technique can help a single Exchange administrator monitor many servers at one time. The Exchange administrator only has to look for the line that jumps up and does not drop back to zero to spot problems with connectivity.

13.7.2. Link Monitor

Link Monitor is a diagnostic and warning system that periodically sends test messages to remote servers or foreign X.400 MTAs to verify connectivity. When the reply returns from the remote site, the local Exchange Server knows that connectivity exists between this site and the remote site. If a non-Exchange system is the target of the Link Monitor, it is important to set up that non-Exchange system to respond to Link Monitor's message. Otherwise, the lack of a reply will mislead Link Monitor into reacting as if the link failed. Link Monitor greatly improves the Exchange administrator's ability to administer an organization. You can use Link Monitor to monitor several Exchange messaging links to multiple sites, including physically remote sites. As is true for Performance Monitor, Link Monitor is not particularly useful for troubleshooting connectivity, but it can give you a warning that something is broken before the phone starts ringing.

13.7.3 Server Monitor

Server Monitor is a diagnostic and warning system that monitors a remote server and its services. It reacts in a predefined manner if the server goes down or a service on that server stops responding. Server Monitor greatly improves an Exchange administrator's ability to administer several Exchange Servers on multiple sites, including physically remote sites and servers. As with the preceding monitors, Server Monitor can tell you if the server or its services are broken, but other than that, its real value is that it provides advanced warning when something breaks.

13.7.4. Site Connectors

Site connectors are the easiest messaging connectors to install and configure. When it comes to configuring a Site Connector, you have to deal with only four or five property pages. With few exceptions, if one of these property pages does not explicitly list the option you want, it is not a configurable option for this type of connector. One of the exceptions is the MTA configuration parameters. Site connectors use the

13

MTA default values set with the site MTA property page. Site connectors do not require a dedicated bridgehead server. Site connectors create associations to one or more target servers on the remote site based on a weighted average of target server costs. A *target server cost* of 0 means that server is used 100 percent of the time. A target cost of 100 means that server is used only if no other path is available. Remember that when you change the Exchange service account password, site connector override accounts are not updated automatically. The Site property page option changes the Exchange Service Account password for the Exchange Server services on each of the Exchange Servers of the site. However, that only changes the services, not things like the overrides on connectors.

Here are a few more things to check out when troubleshooting site connectors:

- Network connectivity and available bandwidth. Site connectors require a minimum of 64 kbps of available bandwidth to function without difficulty. Site connectors do not have any settings that limit their bandwidth usage.

- MTAs connecting over Site connectors that use NT accounts and passwords for their overrides. These NT accounts are usually the Exchange service account. If the Site property page option changes the Exchange service account password, you must change the site connector overrides manually or the overrides will fail.

- RPC connectivity to each target server on the other site. The Site connector will attempt to send messages to any target servers.

- Address spaces for each type of address that leaves the site or passes through the site.

- Verify that the address space scope is correct for the type and addressing of the address space.

Site connectors make a poor first choice when establishing a directory connector for the first time because they lack the Connected Sites property page. All messaging connectors must maintain their X.400 address space and email addresses.

13.7.5. X.400 Connector

The X.400 family of connectorsrequires an MTA stack on each end of the messaging connector. These connectors require a dedicated bridgehead server on each end of the connector. You must make sure that the target MTA name and password match on both ends of the X.400 connector. X.400 connectors use the site MTA defaults, unless the override page is manually changed. The X.400 connectors connect to

TCP/IP, TP4, and X.25 MTA transport stacks. These connectors are very sensitive to address space errors. On virtual private networks, you may have to verify Service Access Point (SAP) entries for Presentation, Session, Transport, and Network (if required) for each X.400 MTA stack and connector. You do not have to verify these entries unless you are using someone else's network backbone.

Troubleshooting TP4 protocol issues is a little more involved. The TP4 protocol requires a network general sniffer. The Microsoft Network Monitor does not support or parse TP4 packets.

Unlike the Site connector, the X.400 connectors can use different MTA settings. There are many MTA settings, and it is important to know what each one does and how it affects the MTA and messaging. If you are not sure what each setting is, review what they do before changing them. Here are some default settings and when you might change them:

- Checkpoint sizes should be smaller than 30KB on unreliable networks and can be larger on more stable or reliable networks.

- Window Size should be less than 5 for unreliable networks and more than 5 for more stable or reliable networks.

- Consider increasing recovery timeouts beyond 60 seconds for messages traveling across slow WAN connections to decrease retransmission of checkpoint files.

- Consider increasing Max Open Retries and Max Transfer Retries on busy or unreliable networks.

If you are unsure whether a value has been changed, write it down and click the Reset Default Values button in the bottom right side of the properties page; compare what was there against the default value. Set X.400 connectors to use two-way alternative connections to reduce the load on the network connections. You can use scheduling and costs to control when non-urgent messaging takes place.

Each X.400 connector requires an X.400 email address. When checking the values for the X.400 address space, the a= (for address space on all X.400 addresses) must contain a value or a single space. Remember that the X.400 Organization value is not the Exchange organization but the Exchange site. The X.400 PRMD value is the Exchange organization. It is important to note that X.400 connectors do not use NT accounts for overrides; they use MTA names and passwords. Verify that each address space that leaves or routes through this connector is present and that the scope is correct.

13

13.7.6. Internet Mail Service

When troubleshooting the Internet Mail Service as a messaging connector, first troubleshoot Internet mail connectivity. The IMS uses SMTP to send and receive messages from other sites. Make sure that the SMTP connectivity to the other site is working correctly. The IMS connector looks a lot like the X.400 connector. There is a good reason for that: The Internet Mail connector and the X.400 connector both came from what used to be called the *X.400 messaging connector* family. You can use the troubleshooting techniques presented in the preceding section, "X.400 Connectors." If Point-to-Point Tunneling Protocol (PPTP) is involved, check for PPTP filtering on the remote RAS server. RAS servers using PPTP filtering drop all packets that are not PPTP protocol packets—including the SMTP packets the IMS uses to connect the sites.

13.7.7. Dynamic RAS Connector

Both Exchange Servers require the Remote Access Service to be installed, even if the local Exchange Serveron this end of the Dynamic RAS connector connects to the remote Exchange Server using a third RAS server. Dynamic RAS connectors require a Dynamic RAS MTA stack. If you are having problems with the Dynamic RAS connector, here is a list of potential problem areas:

- Did you check both the phone book entry and the TAPI location on each end of the Dynamic RAS connector? Make sure that you are calling the right numbers and that the RAS servers are dialing the numbers correctly.

- If you are using Callback security, is the MTA callback number correct? Do you enable Callback security on the remote RAS server? Make sure that the number in the callback setting is a direct inward-dialing number.

- Dynamic RAS does not support multilink connections. It would be nice, but it is just not available with this version of Exchange.

- Double-check that the RAS override has the correct NT domain, service account, and passwords. These accounts must be the Exchange service accounts on the other Exchange Servers. Remember that the Site Properties option to update the service account password does not affect overrides. If possible, use the same service account on both sides of the Dynamic RAS connector.

- Did you ensure that the address space for each type of address leaving or routing through this connector is present and that the scope is correct? Just like any other connector, the Dynamic RAS connector can carry only those messages that fit its address space.

■ Only one side of the Dynamic RAS connector at a time should be able to initiate the connection. Look at the Schedule properties for both sides of the connector. Make sure that both sides alternate which one initiates the connection without overlapping times. You can also schedule it so that only one side initiates the connection.

TCP/IP has many potential issues for RAS servers in general that can also affect the Dynamic RAS connector. Do not install WINS and DNS on a RAS server or an Exchange Server with a Dynamic RAS connector. If TCP/IP is the RAS protocol, ensure that the same site always initiates the RAS connection; if you don't, problems or IP address conflict will show up in the WINS database. In other words, if you are using TCP/IP, you cannot schedule both sides of the connector to alternate which one initiates the connection. Assign or request a static IP address for the incoming Dynamic RAS connections to reduce WINS and DHCP conflicts. You can avoid the whole name resolution issue for each of the Exchange Servers with Dynamic RAS connector. Avoiding name resolution in this case can speed up the initial connection.

Do you remember the stuff about RPC binding order? Just to make things more interesting, Exchange uses a separate RPC connection order for Dynamic RAS. It is just like the other RPC Binding order, except the LPC is missing:

■ NetBIOS over NetBEUI
■ NetBIOS over IPX
■ Native SPX
■ NetBIOS over TCP/IP
■ Native TCP/IP or NCACN_TCPIP

Hub configurations for Dynamic RAS connections offer more efficient message transfers. Much the same way the U.S. Post Office handles mail today, you route all your mail to a central distribution center and then redistribute it to the branches on the second connection. With this arrangement, mail has to make only two hops to get to its final destination.

13.8. Directory Service Connectivity

Some of the top issues related to the Directory Services are orphaned objects, data loss after restoration, and corrupt directories. We'll look at each of these areas in a little more detail.

When we delete an object within the Directory Service, it is actually marked with a *tombstone*, and the tombstone replicates to other Directory Services in all the other sites. When the tombstone expires, the local Directory Service deletes the object from the system. If there are Directory Service replication problems, the tombstones do not replicate properly. If some servers do not receive the tombstone before it expires, the remote Exchange Server does not delete the targeted object. To delete these objects, the Exchange administrator must use the Exchange Administrator program in the RAW mode and delete the local object.

If objects are accidentally marked with tombstones for deletion and then we restore the Exchange Server from backup, the backup does not contain the objects marked with the tombstone. However, the other servers have the tombstones and replicate the tombstones back to the original server. This process eventually removes the objects we want to restore. The Authoritative Restore utility allows us to mark a restored Exchange Server as the *authority*, which means that tombstone requests from other servers are bounced back to protect our restored objects.

Use the EDBUTIL utility with the -r switch on corrupt Directory Service databases. However, before attempting to use the EDBUTIL -r command to repair a Directory Service database, back up the corrupted database in case EDBUTIL cannot repair the damage.

Sometimes, stuff does not show up for a day or so. This problem associated with Directory Services is more of a timing issue. By default, the Knowledge Consistency Check (KCC) checks every three hours for directory changes. Sometimes, we want changes to replicate a little more quickly—for example, when we want stuff to show up all over the organization immediately. Keep in mind that not much is instantaneous in large, multisite Exchange organizations.

After making changes to the site or organization directory structure, do the following:

1. Have each server within the site where the change took place perform the Knowledge Consistency Check (KCC). Wait for the change to show up on all the servers.

2. Use the Directory Replication connector's Request Update feature on the Directory Replication connector's property page to pull the organizational changes throughout the rest of the organization. Start at the point of change and move outwards.

New routes, new connectors, and new foreign mail systems spread more quickly if they are manually pulled through the system. But you must be careful: When making massive changes (such as adding new, large sites) to the Directory Service, the messages carrying this information can sometimes overwhelm existing MTAs and network bandwidth. The MTAcheck utility has an option to remove directory and public folder replication messages from the MTA queue to help move other messages through the system.

Configure Directory Replication connectors in a hub configuration if possible to reduce the time one change takes to reach all sites within the organization. Nevertheless, Directory Replication connectors should follow the messaging connector pattern and the physical network pattern relatively closely. If they do not, you may create a Directory Service messaging bottleneck.

The Directory Replication connector forces messages between the sites to flow against the messaging connector traffic. In the worst case, site A information replicating to site D crosses over three other sites. When sites A and D exchange directory information, the messages travel along the X.400 connectors from A to B to C to D. When site C pulls Directory Service updates from site D, it receives the same messages that its MTAs just transferred to site D. When site B updates from site C, it receives Directory Service updates that its MTAs have routed through to site C from site A earlier.

There is a more efficient Directory Replication model in which the Directory Service updates do not travel through the same sites several times. This replication configuration is better because multiple copies of the same directory messages do not have to travel along the same message route, across sites that in the future will request the same information. Every time we create a directory replication connection, it does not have to follow the exact messaging connector pathway. But when we choose to deviate from the path, we must understand the consequences of the decisions and make sure that we are making a constructive choice.

13.8.1. Message Transfer Agent (MTA)

For each message that arrives in the MTA queue, the MTAs perform both routing and selection. *Routing* is getting the message to the proper destination. *Selection* is choosing the correct route for the message. The Message Transfer Agent resolves the address of each message it retrieves from the queue. Barring any errors, each address resolves in one of three ways:

1. **The address is local to this server.** In this case, the MTA drops the message in the Information Store queue. No further routing is necessary.

13

2. **The address belongs to another server in this site.** In this case, the MTA routes the message to the destination's MTA.

3. **The address does not belong in this site.** In this final case, the MTA routes the message through one of the messaging connectors according to a selection process that uses the site's Gateway Address Routing Table (GWART).

MTAs in sites that use distribution lists heavily can benefit from a dedicated expansion server. *Expansion servers* are servers on which the MTA expands and resolves all distribution lists. These MTAs greatly decrease the workload for MTAs in private and public Exchange Servers.

MTAs create links to other MTAs in the same site to send and receive messages. We call these special links *associations*. Associations are virtual pipelines that carry a stream of messages between two MTAs. As message backlogs build up, MTAs develop additional associations with the same or different MTAs to create parallel message streams. Both of these options are settings on the Site MTA Configuration property page. The Site MTA Configuration property pages set the default MTA setting for all the servers in the site. When you run the Performance Optimizer, this tool sets several configurations in the Registry based on network speeds and other system properties.

The MTAcheck utility is used to troubleshoot and help fix problems with the MTA queue and database. The MTAcheck utility verifies and repairs the integrity of the MTA database. It also can remove public folder replication and directory replication messages from the MTA queue. If an Exchange Server hosting a messaging connector remains offline for an extended period, the MTA queue can overload with messages—including directory and public folder replication messages. Removing these messages from the queue helps clear the queue for other messages and does not cause anything more than a delay in the replication of the directory and the public folders.

You should check several other areas when resolving MTA problems. Most of these are configuration problems that can stop the MTA without too much trouble. Usually, the Event log records a permissions violation or something of that nature.

■ MTA names specified in the X.400 connector are for the remote site and will fail if incorrect.

■ The Transport, Session, and Presentation (TSP) setting for the OSI selector information is normally not used. However, some foreign network systems and hosts such as the Wang or Dec systems may require TSP settings. If you are using virtual private networks on shared backbones, you may have to verify the TSP settings with your network provider.

■ An incorrect X.400 address in the address space will stop routing and selection. Problems with X.400 address space are difficult to spot unless you are familiar with the X.400 addressing conventions. Comparing the address space to the remote server's X.400 email address can help you spot errors.

■ When passwords change on one side of the connector, you must manually change the appropriate overrides on the remote side, too. Remember that although most names are not case-sensitive, almost all passwords are case-sensitive.

■ Dynamic RAS connectors are particularly difficult to set up; sometimes a typo in one of the many settings can cause the connector to fail. Be patient and verify each of the connector settings carefully.

■ If the Exchange Server is restored from a catastrophic failure and the server, organization, or site is incorrect, the MTA from the backups will fail to start until the correct server, organization, and site name are in place.

You can see that the MTA has many potential areas for problems. Determining which MTA is causing problems and then systematically checking each property page for errors can resolve most problems. After making changes to a messaging connector's address space, have the MTA rebuild its routing table. After making changes to the MTA configuration, you may also have to stop and restart the MTA.

13.9. Client Connectivity

There are a few common items to check before getting into the specifics of client connectivity. Unless you happen to be using the Exchange Server itself to log on and check your mail, you are going to be connecting to Exchange across the network. Before you can successfully reach the Exchange Server, you must make sure that you have the appropriate network and RPC connectivity. It does not hurt to make sure that the NT account you log on with has permissions to access the Exchange mailbox you want to check. Ensure that the client is logged on to the network with an account that has permissions to access the mailbox configured in the profile. If possible, limit the client systems to one networking protocol; doing so not only makes Exchange connectivity much easier to work with, it also helps the rest of your network connectivity. Use of offline storage folders and personal storage folders is a potential problem area. Evaluate the systems and users who need this additional flexibility and make sure that they understand the usage limitations and potential problems.

13

13.9.1. Offline Storage Folders

When you need a way to support mobile end-users, offline storage folders (OST) are an excellent choice. Because their mail stays on the server, server backups protect it from laptop crashes. In addition, offline storage folders can work with the synchronized copy when the users disconnect from the network. OST files do not create additional sets of Inbox folders, Outbox folders, sent items folders, journals, contacts folders, or task lists. Users can check their mail from anywhere, using any client, and the mail is always available. However, there are some issues with OST files.

Each OST file must have a unique name for each profile. If a second user attempts to use the same OST file with another profile, the OST locks up that user's server-based mailbox and any PST files on the same system. Deleting, renaming, or moving the OST breaks the lockup the next time the profile reconnects.

Set up only one OST file per account. Multiple OST files can potentially delete mail as they synchronize the server-based mail. To delete your mail on the server, all you have to do is change something in one partially synchronized OST file with a different time stamp.

OST files bind themselves to the profile on the system the first time they attach or synchronize with the server. After the OST files are bound to the profile, the only way to unbind them is to delete, rename, or move the OST file. You must use NT Explore to find and break this binding.

Deleting the original profile breaks the binding between the OST file and the profile and usually renders the OST file unusable. OST does not transport easily; moving the OST to a second machine and attempting to bind it to a new profile can yield the same lockup results.

Many of these issues can be resolved by removing the OST files. When you unbind an OST file, it does not affect the mail on the server. The only potential lost information is any changes in the OST since the client last synchronized.

13.9.2. Personal Storage Folders

Personal storage folders (PST) can remove and store mail on the user's system. This decreases the amount of disk spaced used on the Exchange Server, but it also gives the responsibility of backing up and protecting the users' mail to the users. If, for some reason, you just have to use PST files but need access to your mail from many different systems, you can put all the PST files on network file servers. However, moving the mail from one centralized and efficient storage system to a decentralized, much less efficient storage system may be counterproductive.

PST files can be individually password protected. If the user loses or forgets the password, the mail is lost. Microsoft does not have any password-cracking programs for PST files. Microsoft does not support any password-cracking utilities and does not recommend any third-party utilities that crack PST (or any other passwords for that matter). It is a legal issue: Microsoft does not have the time or manpower to verify the identity and legality of use of password crackers on an individual level. Third-party manufacturers of password-cracking utilities do exist, but Microsoft does not support them or help you find them.

PST files give users the ability to move things onto their systems and to back up or archive mail that the Exchange Server might otherwise delete (if the server-based mail is subject to age limits). However, if the users have to check their mail from any client anywhere in the office, or from the Internet, only the server-based mail is available to those clients.

Unlike OST files, PST files create additional sets of Inbox folders, Outbox folders, sent items folders, and so forth. This causes confusion for some users who do not understand why they have more than one Inbox, contact folder, or sent items folder. When you mix the OST and several PST files on one user's system, it becomes a real mess. Trying to decide which of the contacts, tasks, and calendar information should be stored in the server based (OST) files and which should be stored in the PST files is a real headache.

13.9.3. Client Mail Delivery

The Exchange Server delivers mail to one of three possible destinations each time an Exchange Client connects to the Exchange Server:

- Exchange keeps the mail in the server-based Private Information Store.
- Exchange delivers the mail to one of the PST files configured in the user's mail profile.
- Exchange delivers the mail absolutely nowhere.

If the user has configured his or her profile to deliver mail to a PST file, the mail remains on the server until the user connects to the server and downloads the mail to a PST file. This is true even if the user then checks mail using the Outlook Web client. This is also true if the user configures a POP3 or IMAP client to leave a copy on the server. A user can delete a message before Exchange delivers it to the PST file.

Systems originally set up to support PST file-based mail, such as Internet mail or Microsoft Mail, deliver all the Exchange-based mail in the server-based Inbox folder

13

to the PST files. This includes mail that has already been read and left in the Inbox. If users call and complain that some or all of their mail is missing from their mailboxes, ask whether they checked mail from home or from another system in the office. They may have unknowingly delivered all their Inbox mail to a PST file on that other system. Mail unknowingly pulled down from the server by POP3 or IMAP clients may be more difficult to put back onto the server. Most POP3 and IMAP clients do not use PST files to store mail, which makes it difficult to move the messages from one message storage system to another.

13.9.4. Client Connectivity: Wrapping It All Up

Many factors affect client connectivity in the Exchange environment: networking protocols, RPC methods, name resolution, OST and PST files, and delivery options. Most of these issues can be fixed or avoided altogether during client setup and installation. If you use the auto-profile generator, you can build an installation that generates user profiles without user interaction. Setting the default profile generation to use environmental variables such as %USERNAME% builds uniqueness into the OST and PST filenames. In addition, here are a few more things you can do to keep client connection problems to a minimum:

- Simplify the network issues by choosing one networking protocol. With all of the Internet functionality in today's networking environment, the TCP/IP protocol suite should be your top choice.

- Plan and control client mail delivery. You should limit the number of clients that use PST and OST files, and educate those users on the uses and consequences of using those options.

- As scary as it sounds, your best defense here is a good offense. Provide training resources for your end-users. Some of them will surprise you: They will learn about the mail system.

After you get Exchange up and running, most of your day-to-day problems will revolve around client connectivity. If we build the system to limit client connection problems, we can avoid most of the problems before they arise.

13.10. Mail Delivery Issues

Mail delivery is simple. It eventually gets to its destination or it does not. Non-Deliverable Receipts (NDRs) are Inter Personal Notifications (IPNs) that inform a sender that all possible routes to deliver a message are exhausted or that 24 hours have passed and the mail did not reach its final destination.

Exchange Servers temporarily store messages if the destination servers are unavailable. Messages can also wait in queues scheduled to connect in the future. The length of this temporary storage depends on MTA settings and the urgency of the message.

How fast an NDR returns and what generates the NDR can help you determine where to start looking for reasons for the NDR. There are four different speeds and possible places that generate an NDR:

- If a local MTA returns an NDR quickly, it means that the local MTA could do nothing with the mail. The address should have been local, but there was no recipient mailbox or the MTA could not find a valid route for the message. If we can verify that the address is not local, then we know the NDR is a result of a routing issue: The address space is missing or misspelled. Checking the address space of each of the messaging connectors on the local site is the next step. If no address spaces support this address, have the local MTA recalculate its routing table. After the routing table is complete, check the address spaces again in the GWART. If you cannot find a matching address space and route, you cannot send the mail.

- If the message waited more than a few minutes to return an NDR from a local MTA, look for connectivity problems. The long wait was probably the message waiting for the local side of a message connector before timing out and returning as an NDR.

- If the message returns an NDR from the destination MTA and the NDR returns quickly, verify the address. The MTA routed the message along the path to the correct destination server or gateway, but the recipient address was not valid at the home server or site.

- If an intermediate MTA returns the NDR, check the route for a break in the address space continuity or a connector failure. A fast-returning NDR usually signals a break in address space continuity. For a message to route from the sender to the destination, all the messaging connectors in between must have an address space that supports that message. A slow-returning NDR usually signals a connector failure. Looking at the queues at the site from which the MTA generated the NDR message can tell us whether any messages are backing up.

13

13.11 Mail Migration Issues

Troubleshooting migration issues comes down to two basic areas: addressing and connectivity. We have to move all the addresses over and keep them current during the migration. We also need a connection that moves the mail we want to keep and that supports the cross-messaging of system mail until the migration is complete. Each of the foreign mail systems has unique features, but they do share these two common areas.

13.11.1. Addressing

The Exchange organization dynamically renames and readdresses new mail recipients. The old Personal Address Books contain static entries. These static mail addresses can cause problems if the users continue to use them during and after the migration is complete. Each of the foreign mail systems has email proxy address generators; the setting for the proxy template should reflect the naming conventions of the organization. If the proxy address generator is generating the wrong email address for new mailbox, that mailbox will not receive mail after it is migrated.

Directory synchronization between Exchange and the foreign mail system helps smooth out address issues in the transition. If you maintain a proxy address from the old mail system for a short period after the migration, mail accidentally sent to the old email addresses should still reach you. Do not delete old PAB files, SCD files, CAL files, MMF files, or any other messaging data files until the Outlook client successfully imports them.

The Exchange 5.0 Outlook client cannot make distribution lists; however, the Exchange 5.5 Outlook client can. The old Outlook clients used the Personal Address Books to store personal distribution lists. Your client should have the 8.03 Outlook client installed (not the 8.02 or earlier client) to avoid this problem.

13.11.2. Maintaining Connectivity

Foreign mail systems connect to Exchange using a temporary, or *shadow*, post office to hold mail in transition. Let's use Microsoft mail as an example.

Foreign Mail systems require a connector service. Microsoft Mail connectors use a PC MTA service to connect the shadow post office to the Microsoft Mail system. Other mail systems should have some arrangement like this; for example, cc:Mail also uses a shadow post office.

After creating the service, set it to start up automatically or it will fail. If the connector service does not start, one or more of its components may be corrupt or stalled. The INQUEUE3.KEY and .MDB files can sometimes be corrupted and will stop the Microsoft Mail connector.

Setting up directory synchronization between two foreign messaging systems requires permissions on both sides of the connector. Usually, this implies administrator or supervisor level access. Setting up directory synchronization between Microsoft Mail and Exchange requires configuration on both sides of the connector. An Exchange administrator and a Microsoft Mail administrator should both be involved to ensure that the configuration settings for the mail connections and the directory synchronization are correct. Setting up Exchange as the DirSync server and the Microsoft Mail post offices as remote requesters is the preferred method if the Microsoft Mail system is migrating to Exchange. Setting up Exchange as the requester and the Microsoft Mail post office as the DirSync server is preferred if the Microsoft mail system is stable and DirSync is running without incident.

13

Lab

This lab consists of review questions pertaining to this chapter. It provides an opportunity to apply the knowledge you've gained in this chapter.

Questions

1. You began an Exchange migration six months ago. Your company has Windows 95 clients, a few NT workstations, ten NT servers running file and print services, and various BackOffice products including Exchange. Half of the company's users have migrated to the new Exchange mail client without incident. Last week, after the finance department migrated to Exchange from cc:Mail, the users in the finance department complained that the Exchange Client takes too long to connect to the Exchange Server and that messages take almost 60 seconds to send. What steps can you take to correct this issue?

    A. Upgrade the network in the finance department from a 10BASE-T network to 100BASE-T network and replace the network hubs with 100BASE-T switches and routers.

    B. Install a WINS and DNS server on the network.

    C. Use Regedt32 and set the correct RPC binding order values on the clients.

    D. Set the company's Exchange Clients to use PST files to store mail and decrease the amount of private mail in the Information Store on the Exchange Server.

2. Your POP3 clients complain that they can read their messages from coworkers but that they cannot reply to them. What should you do?

    A. Troubleshoot the Internet Mail Service.

    B. Verify that the site has enabled its POP3 clients to send mail.

    C. Check the address space on the site's POP3 server to see whether the address space is correct to allow users to reply to Internet messages.

    D. Tell the users that POP3 is a read and delete only protocol. They have to use the Outlook Web Access client to reply to their mail.

3. You wanted to check your Exchange mail from home last night. You used dial-up networking to connect to the RAS server. You have Outlook 8.03 installed at home, and you use it to check email from your ISP. You added the

Exchange Service to your profile at home and successfully connected to your Exchange Server and read your new mail. You were careful not to delete anything. When you arrived at the office this morning and opened Outlook, all the mail in your Inbox was gone. How do you get your messages back?

    A. Restore the Exchange Server from the backup tapes from yesterday afternoon to a second NT server and move the PST files. Copy the PST file to your workstation and add it to your Outlook profiles. Finally, drag and drop all your messages back to your server-based mailbox.

    B. Go home and get them.

    C. Send a note to everyone asking them to resend you anything important. Exchange does not support individual mailbox restores from backup.

    D. Log off and log on again. You did not use the correct profile on your workstation.

4. Your company has doubled in size since last year. You have added a second Exchange Server to the site to support the growth. Now some new people are complaining that they cannot check their mail using their IE 3.0 web browsers. They get an `Inbox not found` error. Your IE 4.0 works fine. What is wrong?

    A. Upgrade the users to IE 4.0.

    B. The users are connectingto the wrong web site.

    C. Check to see whether TCP/IP is installed and whether DNS and WINS are configured correctly.

    D. Enable HTTP on their Site Protocol page; it was disabled.

5. You sent a test message to a remote site using a custom X.400 address and almost immediately received an NDR from the remote site. What is most likely the cause of the NDR?

    A. The messaging connector is not working.

    B. The address space on the local Exchange Server is incorrect.

    C. The address space on the remote server is incorrect.

    D. The recipient is not on the remote site.

13

6. You set up a Link Monitor to monitor the connection to your other mail system. The Link Monitor reports that the link is down. But you can send messages to coworkers using their old mail addresses. What is causing the problem?

   A. The link is down. You are not really using the old email addresses; Exchange dynamically changes addresses on messages and sends the messages to your co-workers' Exchange mailboxes.

   B. Nothing is wrong with the link. Link Monitor does not support non-Exchange systems.

   C. Nothing is wrong with the link. Set up a system attendant account on the remote system with auto-reply configured.

   D. The link is down. Exchange intelligently rerouted the message and delivered the message to your coworkers' SMTP gateway.

7. You want to send a test message to your Exchange administrator counterpart at a remote site before you set up directory replication. You and your counterpart set up an X.400 connector and he gave you his X.400 address information. Your organization is Universal.com; his site is EastCoast, his last name is Smith, his first name is John, and his country code is US. All the other fields are blank. You used the following X.400 address: O=EastCoast, C=US, P=Universal.com, S=Smith, G=John, but you keep getting an NDR from his server. What is wrong?

   A. You should have used F=John not G=John.

   B. You have the O and P fields switched. O should be Universal.com and P should be EastCoast.

   C. The X.400 connector is not configured correctly.

   D. You are missing a required field in your X.400 address.

8. Your manager wants you to set up your Exchange Server to support anonymous user access to a small group of newsgroups. How do you do it?

   A. Install and configure the Internet News Service. From the Anonymous tab of the Internet News Service property page, select the Allow Anonymous Access option.

B. You cannot enable anonymous access using Exchange Server. You should get a third-party add-on to support this request.

C. Install and configure the Internet News Service. Install and configure the Outlook Web client. Enable anonymous access to public folders. Select the appropriate public folders to be visible.

D. Install and configure the Internet News Service. Create an NT account called anonymous and give it permissions to log on locally to the Exchange Server. Create a mailbox for the anonymous account and disable all protocol support except for NNTP.

9. You had an important meeting this morning, and several managers flew in from out of town. During the first break, the visiting managers tried to use the local manager's system to check their email. After they checked their mail a few times, they got a message saying that their mailboxes were unavailable. When the local manager tried to log on to send you an email message asking you to check the mail connectivity, she was denied access to her mailbox. What is causing the problem?

A. One Exchange client cannot support users from two different sites.

B. The messaging connectors to the other site are down.

C. The visiting managers' NT accounts do not have the right to log on locally because the correct trust relationship does not exist.

D. The OST files are locked.

10. Last weekend, you had a server go down for almost two days during a migration. When you finally got the system back up, the MTA queue immediately filled with messages. Now the people who use that Exchange Server as their home server cannot send or receive mail because the queues are full. How can you get their mail delivered as quickly as possible?

A. They just have to wait. If you do anything to the queues, you could cause the site to lose its configuration synchronization and crash again.

B. Use the MTAcheck tool to remove the system messages from the queue.

C. Manually delete all the messages in the queues. The system messages will timeout and automatically resend in 30 minutes.

D. Use the Directory Replication connector's Update Now button to get all the directory updates onto the server and out of the queue.

13

Answers to Questions

1. **C**   Exchange Clients thathave slow connection and messaging functions usually come from a bad RPC binding order. Setting the primary RPC connection method at the top of this order should speed up the connection. Answer A is incorrect because changing a few more clients over to Exchange will not suddenly cause a network bandwidth problem. No other complaints other than those related to Exchange suggest that it is an Exchange-only problem. Answer B is incorrect because name resolution may cause network connection slowdowns, but not message sending slowdowns. Answer D is incorrect because the size of the Information Store has nothing to do with connection speed.

2. **A**   The client must use the Internet Mail Service as an SMTP server to reply to mail. The POP3 service runs on the Information Store and is separate from the Internet Mail Service. Answer B is incorrect because the POP3 protocol does not have a send capability; there is no switch to enable users to send mail with POP3. POP3 clients use SMTP to reply to and send mail. Answer C is incorrect because POP3 is a read and delete only protocol. The badly configured address space on the Internet Mail Service may cause problems with certain types of mail, but does not stop Exchange mail replies. Answer D is incorrect because POP3 is a read and delete only protocol. However, POP3 clients use SMTP to reply to and send messages. They can use their POP3 client to connect to the Internet Mail Service and use SMTP to reply to and send messages.

3. **B**   The profile on your home system is set to deliver mail to your PST file. Set the delivery option to your Exchange mailbox and drag and drop your messages onto the server-based mailbox. Answer A is incorrect; technically, it is a possible solution but involves too much work. There are better ways to recover your mail. Answer C is incorrect; technically, it may be a possible solution, but how do you know who sent you important mail? There are better solutions. Answer D is incorrect; sorry, you cannot bury your head in the sand and hope this one goes away.

4. **B**   Each Exchange Server has its own web site. The new people probably have mailboxes on the new Exchange Server. Answer A is incorrect; all that is required to support the Outlook Web Access is frames and JavaScript support. IE 3.0 and IE 4.0 both support frames and JavaScript. Answer C is incorrect; without the correct DNS settings, the users could not connect to the web site at all. Answer D is incorrect because the users are on the same site you are.

Unless you overrode the default settings on their server, they should have the same web access you do.

5. **D**   The X.400 message reached the remote site, but X.400 addressing includes both the user and the site. If the user was not a recipient on the remote site, the message is nondeliverable. Answer A is incorrect; without a working messaging connector, you would not have received the NDR from the remote server. Answer B is incorrect; without the correct address space on the local Exchange Server, the message would not have reached the remote server to trigger the NDR. Answer C is incorrect because the address space on the remote server does not affect incoming messages.

6. **C**   The Link Monitor is not receiving the expected reply from the remote site. Answer A is incorrect because Exchange does not dynamically change email addresses. Answer B is incorrect because Exchange does support Link Monitors for most X.400-compliant mail systems. Answer D is incorrect; technically, Exchange could intelligently reroute the message with the right address spaces and connectors, but you cannot set up a Link Monitor through the Internet to a foreign mail system.

7. **D**   You are missing the required a= field. Even if the a= field is blank, you must still include it but with a single space. Answer A is incorrect; G is the given name, or first name, field. Answer B is incorrect because Exchange sites are the correct value for the X.400 O field and the Exchange organization is the correct value for the P field. Answer C is incorrect; otherwise, the remote server could not have returned the NDR.

8. **C**   Install and configure the Internet News Service. Install and configure the Outlook Web client. Enable anonymous access to public folders. Select the appropriate public folders to be visible. Answer A is incorrect because the INS does not support anonymous access. Answer B is incorrect; although third-party add-ons may be available to do this, you can do it with the web client for no additional cost. Answer D is incorrect; technically, it would work but it would potentially compromise the security of the Exchange Server.

9. **D**   The OST files are locked. One of the visiting managers probably synchronized his or her mailbox. When he or she accessed the local OST file, it locked. Answer A is incorrect because Exchange Clients can connect to as many different Exchange sites and organizations as you can configure. Answer B is incorrect; it is possible, but lots of other alarms and problems would have started up, too. Answer C is incorrect; if the managers were able to check their mail, they had the necessary rights and permissions.

13

10. **B**   The MTAcheck utility can remove directory replication and public folder
replication messages. Answer A is incorrect because it can take three or more
hours for all the sites to synchronize. Answer C is incorrect; although manually deleting the message queue may get new messages through, all messages in
the queue would be lost and the KCC checks would take several hours to
refresh the directories. Answer D is incorrect because forcing the directory
replication would only make the problem worse. The Update Now button
does not move any messages out of the queue.

Day 14

Troubleshooting

by Chris Miller

This chapter takes a look at the kinds of things that can cause problems with Exchange and how you can fix them. Troubleshooting procedures include upgrading hardware, applying service packs, resolving installation problems, dealing with Information Store and backup problems, and detecting and repairing server resource problems.

The chapter starts out with some preventative maintenance tasks, such as applying software service packs, upgrading the server operating system, and adding new hardware to increase server capacity. Then it takes a look at how to fix problems that arise at different points in the life cycle of a server: problems during installation, problems with the Information Store and backup during run time, and lifelong resource problems.

Objectives

This chapter covers the following Microsoft exam objectives:

- Diagnose and resolve upgrade problems
- Diagnose and resolve server installation problems
- Diagnose and resolve Information Store problems
- Diagnose and resolve server directory problems
- Diagnose and resolve server resource problems
- Diagnose and resolve backup problems and restore problems

14.1. Upgrades to Hardware and Software

With the complexity of software today, and the ever-increasing demands of users for more speed and less downtime, it is very important for administrators to stay on top of how to upgrade software and hardware safely and efficiently. Upgrades include adding capacity to servers to enable higher transaction rates and more dependable service as well as adding software patches to increase reliability and reduce downtime, and occasionally adding new features.

14.1.1. Software Service Packs

Microsoft performs an unbelievable amount of testing before a product is released. There are racks upon racks of servers in a building in Redmond that exist solely to install new builds of Exchange Server. These servers are then subjected to punishing loads by racks of client computers that send and receive mail as quickly as they can. Microsoft does everything possible to quality-check their systems. Unfortunately, the products we have today, such as Windows NT and Exchange, are so complex that not every state can be tested. So after a product is released, Microsoft monitors support calls, tracks down bugs, and periodically creates a Service Pack to fix issues that customers have found in their software. Microsoft then runs the same battery of tests against the Service Pack as were run against the original software—plus new tests to ensure that the problems that were discovered by customers are actually fixed in the new software. Then the Service Pack is released.

Each Service Pack contains the following three pieces:

- The instructions on how to apply the Service Pack, along with any limitations that the Service Pack may include.
- A text file that includes a list of all the fixes in the Service Pack. Each fix is tied to a Product Support Services (PSS) article, which explains the problem and any necessary details on how it was fixed.
- The replacement files. In general, when a Service Pack is released, it contains all the files necessary to bring the installation up to the level of the client. In other words, you can apply Service Pack 3 without applying Service Pack 2 or Service Pack 1, and Service Pack 3 will fix everything that Service Packs 1 and 2 did. Sometimes, however, the Service Packs are not cumulative. Read the instructions that come with the Service Pack for details.

There are two types of Service Packs that concern the Exchange administrator. Windows NT Service Packs fix functionality in Windows NT. For example, to install Exchange Service 5.5, you must have Windows NT Server Version 4.0 with Service Pack 3 applied. Exchange Server Service Packs fix various problems with Exchange Server, and may or may not rely on any Windows NT Service Packs you may have applied.

Before applying any Exchange Server service packs, go through the Windows NT Event log carefully to make sure that there are no problems with the Information Store or directory store on the server. If there are problems with any of the databases, the Service Pack application program may fail, resulting in a half-upgraded server with services that may or may not start.

Service Packs are released on an as-needed basis. Usually, there are between four and five Service Packs for a version of Windows NT. They can be found at Microsoft's web site (`http://www.microsoft.com/exchange`). Microsoft does not notify anyone when a Service Pack becomes available, so it is important to check this site periodically to see whether a new Service Pack has been released. Service Packs vary in size from a few megabytes up to 20 or 30 megabytes, depending on the nature of the problems fixed.

Before installing a Service Pack, read through all the documentation for the Service Pack. Some Service Packs may require that all servers in a site be upgraded at the same time. Sometimes, a Service Pack is released that does not upgrade or fix any feature in use in the organization. If this is the case, you must evaluate the value of performing the upgrade. Before you install the Service Pack, perform a full backup of the server. If possible, stop the Exchange Server and back up all the files on the server. Then apply the Service Pack according to the instructions. After the server restarts, monitor it closely to make sure that it comes back up and that it records any events outside the normal startup events in the Windows NT Event log.

14.1.2. Performing Hardware Upgrades

After monitoring a server (and listening to users complain about slow access time), you decide to upgrade the memory/disk space/processor on the Exchange Server. Here are some things to keep in mind about upgrading hardware on an Exchange Server so that the server can be used most efficiently.

If you are increasing the number of processors, make sure that a Hardware Abstraction Layer (HAL) is available for your server that supports multiple servers. The next time you reboot the server, notice whether the NT Server blue screen specifically states Uniprocessor HAL. This means that the Hardware Abstraction Layer for your server is going to recognize and use only one processor. To use multiple processors, you need a new HAL. Usually, multiserver HALs come in the form

14

of software upgrades for the server and are supplied by the server manufacturer. For more information, consult your server documentation or the Windows NT documentation.

Out of space? When adding more disk drives, make sure you do a complete server backup before making any configuration changes to disks to ensure data integrity. Remember that an Information Store can exist on only one logical drive. This means that whenever you add a drive, you have to link it to the other drives somehow. If you are using hardware RAID, use the utilities that come with the server to add the new drive to the array. If you are using a Windows NT stripe set, you must back up all the data on the stripe set, delete the stripe set, rebuild the stripe set with the new disk, and then restore all the data back to the stripe set. If you are not using stripe sets, it is easy to use Disk Administrator to extend the existing Windows NT partition onto a new volume.

Note

Whenever you are adding disk space to a Windows NT server, it is crucial that you assess the impact on backup media. If you have a two gigabyte backup tape, for example, and add four gigabytes of disk space, chances are good that the amount of data to be backed up will soon surpass the capacity of the tape drive, which can negatively impact either the timing or the completion of backups.

One of the easiest upgrades to perform on a server—and the one that usually gives the most "bang for the buck"—is adding memory. Microsoft recommends adding memory to a server as the primary upgrade path. To decide whether adding memory to your server will be beneficial, monitor the memory object in Performance Monitor while the server is under a normal load. The specific keys to watch are Memory/Pages per Second and Memory/Available Memory. To add memory to a server, follow the server manufacturer's directions. What is extremely important for Exchange is that you run the Performance Optimizer after you install the memory to ensure that the memory is used most effectively by Exchange.

Here's how to use Performance Monitor to monitor memory usage:

1. Start the Windows NT Performance Monitor by clicking the Start button, and then selecting Programs|Administrative Tools|Performance Monitor.

2. Click Edit and then select Add to Chart. The Add to Chart dialog box appears.

3. If the computer you want to monitor is not the one you're running Performance Monitor on, type the name of the computer in the Computer field.

4. From the Object drop-down box, choose Memory.

5. Choose Pages per Second (Pages/Sec) from the Counter list and click the Add button.

6. Choose Available Bytes from the Counter list and click the Add button.

7. Click Done to close the Add to Chart dialog box.

It is critical that you run the Performance Optimizer after adding any hardware to Exchange. The Performance Optimizer recalculates the number of execution threads to be used by various Exchange Services based on the amount of memory available and the role of the server in the site. For example, if the server is used only to store mailboxes, the Private Information Store will have a lot more threads than if the server was set up to connect the site to the Internet. In addition, more threads are created on a server with 128M of RAM than one with 32M of RAM. The same is true for a server with two processors instead of one. More threads are created if there is more processor time available to run the threads.

Now that we've examined how to upgrade hardware and software, let's take a look at diagnosing and recovering from problems, starting with problems that occur during installation.

14.2. Troubleshooting Installation Problems

During the installation of Exchange, some problems can crop up. This section takes a look at what those problems are and how you can resolve them. There are three main types of problems that can occur during setup:

■ Problems that occur while setting up the server and copying files

■ Problems that occur while connecting to another server in the site

■ Problems with services that occur immediately after setup

Before running the setup program, you should close all running applications on the server. In some cases, other programs use files that Exchange Server has to replace; if those files are in use when you run setup, the installation program displays a dialog

14

box that says it cannot replace a file necessary for installation and gives you the option to abort the installation, retry the copy, or ignore the problem. Usually, stopping all other applications that are running fixes the problem. After you close all applications other than Exchange Setup, click the Retry button to retry the copy. If the file is still in use, go to Control Panel|Services and stop any non-Windows NT services that are in use (such as SQL Server or SQL Executive, SNA Server, and so on). After all the services are stopped, click Retry again. If the application still won't install, click Abort, reboot the server, and start the installation process again. That should close up any files in use. Make sure that Exchange Setup is the first program that runs after the server is started.

If a server is being added to the site, part of the Setup program replicates all the directory information from an existing server in the site to the new server. There can be problems getting the new server to connect to the old server.

First of all, ensure that the account that is running Setup on the new server is an Exchange administrator's account on the server to which you are connecting. At this point in Setup, the installation program is not using the service account yet—it is still using the account of the person currently logged on. If the user does not have access to the other server, the Setup routine will fail.

After checking the user account, ensure that both servers are using a common network protocol that supports RPC (remote procedure calls). RPC is a protocol for running tasks on remote workstations; it uses any drop-in security authentication (in this case, Windows NT authentication). RPC allows a client and server to communicate with a standard interface and provides the security to make that happen. To check RPC connectivity, make sure that the server is visible in Network Neighborhood and that drives can be attached. Remember that for two servers to be in the same site, they must have a high-bandwidth, constant RPC connection. Without this type of connection at setup time, the setup of the new server will fail. If there is a network problem, fix it before attempting to run Setup.

Another problem that can happen during the installation process is that the services will not start. After the Exchange Server Setup program runs, all the Exchange services will start. If these services fail to start, it is usually because there is not enough memory or a lack of drive space. This condition is usually accompanied by a message such as `An Unexpected Error Occurred in the upgrade process` or `ERROR: Your upgrade did not complete successfully`. These errors occur if there is not enough memory or disk space on the server to accomplish the upgrade. These errors also may occur if there is a corruption problem with any of the databases during upgrade.

> **Note** Don't ever use an upgrade process to attempt to fix database corruption. If there is any database corruption, the upgrade process will fail, and the server may be left in a half-upgraded state. If there is any chance of a problem, use the Fault Tolerant upgrade option, which backs up all files before converting the database.

The first step in resolving the problem of services not starting is to use the System option in Windows NT Control Panel to increase the size of the paging file. A *paging file* is what Windows NT uses for swap space for virtual memory. Increasing the size of the paging file at least allows Windows NT to page its way to enough memory to start the services. If there is not enough disk space, try clearing out some old files. Don't forget to check the TEMP directory and clear out the Internet Explorer temporary cache. These files can unexpectedly use a tremendous amount of disk space. After setup completes, you should have at least 20M of disk space available so that the services can create temporary files.

Here's how to add space to your paging file:

1. Click the Start button and then select Settings|Control Panel.
2. Double-click the System icon.
3. Choose the Performance tab.
4. Click the Change button. A dialog box appears, with a list of disk drives in the top pane. This list shows which disks have paging files and how big the paging files are.
5. Choose a disk with some available space, as shown in the in the Paging File Size for Selected Drive box. Then enter the initial and maximum sizes for the paging file. As a guideline for an Exchange Server, try to make sure that the computer has at least twice the physical memory as it uses page file space.

This section discussed the most common problems that can occur during installation. Installation problems are easy to deal with because there is a low risk of losing data. The next section involves troubleshooting the Information Store services, which is a bit more complex.

14

14.3. Troubleshooting Directory and Information Store Problems

The worst problems that affect Exchange Servers are Information Store problems because the Information Store contains user data, which is usually voluminous and is always critical. The Information Store (IS) service is the service that reads and writes to public folders and private folders (mailboxes).

There are two classes of Information Store problems:

- **Delivery problems.** Mail isn't being delivered to mailboxes correctly.
- **Information store corruption problems.** Information Stores don't start when the server is rebooted, or problems are detected during backup. These problems are the most serious and time consuming to correct.

14.3.1. Delivery Problems

If mail isn't being delivered to a specific mailbox, there is a problem with the mailbox. Sometimes, users set up inbox rules that delete incoming messages as they come in or that remove messages from the inbox and place them into another folder. These types of problems can be fixed from the client.

Another type of delivery error revolves around addressing. The first user in the organization in alphabetical order may receive a huge amount of improperly addressed mail. This is caused by careless addressing of mail; the user at the front of the Address Book becomes, in essence, the default address to send messages to. An easy workaround for this problem is to create a public folder called A Place Holder; set the properties on this folder so that it is available in the Address Book. The name A Place Holder appears in the Address Book before any other addresses, and this folder will then receive all the incorrectly addressed mail. Set up a rule on the folder so that it returns any message it receives with a warning to the user who sent the message to "be more careful."

Other directory-related problems can cause delivery failure. If there are multiple sites in the organization, there can be problems with directory replication. If an address is not appearing in the directory, first check to see whether the problem is within the site or between the sites. Check two different servers in the local site. If the address is missing on both servers, there is a problem with the directory replication connector. If the address is on one server and not another, there is a problem within the site with directory replication.

If there is a problem with the directory replication connector, start by checking the Windows NT Event log on the server that holds the directory replication connector. Look for events that mention communication problems to the target site. Then look for events that involve directory replication failures. In the Exchange Server Administrator program is a Replicate Now button on the directory replication connector properties pages that forces replication to occur. Click this button; if replication still does not occur, check the target servers in the other site to make sure that they are running, and also check their Event logs.

Follow these steps to check the Windows NT Event log for directory replication messages:

1. Click the Start button and then select Programs|Administrative Tools|Event Viewer.

2. If you aren't at the Exchange Server to be viewed, select Select Computer from the Log menu and type the name of the Exchange Server computer you want to work on.

3. From the Log menu, choose Application.

4. A window appears, showing various Exchange Server messages. Select View and then Filter Events. From the Source drop-down list box, select MSExchangeDS.

5. Read through the events by double-clicking the events. Notice that the events are in reverse-chronological order, with the most recent event at the top. To find the event that happened before the current one, click Next; to find the event that occurs after this one, click Previous.

If replication is just running slowly, or if you want more recent data on replication problems, use the Replicate Now button. Here's how:

1. Start the Exchange Server Administrator program.

2. Expand the Organization hierarchy and then the Site hierarchy.

3. Click the Connectors object and choose the proper directory replication connector. All the connectors are listed as Directory Replication (Server), where Server is replaced by the actual server name.

4. Choose Properties from the File menu to display the Properties dialog box for the directory replication connector.

5. Click the Replicate Now button.

14

After you complete this procedure, allow adequate time for replication to occur and then look in the Event log for messages stating whether or not replication was successful. "Adequate time" really depends on the number of objects in the site and the available bandwidth.

If the directory isn't replicating between servers in the same site, check to make sure that the directory service is running on all the servers and then check network connectivity. If the service is running on all the servers and network connectivity checks out, look at the Windows NT Event log for failure messages.

You can use a few different techniques to verify network connectivity. The most common is to open a command prompt and issue a net view *Servername* command. This command returns the names of any shares available on the target server. Figure 14.1 shows an example of what should be returned.

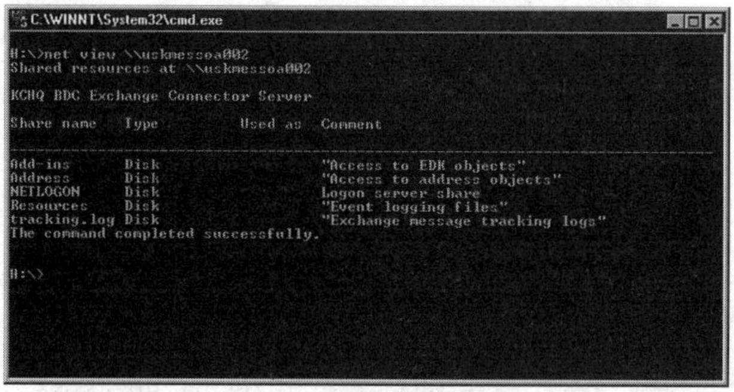

Figure 14.1.

The results of a net view *command.*

As you can see, the net view command shows the name of the server, the server comment, and the available shares. If this command comes back successfully, there is RPC connectivity between the workstation and the server.

Windows NT ServerManager can also be used to determine whether the other server is active. Use the Select Domain option to choose the correct domain and then attempt to pull up properties on the server by double-clicking on them. If this works, RPC connectivity has been established.

Here's a more detailed look at the procedure:

1. Click the Start button and then select Programs|Administrative Tools|Server Manager.

2. From Computer menu, choose Select Domain.

3. Choose the domain in which the Exchange Server to be monitored resides.

4. Double-click the name of the server in question to bring up the server's Properties dialog box.

The RPC Ping utility also works. Ping requires you to run a program on both the local server and the target server. The RPC Ping utility provides timing information, showing how long it takes to get messages from one server to another using RPC. An example of the RPC Ping program is shown in Figure 14.2.

Figure 14.2.

The RPC Ping utility being used to ping the Exchange Server called TRTEST; *this screen shows a successful ping using TCP/IP.*

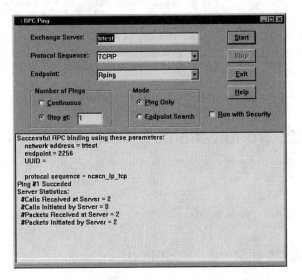

The RPC Ping Utility consists of a client and a server. The Server portion runs only on Windows NT server; there are multiple client versions. At any rate, all the software you need is on the Exchange Server CD-ROM, in the Support directory and the subdirectory called RPC Ping. The files are named RPINGtaa.EXE, where *t* is the type of program (either C for client or S for server) and *aa* is the architecture (16 for 16 bit, 32 for 32 bit, or _A for Alpha).

The following exercise uses the Ping utility to test an Exchange Server, so the client software does not have to be copied.

1. Copy the suitable RPC Ping client-side utility to a client workstation and run it.

14

2. In the window that appears, type the name of the computer running the server program and then choose Admin from the Endpoint drop-down box.

3. Click the Start button to start testing.

Not to be confused with RPC Ping, the TCP/IP PING utility can be used to verify that a network connection exists between two servers; however, TCP/IP PING does not necessarily verify the RPC connection that Exchange services needs. TCP/IP PING comes with Windows NT, Windows 95, and with any TCP/IP protocol implementation on any platform; it verifies that TCP/IP packets can go to a server and come back. To use the TCP/IP PING utility, simply start a command prompt and type PING `<ServerName>`, where `<ServerName>` is the name of the server to be checked. Make sure that the name does not include any backslashes. If there is a problem with the RPC Locator service, the RPC service, or a packet filter on a router between the servers, TCP/IP PING may work but RPC connectivity cannot be established.

14.3.2. Troubleshooting Corruption Problems

Information Stores can become corrupt during normal use because of problems with the Exchange Server software. Information Stores can also be corrupted if a server has an unfortunate disaster, such as a sudden power outage. The following sections look at how you can detect corruption and how you can resolve corruption problems.

Detecting Store Corruption

Corruption can be detected during startup, during operation, and during backup. Most database corruption messages are found during backup because a backup of the IS reads every record in the IS. This is yet another reason to run backups on a regular basis; doing so provides a way to detect problems before they have impact on users.

For problems that don't immediately stop the server, such as problems detected during backup, it is best to move all the users from the server having problems to other servers in the same site, and then rebuild the server that has the corrupt IS. During the move, the unfortunate user who owns the space that is corrupted in the database does not move, but everyone else will. Moving users reduces the impact of the corruption to just a few users, depending on the amount of corruption in the database.

After you move the users, assess the impact of the corruption. Do you have to recover the data the users lost? If so, restore the most recent backup and take the server offline. Then copy the affected user's mailbox to a PST file using the Exchange client software. A *PST file* is a place that isn't on the server in which a user can store messages. The PST file allows the user to have all his or her messages back. Then reinstall Exchange to rebuild the Information Store and begin copying users back to the server.

Some large organizations simply leave a server empty and available; if database corruption occurs, there is a place to quickly move users. The "standby" server reduces the amount of downtime and avoids placing more load on the rest of the servers in the site. When the server that had the corruption problem is rebuilt, it becomes the new standby server.

If the database corruption actually stops the database, or if the server is rebooted and the services won't start, you must follow some steps and make some decisions. First of all, stop any running Exchange services and perform a complete backup. If you have a backup, you will always have a way to get back to the previous state if the following steps make matters worse or have to be attempted again.

The best course of action to repair database corruption is to restore the server from a known clean backup. This is a guaranteed method for bringing the server back online and is the first option you should consider. If this option is not good enough backup is too old or because there is no backup), you can use a few utilities to attempt to fix the problem. Most of these utilities should be used only in conjunction with advice from Microsoft Product Support Services (PSS) because the utilities can cause irreversible data corruption problems. In addition, PSS may have newer versions of the utilities than you do, or more information about them.

The ISINTEG Utility

The ISINTEG utility is a multifunction utility that performs consistency checks on the database. This utility has two functions: It can either test the database for consistency or patch the database. When in test mode, the utility checks the database to make sure that it is consistent. A *consistent database* means that all the tables exist, the record counts match the number of records, and all objects in the database are referenced. You can run the test mode either as a read-only utility (it checks the database, displays errors, and writes errors to a log file) or as a read-write utility (the utility attempts to fix any problems it finds).

The patch mode of ISINTEG is used to restore offline backups. An *offline backup* is a backup either made without NT Backup or made by stopping the Exchange services and backing up the actual PUB.EDB, PRIV.EDB, and associated log files. Run the patch mode if error 2084 appears in the Application section of the Windows NT

14

Event log. The text for error 2084 is `The information store was restored from an offline backup. Run ISINTEG -patch before starting the information store`. The patch mode of the ISINTEG utility will fix the Information Store so that it will work on the current server.

To run ISINTEG in test mode, complete the following steps:

1. Stop the Microsoft Exchange Information Store service.

2. Open a command prompt and change to the `EXCHSRVR\BIN` directory.

3. Type **isinteg -l pri.log -test allfoldertests**. This command runs all the available tests to check the Private Information Store for errors and logs them to the file `PRI.LOG`.

4. To check the Public Information Store, type **isinteg -pub -l pub.log -test allfoldertests**. This command checks the Public Information Store and logs the results to the file `PUB.LOG`.

To run ISINTEG in fix mode, which attempts to fix the Information Store, use the `-fix` switch on the command line. To fix the Public Information Store and log errors to the `PUBFIX.LOG` file, use the command `isinteg -l pubfix.log -pub -fix` (the parameters can be in any order). Sample output from this command is shown in Figure 14.3.

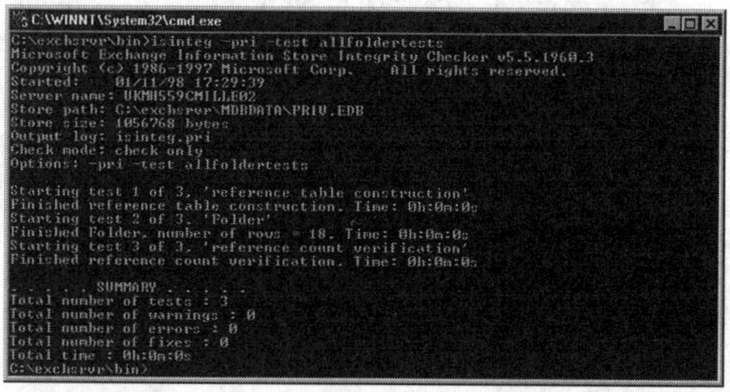

Figure 14.3.

Output from the ISINTEG program.

As you can see in Figure 14.3, the command-line parameters are shown on the top line and are repeated on the `Options:` line. The figure shows a clean test on a server with very few items in it.

To run ISINTEG in patch mode, simply type ***isinteg -patch*** at a command line. The Information Store service must be stopped before running this command, but the directory service must be running. If the directory service is not running, the ISINTEG program can't find the information it needs to update the Information Store.

The ESEUTIL Utility

You use the ISINTEG utility to check the database's contents at the object level; you use the ESEUTIL utility to check the database at the record-by-record level. At this level, the system checks for record readability instead of functionality. ESEUTIL can run in five different modes:

- **Defragmentation mode.** Compacts the database by removing deleted records from the database.
- **Integrity mode.** Checks the database for record integrity.
- **Recovery mode.** Commits the transaction logs to an offline database. Don't use this mode without first checking with Microsoft Product Support Services.
- **Upgrade mode.** Used to upgrade an information store. Don't use this mode without first checking with Microsoft Product Support Services.
- **File Dump mode.** Writes diagnostic header information to an output file. Don't use this mode without first checking with Microsoft Product Support Services.
- **Repair mode.** Repairs databases that have been found corrupt by the Integrity mode checks.

> **Note** It is critical that you check with Microsoft PSS before running any of the modes that change the database. PSS may have updated utilities or newer ideas. Also, the documentation says to always check with PSS.

Really, the only options an administrator has to be concerned with are the defragmentation, integrity, and repair modes. Integrity mode may find some database corruption problems. To run Defragmentation mode, you must have available double the space of the store being processed. Defragmentation mode can be run on any store, including the directory store. If Defragmentation mode finds an invalid record, the defragmentation process stops. To repair a database, use Repair mode. Repair mode is similar to Defragmentation mode, but it does not run database recovery steps before defragmentation.

14

To run the ESEUTIL utility in Defragmentation mode, stop the affected store service (Information Store or directory store) and then run ESEUTIL with the appropriate switches from a command line. Table 14.1 describes the switches for the ESEUTIL utility.

Table 14.1. ESEUTIL command-line switches.

Switch	Description
/ds	Specifies that the directory store should be checked.
/ispriv	Specifies that the Private Information Store should be checked.
/ispub	Specifies that the Public Information Store should be checked.
/d	Runs defragmentation on the specified store.
/r	Runs repair on the specified store.
/g	Runs a check on the specified store. Similar to repair, but the /g switch doesn't fix anything, it only finds problems.
/b pathname	Makes a backup of the database in the specified pathname.
"/p"	Leaves the original Information Store where it is, and puts a defragmented copy in the path \EXCHSRVR\BIN\TEMPDFRG.EDB.
/l pathname	Specifies a log file to use. If /l is specified without pathname, the files are stored in the local directory.
/t filename	Renames the new compacted database with the specified filename; can be used with "/p" to change the location of the new database.

To defragment the Private Information Store, type **eseutil /d /ispriv** at a command line. The /d switch tells ESEUTIL to defragment; the /ispriv switch tells ESEUTIL to work on the Private Information Store. Output from a defragmentation is shown in Figure 14.4.

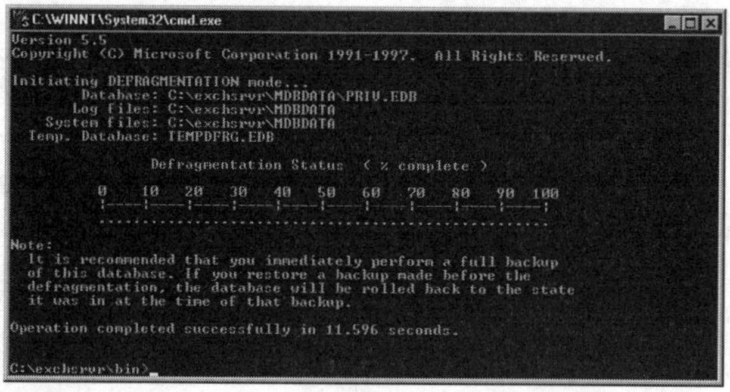

Figure 14.4.

Output from the eseutil /d /ispriv command.

The record checking part of ESEUTIL runs only in read-only mode. To fix problems, use Defragmentation mode and specify the /r option to repair. The ESEUTIL program runs in check mode by specifying /g on the command line. To scan the private information store for bad records, use the command eseutil /g /ispriv. For scan and check modes, the database parameters are the same as they are for Defragmentation mode.

If either ISINTEG or ESEUTIL allows the services to start, immediately begin moving users to another server and rebuild the local Information Store. The real problem may still be there, and these utilities sometimes only serve to buy time between failures to clean up. Moving users also reduces the number of anomalies that you'll have to examine if there is another problem later.

After the problems with the Information Store are found, what happens when the restore process doesn't work? Read on.

14.4. Diagnosing Backup and Recovery Problems

Backup and recovery are critical to data security and maintenance. Regularly scheduled backups with provisions for offsite storage means that the data in the organization is safe from a variety of problems—from software failure to natural disaster. Regular backups also help you find problems with data storage that might otherwise go undetected, as mentioned earlier in this chapter. The following sections focus on what to do when backups don't function properly and the types of things that are likely to cause backup problems. Then we'll take a look at recovery problems and the different techniques you can use during recovery to avoid problems.

14.4.1 Backup Problems

Most of the backup problems an Exchange Server will experience are identical to the problems any other system has. Bad tape media and running out of space on the tape are the two most common problems with backups, followed by various failures of scheduling software including the Windows NT AT command. These problems happen to everyone and aren't unique to Exchange Server.

The preventable problem, running out of space, happens when the administrator isn't monitoring the size of the Information Stores and keeping in mind the amount of tape he or she has to work with. To solve these problems, you can use a different size tape, procure a tape changer, or reduce the amount of data being backed up.

14

Another big problem with Exchange backups is the amount of time it takes to back up a server. Right now, Exchange can back up to only one tape drive at a time. If that tape drive can back up 10M/minute, it will take 800 minutes (13 hours and 20 minutes) to back up an 8-gigabyte Information Store. So if the backup starts at 7 p.m., it won't be finished until after 8 a.m. the following morning. Now imagine that server, already under a load from performing the backup, trying to accept the hundreds of login requests and message reads that take place when users arrive in the morning. Backup planning and equipment quality are critical.

Backups also uncover problems with the Information Store. Because a backup has to read every single record in the database, the backup will catch any errors in these records. These errors can include cross-linked entries and other problems that can be fixed using ESEUTIL. Monitoring the Windows NT Event log for errors of this type can aid in early detection of potentially serious problems. Use the same procedure you used to monitor directory replication (described earlier in this chapter), but filter for MSExchangeIS errors.

14.4.2. Recovery Problems

The restore process is a little different. There are some important rules to remember when running a database restore in Exchange:

- Information Stores can be restored to the server from which they were backed up or onto another server in the same site.
- Directories can be restored only onto the server from which they were backed up. Directories are unique to the server from which they were backed up.
- If an offline backup is restored, the services will not start unless you use the ISINTEG to patch the Information Store.
- If an Information Store is restored onto a server other than the server from which it came (or onto the same server with a different directory), the Information Store service does not start unless you use the ISINTEG utility to patch the Information Store.
- Restoring from a dirty backup is almost pointless.

Let's discuss each of these rules.

Rule 1 states that an information store can be restored onto an Exchange Server other than the server from which it was backed up. Remember that doing so overwrites the current IS on the target server. This rule is used if the directory service or the system files are corrupted on a server but the Information Stores are still intact. The server can be rebuilt, or the standby server can be used to hold the backup.

Rule 2 states that Rule 1 does not apply to the directory store. If the directory store is lost on a given server, it must be restored from a backup from that server. The Windows NT Backup program does not restore the directory to another server. If an offline backup is made of the directory, and the offline backup is restored onto a different server, the services will not start. Here's how to work around this rule: If a new server is built with a new name, taken off the network, and renamed, the directory can be restored to that server. Unfortunately, the server has to remain off the network and separate from the other servers or bad things will happen. But if you need information from the directory, this approach will provide you with the information.

Rule 3 is about the ISINTEG utility and applies to online backups. If an IS is restored to a server other than the server it came from, it will still contain the ID of the server from which it was backed up. Using ISINTEG to patch the file fixes the file so that it will run on the new server.

Rule 4 says that Rule 3 also applies to offline backups. Refer to the section, earlier in this chapter, on troubleshooting Information Store problems for more information on the ISINTEG utility.

Rule 5 says something that should be common sense: If there were errors during a backup, and the backup is restored anyway, the errors will still exist. The backup can still be restored, however, and the ESEUTIL and ISINTEG utilities can be used to attempt to clean up the store.

The key thing to remember is that the only guaranteed and supported way to recover from a disaster is to restore from backup. ISINTEG and ESEUTIL are great when they work, but don't rely on them to fix problems.

14.5. Server Resource Issues: Diagnostics and Recovery

Many problems that arise in Exchange Server are server resource problems. Shortages in resources can cause services to stop. Server resource problems can be grouped into the following categories:

- Memory
- Disk space
- Processor time
- Bandwidth

14

If any of these resources fall below certain threshold levels, services may stop. Monitoring server resources can help determine when problems are going to happen before they cripple a server.

14.5.1. Memory Resource Problems

What does it mean when a server runs out of memory? From a process perspective, a server is out of memory when the process attempts to allocate memory and the operating system returns an error indicating that there isn't any memory to give. From an operating system perspective, there isn't any memory when the amount of paged and physical memory available is zero. That means that not only is the physical memory used up, but the paging file is full as well. Usually, the fastest and easiest way to fix this problem is to expand the paging file. You should also consider adding memory to the server if this is a chronic problem. Once again, monitor the Pages per Second counter as previously described to make a decision on whether or not to upgrade memory.

Memory problems manifest themselves in two ways: First, Windows NT will display a message and write an event to the Event log stating that it is out of memory and that the paging file size must be increased. These events are written before there is an impact on the Exchange services. If the problem is ignored long enough, Exchange services will not be able to allocate memory, and the services will log error messages and stop. To fix the problem, increase the size of the paging file and then restart the service. In some cases, however, the Exchange services may not be able to close down "gracefully" and databases may become corrupt.

Graceful shutdown of a service means that the service was able to close all files and commit all unwritten data to disk. In some cases, this process requires more memory; if there is no memory available, the shutdown won't go as smoothly as it should have.

How big should a pagefile be? Microsoft recommends that the minimum pagefile should be the amount of system RAM plus 12M. However, a more realistic minimum is the amount of system RAM plus 40M; a good pagefile might even be double the amount system RAM or more.

To change the pagefile size, open the Control Panel and select System; from the dialog box, choose the Performance tab and then increase the pagefile size, as described in "Troubleshooting Installation Problems," earlier in this chapter.

14.5.2. Disk Space Problems

Disk space problems occur when a service runs out of space. Unfortunately, there are many different servers and different ways each can run out of space. The primary space-using services are the Information Store, the directory store, and the MTA (Message Transfer Agent).

What happens if the Information Store runs out of disk space? Because of the transaction logging in the Information Store, the service can shut down gracefully but recovery afterwards takes time. Once the store has grown to the point where it is out of space on the current drive and the IS service stops, the only option available is to make more space available on the drive. After space is made available, the affected services restart and read in all the transaction logs necessary for recovery. The service does not start again until there is more space on the drive.

Exchange Server uses a design for storing messages called a single-copy store. *Single-copy store* means that if the same message is sent to 1,000 users on the same server, only one copy of the message is stored on the server and all 1,000 recipients have a pointer to that message. If one user opens the message and makes a change, a new copy of the message is created that contains the edits. This added efficiency is very helpful; Microsoft estimates that every mail message is sent to at least three people, so this may represent a significant savings in disk space.

On UNIX systems, there is considerable danger that the system will not be able to restart if the file systems fill up. An old UNIX system administrator's trick is to put a large, expendable file on the drive; if the system runs out of space, the expendable file is deleted, reducing downtime while the administrator makes plans to add more disk space or reduces demand for space. You can apply this UNIX trick to Exchange Server. Place some expendable files on the drive so that the service can restart after the drive array fills to buy time. Then figure out how to fix the real problem.

If the MTA runs out of space, there are some other issues to consider. The MTA creates temporary files for messages that are in transit. If there is no limit on the size of messages being transferred, the MTA can easily fill up a drive while waiting to deliver messages. This is especially a problem if a link to another site or a connector goes down. In this case, the MTA continues to queue up all the outbound messages until it runs out of space or until the connection comes back up. Even after the connection comes up, it is important to monitor the MTA to make sure that it doesn't get behind.

14

The best way to fix MTA space problems is to put the MTA on a drive with more space or to return messages in the MTA queues back to the users until the messages can be forwarded. In addition, using message size limits can help prevent the problem.

Monitoring available disk space is an important part of maintaining Exchange. Use the Windows NT Performance Monitor counters for LogicalDisk\Free Megabytes and LogicalDisk\% Free Space to monitor available disk space. By monitoring these counters on at least a daily basis, you reduce the chance of filling up a disk volume.

To monitor for free disk space, follow these steps:

1. Start Performance Monitor.
2. From the Edit menu, choose Add to Chart.
3. If the computer to be monitored is not shown in the Computer box, type its name.
4. Choose Logical Disk from the Object drop-down list box.
5. Choose % Free Space from the Counter list, click Add, and then click Done.

14.5.3. Processor Time Problems

When the system is using a high percentage of processor time, message delivery can slow significantly. Also, if a lot of processor time is being used, the MTA process can slow down, affecting message delivery to other sites and connectors and causing problems with disk space availability as the MTA queues back up. If a system is using a large amount of processor time, the first step is to find out what processes are using processor time, and then find out why.

To find out what processes are using processor time, complete the following steps:

1. Open the Windows NT Performance Monitor.
2. Choose Add to Chart from the Edit menu. The Add to Chart dialog box appears.
3. Choose Process from the Object drop-down list box.
4. Verify that % Processor Time is selected from the Counter list.
5. Click the second item from the top in the Instance list. (The first item should be _Total; you don't have to monitor that.)
6. Press and hold the Shift key and scroll down the Instance list; click the last item in the list. This action selects all the items in the list.

7. Click the Add button to add all these items to the chart.

8. Click the Done button to close the Add to Chart dialog box.

   Notice that at least one of the lines in the chart is at or close to 100 percent. There may be multiple lines that contend for the 100-percent mark.

9. You should be at the main screen for Performance Monitor, with a virtual spaghetti bowl of lines in the chart. Press the Backspace key to highlight the graph line for the currently chosen object (in this case, the first counter in the list).

10. Using the arrow keys, select each counter in the list to see whether that is the process using a lot of processor time. Note the names of the processes that consume a lot of processor time and move on until you've checked all the counters.

You now have a list of the processes using the most processor time. There are two special processes that you should be aware of: The Idle process is what Windows NT runs when nothing else is running. The Idle process runs at such a low priority that any other process that has to run will pre-empt it. The Idle process consumes whatever is left of the processor's time; it is normal for this process to use a lot of processor time. The other process is perfmon, the Windows NT Performance Monitor. It usually doesn't use a lot of processor time unless the Counters box is being scrolled very quickly, or it is monitoring too many counters. These conditions make the processor time jump for the perfmon executable. The perfmon process is special because it is not part of the normal operating load of the server; any effects it causes can be ruled out of a diagnosis.

Most of the processor time on an Exchange Server should be used by the processes dsmain, emsmta, mad, and store. The dsmain process is the directory store; emsmta is the MTA process; mad is the System Attendant, and store is the Information Store. If one of these processes isn't at the top of the list for the Exchange Server, there is a process on the server that probably shouldn't be running.

Test Tip

Under no circumstances should an OpenGL screen saver be run on *any* server. OpenGL screen savers, such as the 3D Pipes, 3D Text, and any other Windows NT 4.0 screen saver that starts with *3D*, will consume 100 percent of the available processor time to draw pretty pictures on the screen. This brings user performance to a standstill and is one of the few things that will get the Microsoft PSS to laugh out loud at you.

14

14.5.4. Bandwidth Issues

One crippling problem that can occur on any Exchange Server at any time and with no warning is network congestion. Network congestion can cause every performance problem that has been mentioned, as well as slow delivery times, slow connector delivery times, and poor user response time. Like any other server, an Exchange Server is only as fast as the network allows it to be.

A variety of things can cause network congestion:

- When a network card in a computer or router goes bad, it may start sending out garbage.

- Users attaching to servers and retrieving huge amounts of data consume bandwidth.

- Network cabling faults can cause errors in packet delivery, resulting in a huge increase in retransmissions.

- Computers set at half duplex connected to routers, or switches set to full duplex (or vice versa) will cause a huge increase in retransmissions.

- Unnecessary network protocols or file and print sharing enabled on Windows 95 workstations can cause some bandwidth issues. Most routers filter out bad protocols; however, resource sharing is broadcast throughout the network.

- Bad router configuration, including unnecessary broadcast forwarding, can cause bandwidth problems to propagate over an entire network.

- Streaming video eats a huge amount of bandwidth.

Tracking these problems down to a root cause is beyond the scope of this book, but knowing how to recognize a network problem is vitally important.

About the only way to monitor network usage is with a network monitoring tool. Starting with Windows NT Server 4.0, Microsoft is bundling a limited-use edition of Network Monitor to help administrators monitor network traffic originating from or terminating on the local server. Other tools, such as the version of Network Monitor that comes with Microsoft Systems Management Server or Network General's Sniffer product, allow the network to be sampled to discover what is going on that is causing the network to slow down. You can find many books on network analysis and design, and you can use network protocol analyzers to find problems. There isn't enough room in this book to go through the use and analysis behind using such tools.

If you are using a TCP/IP network, it is easy to track down network problems using the PING utility. This utility sends a packet of information to any other TCP/IP host on the network. The receiving host then returns the message to the sender. Before you experience any problems, create a set of baseline statistics so that you can identify abnormalities. Use the PING utility to get a feel for the time it takes to send data to the farthest reaches of the network. Use the -1 flag (that's a lowercase *L*, not a number *1*) followed by a size value to specify how big the packet being sent will be. Usually, a 1K or 2K packet is sufficient to test most network connections.

If a non-TCP/IP connection is being used, use the RPC Ping utility in the Support directory on the Exchange Server CD-ROM. This utility provides similar functionality to that of the TCP/IP PING utility but requires that the other side of the connection run a client-side RPC Ping utility to answer back. RPC Ping also doesn't allow you to send large packets, as you can with the TCP/IP PING -1 switch.

Proper network design and monitoring can prevent most bandwidth problems or will arrest them before they cause too many other problems.

14

Lab

This lab consists of review questions pertaining to this chapter and provides an opportunity to apply the knowledge you've gained in this chapter.

Questions

1. At the end of the installation process, Exchange services are attempting to start and fail with the error message `An unexpected error occurred in the upgrade process`. What is a likely cause of this error?

   A. Bad RAM in the server.

   B. The Windows NT Service Pack on the server is not the correct version.

   C. There is not enough disk space on one of the server drives that holds Exchange Server data.

   D. There is a network problem.

2. While installing an Exchange Server into an existing site, the installation program reports that it cannot connect to the other server specified. Both systems are running TCP/IP, and RPC connectivity has been ensured between the two systems. What else can prevent communications?

   A. The two computers have different IP addresses, so they cannot communicate.

   B. The two computers are in different domains, and the account of the logged-on user is not valid in the target domain.

   C. There is a physical-layer network problem between the two computers, such as a bad cable.

   D. The user account being used to install Exchange does not have the Log On as a Service right.

3. After rebooting a server, the administrator sees the following message: `One or more services failed to start. Please check the Windows NT Event log`. After checking the Event log, the administrator notices the following error message: `Error: Non-database file or corrupted database initializing the Microsoft Exchange Server Information Store database`. What should the administrator do?

   A. Restore the Information Store from a known clean backup.

   B. Reboot the server in hopes that the error will go away.

C. Delete the log files from \EXCHSRVR\MDBDATA.

D. Reinstall Exchange.

4. After losing an Exchange Server because of a fire-sprinkler malfunction, the administrator attempts to restore the directory onto the server. But he or she finds that the directory backup is corrupt and can't be restored. What can the administrator do to bring the server back up?

    A. All the directories replicate to each other, so it's okay to pull a backup from another server's directory onto this server.

    B. Reinstall Exchange as a new server in the site and then restore the information stores to the server.

    C. Run ESEUTIL on the directory store.

    D. Run ISINTEG on the directory store.

5. A careful administrator has delayed installing Service Pack 1 for Exchange 5.5 because nothing in his or her environment was affected by the service pack. Service Pack 2 has now been released, and the administrator notices that it fixes some anomalies he or she has noticed. What should the administrator do?

    A. Service Pack 2 can be installed without Service Pack 1, so the administrator can install Service Pack 2.

    B. Service Pack 1 must be installed before installing Service Pack 2.

    C. Read and follow the instructions in Service Pack 2.

    D. Reinstall Exchange Server before installing any Service Packs.

6. An administrator is called by a user. The user is not receiving any mail even though other users are sending him or her mail. The administrator can view the user's mailbox, and everything seems to be in order from the server; the user can log on to Exchange using the Outlook client. The administrator discovers that the users who are sending mail are not receiving any non-delivery reports. What should be done first to resolve this problem?

    A. Check to see whether the user has any inbox rules that are deleting or moving messages.

    B. Check to see whether the user's address has been changed in the global address list.

14

C. Delete the user's mailbox and re-create it.

D. Delete the user's mailbox and Windows NT account and re-create them.

7. After adding 128M of RAM to an Exchange Server that is responding very slowly to user requests, the administrator is disappointed in the performance of the server. The problem has improved a little, but not as drastically as was hoped after doubling the amount of memory in the server. What is a likely cause of the disappointing performance?

A. The memory is not functioning properly.

B. Windows NT must be configured to recognize the new memory.

C. The virtual memory file must be expanded to allow access to the additional memory.

D. The Exchange Performance Optimizer must be used to reconfigure Exchange to access the new memory.

8. What should be done immediately before installing an Exchange Service Pack?

A. Back up the server.

B. Delete all the log files from \EXCHSRVR\MDBDATA.

C. Run the Performance Optimizer.

D. Reboot the server.

9. The Public Information Store on an Exchange Server has filled its disk drive. The drive is not part of a hardware RAID array or a Windows NT stripe set. How can you add disk space to the server that the public store can use?

A. Add a new disk and create a new Public Information Store on the server.

B. Add a new disk and create a volume set that includes the disk that the public folder is already on.

C. Add a new disk and create a stripe set that includes the disk that the public folder is already on.

D. Add a new disk; Exchange will automatically start using the space for the public folder store.

10. An administrator is trying to figure out what to put into the Exchange Server to make it perform better. The administrator notices that the disks are almost always busy, memory pages per second is low, and processor time never goes above 75 percent. The server is already using hardware RAID. What would be a good purchase to increase performance?

   A. Add memory.

   B. Add a new processor.

   C. Add another disk.

   D. Add a faster network card.

14

Exercises

Exercise 1: Troubleshooting Directory Store Problems

This exercise addresses the following Microsoft exam objective:
- Diagnose and resolve Exchange Server issues

In this exercise, you create a problem for starting the Information Store services, and then go through the steps of troubleshooting it.

1. Stop all Exchange services. The easiest way to do this is to stop the Microsoft Exchange System Attendant service.

2. Use Windows NT Explorer to go to the Exchange database files on the Exchange server. These files are located in the \EXCHSRVR\DSADATA directory. Create a new subdirectory called BACKUP and move the contents of the current directory into the BACKUP directory.

3. Reboot the server. When the server starts, you will receive an error message that says that some services failed to start. Log in and open the Event log (click the Start button and select Programs|Administrative Tools|Event Viewer). From the Event Viewer, choose Log|Application to look at the Application log.

4. In the Application log, you'll notice several events. There will be at least one event with a stop-sign icon. Double-click this event to bring up the event details. The error message will be The Microsoft Exchange Server database (EDB) could not be initialized and returned error -1811. Unrecoverable error, the directory can't continue. The directory service will then shut itself down.

5. Restore the files from the backup you made in Step 2 by moving the files back to the original directory. Then restart the Microsoft Exchange Directory service.

Exercise 2: Resolving Service Account Problems

This exercise addresses the following Microsoft exam objective:
- Diagnose and resolve Exchange Server issues

In this exercise, you'll create an error condition to simulate a password change problem with the Exchange service account. To avoid confusion, please write down the Exchange service account password that works before starting this exercise.

1. Open the Control Panel and then open the Services application.

2. Scroll down to the Microsoft Exchange directory and choose Startup.

3. Type a new password into the Password and Confirm Password boxes and click OK to save the changes.

4. Stop the Directory if it is running and then restart it. You will get the following error message: `Error 1069: The service could not start due to a logon failure.`

5. Open the Event Viewer and check the Application log to see the same message there.

6. In the Services application, fix the password for the Exchange Directory service and restart the service.

Answers to Questions

1. **C** The Service Pack issue is detected before any files are installed with a different message. Bad RAM in the server almost always causes a "blue screen of death" (the Windows NT Stop message). Network problems are usually documented by a message in Event Viewer that states that there were network problems. In addition, the stranger the error message, the more likely it is that a low-memory condition caused it (because the programmers usually don't have enough memory available to call the routines that write pretty error messages).

2. **B** If the two systems don't have different IP addresses, they will not communicate. If there was a problem with the cabling, the TCP/IP and RPC connectivity wouldn't have worked. In addition, the Exchange Setup program assigns Log On as a Service rights during setup.

3. **A** The only supported and correct way to recover from store corruption is to restore from backup. Rebooting does not help—and even if the store comes back up, you'll always wonder why the message came up in the first place. Don't ever delete the log files from the MDBDATA directory or the store won't recover properly. Reinstalling Exchange deletes all the data files, which won't help users much.

14

4. **B**   The Information Stores are not unique to a particular server and can be moved to a new server with a new name without any problems other than patching the store using the `isinteg -patch` command.

5. **C**   Always read the directions. Although answer A is generally true, it is not always the case. For example, Exchange 4.0 Service Packs after Service Pack 2 couldn't be installed without first installing Service Pack 2.

6. **A**   If the address had changed, the senders would receive non-delivery reports. Deleting and recreating the mailbox, or the mailbox and the NT account, would fix the problem, but that's not the best way to fix the problem.

7. **D**   It is imperative that you run the Performance Optimizer after making changes to hardware.

8. **A**   That goes for any Service Pack on any system anywhere.

9. **B**   Of the given choices, this one represents the smallest amount of work and risk. A server can only have one Public Information Store. If a stripe set is built, the store must be backed up before the build and then restored afterwards. Most unfortunately, an Information Store can exist on only one logical drive, so choice D won't work either.

10. **A**   If the disk time is always high, adding more memory will increase the amount of caching on the server, causing fewer disk reads.

Appendix

Sample Exam

Here is a sample MCSE exam for Exchange Server 5.5. You have 105 minutes to complete the real exam. The answers and their explanations are located at the end of this appendix.

1. During routine monitoring, the administrator notes that the Private Information Store is approaching the amount of available disk space. The number of users in the organization is reasonably constant. Which of the following is not a good long-term solution to this problem?

    A. Use Information Store size limits to limit the amount of information a user can keep.

    B. On a monthly basis, remove all messages over six months old.

    C. Route the messages from private folders to public folders using Inbox rules.

    D. Add another server to the site and move half the users.

    E. Limit message sizes.

2. ___ determines whether information about a public folder is replicated to other mail systems during directory synchronization.

    A. Replication Message Importance

    B. Directory Synchronization Replication Information

    C. Replication Level

    D. Trust Level

    E. Public Folders

3. The administrator is receiving complaints about problems with messages to the Internet taking an excessive amount of time to deliver. Which of the following is not a likely source of the problem?

   A. Message size

   B. Bad addressing on outgoing messages

   C. Lack of bandwidth to the Internet

   D. Failure to convert to X.400 addressing

   E. Lack of disk space on the connector server

4. Which of the following is the primary reason to use X.509 v3 Certificates when configuring Advanced Security?

   A. Exchange Server only supports X.509 v3 certificates.

   B. The other types of certificates cause performance problems and may corrupt the key management database.

   C. The X.509 v3 certificates are the only ones compatible with the Exchange 4.0 and 5.0 client.

   D. The X.509 v3 certificates maximize compatibility with S/MIME, so they can be shared with people outside the organization.

   E. X.509 v3 certificates will encrypt better than other types.

5. A user, Joe, is complaining that Susan, another user, is sending him messages but he is not receiving them. Joe and Susan are in different Exchange sites within the same organization. Which two steps should be taken to troubleshoot the problem?

   A. Delete and rebuild Joe's mailbox.

   B. Determine whether there are any other users having similar problems to see if there is a connector failure.

   C. Delete and rebuild Susan's mailbox.

   D. Check to see whether Joe has an Inbox rule that may be obstructing the delivery of mail from Susan.

   E. Check to see whether Susan has an Inbox rule that may be obstructing the delivery of mail to Joe.

6. During migration, the organization needs to support existing advanced security certificates but wants to change to the new X.509 v3 standard to allow S/MIME to be used in Internet messaging. How can these requirements be met?

   A. Enable both X.509 v3 and the old certificate types in the Advanced Security Setup process.

   B. Because only one certificate type can be issued in an organization at a time, use the old standard until all the advanced security users are updated, and then update all users with new X.509 v3 certificates.

   C. Allow the users to acquire their own certificates directly from VeriSign.

   D. Use PGP security on every client, and use Exchange Server to manage the keys.

   E. Exchange Server 5.5 does not support the old keys, so all the users must be upgraded at once.

7. What is the purpose of public folder affinity?

   A. To permit proper routing of information contained in public folders.

   B. To enable users in one site to open public folders on servers in other sites.

   C. To control the replication of public folders across sites.

   D. To permit users to move information between private and public folders.

   E. To control the replication of public folders across organizations.

8. What are the minimum hardware requirements for a Microsoft Exchange Server installation?

   A. 80486 66-MHz processor with 32M DRAM

   B. 60-MHz Pentium processor with 64M DRAM

   C. 90-MHz Pentium processor with 24M DRAM

   D. 166-MHz Pentium processor with 64M DRAM

   E. 166-MHz Pentium processor with 32M DRAM

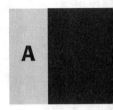

9. The outbound mail for your Internet Mail Service stops working, with the error message `No Route to Intended Recipient`. What is the most likely cause of this system error?

   A. The server has crashed.

   B. The MTA has no routing information for SMTP mail.

   C. The TCP/IP addressing is set up incorrectly.

   D. The `HOSTS` file contains invalid information.

   E. The MIME router information is incorrect.

10. Exchange Servers duplicate directory information across sites through a process known as what?

    A. Directory duplication

    B. Directory synchronization

    C. Directory replication

    D. Site synchronization

    E. Site duplication

11. The purpose of the offline Address Book is:

    A. To keep the Exchange Server operational in case of a primary Address Book failure.

    B. To allow remote users to use Exchange address lists, because the current versions of these lists are stored in the offline Address Book.

    C. To permit LAN-based Exchange users to use their local Exchange Server when it is being backed up.

    D. There is no offline Address Book.

    E. To track system addresses during server down times.

12. A ___ in Microsoft Exchange terminology refers to a marker that represents a deleted directory object.

    A. Deletion badge

    B. Garbage collector

    C. Tombstone

    D. DS site

    E. SMTP

13. You are the administrator of both an Exchange Server and a Microsoft Mail (PC) system. You attempt to start the Schedule+ Free/Busy Connector, but it will not start. Select all the appropriate possibilities for why the connector will not start.

    A. The Schedule+ Free/Busy Connector cannot be used with Microsoft Mail systems.

    B. An administrator's mailbox (ADMINSCH) has not been specified.

    C. The distribution list of accounts to whom the connector will send scheduling updates from Microsoft Exchange users is empty.

    D. There is no supervisor account on the Microsoft Mail system.

    E. The Schedule+ Free/Busy Connector is busy.

14. How is directory replication between servers within a site performed?

    A. Directory replication only occurs between sites.

    B. By clicking the Directory Replication option in the Exchange Administration program.

    C. It is a part of the directory synchronization function.

    D. Directory replication is done automatically.

    E. There is no directory replication within a site.

15. The Microsoft Exchange ESEUTIL.EXE program's primary function is to ___.

    A. Perform manual defragmentation and optimization of disk space allocation for an Information Store

    B. Delete all the temporary Exchange database files

    C. Manually back up all the Information Stores

    D. Maintain the Message Transfer Agents

    E. None of the above

16. To verify a messaging connection, one must first set up and configure ___.

    A. Exchange monitors

    B. Messaging monitors

    C. Link monitors

    D. MTA monitors

    E. Server monitors

17. What are the fundamental ways in which an Exchange Administrator may be notified of a downed messaging link?

  A. A user sends a message and it comes back undelivered; the user then informs the administrator of the messaging problem.

  B. A user sends a message and it comes back undelivered; the user then informs the administrator of the messaging problem using a specially configured link monitor that detects delays and errors in messaging flows.

  C. Through a specially configured link monitor that detects delays and errors in messaging flows.

  D. A message box appears on the Exchange administrator's screen, informing him or her of a downed message link.

  E. Both A and D.

18. How can the routing table for the Message Transfer Agent be rebuilt?

  A. It is done automatically daily and after a change has been detected.

  B. By selecting the manual rebuild option from the MTA Site Configuration Properties screen.

  C. By reinstalling Microsoft Exchange.

  D. By reinstalling the MTA.

  E. There is no routing table for an MTA.

19. What are the authentication options available for Microsoft Exchange POP3 mailboxes?

  A. Basic (Clear Text)

  B. Basic (Clear Text) using Secure Socket Layer

  C. Windows NT Challenge/Response

  D. Windows NT Challenge/Response using Secure Socket Layer

  E. All of the above

20. The Lightweight Directory Access Protocol (LDAP) permits clients with access to ___.

    A. Browse, read, and search the listings found in an Exchange Server directory

    B. Browse, read, and search the listings found in an Exchange Server directory and write new directory entries

    C. Perform read, write, and delete functions on an Exchange 5.0 directory structure

    D. Search Exchange Server directories

    E. None of the above

21. LDAP supports which type(s) of security authentication?

    A. Basic (Clear Text)

    B. Basic (Clear Text) using Secure Socket Layer

    C. Windows NT Challenge/Response

    D. Both B and C

    E. Both A and B

22. The Microsoft Outlook Web Access feature permits

    A. Anonymous users to access the anonymous public folders.

    B. Anonymous users to access the anonymous public folders and to browse the global address list.

    C. All users to access the anonymous public folders.

    D. All users to access the anonymous public folders and to browse the global address list.

    E. None of the above.

23. What are the authentication options available for the Exchange Network News Transfer Protocol?

    A. Basic (Clear Text)

    B. Basic (Clear Text) using Secure Socket Layer

    C. Windows NT Challenge/Response

    D. Windows NT Challenge/Response using Secure Socket Layer

    E. All of the above

24. What is required for aWeb Outlook Access server installation?

    A. Windows NT 4.0 with SP3 or later, Exchange 5.5

    B. Active Server Pages for IIS 3.0, Windows NT 4.0 with SP3 or later, Exchange 5.5

    C. Windows NT 4.0 with SP3 or later, Exchange 5.5, Internet Information Server 3.0

    D. Exchange 5.5

    E. An Internet browser and Outlook 8.01

A

25. You are an Exchange administrator who has been setting up users with mail delivery to the server and using .OST files for their local copy. However, synchronization appears to be very slow. What can be done to improve the performance for .OST synchronization?

    A. Limit folder sizes, most notably the Inbox and Deleted Items folders.

    B. Limit the number of folders being synchronized.

    C. Limit folder sizes (most notably the Inbox and Deleted Items folders) and limit the number of folders being synchronized.

    D. Limit folder sizes (most notably the Inbox and Draft folders) and limit the number of folders being synchronized.

    E. Limit folder sizes (most notably the Inbox and Draft folders), eliminate the Outbox folder, and limit the number of folders being synchronized.

26. What are the additional core component troubleshooting tools provided with the Exchange Server software?

    A. MTACHECK.EXE

    B. ISINTEG.EXE

    C. MTACHECK.EXE, ISINTEG.EXE, IMSCHECK.EXE

    D. MTACHECK.EXE, ISINTEG.EXE, EDBUTIL.EXE

    E. MTACHECK.EXE, ISINTEG.EXE, ESEUTIL.EXE

27. What situations may justify the use of the MTACheck utility?

    A. A weekly integrity check of MTA queue databases

    B. A weekly integrity check of MTA queue databases; to help troubleshoot a downed MTA

    C. To help troubleshoot a downed MTA

    D. For routine testing of an MTA transfer link

    E. None of the above

28. The ___ tool will perform diagnostic and repair functions on Information Store databases.

    A. IMSCheck

    B. ISInteg

    C. MTACheck

    D. DIAGS

    E. Statistics

29. The Exchange core components allow an administrator to set specific levels of diagnostic logs. What does a Level 5 setting mean?

    A. Log everything

    B. Log only the required events

    C. Log low-level events only

    D. Log security breaches

    E. Log nothing

30. Diagnostic logging tools are available for which of the following Exchange components?

    A. Directory Service

    B. Directory Synchronization

    C. Message Transfer Agent

    D. Public and Private Information Stores

    E. All of the above

31. What is/are the primary advantages for using several low-powered servers, instead of a single high-powered computer?

    A. No single point of failure for the entire network

    B. Usually, additional increases in capacity are less expensive to add

    C. Lessened network overhead and storage for replicated data

D. All of the above

E. Both A and B

32. What are some things to consider when attempting to estimate the hardware requirements for a Microsoft Exchange Server installation?

    A. Disk transfer bandwidth for potential read and writes to hard drives

    B. Number of Gateways required

    C. NIC bandwidth requirements

    D. Communication with remote clients

    E. All of the above

33. As the Exchange Administrator, what should you do if you think that someone else is signing email messages on behalf of one of your users without his or her permission?

    A. Delete that user's mailbox and then recreate it with a new password.

    B. Ignore the problem; it will go away in time.

    C. Tell the user to change his or her password.

    D. Revoke advanced security for that user and then re-enable it after you give the user a new token.

    E. Inform the user of the security breach and have that person reissue himself a new security token.

34. Microsoft Exchange's X.400 Connector is able to transmit messages using what network transport protocols?

    A. TP0/X.25

    B. TP4/CLNP

    C. TCP/IP, TP4/CLNP, TP0/X.25

    D. TP0/X.25, TP4/CLNP

    E. TCP/IP

35. An X.400 message consists of body parts and header information. Under Microsoft Exchange Server, how many body parts can be associated with any one X.400 mail message?

    A. 1

    B. 2

    C. 16

    D. 32

    E. As many as required by the Exchange message

36. How does one configure the RAS MTA stack for use with X.400 connections?

    A. From the Exchange Administrator's File menu, click New Other and then select MTA Transport Stack. Then choose the RAS MTA Stack and click OK.

    B. From the Exchange Administrator's File menu, click New Other and then select MTA Transport Stack. Then select the RAS MTA Stack and right-click it to display the Configure menu option.

    C. From the Exchange Administrator's File menu, click New Other and then select X.400 Transport Stack. Then choose the RAS MTA Stack and click OK.

    D. From the Exchange Administrator's File menu, click New Other and then select X.400 Transport Stack. Then select the RAS MTA Stack and right-click it to display the Configure menu option.

    E. The RAS MTA Stack cannot be configured for X.400 connections.

37. How can an Exchange Server's name be changed, once it has been named?

    A. It cannot be changed.

    B. Remove the Server from the site, rename the Server, and then reinstall Microsoft Exchange Server.

    C. Remove the Server from the site, rename the Server, and then reinsert the Server back into the site.

    D. Click once on the site; then click the server name to rename it.

    E. From the Exchange Administrator's File menu, click Rename Other and then select Server Name. Then choose the Rename function and click OK.

38. What is the primary downfall of using the X.400 Connector to connect two Exchange Server sites?

    A. It does not support the TCP/IP protocol.

    B. It requires the use of multiple bridgehead servers in each location.

    C. Because specific network protocols are used by the X.400 Connector, the Exchange administrator must first verify that the existing network infrastructure will support these protocols.

    D. None of the above.

    E. All of the above.

39. What are some of the advantages of using the Internet Mail Service to connect Exchange Server sites?

    A. It permits scheduling of connections.

    B. The Internet can be used as a messaging backbone in place of your company's LAN or WAN.

    C. Message sizes can be specified.

    D. Message format conversions are not required.

    E. Both B and C.

40. What are some of the advantages of using the Dynamic RAS Connector to connect Exchange Server sites?

    A. It permits scheduling of connections.

    B. It supports ISDN connections.

    C. It supports Async connections.

    D. It does not require a permanent LAN or WAN connection between the sites.

    E. All of the above.

41. Why would an Exchange administrator want to dedicate an Exchange Server for all the public folders for a site?

    A. It reduces the hardware requirements on the mailbox server.

    B. Backup and recovery procedures for the public folders will become easier.

    C. There should be a performance increase in the mail delivery processes.

D. It makes the overall administration of the servers easier.

E. All of the above.

42. A message routing cost with a value of 1 means what?

A. The message route is to be used only if no other routes are available.

B. The message route is to be shared on a 50-50 basis with other message routes.

C. The message route is to be used even though other routes are available.

D. The message route is to be used only if the message is being sent to an Internet address.

E. All message routes with a cost of 1 will be used all the time.

43. What is the easiest way in which to connect two Microsoft Exchange Server sites?

A. The X.400 Connector

B. The MS Mail (PC) Connector

C. The Dynamic RAS Connector

D. The Site Connector

E. The Internet Mail Service Connector

44. An Exchange Server that has been specifically designated to manage communication between Exchange Sites is known as a ___.

A. Primary domain controller

B. Backup domain controller

C. Bridgehead server

D. Site server

E. Point server

45. What is the purpose of an address space?

A. To balance the messaging load of an Exchange Server when using multiple connectors on that server.

B. To determine what type of connector is to be used.

C. To determine the outbound message routing.

A

D. To determine the inbound message routing.

E. To optimize the inbound message routing.

46. Microsoft Exchange Server supports which data encryption standard(s)?

   A. Data Encryption Standard (DES)

   B. CAST encryption algorithms

   C. Data Encryption Standard (DES), CAST encryption algorithms

   D. PGP encryption standards

   E. Data Encryption Standard (DES), CAST encryption algorithms, PGP encryption standards

47. What is the purpose of an age limit on a public folder?

   A. It determines the length of time a message remains in the MTA's outbound queue before being sent.

   B. It sets the number of days a message can stay in a public folder before it will automatically be deleted.

   C. It sets the number of weeks a message can stay in a public folder before it will automatically be deleted.

   D. It sets the number of months a message can stay in a public folder before it will automatically be deleted.

   E. There is no such thing as an age limit.

48. When the ExchangeMigration wizard is used, it has the capability to do what?

   A. Create the Windows NT user accounts for every mailbox, while generating random passwords.

   B. Create the Windows NT user accounts for every mailbox, while using the alias name of the account for the password.

   C. Create the Exchange mailbox, but not the Windows NT user account.

   D. Select the Windows NT domain in which the user accounts are to be created, or to find where the existing accounts are.

   E. All of the above.

49. What is the purpose of a template account?

    A. It permits the NT administrator to use this "copy" account as the basis for Exchange administration accounts.

    B. It permits the Exchange administrator to use this "copy" account as the basis for all other accounts he or she manually creates.

    C. This account has the default restrictions and properties that form the basis for the accounts created by the Migration wizard.

    D. Both A and B.

    E. Both A and C.

50. How many users can be supported by a single Microsoft Exchange messaging system?

    A. 500

    B. 1,000

    C. 3,000

    D. 12,000

    E. It varies by organization.

51. What does it mean when a message is referred to as a "local delivery message"?

    A. That the message was sent to a user by himself or herself using a CC: or Bcc: method.

    B. That the message was sent from one user to another user who are both in the same Exchange site.

    C. That the message was sent from one user to another user who are both in the same Exchange organization.

    D. That the message was sent from one user to another user who both share the same home server.

    E. That the message was sent from one user to another user who both share the same public folder.

52. A ___ is a user who logs on to the Exchange Server client from multiple PCs within an organization.

    A. Hacker

    B. Ghost user

C. Roving user

D. Remote user

E. It is not possible to log on to an Exchange Server client from various computers in an organization.

A

53. What is meant by "message spoofing"?

A. Message spoofing occurs when someone is able to make it appear that messages are sent from the Internet when they are actually coming from a recipient inside the organization.

B. Message spoofing is the art of hacking someone else's email messages in order to read or change the content of the messages.

C. Message spoofing permits a person from outside the organization to transmit a mail-based virus to a recipient inside the company.

D. All of the above.

E. None of the above.

54. Why would a person outside of the organization issue an SMTP Verify command against an Exchange Server that is running an IMS connector?

A. Because they want to learn the mailbox of a user and that user's full name.

B. Because they want to delete the mailbox of a user.

C. Because they want to change the mailbox of a user and that user's full name.

D. Because they want to copy the contents of a specific user's mailbox.

E. It is not possible to issue an SMTP Verify command against an Exchange Server.

55. To use SSL encryption for a POP3 client, what additional application must be installed on the Exchange Server computer?

A. Active Server Pages

B. Internet Information Server (IIS) 3.0

C. Personal Web Services

D. FrontPage for NT

E. It is not possible to use SSL encryption with an Exchange POP3 client.

56. If POP3 clients in your Exchange organization received non-delivery reports (NDRs) for any message submitted for delivery to recipients outside of the organization, what is the most likely cause of the problem?

    A. The Reroute Incoming SMTP Mail feature within the IMS may not be configured properly, or the SMTP domain name of the organization may have been input incorrectly.

    B. The Reroute Outbound SMTP Mail feature within the IMS may not be configured properly, or the SMTP domain name of the organization may have been input incorrectly.

    C. All of the above.

    D. None of the above.

    E. POP3 clients do not possess the ability to send messages to recipients outside the organization.

57. How can the Microsoft Exchange Server Setup program be run in an automated batch mode?

    A. By using the /b command line option.

    B. By using the /a command line option.

    C. By using the /q command line option.

    D. By using the /a /b command line option.

    E. It cannot be run in an automated batch mode.

Answers

1. **C** Answer C isn't technically feasible and isn't directly controlled by the administrator, and therefore is suspect. The other choices all represent effective methods for getting out of the trouble represented by a lack of disk space.

2. **D** Trust level determines whether or not a site receives a replica of an object. Any time "directory synchronization" is mentioned, it applies to Microsoft Mail. The rest of the choices are made up.

3. **D** Incoming and outgoing message size, along with a lack of bandwidth, are the most common problems. Users sending messages to bad addresses can also cause problems. Lack of disk space can cause all kinds of problems because any binary attachments have to be saved and converted from either MIME or UUENCODE format to binary format. Because the Internet doesn't use X.400 addressing, there can't be any conversion failure there.

4. **D** Exchange Server 5.5 supports X.509 v1 and v3 certificates, as well as the certificates used in Exchange 4.0 and 5.0. That rules out answers A and C. Because the security certificate type does not rule out any type of encryption, that rules out answer E. Microsoft would not make a certificate type available that could cause the problems outlined in answer B. So answer D is the only option left.

5. **B, D** Deleting and rebuilding mailboxes is too drastic (and isn't really troubleshooting), so answers A and C won't work. Inbox rules only effect incoming messages, so checking Susan's client for Inbox rules won't solve the problem either.

6. **A** Because Exchange advanced security supports multiple security types, answers B and E aren't valid. VeriSign doesn't issue certificates that Exchange Server can use without using advanced security, so answer C isn't valid. PGP isn't supported by advanced security, so answer D won't work either.

7. **B** Public folder affinity is very useful when multiple sites are on the same WAN and the folders aren't accessed enough to justify replication. Routing information in public folders is either folder replication or a folder rule, so answer A doesn't apply. Public folder replication is controlled by managing the public folder replication properties and trust levels, not by adjusting affinity levels, so answer C does not apply either. Moving information from public to private folders or vice versa is done with folder rules, so answer D won't apply. Answer E is basically a repeat of answer B.

8. **C** The other options don't meet the requirements. It's probably better to go with the recommended configuration of a Pentium 166 with 32MB of RAM.

9. **B** Usually this happens when the connector is set up and does not have an address space assigned to it. If the server had crashed, other messages would be displayed on the client, so answer A does not apply. If TCP/IP is not set up correctly, there would be no connectivity from the server to *any* address, so the error would be a network error and a different non-delivery report. HOSTS files are rarely if ever used for Internet mail routing; DNS is usually used. If a HOSTS file was used in this case, incorrect entries would cause the same problems as a bad TCP/IP setup, cutting out answer D. There is no such animal as a MIME router, so answer E is gone as well.

10. **C** Directory synchronization is the process used by Microsoft Mail to transfer directory information. The rest of the terms are made up.

11. **B** The offline Address Book has to be created using the DS Site Configuration tab in every site that will be accessed by offline clients. It is not a backup of the directory store, as suggested by answers A, C, and E. It exists, so that rules out answer D.

12. **C** Garbage collection is the process that clears the tombstones and makes the space available again. The rest of the choices are made up or are so far-fetched that they don't apply.

13. **B, C** Both of these answers happen if the connector has not been configured at all or if the connector has been configured incorrectly. For this type of question, most of the time the answer is any condition that happens if a service is started from its default, unconfigured state. The Schedule+ Free/Busy connector will work very nicely with Microsoft Mail, so answer A doesn't apply. The administrator account on Microsoft Mail cannot be deleted, so answer D doesn't apply; and if it was busy, it wouldn't start in the first place, so answer E won't work either.

14. **D** Within a site, directory replication is performed automatically. If there was no directory replication within a site, the Address Book within a site would constantly be out of date, so answers A and E are wrong. Because it is automatic, answer B won't work. Anything that mentions directory synchronization applies to Microsoft Mail, and the question isn't about MS Mail, so throw out answer C.

15. **A** Defragmentation runs automatically as part of scheduled maintenance by the system administrator, but it is not as efficient as the offline manual process in ESEUTIL. There are no temporary database files, so answer B isn't valid.

A

Backups are done using NTBackup, and the MTA is maintained with MTACheck.

16. **C** There are only two types of monitors: link and server. That rules out answers A, B, and D. Server monitors watch services running on servers, so link monitors must be the correct answer.

17. **B** Users usually bring problems like this to the administrator's attention. If link monitors are running, they can back up the user's story and help pinpoint the problem.

18. **A** There is no rebuild option on the MTA Site property pages. It is located on the MTA object in the Server container.

19. **E** The POP3 interface supports all the specified authentication protocols.

20. **A** It is not really a good idea to have users on the Internet making changes to your directory database, so answers B and C are not valid. Because search and read options are allowed, answer D is not the correct answer either.

21. **E** LDAP is a very specific specification and does not allow plug-in authentication as many specifications do.

22. **B** This is the default and can be changed to limit or eliminate access to anonymous users.

23. **E** NNTP has been around long enough that there are versions of it to do just about anything, so all options are valid.

24. **C** IIS 3.0 includes Active Server Pages and must be installed on the server that will be running Outlook Web Access. IIS 3.0 requires Windows NT 4.0 SP3. That makes answer C the most complete choice.

25. **C** The .OST file contains copies of specified folders; by limiting the sizes of the mailboxes, you reduce the amount of time to transfer messages.

26. **E** The EDBUTIL program was superseded by ESEUTIL in Exchange 5.5. Because all three of these components are provided, the rest of the choices must be incorrect.

27. **B** The MTACHECK utility checks data structures on a server and does not check links, so answer D is not correct.

28. **B** ISInteg checks the Information Store integrity; the rest of the names are made up.

29. **A** The logging levels go from 0 (which means "log nothing") to 5 (which means "log everything").

30. **E** Remember that all services in Exchange have logging that can be activated for them.

31. **E** In addition, if one server fails, fewer users are impacted, resulting in fewer angry phone calls. If there are several servers, the amount of communications between servers (that is, network traffic) will be increased, ruling out answer C.

32. **E** Exchange is very difficult to analyze for performance because there are a lot of variables.

33. **D** Revoking advanced security is much easier and less obtrusive to the user than any other options. Answer B is a definite security problem. Changing the password won't work because the password encrypts the key, so if a user has a copy of the key file that is encrypted with the old password, it will still work. Answer D is the best option.

34. **C** It includes all the correct protocols.

35. **E** Message size canbe limited, however.

36. **E** Dynamic RAS cannot be used for an X.400 connection; only TP0/X.25, TP4, and TCP/IP can be used.

37. **B** Never choose an answer that says "It cannot be changed," because it is always possible to rebuild the server—or every server in the environment. The directory name cannot be changed, but the display name can be changed.

38. **C** X.400 works on TCP/IP and requires only one bridgehead server per site.

39. **E** Message format conversions are required, which may slow performance if a lot of binary files are sent. Also note that the X.400 connector can also be used over the Internet because it supports TCP/IP.

40. **E** But the Dynamic RAS Connector is usually the least desirable of the connector options.

41. **E** Consolidating public folders in large organizations, or in organizations that make extensive use of public folders, simplifies disaster recovery as well as increasing performance.

42. **E** A cost of 1 is the lowest cost and so will be used by default; if there are multiple routes to the same destination with the same cost, they will be balanced.

43. **D** The site connector has the fewest restrictions on network protocol and the fewest property pages to configure.

A

44. **C**   However, a bridgehead server can also handle other tasks such as mailboxes or public folders. *Primary domain controller* and *backup domain controller* are Windows NT domain security terms and are irrelevant to the handling of messages. Site and point server do not apply to Exchange either.

45. **C**   The use of a connector for transmitting mail is determined by its address space. Because Exchange uses a "push" type of routing, where an MTA sends a message to another MTA, there isn't a possibility of inbound routing, which eliminates answers D and E. Answers A and B are essentially restatements of answer C, but answer C is the clearest statement of the answer.

46. **C**   Exchange Server doe not support the use of PGP encryption.

47. **B**   Age limits are used to determine how long a message will remain in a public folder—in days—eliminating answers A, C, and D.

48. **E**   The Migration wizard has a lot of options, so it can either create or not create an NT account for each mailbox.

49. **C**   Template accounts are useful for setting default options. The NT administrator should not be making a bunch of Exchange administrator accounts, so answer A does not apply; although answer B is valid, it is not as good as answer C.

50. **E**   Microsoft has reported testing over 20,000 users on a single server.

51. **D**   A local delivery message is a message that stays on one server, which eliminates all other choices. One measure of Exchange performance is the delivery time for local delivery messages.

52. **C**   A *hacker* is someone who breaks into computer systems; a *ghost user* is slang for a user who is hidden from the Address Book. *Remote users* are users who dial in and access Exchange. That only leaves *roving users*.

53. **A**   Reading and changing content, or transmitting viruses through email, is just miscellaneous hacking that can be resolved by using advanced security options.

54. **A**   The VRFY command verifies a user by reporting back the user's full name.

55. **B**   SSL is part of IIS, not Exchange, so IIS must be installed for SSL to work.

56. **A**   The ability to use Exchange as a message router is required to send messages from a POP3 client to the Internet using an Exchange Server.

57. **C**   This is standard with newer Microsoft installation programs.

Index

A

F - G

networks

bandwidth problems, troubleshooting, 512-513

sites, directory replication, 284-285

**NNTP (Network News Transfer
Protocol)**

configuring, 324-326

connectivity, troubleshooting,
462-464

dialog box, 324-326

messaging process, 323-324

overview, 322

Usenet nodes, 322

**Non-Deliverable Receipts (NDRs),
477**

notable files, troubleshooting, 78-79

Novell GroupWise, 4

data mappings, 433

migrating user accounts, 430-431

multiphase migration, 433

single phase migration, 431-432

source extractor, 430

O

object permissions

displaying, 377

modifying, 380-383

**object types (Exchange
Administrator), 81-82**

objects

organization, 99

server, 101

site, 100

offline data backups, 119

database restoration, 122

offline storage folders (OST), 474

versus personal storage folders
(PST), 474-475

one-way trust relationships, 43-44

online data backups, 119

database restoration, 123

log files, 120

organization objects, configuring, 99

organizing servers into sites, 232

outbound sites, 286

Outlook

clients, 196

16-bit, 196

32-bit, 196

configuring connectivity,
202-203

interoperability, 199

Macintosh, 196

profiles, 204-208

command line options, illegal
combinations, 215

installation options, 212-215

Internet Mail Service, configuring,
210-211

messaging profiles, modifying, 195

network installation points,
creating, 215-216

Network Installation Wizard, 215

public folders

configuring, 92-93

creating, 92-93

setup files, 212-215

command line options, 213-214

Setup Wizard functions, 202-203

**Outlook for Macintosh, clients,
interoperability, 200-201**